Global Responsibilities

Global Responsibilities

Who Must Deliver on Human Rights?

JC
571
.G5825
2005
WEST

Edited by
ANDREW KUPER

Routledge
Taylor & Francis Group

NEW YORK AND LONDON

Published in 2005 by
Routledge
Taylor & Francis Group
270 Madison Avenue
New York, NY 10016

Published in Great Britain by
Routledge
Taylor & Francis Group
2 Park Square
Milton Park, Abingdon
Oxon OX14 4RN

© 2005 by Andrew Kuper
Routledge is an imprint of the Taylor & Francis Group

Printed in the United States of America on acid-free paper
10 9 8 7 6 5 4 3 2 1

International Standard Book Number-10: 0-415-95126-7 (Hardcover) 0-415-95127-5 (Softcover)
International Standard Book Number-13: 978-0-4159-5126-5 (Hardcover) 978-0-4159-5127-2
(Softcover)

No part of this book may be reprinted, reproduced, transmitted, or utilized in any form by any
electronic, mechanical, or other means, now known or hereafter invented, including photocopying,
microfilming, and recording, or in any information storage or retrieval system, without written
permission from the publishers.

Trademark Notice: Product or corporate names may be trademarks or registered trademarks, and
are used only for identification and explanation without intent to infringe.

Library of Congress Cataloging-in-Publication Data

Global responsibilities : who must deliver on human rights? / edited by Andrew Kuper.
    p. cm.
Includes bibliographical references and index.
ISBN 0-415-95126-7 (hb : alk. paper) – ISBN 0-415-95127-5 (pb : alk. paper)
    1. Human rights. 2. Justice. 3. Responsibility. 4. Globalization. 5. World politics. I. Kuper,
Andrew.

JC571.G5825 2005
323–dc22

2004022283

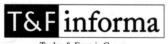

Taylor & Francis Group
is the Academic Division of T&F Informa plc.

Visit the Taylor & Francis Web site at
http://www.taylorandfrancis.com

**and the routledge Web site at
http://www.routledge-ny.com**

Contents

Acknowledgments

As editor, I thank all the contributors for their thoughtful work, swift cooperation, and willingness to tolerate editorial chutzpah. I am especially grateful to Onora O'Neill, Thomas Pogge, and Christian Barry for discussions that did much to shape this volume and for their inspiring friendship over the years.

All of the chapters that follow were written or published in the past three years. Most of the contributors refer to each other's work, often at length. As such, the volume represents the latest, most self-conscious and interconnected work on obligations, rights, and globalization.

The editor, contributors, and publisher are grateful to several journals and editors for kind permission to reprint original or revised versions of the articles listed in the Appendix. We are also indebted to Robert Tempio at Routledge, who immediately recognized and amplified the value of the book, even while ensuring speedy publication. I am personally indebted to Trinity College, Cambridge University. This volume would not have been possible without the unstinting support of the other Fellows and the staff of the College. Finally, I am grateful to my family and close friends, who have taught me much about the global reach of responsibility and humanity.

The "responsibilities approach" to human rights explored in these pages is in its relative infancy. It will develop and have a great impact only as a collective project. I warmly invite comments and criticisms, which may be sent to: akuper@ashoka.org

Andrew Kuper

Introduction:
The Responsibilities Approach to Human Rights

ANDREW KUPER

One moral discourse now dominates international law and politics: the language of rights. It is the basic normative currency for addressing political, social, and economic injustices and insecurity. There are many benefits to this common currency. On its own, however, it is prone to spirals of devaluation. When we call something a *right*, we are at least claiming that it is urgent and deserving of priority in reasoning and action; but when almost every personal and political demand is couched as a right, this sense of overriding importance is lost, and the meaning and value of rights-talk can be undermined. We care about human rights because we understand them to be more than careless rhetoric or gestures that are so vacuous as to be "a bitter mockery to the poor and needy."[1] Human rights must be practical entitlements that potentially make a difference to the people who hold them.

Why is the language of rights so vulnerable to profligacy and devaluation, and how can it be brought under control? Few questions are more important. A number of theorists have recently converged on a striking answer: The proliferating language and politics of rights has often obscured the need to specify *who bears the counterpart obligations to deliver on those rights*. In a world of severe deprivation, in which absolute poverty and violence blight the lives of billions of people, it is relatively uncontentious to insist that someone must do something. It is far more difficult, both conceptually and politically, to identify particular agents who are able and obliged—let alone willing—to relieve such suffering.[2] But it is not a task that can be responsibly avoided.

Unless a person or her representative can identify the agents against whom her right is held, her right may amount to little more than useless words. If, on the other hand, there is an identifiable agent or set of agents that has obligations to her—and is failing to live up to those obligations—then the situation and possibilities are quite different: There is someone at fault, someone against whom she or her representative could lay a complaint or approach with a complaint, and perhaps even an effective procedure through which to ensure enforcement of her rights and remedies for any rights violations. In this way, accounts of the concrete obligations of particular agents, which correlate with specific rights, could dramatically reduce the vagueness and idealization that beset our practical thinking about human rights.

The pressing conceptual and political task of this volume is to begin to consider, in a consistent and systematic way, the question: "*Who* must do *what* for *whom*?"[3] This task must be understood in historical context. The discourse of rights achieved preeminence at a time when the state was generally assumed to be the only agent tasked with meeting rights-claims. This assumption is explicit in the Universal Declaration of Human Rights of 1948. Yet it proved a notoriously simplistic assumption, out of kilter with messy realities. Because of what is bluntly called globalization, the political picture has become even more complex. Effective and legitimate power is no longer solely attributed to states, but is ascribed also to a variety of non-state actors such as non-governmental organizations (NGOs), corporations, and intergovernmental institutions. Intensified global communication, legal rules, economic interactions, networks, as well as multilateral institutions have contributed also to a dramatic rise in the number of groups claiming that they have certain rights and that those rights are being violated. The usefulness and resonance of the language of rights has led, moreover, to numerous other claims—previously articulated in terms of needs or interests—being articulated or reformulated as rights-claims. In short, an unprecedented increase has occurred in the *number* and *kinds* of rights-claims made, as well as the *range of agents* and *institutions* that potentially could and should meet those claims. The international arena lacks a principled basis, let alone the governmental powers and political will, to formally assign responsibilities to this multiplicity of agents and institutions.

The problem—and the challenge—does not stop there. Distributing responsibilities is one thing, ensuring that those obligations are fulfilled is quite another. Agents must not only exercise power in the pursuit of human rights, but they must be held *accountable* for the use and abuse of that power. Yet non-state actors are not subject to the direct discipline of elections; moreover, organizations and networks often operate across multiple state borders and are peculiarly adept at avoiding state-based regulatory efforts to get them to obey and advance human rights norms. In such a global context, it proves notoriously difficult to achieve accountability and its adjuncts: adequate transparency, information flow, standard setting, monitoring, and enforcement.[4] The need and demand for such accountability grows greater by the day, but is not matched by an equally intensive outpouring of proposals as to how the "accountability gap" might be filled. Paradigms of accountability that were constructed for a world of state-based multilateralism suddenly seem inadequate, even obsolete, in a world rapidly morphing into a multilevel complex of institutions, networks, coalitions, and informal arrangements.

In the face of these global transformations, there is an evident need for new, principled frameworks to secure human rights and accountability—principles that recognize the complexity of agency and of rights-claims—yet simultaneously rein in the use, and reduce the abuse, of rights discourse.

In this volume, thirteen practical thinkers together show (a) how human rights can be plausibly linked to accounts of corresponding obligations, (b) how such obligations can be allocated to diverse potential agents of justice, and (c) how those agents might be held accountable for fulfilling those obligations. This approach—always asking "who should do what for whom?"—is developed and applied in different ways by the contributors, each of whom addresses one or more concrete problems: poverty relief, multiculturalism, corporate social responsibility, trade standards, and reforming major political and economic institutions. The net result is an unprecedented articulation of what I shall call the *responsibilities approach* to human rights and—more broadly—the effort to understand accountability anew and achieve global justice.

The Nature of Responsibility

The volume is divided into four parts. In Part I, the contributors together show why we need to shift our approach to human rights, from a recipient-centric articulation of rights to an agent-centric approach, focusing on identifying those with the capacities and obligations to deliver on rights.

Thomas W. Pogge begins by arguing that the richest one-tenth of humankind could abolish severe poverty at minimal cost; for these people, and for developed states, the question is not one of capacity, but of whether they have any responsibilities that are correlative to the massively underfulfilled human rights of the global poor. He considers the recently proposed Draft Declaration of Human Responsibilities, which expresses the compelling idea that rights may be meaningless without specifying corresponding duties. Unfortunately, the document proves to be, if anything, less specific about responsibilities than existing human rights documents that it seeks to complement. Simply speaking, the language of obligations is not enough. In the search for greater specificity, Pogge returns to the Universal Declaration of Human Rights, and reinterprets it from a perspective that is not solely recipient-oriented. He argues that Article 28 in particular suggests that human rights give persons who are subject to an institutional order certain moral claims against those who impose it. This implies that the more powerful states imposing the international order must shape it so that (insofar as is reasonably possible) all persons subjected to it have secure access to the objects of their human rights. If those states lived up to this responsibility, much of the current vast underfulfillment of human rights would be avoided.

Pogge draws strong conclusions about individual duties in this context. When an institutional order avoidably fails to realize human rights, then those of its members who significantly collaborate in its imposition are violating a negative duty of justice—they are not merely failing to help, but are participating in unjustified coercion. As it stands, then, wealthy and influential citizens and states spuriously "present themselves as the most advanced in terms of human rights and are chiefly responsible for the fact that most human beings still lack secure access to the most vital goods." Pogge's emphasis on negative duties aims to undermine the widespread view that civil and political rights require only restraint, while social, economic, and cultural rights demand positive efforts and costs. His approach thus promises to reduce philosophical and political controversies between supporters of these different kinds of rights, and to focus attention on some key proposals to reform the global order so as to secure both kinds of rights.

Onora O'Neill points out, however, that most approaches to global justice assume that *states* are "the primary agents of justice," viewing all other actors as secondary agents of justice whose main contribution to justice is to conform to the just requirements of states. She traces this problematic background picture to the Universal Declaration of Human Rights, which, while universalist in its aspirations, looks at justice from the perspective of recipients and rights, to the exclusion of the perspective of actors and obligations. This commitment to a statist conception of obligations is equally reflected in influential political theories, such as that of John Rawls.

O'Neill concentrates on how this conceptual framework runs into particular difficulties when states are unjust or weak (in our world, much of the time). Here, non-state actors may have significant capabilities that states lack, and may have opportunities to contribute to the construction of justice precisely *because* they have greater relative powers and face fewer restrictions than they would in strong states. In such contexts, it is sociologically simplistic to presume that these agents (including transnational corporations) are ill motivated or indifferent to justice (merely intent on maximizing profit), or to presume that the state is a force for justice. Any simple division between primary and secondary agents of justice blurs. Justice has to be built by a diverse set of agents with different capabilities and correspondingly varied obligations.

Amartya Sen takes up this gauntlet by considering the appropriate standpoint or *evaluative perspective* for judging—in an impartial fashion—which obligations and rights fall to which agents. Sen's main target of attack is, again, the view of impartiality pioneered by John Rawls. On this view, we derive fair principles of justice by considering what principles would be chosen in an *intra*societal or *intra*polity contract, where the parties are ignorant of their exact identity within that focal group (generally, a nation or a state). Sen maintains that this procedure, which he calls "closed impartiality," may be effective in overcoming individual partialities within a group, but still fails in three crucial respects:

1. It fails to overcome the shared prejudices or biases of the focal group.
2. It results in inconsistencies when the decisions to be taken influence the size and composition of the focal group.
3. It excludes the voice of outsiders whose lives are affected by the decisions of the focal group.

Sen adds the empirical point that any initial identification of the focal group is deeply problematic: "The world is divisive all right, but it is diversely divisive, and the partitioning of the global population into distinct 'nations' or 'peoples' is not the only line of division." Neither principles of justice nor human rights and obligations can be adequately conceived and realized through "a nationally derived social contract."

Sen's positive proposal is that we avoid parochial contractarian reasoning not by imagining a single global contract, as some have suggested, but by reviving Adam Smith's device of the impartial spectator. This fair and impartial observer is not necessarily a member of the focal group, does not share their assumptions and biases, and can take the views of outsiders into account. Nevertheless, Sen adds a crucial modification: It is necessary to examine "the perspectives of differently situated spectators—from far and near—to overcome partiality in general." This complex "open impartiality" has vital practical implications because, according to Sen, it leads to the recognition of imperfect obligations to outsiders and not merely to group members, obligations "falling broadly on anyone who is in a position to help."

But who is in a position to help? What are the principles that enable us to determine whether, to what extent, and how any particular agent *ought* to help remedy a morally unacceptable situation?

Allocating Responsibilities

Sen, Pogge, and O'Neill could agree that powerful states have extensive obligations, and that obligations also fall on non-state actors where states are weak, unjust, or unwilling to act. Yet, even assuming an impartial standpoint, how do we pick out particular states or non-state actors and define their concrete obligations? Sometimes, as with "a right to aid" in a remote region, we may find it difficult to identify any capable agent who should deliver on purported rights (the problem of *emptiness*). Sometimes, as with "a right to development," we may find that there are multiple agents who could deliver on one or another rights-claim (the problem of *multiplicity*). The contributors to Part II develop a range of principles and strategies for allocating obligations when faced with these two problems.

Susan James examines the core idea that, if rights are to avoid the charge of emptiness, there must be identifiable agents who would be at fault for unfulfillment of the right. She argues that even this requirement is not sufficiently demanding. Certainly, there must be someone against whom to complain, and a minimal procedure of complaint, but there must also be someone or some mechanism to ensure that such agents fulfill their obligations. Rights must be not merely claimable, but effectively enforceable. Indeed, James is prepared to say that, where there is *no* agent in a position to help or no effective method of implementation, it does not make sense to talk of rights at all, and we should use different moral language. Rights are not freestanding but are "created" by individual and institutional capabilities to fulfill some moral claims and not others.

James proposes to narrow and clarify the meaningful use of rights-talk by identifying three conditions of enforceability:

1. Elaborate and interlocking sets of institutions.
2. Agents who understand what they are obliged to do and are able to do it.
3. Agents capable of claiming those rights.

She identifies four circumstances in which these conditions can be met:

1. There must be an overarching source or set of political authorities, which implies that there are fewer rights in the absence of such institutions.
2. Power must be distributed fairly evenly, otherwise some groups will be unable to claim their rights.
3. Agents to whom obligations are attributed must command the relevant resources to fulfill their duties; this often rules out weak and failed states.
4. Finally, those agents must be willing to contribute to the process of realizing rights; rights become mere words in the absence of crucial social attitudes and dispositions.

These conditions radically limit our capacity to generate rights. However, James seeks to illustrate that her stark approach enables us to better describe and deal with human rights dilemmas, such as those that arise when multicultural societies threaten to oppress women. To many human rights theorists and practitioners, including contributors to this volume, James's view may seem much too demanding. However, it serves as a lucid marker at one end of the continuum of the responsibilities approach.

David Miller marks out the other end of the continuum. He argues that where there is severe deprivation and suffering that can be alleviated, it is morally intolerable to allow it to continue and implausible to maintain that no one has the responsibility to help. We must ensure that, in grave cases, there is always some agent to whom responsibility can be assigned. The question, then, is not one of emptiness, but of how to pick out those who are responsible from the multiplicity of possible agents of justice.

Miller coins the term "remedial responsibilities" to refer to special obligations—obligations that do not fall equally on all agents—to remedy rights violations and deprivations such as severe poverty. He considers four principled answers to the question of how to establish who bears these special obligations: the agent who caused the deprivation, the agent who is morally responsible for the deprivation, the agent with the greatest capacity to remedy it, and the agent most closely connected by ties of community. None of these answers alone proves adequate because they do not capture our intuitions about simple paradigmatic situations of responsibility, nor do they resolve complex real-life quandaries, such as establishing who bears responsibility for causing and alleviating the plight of malnourished Iraqi children.

Should we therefore abandon the search for a general theory of remedial responsibility? Should we defend one principle despite seemingly intolerable implications? Should we attempt to rank principles once and for all? Miller rejects these unpalatable solutions. Instead, we should adopt a theory that is more openly pluralist, allowing us to weigh the respective strengths of principles in context. He sketches a *connection* theory of remedial responsibility that might meet this challenge. The idea is to fix responsibility on the agent who is already connected to the suffering person in some way; if several agents are so connected, we distribute responsibility according to the relative strength of the connection between potential relievers and suffering people. The four principles above then serve to establish the kind and importance of the special links involved, eliciting and clarifying our moral intuitions about which principles weigh more heavily in each empirical context. For Miller, this theoretical intricacy is not a drawback, but an appropriate mirroring of the complexity of real-world cases.

Michael Green is also concerned to overcome the problems of emptiness and multiplicity through what he calls "a complete attribution of responsibility." The central obstacle to such attribution, in his view, is nothing less than our commonsense conception of moral responsibility, which is too restrictive to capture and address large-scale social problems. Its individualism, its distinction between positive and negative duties, and its emphasis on special obligations owed to those close to us are analytically inadequate and implausible in the face of global harms, such as climate change, which transcend the intentions, powers, and interests of any individual or organized group. How, then, are we to avoid a counsel of despair?

Green proposes that we opt for an alternative conception of responsibility for large-scale problems, one that focuses on institutional agents—such as governments, corporations, labor unions, and international agencies—that do not face the same limitations as individual agents, and so can be subject to a less restrictive conception of responsibility. Institutional agents are better than individuals at collecting and processing information about the distant or indirect consequences of their actions, they are more often able to alter mass behavior, and they can spread the costs of regulating a problem. These capabilities give rise to obligations of greater scope. His distinctive claim, however, is that the special character of institutional capabilities also alters the *structure* of the obligations attributable to institutions. For instance, failures to act may be more deliberate, impactful, and unnecessary, thus omissions may be more blameworthy. Institutions cannot plausibly regard themselves as mere bystanders; they can and must act accordingly. In contrast to Pogge, however, Green wants to construe the negative obligations of individuals quite narrowly, and is prepared to do so because the distinctive obligations of institutional agents will take up the slack.

Christian Barry points out, however, that leaders of institutions are quick to disclaim responsibility for global harms on seemingly plausible grounds: Millions of agents may have contributed to these harms, often in highly mediated ways, and the empirical evidence concerning whether and to which extent some particular agent has contributed is far from conclusive. In the absence of such conclusive evidence, some might argue, each agent lacks strong moral reasons to rectify the situation. In order to assess this claim, Barry first explicates what he calls "the contribution principle"—the principle that we are responsible for addressing or preventing acute deprivations insofar as we have contributed or are contributing to them. He points out that this principle has great weight in our everyday moral thinking.

Barry then argues that agents who disclaim responsibility for addressing acute deprivations on the grounds that there is no conclusive evidence of contributing to such harms are committed to implausible doctrines concerning the burden of proof, the standard of proof, and the standards of evidence that are relevant in the context of assigning such ethical responsibilities. Appropriate thresholds are not determined by fiat, but rather by considering the context of inquiry and the goals of the practice in which the inquiry is undertaken. In a criminal trial, for instance, it may make sense to err on the side of letting the guilty go free rather than punishing the innocent; but Barry shows that such strictures are far less plausible when applied outside limited legal settings. When our concern is to determine ethical responsibilities to alleviate widespread and avoidable suffering and death, the application of the principle of contribution instead must express a much greater willingness to err in favor of those who are acutely deprived. When agents have reason to suspect that they contributed to such harms, this alone may be sufficient to impose moral requirements to change their policies and conduct. Powerful agents cannot let themselves so easily off the hook.

Part II leaves us, then, with at least five principles to consider in allocating responsibilities, as well as a more nuanced grasp of how those principles might be connected and applied in the real world of justice and injustice. There remain significant and revealing differences of opinion between the contributors. Yet, we are now better equipped to judge both when it is pointless or misleading to invoke rights and when it is fruitful and plausible to do so.

Individual Responsibility for Poverty Relief

Engaging more closely with the pragmatic quandaries of human development, Andrew Kuper and Peter Singer debate the nature and extent of responsibilities to relieve global poverty. Singer has proposed an unusually clear "solution to world poverty": Individuals should give away every cent in their possession not devoted to buying necessities. For the average American household, that means donating all income over $30,000 to charities. Are we obliged to sacrifice so much?

Kuper argues that the main problem with this charity-based approach is not so much that it is too demanding as that it will not work. We interact with one another globally through a complex web of political and economic arrangements; the poor remain poor because these arrangements exclude them in important ways. When well-off individuals beneficently dispense charity, it can help to redistribute wealth (and make us feel better), but it is a limited vehicle for improving poor people's situations on a sustainable basis. For that, we need some fundamental reforms to the rules and institutions of global order, such that the poor also come to benefit systematically from mechanisms of social cooperation. Thus, we need to avoid the narrow language of "selfishness versus sacrifice" (to which Singer directs us) in favor of a responsibilities approach that emphasizes "exclusion versus inclusion." Drawing on insights from the very different philosophies of John Rawls and Karl Marx, Kuper explicates key dimensions of the agenda for a political philosophy that might meet this challenge—one that moves us beyond both liberal and Marxist pieties. He then proposes some exemplary reforms in production (such as linking mining concessions to management of HIV/AIDS obligations), consumption, activism, and aid.

Singer does not see the disagreement as this fundamental. He points out, first, that Kuper accepts the cosmopolitan claims that the interests of everyone count equally and that our obligations to assist those in need do not stop at the borders of our nation or state. Second, he argues that Kuper's counterexamples are often irrelevant because Singer does not regard himself as indissolubly tied to any one way of overcoming poverty and starvation; if better strategies can be found, so be it. However, third, since most individuals do not know how to make deep structural changes that will end desperate poverty, it is still better to help some people rather than none. We are therefore obliged to dispense large portions of our income and wealth as immediate aid to organizations like Oxfam and UNICEF unless and until we know of better ways to address acute deprivations.

Kuper replies that there is a methodological disagreement here between a more "interactional" and a more "institutional" conception of obligations—a disagreement that has vital practical import. Charity from individuals can make a difference, but chronic reliance on this one strategy (until something better comes up) could harm the poor and vulnerable. We must dispense with the fantasy of a royal road to poverty relief, and address the causes of exclusion directly by contributing to institutional reform that generates sustained inclusion in governance and the global economy. Theory-informed analysis of institutional capabilities and obligations is indispensable to this task.

Singer, in his final rejoinder, is unconvinced. Indeed, he is skeptical of this kind of grand theoretical orientation because it threatens to distract attention from the immediate plight of real individuals. We can act now to reduce poverty, at little or no cost to ourselves, and we should do it.

Accountability of Actors in the Global Economy

The contributors to Part IV turn to examining the obligations of global economic organizations and how they can be held accountable for effectively discharging those obligations. According to the Institute for Public Policy Research, 51 of the 100 most powerful economic entities are now corporations and only 49 are states.[5] Meanwhile, the shape and direction of globalization is heavily influenced by three multilateral economic organizations (the World Bank, International Monetary Fund, and World Trade Organization). Thus, while contributors might have taken up many pressing practical problems, the case for paying particular attention to the capabilities and responsibilities of these economic institutions can hardly be countermanded.

David Held begins by charting crucial changes in the nature and forms of globalization. He argues that markets and business activities are being reframed through the introduction of cosmopolitan social standards embedded in human rights regimes and other legal instruments. He examines how these standards tend to emerge and he argues that they do delimit the obligations of different actors in important ways. However, he finds that the reach and impact of cosmopolitan standards is uneven, creating acute moral and competitive problems for socioeconomic agents and institutions of economic governance. This gives us a strong and pragmatic rationale for a politics of intervention in economic life. Held maintains that two interrelated sets of transformations are required, above all, if there is to be a better basis for global economic accountability. First, new principles based on rightful public authority must be institutionalized—to enable the effective exercise of legitimate power beyond the nation-state—at multiple levels and locales. Second, revised rules, codes, and procedures (concerning health, labor, the environment, corporate governance, and more) must be entrenched in the very articles of association and terms of reference of economic organizations and trading agencies. On the whole, previous chapters have addressed the first of these topics; the remaining three chapters of the volume address the second.

S. Prakash Sethi highlights how globalization in its current form is justified by invoking free trade and yet does not conform to that notion in a crucial respect: Multinational corporations have an unfair advantage in expropriating a greater share of gains from international trade than would be possible if organized labor and developing countries could bargain on fairer terms. Sethi considers corporate arguments to justify not remedying the current situation (e.g., it protects jobs and improves conditions in developing countries; it benefits customers and shareholders) and shows those arguments to be flawed and often disingenuous. He then focuses on how corporations can dramatically reduce the adverse effects of their operations on the rights of the poor, and substantially enhance the benefits, through the adoption of corporate codes of conduct. He sharply criticizes group-based approaches to developing effective codes—the Sullivan Principles, the UN Global Compact, and the Fair Labor Association—and favors instead individual company codes. The latter "go-it-alone" approach, he argues, is less susceptible to free-rider problems and to unwarranted charges of wrongful conduct, and can be better tailored to the needs of the company. Sethi outlines a framework for multinationals to undertake meaningful actions of this kind, thereby building public trust and producing worthwhile reputational effects for corporations that are agents of positive change. He also warns that corporate failure to act endangers private enterprise and property rights just as much as it endangers respect for individual freedom and human rights.

The final two chapters turn to the notion of "accountability"—undoubtedly the framing mantra for those who wish to advance institutional transformations of the kinds elaborated by Held and Sethi. Yet, accountability has been a fairly marginal and technical concept in political thought to date, and requires much clarification and development if it is to play a pivotal role in global political legitimacy. Melissa Lane and Ngaire Woods contribute to this broad project by elaborating the links between accountability and the responsibilities of economically powerful actors.

Lane distinguishes three aspects of accountability—legal, social, and moral—and seeks to understand their respective roles in holding corporations to account. While legal accountability has an unequalled clarity, force, and effectiveness, she finds that it leaves gaping holes for corporate malfeasance in both weak states and mature democracies. Social accountability, such as civil society processes of publicity, pressure, and boycott (often led by NGOs), fills some of these gaps, but it often degenerates into NGOs proclaiming their virtue and corporations defending theirs, since there is no "objective account or arbiter" of the legitimacy of competing claims. Only moral accountability can provide that much-needed standard of expectation and assessment. The key feature of moral accountability, an emphasis on (self-imposed) responsibility instead of sanction imposed from the outside, has provoked much skepticism from corporations as well as their critics. Lane addresses both sorts of doubt. First, she argues that neither duties to shareholders nor efficiency considerations justify corporations limiting their responsibilities to the relatively small set prescribed in the law. Second, she offers some procedural and substantive principles that provide more definite descriptions of the content of the moral responsibilities of corporations. This approach reduces the room for corporate maneuvering, while also insisting that these moral standards are not best enshrined as legal forms of accountability.

Finally, Ngaire Woods concentrates on what can be done to improve the accountability of multilateral economic institutions such as the World Bank, International Monetary Fund, and World Trade Organization. As the powers and formal responsibilities of these organizations have expanded, they have faced ever-increasing crises of both effectiveness and legitimacy; Woods warns, however, that we need to recognize the limits of various forms of accountability, otherwise we risk worsening the situation. She goes on to delineate four sorts of accountability deficits that beset these organizations—constitutional, political, financial, and internal—as a prelude to proposing reforms that she maintains will produce accountability of the right kinds. The proposals include dramatic changes, such as an overseer Economic and Security Council, extended representation of debtors in governing bodies, as well as more modest procedural changes, such as new rules of transparency on high-level decision making, more meritocratic forms of appointment to senior management positions, and more actionable internal operating guidelines.

If such accountability cannot be brought about, then must these responsibilities be redistributed to other agents or relinquished? If such reforms can be achieved, however, then need we stop there, or is it justifiable to assign obligations that are even more extensive to powerful agents such as corporations and intergovernmental organizations? Woods's contribution offers further general guidance in addressing these larger questions because her proposals are structured by two overriding imperatives:

1. To bring the capabilities of multilateral economic institutions into line with their newly assumed responsibilities.
2. To establish clearer lines of responsibility for both performance and oversight.

Responsibility—The Bridge between Rights and Accountability

In our world, immense wealth and power exist alongside widespread poverty and severe deprivation; nation-states regularly fail to provide an enabling environment for survival, freedom, and flourishing for all; and the potentially liberating language of human rights is often debased by overuse, misuse and abuse. In the face of these challenges, we must look for alternatives. Above all, we must begin to understand the potential inherent in a new constellation of power, where multinational corporations, nongovernmental organizations, intergovernmental institutions, cross-border networks, and informal arrangements are shaping our lives in unprecedented ways. We must begin to explore, systematically, what these powerful actors can and should do to improve the situation of the world's people, especially those who are acutely deprived. We must understand how, and ensure that, such powerful actors can be held accountable for their actions to remedy this brutal and distressing situation.

These imperatives require that we think outside of the usual boxes to which human rights discourse is confined. And the responsibilities approach to human rights—where we demand, in every context, to know "who must do what for whom?"—provides the conceptual resources to move beyond conventional pieties and statist strictures. It provides a much-needed bridge that at once *strengthens* the discourses of rights and accountability and *links* them to one another: Responsibility becomes the middle term that allows us to delineate justifiable and feasible rights-claims and to identify and hold to account agents who can and should deliver on those rights.

The responsibilities approach to human rights, articulated collectively, promises to renew our understanding and pursuit of global justice—in the conviction that our shared future may yet be made more humanly controllable and humane.

Notes

1. Onora O'Neill, *Towards Justice and Virtue: A Constructive Account of Practical Reasoning* (Cambridge: Cambridge University Press, 1996), p. 133.
2. This is an important part, not the whole, of the explanation for overuse and dilution of rights discourse.
3. This crisp formulation was provided first by Onora O'Neill (ibid.).
4. I have discussed this nexus of problems around defining and extending accountability—and have explored some interconnected solutions—in *Democracy Beyond Borders: Justice and Representation in Global Institutions* (Oxford: Oxford University Press, 2004).
5. S. Anderson and J. Cavanagh, *Report on the Top 200 Corporations* (Washington, D.C.: Institute for Policy Studies, 2000). The United Nations Conference on Trade and Development (UNCTAD) provides the rather more conservative estimate of 29 out of 100 (Associated Press, "UN Rates Top 100 Economic Entities," *Financial Review*, 13 August 2002).

PART I

The Nature of Responsibility

CHAPTER 1

Human Rights and Human Responsibilities[1]

THOMAS W. POGGE

The Problem

Various international declarations and treaties offer formulations of human rights that are, for the most part, clear enough to support reasonably precise estimates of the extent to which human rights are unfulfilled worldwide. Piecing together this global human rights record from the available data, we find that most of the current underfulfillment of human rights is more or less directly connected to poverty. The connection is direct in the case of basic social and economic human rights, such as the right to a standard of living adequate for the health and well-being of oneself and one's family, including food, clothing, housing, and medical care.[2] The connection is more indirect in the case of civil and political human rights associated with democratic government and the rule of law. Desperately poor people, often stunted, illiterate, and heavily preoccupied with the struggle to survive, can do little by way of either resisting or rewarding their rulers, who are therefore likely to rule them oppressively while catering to the interests of other (often foreign) agents more capable of reciprocation.

We have a great wealth of data about how widespread and severe global poverty is today: Out of a total of 6.2 billion human beings (2002), some 799 million are malnourished, more than 880 million lack access to basic health services, 1 billion are without adequate shelter, 1.1 billion without access to safe drinking water, 2 billion without electricity, and 2.4 billion without access to basic sanitation. In addition, 876 million adults are illiterate,[3] and over 200 million children between 5 and 14 do wage work outside their household, often under harsh or cruel conditions.[4] Some 50,000 human deaths per day, fully a third of all human deaths, are due to poverty-related causes and therefore avoidable insofar as poverty itself is avoidable.[5]

That a large segment of humankind is living in extreme poverty is nothing new. What is comparatively new, however, is that another large segment is living in considerable affluence. "The income gap between the fifth of the world's people living in the richest countries and the fifth in the poorest was 74 to 1 in 1997, up from 60 to 1 in 1990 and 30 to 1 in 1960." Earlier estimates are 11 to 1 for 1913, 7 to 1 for 1870, and 3 to 1 for 1820.[6] With this tremendous upsurge in global inequality comes a dramatic increase in human capabilities to eliminate severe poverty. It would not cost us much to eradicate the deprivations I have highlighted in the preceding paragraph—perhaps around one percent of the disposable incomes of the most affluent tenth of humankind. And this cost would decline over time, as adults who do not have to bear the horrendous mental and physical effects of childhood malnutrition, childhood diseases, child labor, and lack of basic education would be much better able to fend for themselves and to provide for their families. Our opportunity to abolish severe poverty worldwide starkly confronts us then with the question whether we have any responsibilities correlative to the internationally recognized, but massively underfulfilled, human rights of the global poor.

The world's governments faced up to this question at the World Food Summit in Rome, organized by the UN Food and Agriculture Organization (FAO) in November 1996. The principal achievement of this summit was a pledge by the 186 participating governments to reduce the number of undernourished people worldwide by about one-half, to 400 million, by the year 2015. The opening sentences of this Rome Declaration on World Food Security read as follows: "1. We, the Heads of State and Government, or our representatives, gathered at the World Food Summit at the invitation of the Food and Agriculture Organization of the United Nations, reaffirm the right of everyone to have access to safe and nutritious food, consistent with the right to adequate food and the fundamental right of everyone to be free from hunger. 2. We pledge our political will and our common and national commitment to achieving food security for all and to an on-going effort to eradicate hunger in all countries, with an immediate view to reducing the number of undernourished people to half their present level no later than 2015. 3. We consider it intolerable that more than 800 million people throughout the world, and particularly in developing countries, do not have enough food to meet their basic nutritional needs. This situation is unacceptable."[7] The represented governments could not, however, agree on concrete steps toward achieving such progress and did not sign or officially commit to the final document articulating the Summit goals.

Events since 1996 likewise indicate no special eagerness for implementation. The United States has issued an "Interpretive Statement" to clarify *its* understanding of the Rome pledge: "the attainment of any 'right to adequate food' or 'fundamental right to be free from hunger' is a goal or aspiration to be realized progressively that does not give rise to any international obligations."[8] Challenging the FAO's claim that achieving the Summit goals would require all developed countries combined to increase their annual official development assistance (ODA) in agriculture by $6 billion,[9] the United States published a competing calculation according to which an increase of US$2.6 billion per annum—that is, only $3.30 rather than $7.60 annually for each malnourished person—should be sufficient.[10] The affluent states' foreign aid budgets continued their downtrend.[11] And the widely publicized millennial restatement of the pledge weakened its ambition quite dramatically.[12]

It appears then that the developed countries do not accept any responsibility with regard to severe poverty abroad, either in principle or in practice. Yet, they also seem reluctant to publicize and defend this position, and even suggest the opposite in their rhetorical employment of words such as "intolerable" and "unacceptable." This should heighten interest in the question before us: What are our responsibilities in regard to the massive and avoidable underfulfillment of human rights abroad?

A New Universal Declaration?

Great expectations are raised, then, when a prominent group of former heads of state, calling itself the InterAction Council, proposes a Universal Declaration of Human Responsibilities for worldwide discussion and for adoption by the General Assembly of the United Nations with the express aim to "complement" the 1948 Universal Declaration of Human Rights on the occasion of its 50th birthday.[13] In its preamble, the Draft Declaration has the United Nations announce that: "We, the peoples of the world thus renew and reinforce commitments already proclaimed in the Universal Declaration of Human Rights." The new declaration is nevertheless necessary, as the accompanying report points out, for clarifying that human rights correlate with human duties: "Because rights and duties are inextricably linked, the idea of a human right only makes sense if we acknowledge the duty of all people to respect it."

Looking at the Draft Declaration in search for a clarification of the responsibilities for the realization of human rights, one cannot but be severely disappointed. Although one purpose of this Declaration is expressed by the compelling idea that rights are meaningless without the specification of corresponding duties, the Draft Declaration is, if anything, *less* specific about responsibilities than the human-rights documents it seeks to complement. Consider the various articles that spell out our responsibilities with regard to poverty.

Article 7 begins in a promising way: "Every person is infinitely precious and must be protected unconditionally." So who must effect this unconditional protection, how, and against what threats? What are our responsibilities? Article 7 continues: "The animals and the natural environment also demand protection. All people have a responsibility to protect the air, water and soil of the earth for the sake of present inhabitants and future generations." So the only responsibility assigned to us, it seems, is to protect air, water and soil: Animals merely "demand" protection; and humans "must be" protected, though apparently by no one in particular.

Article 9 does somewhat better: "All people, given the necessary tools, have a responsibility to make serious efforts to overcome poverty, malnutrition, ignorance, and inequality." But again, the main issues raised by this statement remain unaddressed: Is the directive to *overcome* poverty, malnutrition, etc., addressed to the poor themselves or to others as well? If the latter, which others: compatriots, all human beings? What counts as making a "serious effort"? And what is the import of the qualification "given the necessary tools"? The other sentence of Article 9 offers little help: "[All people] should promote sustainable development all over the world in order to assure dignity, freedom, security and justice for all people." Nothing is said about what "sustainable development" means or about what counts as promoting it.

Article 10 adds that "Everyone should lend support to the needy, the disadvantaged, the disabled and to the victims of discrimination." Nothing is said about the amount of support, nor about its targeting to ensure that the most urgent needs are actually met.

Article 11, finally, proclaims that "economic and political power must . . . be handled . . . in the service of economic justice and of the social order." The Draft Declaration provides no guidance with respect to the highly controversial notion of economic justice. Moreover, since the social order is often itself a major contributor to oppression and economic injustice (however one may wish to understand this notion), the Draft assigns potentially counterproductive and conflicting duties to people wielding economic and political power.

While the Draft Declaration expresses awareness of disadvantage and poverty, it fails then to clarify what responsibilities arise therefrom. Perhaps this should not be surprising in a declaration proposed by former heads of state for adoption by present political leaders. For these politicians, any more specific statement of responsibilities might raise awkward questions about how their own decisions have affected global poverty. The former leaders proposing the Draft Declaration can at least adduce the pressures of the Cold War as an excuse. It is unclear what could possibly excuse the increasing tolerance for starvation in the 1990s, when half of the so-called peace dividends would have sufficed to eradicate most of the world hunger problem.[14]

The excessive generality and vagueness of these middle articles is typical of the Draft Declaration as a whole, and especially evident also in the opening articles, which have the pomposity and emptiness one might expect in a teenager's first writing attempts. The first four articles are billed as "Fundamental Principles for Humanity." Of these, the third one best exemplifies the problem when it declares that nobody stands above good and evil and that everybody has a responsibility to promote good and to avoid evil "in all things." But the others are not much more meaningful either. The first principle of humanity says that every person has a responsibility to treat all people in a humane way. What does this mean? There are six billion other people out there, and with the vast majority of these I never interact except very indirectly. In these cases, am I discharging my responsibility to treat them in a humane way? What if some of them are starving or being tortured for their religious or political views and I do nothing for them—am I treating them humanely? Does it matter here whether they are compatriots or foreigners, or whether I have any general or particular knowledge of their plight? Or consider the people around me: Am I discharging my responsibility if I treat them in a humane way at some times and fail to do so at other times? And, most important, how is the distinction between humane and inhumane treatment to be drawn? As if to make up for the vagueness of the prescription, the drafters then add that it applies to every person "regardless of gender, ethnic origin, social status, political opinion, language, age, nationality, or religion." This addition would have a point if it referred to the *objects* of the proclaimed responsibility: to those who are to be treated humanely. It could naturally be taken to mean, then, that one's responsibilities are *equally* strong with regard to all others: The treatment I owe to compatriots, I also owe to foreigners; the treatment I owe to men, I also owe to women; and so forth. The addition is in fact attached, however, to the *subjects* of the proclaimed responsibility: to those who are to accord humane treatment. Here the long verbal addition adds no content at all: The statement that *every person* has a responsibility to treat all people humanely already entails that this responsibility is asserted for male and female persons, rich and poor persons, old and young persons, and so on.

One might think that more clarity can be derived from the Draft Declaration's endorsement of the Golden Rule in Article 4: What you do not wish to be done to yourself, do not do to others. This, of course, is the *negative* version of the Golden Rule. Its *positive* version—do unto others as you would have them do unto you—is not endorsed, although it is much closer to the "spirit of solidarity" invoked in Article 4. Endorsement of the positive version would have made it difficult to deny that persons have a responsibility to help others in distress, even across large distances, when they can do so at comparatively small cost to themselves. Endorsement of the negative version makes this far easier to deny: By *ignoring* the distress of others, I am not *doing* anything to them and hence a fortiori not doing anything I would not wish to be done to myself. What could the point of the selective endorsement of the negative version possibly be, if not to buttress this denial?

To make matters worse, the Golden Rule, in its negative version, often tends to shield and entrench immorality and injustice in situations where exposing them would be painful to their practitioners and beneficiaries. If I had violated some law or some significant ethical rule or principle, or had benefited from another's such violation, I would not wish this fact to become widely known. Does it follow therefrom that I should never expose such violations? Or, to take Kant's related example: Should a judge follow the Golden Rule when it enjoins her not to inflict on a defendant any punishment that this judge would not wish inflicted on herself?[15] To be sure, these problems do not defeat the view that the Golden Rule can be developed into a useful and plausible ethical standard that avoids these and other difficulties. Perhaps it can be. But without such a development, the Golden Rule cannot accomplish any of the purposes appealed to by the drafters. It is far too unclear.[16]

However timely and praiseworthy the project of drafting a universal declaration of human responsibilities may be, this particular Draft Declaration will not do. It gives no guidance about what our responsibilities are with respect to the massive underfulfillment of human rights today. Let us see, then, whether further reflection on the idea of human rights may lead to a clearer sense of our responsibilities.

Understanding Human Rights

It makes sense to begin this inquiry by outlining some plausible competing understandings of human rights while attending especially to how these differ in their implications about responsibilities for the realization of human rights. This exercise involves distinguishing two different components of any conception of human rights:

1. The *concept* of a human right used by this conception, or what one might also call its *understanding* of human rights
2. The *substance* or content of the conception, that is, the goods it selects as objects for a set of human rights

A conception of human rights addresses then two questions: What are human rights? And what human rights are there? I believe that these two questions are asymmetrically related, in this sense: We cannot convincingly justify a particular list of human rights without first making clear what human rights are. Yet we *can* justify a particular understanding of human rights without presupposing more than a rough idea about what goods are widely recognized as worthy of inclusion. This, in any case, is what I will attempt to do.

Even a fully comprehensive answer to the first question does not preempt the second. The fact that some formulated right has all the conceptual features of a human right does not entail that it exists (can be justified as such) any more than the fact that Robinson Crusoe as described has all the conceptual features of a human being entails that there is (atemporally) such a person. Settling what human rights there are requires not merely careful conceptual explication, but also substantive moral argument pro and con. It will be easier to engage in such substantive moral argument, however, once we have a shared understanding of what human rights are and hence of what the assertion of some particular human right actually amounts to, especially in regard to correlative responsibilities.

A straightforward answer to our question proposes that human rights are whatever governments—individually, in domestic law, or collectively, in international law—create under this title. The expression "human rights" is often used in this sense by lawyers, politicians, activists, and others. Without objecting to this use in the slightest, I am here interested in human rights as moral rights. That there are such rights is a widely shared presumption, which manifests itself, for instance, in the common phrase "internationally recognized human rights." That international legal documents *recognize* human rights suggests that people have human rights quite apart from such recognition—already in the Nazi era, for example—and that people would continue to have human rights even if governments decided to repeal and abrogate all national and international human-rights legislation. More generally, this common phrase leaves open the possibility that, even today, some human rights may not be legally recognized as such and also the converse possibility that some legal texts may be recognizing as human rights what are not human rights at all. Where legal texts confer recognition correctly, they create then a second legal right in addition to the moral one they "recognize" and thus present as preexisting: A government that used torture against its political opponents violated a (moral) human right of the persons it tortured—and, if it did so after March 23, 1976, it also breached its legal obligation under Article 7 of the International Covenant on Civil and Political Rights, violating a legal right (or a legal human right) of the tortured persons. My attention in what follows is focused exclusively on human rights of the first kind.

How should we understand the assertion that something is a human right in this moral sense? The moral concept of a human right has six rather uncontroversial elements that any plausible understanding of human rights must incorporate. First, human rights express *ultimate* moral concerns: Agents have a moral duty to respect human rights, a duty that does not derive from a more general moral duty to comply with national or international laws. (In fact, the opposite may hold: Conformity with human rights is a moral requirement on any legal order, whose capacity to create moral obligations depends in part on such conformity.) Second, human rights express *weighty* moral concerns, which normally override other normative considerations. Third, these moral concerns are focused on *human beings*, as all of them and they alone have human rights and the special moral status associated therewith. Fourth, with respect to these moral concerns, *all* human beings have *equal status*: They have exactly the same human rights, and the moral significance of these rights and of their fulfillment does not vary with whose human rights are at stake.[17] Fifth, human rights express moral concerns whose validity is *unrestricted*, that is, they are conceived as binding on all human agents irrespective of their particular epoch, culture, religion, moral tradition, or philosophy. Sixth, these moral concerns are *broadly shareable*, that is, capable of being understood and appreciated by persons from different epochs and cultures as well as by adherents of a variety of different religions, moral traditions, and philosophies. These last two elements of unrestrictedness and broad shareability are related in that we tend to feel more confident about conceiving of a moral concern as unrestricted when this concern is not parochial to some particular epoch, culture, religion, moral tradition, or philosophy.[18]

Various understandings of human rights are consistent with these six points. Though I cannot here examine all such understandings in detail, I want briefly to present three of the more prominent ones as a backdrop to the one I will endorse. I have tried to arrange the four understandings so that their sequence can be seen as a dialectical progression.

The first understanding, U_1, conceives human rights as moral rights that every human being has against every other human being or perhaps, more generally, against every other human agent (where this also includes collective agents, such as groups, firms, or governments).[19] Given this understanding of human rights, it matters greatly whether one then postulates human rights that impose only negative duties (to avoid depriving) or whether one instead postulates human rights that in addition impose positive duties (to protect and/or to aid).[20] A human right to freedom from assault might then give every human agent merely a weighty moral duty to refrain from assaulting any human being or also an additional weighty moral duty to help protect any human beings from assaults and their effects.

I do not deny that there are such universal moral rights and duties, but it is clear that we are not referring to them when we speak of human rights in the modern context. To see this, consider first some ordinary criminal assault. Though the victim may be badly hurt, we would not call this a human rights violation. A police beating of a suspect in jail, on the other hand, does seem to qualify. This suggests that, to engage human rights, conduct must be in some sense official. This suggestion is confirmed, secondly, by the human rights that have actually been recognized in various international documents. Many of them do not seem to be addressed to individual agents at all in that, rather than forbearance or support of a kind that individuals could provide, they demand appropriately constrained institutional arrangements such as equality before the law (§7), a nationality (§15.1), and equal access to public service (§21.2).[21] Finally, these documents also envisage the possibility of human rights that are limited in scope to the territory of the state to which the right holder belongs, or in which she or he resides, and thus do not impose duties upon foreigners. Examples are the right to equal access to public service in his country (§21.2) and the right to an education (§26.1).[22]

These problems with U_1 suggest another understanding, U_2, according to which human rights are moral rights that human beings have specifically against governments, understood broadly so as to include their various agencies and officials. This understanding solves the first problem with U_1 by supporting a distinction between official and nonofficial violations, between assaults committed by the police and those committed by a petty criminal or a violent husband. It solves the second problem insofar as governments are in a position to underwrite and reform the relevant institutional arrangements, at least within their own territory. And it facilitates a solution to the third problem by allowing a distinction between human rights persons have against their own government only and those they have against any government: A human right to education could be conceived as a right that every human being has against his or her own government (which thus is thought to have a weighty moral duty to ensure that each national or resident in its territory receives an appropriate education).

A human right not to be subjected to arbitrary arrest (§9), by contrast, could be conceived as one that every human being has against every government (which thus is thought to have a weighty moral duty to refrain from arbitrarily arresting any human being at all).[23]

The main problem with U_2 is that it unburdens private human agents. So long as one is not a government official, one need not worry about human rights at all. In response, it might be said that in a democracy it is ultimately the people at large who, collectively, constitute the government. But this response does not help with other kinds of regime. Persons who live under an undemocratic government need not worry about human rights because it is the duty of that government alone to fulfill these rights—including the human right of its subjects to take part in government (§21.1). On this understanding, wealthy and influential nationals would have no moral duty to do anything to prevent or to mitigate human-rights violations that their non-democratic government is committing against their compatriots or against foreigners—at least they would have no moral duty arising from the human rights of the victims. This limitation is not only morally implausible; it also goes against common parlance, as when people speak of a country's human rights record, thereby suggesting that the government does not bear sole responsibility for human rights.

This problem is avoided by yet another understanding, U_3, according to which human rights are basic or constitutional rights as each state ought to set them forth in its fundamental legal texts and ought to make them effective through appropriate institutions and policies.[24] So understood, a human right to X might be said to have two distinct components: juridification and observance. Through its *juridification* component, a human right to X would entail that every state ought to have a right to X enshrined in its constitution (or comparable basic legal documents). A human right to X would contain, then, a moral right to effective legal rights to X, which gives all citizens of a state a weighty moral duty to help ensure that an effectively enforced and suitably broad legal (or better: constitutional) right to X exists within this state.[25] Through its *observance* component, a human right to X would give a weighty moral duty to each government and its officials to ensure that the right to X—whether it exists as a legal right or not—is observed.

Though a definite improvement over U_1 and U_2, this understanding still faces three problems. First, in regard to some human rights, the juridification component of U_3 would seem to be excessively demanding. Consider a human right to adequate nutrition (§25.1). A society may be so situated and organized that all its members have secure access to adequate nutrition, though not a legal right thereto. Would this be a human rights problem?

I think not. Having the corresponding legal right in addition may be a good thing, to be sure, but it is not so important that this and every other human right must constitutively require its own juridification. Secure access is what really matters, and if secure access can be maintained through a culture of solidarity among relatives, neighbors, friends, or compatriots, say, then an additional legal right to adequate food when needed is not so important. The juridification component of U_3 is likely, then, to lead to a conception of human rights diluted by elements that are not truly essential.[26] Moreover, insistence on the juridification of human rights also provokes the familiar communitarian and East Asian criticisms, to be further discussed below.

In reply to this first criticism, a proponent of U_3 might point out that poor people may have secure access to food through reliable charities that do, however, require demeaning forms of supplication. Legal rights to food would protect poor people from having to choose between hunger and humiliation.[27] This reply does not, however, block the first criticism of U_3. For suppose it is right that people must be protected from facing such a choice, and suppose people thus have not merely a human right to adequate food, but a human right to adequate food without humiliation. (Since I am leaving aside here the substantive question what human rights there are, I am in no position to dispute these suppositions.) The first criticism can then still be reapplied to how U_3 would understand this stronger human right: A society may be so situated and organized that all its members have secure access to adequate nutrition without humiliation, though not a legal right thereto. Legal rights to food without humiliation are not necessary to protect people from facing a choice between hunger and humiliation. And U_3 is then too demanding by requiring legal rights to what really matters, even when secure access thereto is achievable in other ways.

The remaining two problems show that U_3 is, in other ways, not demanding enough. Thus a second problem with U_3 is that, even when a human right is appropriately juridified and the corresponding legal rights are observed and reliably enforced by the government and the courts, citizens may nevertheless be unable to insist on their rights. Being illiterate or uneducated, they may not know what their legal rights are, or they may lack either the knowledge or the minimal economic independence necessary to claim these rights through the proper legal channels. In this way, a human right to freedom from inhuman and degrading treatment (§5) may remain unfulfilled for most of a society's domestic servants, even if the state provides them an effective legal path on which they could defend themselves against abuse by their employers. This problem can be avoided by interpreting "observance" in a demanding sense as requiring that human rights be made fully (not merely legally) effective so as to ensure secure access to their objects.[28] I use "fulfillment" for this demanding sense of "observance" and develop this notion further below.

The third problem with U_3 is that it excessively unburdens agents with regard to human rights fulfillment abroad. According to U_3, our task as citizens or government officials is to ensure that human rights are juridified and observed (or fulfilled) in our own society and also observed by our government abroad. We have no human rights-based duties to promote the fulfillment of human rights in other countries or to oppose human rights violations by foreign governments—though it may be morally praiseworthy, of course, to work on such projects.[29] But, you will ask, what is wrong with this unburdening? To what extent, and on what grounds, should we be held responsible for the underfulfillment of human rights abroad?

An Institutional Understanding of Human Rights Based in §28

We find the beginnings of an answer to these questions in what may well be the most surprising and potentially most consequential sentence of the entire Universal Declaration: "Everyone is entitled to a social and international order in which the rights and freedoms set forth in this Declaration can be fully realized" (§28). This article has a peculiar status. As its reference to "the rights and freedoms set forth in this Declaration" indicates, §28 does not add a further right to the list, but rather addresses the concept of a human right, says something about what a human right is. It is then consistent with any substantive account of what human rights there are—even while it significantly affects the meaning of any human rights postulated in the other articles of this Universal Declaration: They all are to be understood as claims on the institutional order of any comprehensive social system.[30]

Section 28 suggests then a fourth, institutional, understanding of human rights, U_4, according to which human rights are moral claims on any coercively imposed institutional order. This understanding can be further specified through four plausible interpretive conjectures:

1. Alternative institutional orders that do not satisfy the requirement of §28 can be ranked by how close they come to enabling the full realization of human rights: Social systems ought to be structured so that human rights can be realized in them as fully as possible.
2. How fully human rights *can* be realized in some institutional order is measured by how fully these human rights generally are, or (in the case of a hypothetical institutional order) generally would be, realized in it.

3. An institutional order *realizes* a human right insofar as (and fully if and only if) this human right is *fulfilled* for the persons upon whom this order is imposed.

4. A human right is fulfilled for some person if and only if this person enjoys *secure access to the object of this human right.* Here the *object* of a human right is whatever this human right is a right to—adequate nutrition, for example, or physical integrity. And what matters is *secure access* to such objects, rather than these objects themselves, because an institutional order is not morally problematic merely because some of its participants are choosing to fast or to compete in boxing matches.

Taking these four conjectures together, I thus read §28 as holding that the moral quality, or *justice*, of any institutional order depends primarily on its success in affording all its participants secure access to the objects of their human rights: Any institutional order is to be assessed and reformed principally by reference to its relative impact on the realization of the human rights of those on whom it is imposed.[31] Postulating a human right to X is then tantamount to declaring that every society and comparable social system ought to be so organized that, as far as possible, all its members enjoy secure access to X.

When an institutional order avoidably fails to realize human rights, then those of its members who significantly collaborate in its imposition are violating a negative duty of justice. This duty should not mandate in all cases that such persons discontinue their participation. It may indeed come to this in extreme cases—toward the end of Nazi rule in Germany, for instance, when citizens, as far as possible, ought to have ceased all support, including payment of taxes and performance of services useful to the state. In most cases, however, it is better for the victims of injustice if we continue participation while also working toward appropriate institutional reforms or toward shielding these victims from the harms we also help produce. The duty in question should then afford this option. It should be formulated as a duty not to contribute to the coercive imposition of any institutional order that avoidably fails to realize human rights, unless one also compensates for one's contribution by working toward appropriate institutional reforms or toward shielding the victims of injustice from the harms one helps produce. Pursuant to U_4, a person's human rights are then not only moral claims *on* any institutional order imposed upon her, but also moral claims *against* those (especially more influential and privileged) persons who collaborate in its imposition.[32]

Given this understanding, a human right may be fulfilled for some and unfulfilled for other members of the same society. This is so because security of access to the object of some human right may vary across social groups. For example, only women may be facing a significant risk of assault, only rural dwellers may be in any real danger of hunger, and only persons with a certain skin color may be excluded from the franchise. Because an institutional order ought to be such that the human rights of all its participants are fulfilled, a human right is *fully realized* by some institutional order if and only if *all* of its participants have secure access to its object.

To be sure, no society can make the objects of all human rights *absolutely* secure for all. And making them as secure as possible would constitute a ludicrous drain on societal resources for what, at the margins, would be very minor increases in security. To be plausible, any conception of human rights employing the proposed concept must therefore incorporate an idea of reasonable security thresholds: Any human right of some person is *fulfilled* (completely) when access to its object is sufficiently secure—with the required degrees of security suitably adapted to the means and circumstances of the relevant social system. Thus, your human right to physical integrity (§3) is fulfilled by some institutional order, when it is sufficiently unlikely that you suffer a violation of your physical integrity without your consent.[33] Of course, what is sufficiently unlikely, within a well-designed institutional order, may nevertheless happen. We should allow then for the possibility that a person is actually assaulted even while his human right is fulfilled (because he is sufficiently secure from assault)—and also, conversely, for the possibility that someone's human right is not fulfilled (because his physical integrity is endangered) even though he never actually suffers an assault.

We have seen how U_4 goes beyond U_3 by insisting that, to realize human rights, a national institutional order must secure the objects of all participants' human rights not only against abuse by their government and its officials, but also against other social threats arising, for example, from death squads, criminals, domestic violence, or economic dependency. U_4 may and (I believe) should nevertheless hold that insecure access is more serious when its source is official. It is, other things equal, more important that our laws and the agents and agencies of the state should not themselves endanger the objects of human rights than that they should protect these objects against other social dangers. The need for this differential weighing shows itself, for instance, in our attitudes toward the criminal law and the penal system.[34] The point can be communicated most quickly, perhaps, by distinguishing, in a preliminary way, six ways in which an institutional order may affect the lives of its participants. The following illustration uses six different scenarios, arranged in order of their intuitive moral significance, in which, due to the prevailing institutional order, certain innocent persons are avoidably insecure in their access to some vital nutrients V (the vitamins contained in fresh fruit, say).[35] In scenario 1, the deficit is *officially mandated*, paradigmatically by the law: Legal restrictions bar certain persons from buying foodstuffs containing V. In scenario 2, the deficit results from *legally authorized* conduct of private subjects: Sellers of foodstuffs containing V lawfully refuse to sell to certain persons. In scenario 3, social institutions *foreseeably and avoidably engender* (but do not specifically require or authorize) the deficit through the conduct they stimulate: Certain persons, suffering severe poverty within an ill-conceived economic order, cannot afford to buy foodstuffs containing V. In scenario 4, the deficit arises from private conduct that is *legally prohibited but barely deterred*: Sellers of foodstuffs containing V illegally refuse to sell to certain persons, but enforcement is lax and penalties are mild. In scenario 5, the deficit arises from social institutions *avoidably leaving unmitigated the effects of a natural defect*: Certain persons are unable to metabolize V due to a treatable genetic defect, but they avoidably lack access to the treatment that would correct their handicap. In scenario 6, finally, the deficit arises from social institutions *avoidably leaving unmitigated the effects of a self-caused deficit*: Certain persons are unable to metabolize V due to a treatable self-caused disease and avoidably lack access to the treatment that would correct their ailment. [36]

Behind the moral significance we attach to these distinctions—and one could easily maintain that a human rights standard should not be sensitive to scenario 6 (and scenario 5?) deficits at all—lies the idea that an institutional order and the political and legal organs established through it should not merely *serve* justice, but also *symbolize* it. The point is important, because it undermines the plausibility of consequentialist (e.g., utilitarian) and hypothetical-contract (e.g., Rawlsian) moral conceptions that assess alternative institutional orders from the standpoint of prudent prospective participants who, of course, have no reason to care about this distinction among sources of threats.[37] A conception of human rights should avoid the mistake of such recipient-oriented approaches. To do so, it must, for each human right, distinguish and measure separately the different ways in which access to its object can be insecure; and it must then give more weight to first-class insecurities than to second-class insecurities, and so on.

The Global Normative Reach of Human Rights

Human rights are often said to be "universal"—a word used also in the title of the Universal Declaration. I have listed two senses in which human rights are universal among the uncontroversial elements of the concept of a human right: Human rights are equally possessed by, and are also equally binding upon, each and every human being. These two features are compatible with a "nationalistic" interpretation of human rights, according to which any person's responsibility for the fulfillment of human rights is limited by the boundaries of his or her society.[38] Yet §28 specifically excludes this interpretation by requiring that the *international* institutional order, as well, must be hospitable to the realization of human rights. Pursuant to U_4, human rights are then universal also in the further sense of having global normative reach: Human rights give persons moral claims not merely on the institutional order of their own societies, which are claims against their fellow citizens, but also on the global institutional order, which are claims against their fellow human beings. Any national *and any global* institutional order is to be assessed and reformed principally by reference to its relative impact on the realization of the human rights of those on whom it is imposed. Human rights-based responsibilities arise from collaboration in the coercive imposition of any institutional order in which some persons avoidably lack secure access to the objects of their human rights. For persons collaborating in the coercive imposition of a global institutional order, these responsibilities extend worldwide.[39]

This view presented by U_4 must be distinguished from the more common, but also less plausible, position that emerges when, in the context of U_1, human rights are interpreted as entailing duties to protect—the position, namely, that we ought to defend, as best we can, the objects of the human rights of any person anywhere. This position is less demanding in that it postulates merely positive duties, whereas U_4 supports a stronger negative duty not to impose an institutional order under which human rights avoidably cannot be fully realized. In another respect, this position is also more demanding by making the global normative reach of human rights unconditional—specifically, independent of the existence and causal significance of a coercively imposed global order. By contrast, what §28 is asking of the citizens and governments of the developed states is not that we assume the role of a global police force ready to intervene to aid and protect all those whose human rights are imperiled by brutal governments or (civil) wars. It requires instead that we support institutional reforms toward a global order that would strongly support the emergence and stability of democratic, rights-respecting, peaceful regimes and would also tend to reduce radical economic deprivations and inequalities, which now engender great vulnerabilities to civil rights violations as well as massive premature mortality from malnutrition and easily preventable diseases.

Unmoved by §28, influential citizens and politicians in the wealthy countries tend to regard the massive global underfulfillment of human rights with self-satisfied detachment. They are not unaware of the basic facts I have presented about the extent of poverty. But they do not see themselves as connected to, let alone responsible for, massive global poverty. They might give three reasons for their supposed innocence. First, they might say that the massive underfulfillment of human rights is caused by a variety of local factors endemic to particular developing countries and is thus quite independent of the existing global order.[40] Second, they might say that this global order is so complex that it is impossible, even with the good will of the world's rich and mighty, to reform it in a way that would reliably improve human rights fulfillment. Third, they might say that this global order is upheld by very many persons acting together so that the contribution of each is negligible or even naught.

The third of these reasons is a bad one. Even a very small fraction of responsibility for a very large harm can be quite large in absolute terms, and would be in the case before us.[41] To be sure, nearly every privileged person might say that she bears no responsibility at all because she alone is powerless to bring about a reform of the global order. But this, too, is an implausible line of argument, entailing as it does that each participant in a massacre is innocent, provided any persons he killed would have been killed by others, had he abstained. It is true that we, as individuals, cannot single-handedly reform the global order, and would find it very difficult to give up our privileged position in it so as to avoid making further contributions to its imposition. But we can clearly indicate our willingness to support institutional reforms, urge others to participate, and make efforts to facilitate cooperation. In addition, thanks to international human rights organizations like UNICEF, Oxfam, or Amnesty International, we can also help prevent or mitigate some of the harms caused by the global order—thereby making up, as it were, for our contribution to their production.

The first two reasons are harder to disprove. It is quite true that national factors (such as political and economic institutions, entrenched power structures, culture, contingencies of history, population density, climate, soil conditions, and mineral wealth) significantly affect a society's levels of poverty and human rights fulfillment. Yet, it is also true that the existing global order plays a profound role both in shaping many of these local factors and in influencing their effects. Let me illustrate this point by focusing on one consequential and reform-worthy feature of this order: Any group controlling a preponderance of the means of coercion within a country is internationally recognized as the legitimate government of this country's territory and people—regardless of how that group came to power, of how it exercises power, and of the extent to which it may be supported or opposed by the population it rules. That such a group exercising effective power receives international recognition means not merely that we are prepared to negotiate with it. It means also that we acknowledge this group's right to act for the people it rules, that we, most significantly, confer upon it the privilege freely to borrow in the country's name (international borrowing privilege) as well as freely to dispose of the country's natural resources (international resource privilege).

The *international borrowing privilege* includes the power to impose internationally valid legal obligations upon the country at large. Any successor government that refuses to honor debts incurred by an ever so corrupt, brutal, undemocratic, unconstitutional, repressive, unpopular predecessor will be severely punished by the banks and governments of other countries; at minimum it will lose its own borrowing privilege by being excluded from the international financial markets. Such refusals are therefore quite rare, as governments, even when newly elected after a dramatic break with the past, are constrained to pay the debts of their ever so awful predecessors.

The international borrowing privilege has three important detrimental effects on human rights fulfillment in the developing countries. First, this privilege facilitates borrowing by destructive governments. Such governments can borrow more money and can do so more cheaply than they could do if they alone, rather than the entire country, were obliged to repay. In this way, the borrowing privilege helps such governments maintain themselves in power even against near-universal popular discontent and opposition. Second, the privilege imposes upon democratic successor regimes the often huge debts of their corrupt predecessors. It thereby saps their capacity to implement institutional reforms and other political programs, thus rendering these democratic governments less successful and less stable than they would be otherwise. Third, the international borrowing privilege provides incentives toward coup attempts: Whoever succeeds in bringing a preponderance of the means of coercion under his control gets this privilege as an additional reward.

The *international resource privilege* enjoyed by a group in power is much more than our mere acquiescence in its effective control over the natural resources of the country in question. This privilege includes the power to effect legally valid transfers of ownership rights in such resources. Thus a corporation that has purchased resources from the Saudi or Suharto families, or from Mobuto or Sani Abacha, has thereby become entitled to be—and actually *is*—recognized anywhere in the world as the legitimate owner of these resources. This is a remarkable feature of our global order. A group that overpowers the guards and takes control of a warehouse may be able to give some of the merchandise to others, accepting money in exchange. But the fence who pays them becomes merely the possessor, not the owner, of the loot. Contrast this with a group that overpowers an elected government and takes control of a country. Such a group, too, can give away some of the country's natural resources, accepting money in exchange. In this case, however, the purchaser acquires not merely possession, but all the rights and liberties of ownership, which are supposed to be—and actually *are*—protected and enforced by all other states' courts and police forces. The international resource privilege, then, is the power to confer globally valid legal ownership rights in the country's resources.

The international resource privilege has disastrous effects on vast numbers of people, especially in the poorest countries in which the resource sector often constitutes a large segment of the national economy. Whoever can take power in such a country by whatever means can maintain his rule, even against widespread popular opposition, by buying the arms and soldiers he needs with (funds borrowed abroad in the country's name and) revenues from the export of natural resources. This fact in turn provides a strong incentive toward the undemocratic acquisition and unresponsive exercise of political power in these countries. And the international resource privilege also gives foreigners strong incentives to corrupt the officials of such countries who, no matter how badly they rule, continue to have resources to sell and money to spend. This shows how the local causal chain (persistent poverty caused by corrupt government caused by natural resource wealth) can itself be traced back to the international resource privilege. It is on account of this privilege that resource-rich developing countries are more likely to experience coup attempts and civil wars and more likely also to be ruled by corrupt elites, so that—despite considerable natural wealth—poverty in these countries tends to decline only slowly, if at all.[42]

It is hardly surprising that the causal role of global institutional factors is so often overlooked. We have a very powerful personal motive to want to see ourselves as unconnected to the unimaginable deprivations suffered by the global poor. This motive produces self-deception and automatic rejection of politicians, academics, and research projects that explore the wider causal context of global poverty. Moreover, we have a general cognitive tendency to overlook the causal significance of stable background factors (e.g., the role of atmospheric oxygen in the outbreak of a fire) in a diverse and changing situation. Looking at human rights fulfillment worldwide, our attention is thus drawn to local factors, which sometimes change dramatically (e.g., recently in Eastern Europe) and which vary greatly from country to country. Through an exhaustive analysis of these factors, it seems, all phenomena relevant to the realization of human rights can be explained.

And yet, it is not so: When human rights are more fully realized in one country than in another, then there must be, of course, some difference that contributes to this discrepancy. But an explanation that merely points to this difference leaves many questions open. One question concerns the broader context which determines that national factors have these effects rather than others. It is quite possible that in the context of a different global order the same national factors, or the same international differences, would have quite another impact on the realization of human rights. Another question concerns the explanation of the national factors themselves. It is quite possible that, within a different global order, national factors that tend to undermine the fulfillment of human rights would occur much less often or not at all.[43] These considerations show that the global level of human rights fulfillment cannot be explained in terms of national factors alone.

My discussion of some central features of the existing global order was meant to illustrate the following important points:

1. The fulfillment of human rights in most countries is strongly affected not merely by national factors, but also by global ones.
2. Explanations in terms of national and global factors do not simply compete with each other. Only their synthesis—*one* explanation that integrates factors of both kinds—can be a true explanation. This is so because the effects of national factors are often strongly affected by global factors (and vice versa) and because global factors strongly shape those national factors themselves (though the inverse influence is generally slight).
3. The influences emanating from our global order are not necessarily the way they are, but are co-determined by reformable institutional features, such as the two privileges I have discussed.

These points can help refute the first two reasons that influential citizens and politicians in the wealthy countries might adduce in support of their innocence: The global order we uphold does play a major role in causing the massive underfulfillment of human rights today. It does so in four main ways: It crucially affects what sorts of persons shape national policy in the developing countries, what incentives these persons face, what options they have, and what impact the implementation of any of their options would have on domestic poverty and human rights fulfillment. Once the causal effects of specific global institutional arrangements are appreciated, it is not too difficult to take on the second reason by developing plausible proposals for reform—though space constraints do not allow me to do this here.[44]

Pursuant to U_4, human rights support then a severe critique of the more influential citizens and politicians in the wealthy countries. We are quite wrong to present ourselves as the most advanced in terms of human rights and are chiefly responsible for the fact that most human beings still lack secure access to the most vital goods.[45] And we are also the chief beneficiaries of the existing global order. This order perpetuates our control over the weaker developing countries. And it also guarantees us a reliable and cheap supply of natural resources, because we can acquire ownership rights in such resources from anyone who happens to exercise effective power and because the resource consumption of the majority of humankind is severely constrained by poverty.[46]

The discussion of the international borrowing and resource privileges thus illustrates the empirical background against which the global demand of §28 makes sense. It is the point of human rights, and of official declarations thereof, to ensure that all human beings have secure access to certain vital goods. Many persons currently lack such security.[47] We can assign responsibility for such insecurity to the governments and citizens of the countries in which it occurs, and doing so makes good sense. But leaving it at this does not make good sense. For the hope that these countries will, from the inside, democratize themselves and abolish the worst poverty and oppression is entirely naïve so long as the institutional context of these countries continues to favor so strongly the emergence and endurance of brutal and corrupt elites. And the primary responsibility for this institutional context, for the prevailing global order, lies with the governments and citizens of the wealthy countries because we maintain this order, with at least latent coercion, and because we, and only we, could relatively easily reform it in the directions indicated. §28 should be read as a recognition of these points: a clear repudiation of the common and ever so dear conviction that human rights do not reach beyond national borders, that we normally have no responsibilities for the fulfillment of the human rights of foreigners (living abroad).[48]

In the world as it is, U_4 thus tends to undermine the self-satisfied detachment with which the governments and peoples of the wealthy countries tend to look down upon the sorry state of human rights in many of the so-called less developed countries: This disaster is the responsibility not only of their governments and populations, but also ours, in that we continuously impose upon them an unjust global order without working toward reforms that would facilitate the full realization of human rights.

The Universality of Human Rights

Having shown that it makes sense to conceive of human rights, as U_4 suggests, as having global normative reach, let me proceed to survey the advantages of this understanding. Some advantages have already been touched upon in the preceding discussion: U_4 is more suitable than U_1–U_3 for singling out the truly essential elements in human quality of life and it incorporates a more plausible assignment of responsibilities in regard to the underfulfillment of human rights. In the three ensuing sections, I lay out three further important advantages, showing that U_4 can make a much greater contribution toward facilitating agreement on how to specify and to pursue the realization of human rights worldwide.

The first of these additional advantages lies in the profound implications of U_4 for the debate about the universal validity of human rights. Many people see the fact that human rights are understood as universal as a strong reason for denying them. They view human rights as an outgrowth of a provincial morality whose pretension to universal validity is yet one more variant of European imperialism. They might say the following: "Non-European peoples have cultural traditions of their own from which they construct their own moral conceptions, perhaps wholly without the individualistic concept of a right. If you Westerners want to make a conception of human rights the centerpiece of your political morality and want to realize it in your political system, then go ahead, by all means. But do leave other peoples the same freedom to define their values within the context of their own culture and national discourse."

Even if such admonitions are often put forward in bad faith,[49] they nevertheless require a reasoned response, which, pursuant to U_4, can be formulated as follows: When human rights are understood as a standard for assessing only national institutional orders and governments, then it makes sense to envision a plurality of standards for societies that differ in their history, culture, population size and density, natural environment, geopolitical context and stage of economic and technological development. But when human rights are understood also as a standard for assessing the *global* institutional order, international diversity can no longer be accommodated in this way. There can be, at any given time, only *one* global order. If it is to be possible to justify this global order to persons in all parts of the world and also to reach agreement on how it should be adjusted and reformed in the light of new experience or changed circumstances, then we must aspire to a *single, universal* standard that all persons and peoples can accept as the basis for moral judgments about the global order that constrains and conditions human life everywhere.

Consider a domestic parallel. Imagine someone setting forth a moral conception of decent family life in the hope of achieving nationwide agreement. Our first reaction might be that we do not need such agreement, need no shared conception how all families should live. We can happily live together in one society even while we differ in many of our deepest aspirations, including those about family life. Having received this response, our interlocutor says that she meant to raise a quite different issue: The institutional rules of our society affect family life in countless ways. A few do so very directly—they define and limit the legal freedoms of spouses with regard to how they may treat each other and their children, how they may use and dispose of individually or jointly owned property, what kinds of education and medical care they may give to or withhold from their children, and so forth. Many other rules influence family life more indirectly. Social rules may, for instance, affect the economic burdens of child rearing, shape the physical and social environment within which families exist, and determine the extent to which women are respected as the full equals of men (can successfully participate in the economy, can present their concerns within the political process, etc.). Since a society's social rules are subject to intelligent (re)design and also exert a profound influence upon family life within this society, its citizens have a responsibility to bring their sharable values concerning family life to bear upon the design of their shared institutional order. This, concludes our interlocutor, was her point in proposing a moral conception of decent family life.

As the domestic parallel shows, attaining a common standard for assessing a shared institutional order does not presuppose thoroughgoing agreement. Thus, our interlocutor in the domestic case need not decide what kinds of relationships among spouses and children are best. She may merely advocate certain constraints, insisting, for example, that wives must be secure from coercion by their husbands, which can be achieved by promoting through the education system equal respect and equal opportunities for women, by criminalizing interspousal rape, by safeguarding the voluntariness of religious practices, and by guaranteeing an economically safe option of divorce.

The analogous point holds for human rights as a moral standard for our global order. This standard does not presuppose agreement on all or even most moral questions. It may merely demand that this global order be so designed that, as far as possible, all persons have secure access to a few goods vital to human beings. Now it is true that designing an institutional order with an eye to a few key values will have collateral effects on the prevalence of other values. A solidly Catholic (or Muslim) family life may well be harder to sustain within a society that safeguards freedom of religion than in one in which Catholicism (or Islam) is the official state religion. Similarly, the choice of a global order designed to realize human rights would have a differential impact on the cultures of various societies and on the popularity of various religions and ways of life. But such collateral effects are simply unavoidable: *Any* global (and national) institutional order can be criticized on the grounds that some values do not optimally thrive in it. So long as there is any global order at all, this problem will necessarily persist.

Still, the problem can be mitigated by formulating a common moral standard so that the global order it favors will allow a wide range of values to thrive locally. Human rights meet this condition because they can be fully realized in a wide range of countries that differ greatly in their culture, traditions, and national institutional order.

The crucial thought here is this: Once human rights are understood as moral claims on our global order, there simply is no attractive, tolerant, and pluralistic alternative to conceiving them as valid universally. While the world can contain societies that are structured in a variety of ways (according to diverse, even incompatible values), it cannot itself be structured in a variety of ways. If the Iranians want their society to be organized as an Islamic state and we want ours to be a secular democracy, we can both have our way.[50] But if the Iranians wanted our *global* order to be designed on the basis of the Koran, while we want it to secure the objects of everyone's human rights, then we cannot both have our way. Our global order cannot be designed so as to give all human beings the assurance that they will be able to meet their most basic needs *and* so as to give all governments maximal control over the lives and values of the peoples they rule *and* so as to ensure the fullest flourishing of Islam (etc.). Among competing plans for the future of our global order, *one* will necessarily win out—through reason or through force. Neutrality is not an option here. The policies of the major societies will necessarily affect the outcome. It is, for the future of humankind, the most important and most urgent task of our time to set the development of our global order upon an acceptable path. In order to do this together, peacefully, we need international agreement on a common moral standard for assessing the feasible alternatives. The best hope for such a common moral standard that is both plausible and capable of wide international acceptance today is a conception of human rights. At the very least, the burden now is on those who reject the very idea of human rights to formulate and justify their own alternative standard for achieving a global order acceptable to all.

Making Human Rights More Broadly Sharable

In order to serve as a common moral standard, a conception of human rights must meet the sixth condition of broad shareability. Whether it does depends not only on its content (the specific human rights it postulates), but also on the concept of a human right it employs. U_4 renders human rights significantly less vulnerable to critical doubts and hence more broadly shareable. Let me briefly indicate why this is so.

One important communitarian critique, often claimed to show that human rights are alien to communal cultures (for instance in Southeast Asia), asserts that human rights discourse leads persons to view themselves as Westerners: as atomized, autonomous, secular, and self-interested individuals ready to insist on their rights no matter what the cost may be to others or to society at large.[51]

This critique may have some plausibility when human rights are understood as demanding their own juridification as basic legal rights held by individuals (U_3). But it has much less force when, as I have proposed, we avoid any conceptual connection of human rights with legal rights. We are then open to the idea that, in various economic and cultural contexts, secure access to the objects of human rights might be established in other ways. Yes, secure access to minimally adequate nutrition can generally be maintained through legal rights to food when needed. But it can also be maintained through other legal mechanisms—ones that keep land ownership widely dispersed; ban usury or speculative hoarding of basic staples; or provide child care, education, retraining subsidies, unemployment benefits, or start-up loans. And non-legal practices—such as a culture of solidarity among friends, relatives, neighbors, and compatriots—may also play an important role. Even those hostile to a legal-rights culture can, and often do, share the goal of realizing human rights as understood by U_4; and they may be quite willing to support a legally binding international commitment to shape national and international institutional arrangements so that all human beings can securely meet their most basic needs. We have reason then to conceive the realization of human rights in this broad way, rather than insist on conceiving it narrowly as involving individual legal rights of matching content. We may feel strongly that such matching individual legal rights ought to exist in our own culture. But there is no good reason for requiring that secure access to the objects of human rights must be maintained in the same way everywhere on earth.

One important libertarian critique, which is often claimed to show that human rights are alien to individualist (especially Anglo-American) cultures, asserts that human rights impose excessive restrictions on individual freedom by requiring all human agents to defend, as best they can, the objects of the human rights of any person anywhere (U_1). Libertarians reject such a requirement not merely because it would be excessively burdensome in a world in which the human rights of so many remain unfulfilled, but mainly because they hold that all moral duties must be *negative* ones, that is, duties to refrain from harming others in certain ways. Libertarians may acknowledge that it is morally good to protect, to aid, or to benefit others, but they deny that anyone has a duty to do such things. And since they recognize no positive moral duties, libertarians also deny the existence of any moral rights to be protected, aided, or benefited.

U_4 can help accommodate this critique as well. U_4 does not assume that human agents have human-rights-based obligations merely by virtue of the fact that the human rights of some persons avoidably remain unfulfilled. U_4 envisions such obligations specifically for agents who significantly collaborate in imposing an institutional order that produces this human-rights problem. Such agents must either stop contributing to this imposition or else compensate for this contribution by working toward appropriate institutional reforms and toward shielding the victims of injustice from the harms they help produce.[52] This is a *negative* duty on a par with the libertarians' favorite duty not to defraud others by breaking a contract or promise one has made. One can avoid all obligations arising from these duties by, respectively, not taking part in the coercive imposition of an unjust institutional order, and not making any contracts or promises. But if one does contribute significantly to imposing an institutional order upon others, one is obligated to help ensure that it fulfills the human rights of these others as far as possible—just as, if one does make a promise, one is obligated to keep it.

Reconciling Conflicting Priorities Among Human Rights

The substance of a conception of human rights continues to be controversial. Prominent here is the debate between those who, like many Western governments, emphasize civil and political rights and those who, like many developing and socialist states, emphasize social, economic, and cultural rights. I have shown already how U_4 can be detached from such controversies and defended with powerful, independent arguments. I will now show how its acceptance would also greatly reduce the significance of such controversies, which have occasioned much discord in the UN and elsewhere. The third further advantage of U_4 is then that it can facilitate agreement on the substance or content of our conception of human rights.

U_4 does not lead to the idea that civil and political rights require only restraint, while social, economic, and cultural rights also demand positive efforts and costs. Rather, it emphasizes negative duties across the board: We are not to collaborate in the coercive imposition of any institutional order that avoidably fails to realize human rights of whatever kind. Moreover, there is no systematic correlation between categories of human rights, understood pursuant to U_4, and effective institutional means for their realization, which may vary in time and place. Thus, in order to realize the classical civil right to freedom from inhuman and degrading treatment (§5), for instance, a state may have to do much more than create and enforce appropriate criminal statutes. It may also need to establish adequate social and economic safeguards, ensuring perhaps that domestic servants are literate, know about their rights and options, and have some economic security in case of job loss. Conversely, in order to realize a human right to adequate nutrition, perhaps all that is needed is an effective criminal statute against speculative hoarding of foodstuffs.

These considerations greatly narrow the philosophical gap between the friends of civil and political rights and the friends of social, economic, and cultural rights. Let me now show how they may also greatly reduce the practical significance of such controversies.

Suppose that only civil and political human rights are worthy of the name, that the social, economic, and cultural rights set forth in the Universal Declaration (foremost the much ridiculed right to "periodic holidays with pay" of §24) should hence be repudiated. Conjoining this view with U_4 yields the moral assertion that every human being is entitled to a national and global institutional order in which civil and political human rights can be fully realized. The existing global order falls far short in this respect, and does so largely on account of the extreme poverty and inequality it reproduces: In most developing countries, the legal rights of ordinary citizens cannot be effectively enforced. Many of these countries are so poor that they cannot afford properly trained judges and police forces in sufficient numbers; and in many of them social institutions as well as politicians, officials, and government agencies are in any case (partly through foreign influences) so thoroughly corrupted that the realization of civil and political human rights is not even seriously attempted. And even in those few countries where the legal rights of ordinary citizens can be effectively enforced, too many citizens are under too much economic pressure, too dependent on others, or too uneducated to effect the enforcement of their rights. Thus, even the goal of realizing only the recognized civil and political human rights—if only they were interpreted in the light of §28—suffices to support the demand for global institutional reforms that would reduce global poverty and inequality.

Or suppose that only social, economic, and cultural human rights are worthy of the name. Conjoining this view with U_4 yields the moral assertion that every human being is entitled to a national and global institutional order in which social, economic, and cultural human rights can be fully realized. The existing global order falls far short in this respect as billions live in poverty, with little access to education and health care, and are in constant mortal danger from malnutrition and diseases that are easily controlled elsewhere. Their suffering is in large part due to the fact that the global poor live under governments that do little to alleviate their deprivations and often even contribute to them. The global poor are dispersed over some 150 countries, of which many are ruled not by general and public laws, but by powerful persons and groups (dictators, party bosses, military officers, and landlords), often sponsored or assisted from abroad. In such societies, they are unable to organize themselves freely, to publicize their plight, or to work for reform through the political or legal system. Thus, even the goal of realizing only the usual social and economic human rights—if only they were interpreted in the light of §28—suffices to support the call for a global order that would strongly encourage the incorporation of effective civil and political rights into national constitutions.

I certainly did not mean to contend in this section that it makes no difference which rights we single out as human rights. I merely wanted to show that both the philosophical and practical–political importance of the actual controversies about this question would diminish, if human rights were understood pursuant to U_4: as moral claims on any coercively imposed institutional order. Even if we continue to disagree about which goods should be included in a conception of human rights, we will then—provided we really care about the realization of human rights rather than about ideological propaganda victories—work together on the same institutional reforms instead of arguing over how much praise or blame is deserved by this state or that.

Conclusion

In the aftermath of the Second World War, a fledgling United Nations issued a Universal Declaration of Human Rights as the preeminent moral standard for all of humankind. This declaration, in its §28, specifically suggests that the realization of human rights will crucially depend on the achievement of a just global order.[53] In the intervening half-century, the dominant powers, led by the United States, have indeed created a far more comprehensive global order that severely constrains and conditions the political and economic institutions and policies of all national societies and governments. It is hardly surprising that these powers have tried to shape this order in their own interest. They have done so quite successfully, bringing peace and unprecedented prosperity to their populations.

And yet, if we judge this global order from a less parochial moral standpoint, one that makes the fulfillment of everyone's human rights the central concern, then we must conclude that this order is still deeply flawed and quite avoidably so. Yes, the last fifty years project a strong image of brisk progress from one declaration, summit, and convention to the next. There has been significant progress in formulations and ratifications of human rights documents, in the gathering and publication of statistical information, and even in the realization of some human rights. But these fifty years have also culminated in unprecedented economic inequality between the most affluent tenth of humankind and the poorest fifth. What makes this huge and steadily growing inequality a monstrosity, morally, is the fact that the global poor are also so incredibly poor in absolute terms. They lack secure access to food, safe water, clothing, shelter, and basic education, and they are also highly vulnerable to being deprived of the objects of their civil and political human rights by their governments as well as by private agents. Some 18 million of them die prematurely every year.

Since features of the global order are the decisive variable for the realization of human rights today, the primary moral responsibility for the realization of human rights must rest with those who shape and impose this order, with the governments and peoples of the most powerful and affluent countries. We lay down the fundamental rules governing internal and external sovereignty, national property rights in land and resources, global trade, international financial transactions, and so on. And we enforce these rules through economic sanctions and occasional military interventions. These rules and their foreseeable effects are then our responsibility. And our failure to initiate meaningful institutional reforms that would drastically reduce global poverty is all the more appalling as the opportunity costs such reforms would impose upon us have declined steeply with the end of the Cold War and the great economic and technological advances of the last decade.

Against this background, I conclude, then, that the understanding of human rights and correlative human responsibilities, which I have presented here in explication of §28, is more compelling than the three competing understandings and the Draft Universal Declaration of Human Responsibilities. U_4 correctly identifies the crucial human-rights-based responsibility in this world: the responsibility of the affluent states and their citizens for the global economic and political order they impose. This order is the key obstacle to the realization of human rights. Our preeminent moral task is to reshape this order so that all human beings have secure access to the basic goods they need to be full and respected members of their communities, societies, and of the wider world.

Notes

1. I am indebted to Christian Barry, Pablo de Greiff, Cecile Fabre, Thomas Mertens, Andrew Nathan, Guido Pincione, Markus Pins, and Ling Tong for their very helpful critical comments. Composition of the essay was supported by a generous grant from the Research and Writing Initiative of the Program on Global Security and Sustainability of the John D. and Catherine T. MacArthur Foundation.
2. §25, Universal Declaration of Human Rights, adopted and proclaimed by the General Assembly of the United Nations on December 10, 1948, as resolution 217A(III). I use the symbol "§" throughout to refer to articles of this document.
3. This information is collated in the annual *Human Development Reports* (henceforth *HDR*) produced by the United Nations Development Programme (with most data supplied by the World Bank) and published by Oxford University Press. The information I have cited is from *HDR 2003*, 6, 9, 87; *HDR 1999*, 22; and *HDR 1998*, 49.
4. World Bank: *World Development Report 1999/2000* (New York: Oxford University Press 1999), 62, also available at www.worldbank.org/wdr/2000/fullreport.html. I will cite these annual reports as *WDR*. For more recent figures, see www.ilo.org/public/english/standards/ipec/simpoc.
5. *Cf.* U.S. Department of Agriculture (USDA): *U.S. Action Plan on Food Security* (www.fas.usda.gov:80/icd/summit/usactplan.pdf; March 1999), p. iii: "Worldwide 34,000 children under age five die daily from hunger and preventable diseases." For full details, see more recently World Health Organization (WHO): *The World Health Report 2004* (www.who.int/whr/2004), especially Annex Table 2.

6. *HDR 1999*, 3.
7. www.fao.org/documents/show_cdr.asp?url_file=/DOCREP/003/W3613E/W3613E00.HTM
8. "Interpretive Statement" filed by the U.S. Government in reference to the first paragraph of the Rome Declaration on World Food Security (www.fas.usda.gov:80/icd/summit/interpre.html).
9. Nikos Alexandratos, ed.: *World Agriculture: Toward 2010, an FAO Study* (Chichester, U.K.: J. Wiley & Sons, and Rome: FAO, 1995).
10. USDA: U.S. Action Plan on Food Security, Appendix A.
11. HDR 2003, 290. At 0.11 percent of its GNP in 2001, versus 0.21 percent under Ronald Reagan in 1987/8, the United States provides the lowest level of net ODA among developed countries. Moreover, as the USAID itself had, until recently, stated on its website: "The principal beneficiary of America's foreign assistance programs has always been the United States. Close to 80 percent of the U.S. Agency for International Development's (USAID's) contracts and grants go directly to American firms."
12. *Cf.* my "The First UN Millennium Development Goal," *Journal of Human Development* 5 (2004), 377-97.
13. See *Ethics and International Affairs* 12 (1998), 195–9, or www.philia.ca/Caring_citizen/universal-responsib.htm, for full text. The InterAction Council was founded in 1983 by the late Takeo Fukuda, former Prime Minister of Japan. Among the "high-level experts" consulted in drafting the declaration are Hans Küng (Tübingen University) and Richard Rorty (Stanford Humanities Center).
14. After the end of the Cold War, the developed countries were able to reduce their military expenditures from 4.1 percent of their combined GDPs in 1985 to 2.2 percent in 1998 (*HDR 1998*, 197; *HDR 2000*, 217). With their combined GDPs at $24,563 billion in the year 2000 (*HDR 2002*, 193), their peace dividend in that year came to about $467 billion.
15. Immanuel Kant: *Grundlegung zur Metaphysik der Sitten*, (1784), in *Preussische Akademieausgabe*, vol. IV (Berlin: Georg Reimer 1911), 430n.
16. In addition, the negative version of the Golden Rule is subject to numerous well-known further problems. On its face, it would seem to rule out many ordinarily accepted activities, such as one person entering into competition with another (for customers, a job, a house, a spouse, or whatever), an officer sending a soldier on a dangerous mission, a lawyer asking a witness embarrassing questions, and so on. This problem is aggravated by the Draft Declaration's insistence (in Article 13) that general ethical standards, such as the Golden Rule, must take precedence over specific ethical standards appropriate in particular contexts (e.g., business, military, or law).
17. This second component of equality is compatible with the view that the weight agents ought to give to the human rights of others varies with their relation to them—that agents have stronger moral reasons to secure human rights in their own country, for example, than abroad—so long as this is not seen as being due to a difference in the moral significance of these rights, impersonally considered. (One can believe that the flourishing of all children is equally important and yet be committed to showing greater concern for the flourishing of one's own children than for the flourishing of other children.)
18. These six central elements are discussed in greater detail in my *World Poverty and Human Rights* (Cambridge: Polity Press, 2002), 54–9. If we can agree that these are indeed elements of the moral concept of human rights, then each human right will have these six features. The converse, however, does not hold, as alternative conceptions of human rights go beyond the shared core in two ways: (a) by further specifying the concept of human rights through additional elements and (b) by selectively postulating a list of particular human rights (*cf.* second paragraph of this section).
19. Here is an example of U_1: "A human right, then, will be a right whose beneficiaries are all humans and whose obligors are all humans in a position to effect the right"—David Luban: "Just War and Human Rights" in Charles Beitz, Marshall Cohen, John Simmons, and Thomas Scanlon, eds.: *International Ethics* (Princeton, N.J.: Princeton University Press, 1985), 209.
20. The first of these possibilities is exemplified by Robert Nozick: *Anarchy, State and Utopia* (New York: Basic Books, 1974), the second by Henry Shue: *Basic Rights* (Princeton, N.J.: Princeton University Press, 1996 [1980]). Nozick and Shue prefer to write in terms of, respectively, *fundamental* and *basic* rights. U_1 leads to views like theirs but phrased in terms of *human* rights.

21. By drawing on the Universal Declaration of Human Rights for examples and illustrations, I am not implying that all the rights it lists are human rights or that its list is complete. Rather, I am using these rights as evidence for how the concept of a human right has been understood, on the assumption that any plausible understanding of human rights must be critically developed out of this established and customary notion.

22. The right to equal pay for equal work (§23.2) seems intended to be doubly limited in scope. Equality needs to be achieved only within each state, not internationally—equal work need not be paid the same in Bangladesh as in Switzerland. And the duty to help maintain such equality within each country is confined to its citizens—we have no duty to help implement the equal pay principle in foreign countries. Of course, a defender of U_1 could respond that the international human rights documents are mistaken on this point: Every human agent has a moral responsibility to promote the fulfillment of every human right of every human being.

23. This distinction will not be clear-cut because some human rights may have components that differ in scope. Pursuant to U_2, the human right not to be subjected to torture (§5), for example, would presumably be interpreted as giving each government negative duties not to use torture as well as positive duties to prevent torture. The negative duties would most plausibly be construed as being equal in content and strength toward all human beings: A government must not order or authorize the torture of any human being at all. But not so for positive duties: A government has much stronger duties to prevent the torture of persons within the territory it can effectively control than to prevent the torture of persons elsewhere.

24. See, for example, Jürgen Habermas: "Kants Idee des ewigen Friedens—aus dem historischen Abstand von 200 Jahren," *Kritische Justiz* 28 (1995) 3, 293–319. He claims that "the concept of human rights is not of moral origin, but . . . *by nature* juridical" (310) and that human rights "belong, through their structure, to a scheme of positive and coercive law which supports justiciable individual right claims. Hence it belongs to the meaning of human rights that they demand for themselves the status of constitutional rights" (312; my translations, italics in the original). Though Alexy explicitly refers to human rights as moral rights, he holds an otherwise similar position which equates the institutionalization of human rights with their transformation into positive law. See Robert Alexy: "Die Institutionalisierung der Menschenrechte im demokratischen Verfassungsstaat" in Stefan Gosepath and Georg Lohmann, eds.: *Die Philosophie der Menschenrechte* (Frankfurt: Suhrkamp 1997), 244–64.

25. The expression "suitably broad" alludes to how U_2 had solved the third problem with U_1. Some human rights—such as the human right not to be subjected to arbitrary arrest (§9)—are meant to protect every human being regardless of location or citizenship. Such human rights would be only partially juridified through a constitutional right that prohibits the government's arbitrary arrest merely of its own citizens or residents but not the arbitrary arrest of foreigners. The juridification component of a human right not to be subjected to arbitrary arrest would then give a weighty moral duty to all citizens of every state to help ensure that their state affords all human beings a legal right not to be arbitrarily arrested by its government.

26. This is not to deny that some human rights are difficult or impossible to fulfill without corresponding legal or even constitutional protections. This seems manifestly true, for instance, of a human right to an effective remedy by the competent national tribunals for acts violating fundamental rights granted by the constitution or by law (§8). It is also hard to imagine a society under modern conditions whose members are secure in their property or have secure access to freedom of expression even while no legal right thereto exists. I assume below that secure access to the objects of civil and political human rights generally requires corresponding legal protections.

27. I am grateful to Pablo de Greiff for suggesting that I address this reply.

28. As the examples indicate, my notion of *secure access* involves a knowledge condition: A person has secure access to the object of a human right only when she is not prevented by social obstacles from acquiring the knowledge and know-how necessary to secure this object for herself.

29. In response to this objection, U_3 might be amended to say that human rights require their *supranational* juridification as well. Habermas appears to leave room for this amendment

when he writes the following: "in spite of their *claim* to universal validity, these rights have thus far managed to achieve an unambiguous positive form only within the national legal orders of democratic states. Beyond that, they possess only a weak force in international law and still await institutionalization within the framework of a cosmopolitan order that is only now beginning to take shape" (Habermas, *op. cit.*, 312). Again, I am grateful to Pablo de Greiff for this point.

30. My reading of §28 emphasizes its statement that all human beings have a claim that any institutional order imposed upon them be one in which their postulated rights and freedoms can be fully realized. §28 could be read as making the additional statement that human beings have a claim that such an order be newly established in any (state-of-nature or "failed state") contexts in which no effective institutional order exists. I do not, however, read §28 as including this additional statement.

31. "*Relative* impact," because a comparative judgment is needed about how much more or less fully human rights are realized in this institutional order than they would be realized in its feasible alternatives.

32. This understanding of human rights is laid out more extensively in chapter 2 of *World Poverty and Human Rights* (*op. cit.*, note 18).

33. The task of specifying, for the object of each particular human right, acceptable probabilities for threats from various (official and nonofficial) sources belongs to the second, substantive component of a conception of human rights, which is not discussed in the present essay.

34. We do not believe that the police should be authorized to beat up suspects in its custody, say, if such authorization (by deterring criminal beatings) reduces the number of beatings overall.

35. Other things must be presumed to be equal here. Deficits become less weighty, morally, as we go through the list. But greater low-weight deficits can still outweigh smaller high-weight deficits.

36. This might have been caused, for instance, by their maintaining a long-term smoking habit in full knowledge of the medical dangers associated therewith.

37. This critique of such recipient-oriented moral conceptions is presented more fully in my essays "Three Problems with Contractarian-Consequentialist Ways of Assessing Social Institutions," *Social Philosophy and Policy* 12 (1995), 241–66, and "Equal Liberty for All?," in *Midwest Studies in Philosophy* 28 (2004), 266–81.

38. *Cf.* note 17.

39. On the stronger reading of §28 (*cf.* note 30), human agents would also have a duty to establish a global institutional order that fulfills human rights even if no such order presently exists. It is doubtful, however, whether this duty could, in such a context, be considered a negative one. Kant suggests how it might be: "A human being (or a people) in a mere state of nature robs me of this assurance and injures me through this very state in which he coexists with me—not actively (facto), but through the lawlessness of his state (statu iniusto) through which I am under permanent threat from him—and I may compel him either to enter with me into a common juridical state or to retreat from my vicinity." Immanuel Kant: "Zum ewigen Frieden" (1795), in *Preussische Akademieausgabe*, vol. VIII (Berlin: de Gruyter, 1923), 349n (my translation).

40. Typical here John Rawls: *The Law of Peoples* (Cambridge, MA: Harvard University Press 1999), 108: "the causes of the wealth of a people and the forms it takes lie in their political culture and in the religious, philosophical, and moral traditions that support the basic structure of their political and social institutions, as well as in the industriousness and cooperative talents of its members, all supported by their political virtues. . . . Crucial also is the country's population policy."

41. *Cf.* Derek Parfit: *Reasons and Persons* (Oxford: Oxford University Press 1984), Chapter 3 titled "Five Mistakes in Moral Mathematics." Even if each privileged person typically bears only one billionth of the moral responsibility for the avoidable underfulfillment of human rights caused by the existing global order, each of us would still be responsible for very significant harms (*cf.* note 3 and accompanying text).

42. This is confirmed by the—otherwise startling—empirical finding of a *negative* correlation between developing countries' resource endowments and their rates of economic growth, exemplified by the relatively low growth rates, over the past 40 years, of resource-rich Nigeria,

Kenya, Angola, Mozambique, Zaire, Venezuela, Brazil, Saudi Arabia, Burma, and the Philippines. *Cf.* Ricky Lam and Leonard Wantchekon, 1999. "Dictatorships as a Political Dutch Disease." Working Paper 795 (1999). Yale University, http://econpapers.hhs.se/paper/wopyalegr/

43. This point is frequently overlooked in the manner exemplified by Rawls (*cf.* note 40).

44. For a somewhat more extensive discussion with additional data and reform proposals, see chapter 6 of *World Poverty and Human Rights* (*op. cit.*, note 18).

45. Participants in an institutional order will be differentially responsible for its moral quality: Influential and privileged participants should be willing to contribute more to the maintenance of a just, or the reform of an unjust, institutional order. Moreover, we must here distinguish responsibility from guilt and blame. Our substantial causal contribution to the imposition of an unjust institutional order means that we share moral responsibility for this imposition and the avoidable harms it entails. It does not follow from this that we are also guilty or blameworthy on account of our conduct. For there might be applicable excuses such as, for instance, factual or moral error, or ignorance.

46. All this does not diminish in any way the responsibility of repressive and corrupt rulers in the developing countries who also strongly support, and greatly benefit from, the international borrowing and resource privileges. These two groups should be seen as a symbiotic unit, a global elite who are together imposing a mutually agreeable institutional order that allows them to exploit the natural wealth of this planet at the expense of the excluded majority of humankind.

47. This is so no matter which of the available substantive accounts of human rights one might endorse.

48. For a different argument, which attacks the same conviction by appeal to the inherently regrettable incentives it provides, see chapter 3 of *World Poverty and Human Rights* (*op. cit.*, note 18).

49. For example, by representatives of Western governments and corporations who benefit from or support sweat shops, child prostitution, or torture in developing countries and seek to defend their involvement in such practices against moral criticism from other Westerners.

50. Mutual toleration with regard to this question is at least *possible*. This is not to say that we *ought* to tolerate the national institutional order of any other country no matter how unjust it may be.

51. This criticism has been voiced by Singapore's patriarch Lee Kuan Yew, by Mary Ann Glendon: *Rights Talk: The Impoverishment of Political Discourse* (New York: The Free Press, 1991), and by many others as well.

52. We might try to initiate appropriate changes in our global order, for example, by publicizing its nature and effects and by formulating feasible paths of reform. And we might help preempt or undo some of the harms through volunteer work or donations to effective relief organizations. How much should one contribute to such reform and protection efforts? In proportion to one's affluence and influence, at least as much as would suffice for the full realization of human rights if most similarly situated others followed suit. Thus, if one percent of the income of the most affluent tenth of humankind would suffice to eradicate world hunger within a few years, then we should give at least one percent of our incomes to fight hunger. For an extensive discussion of the fair distribution of demands, see Liam Murphy: *Moral Demands in Nonideal Theory* (New York: Oxford University Press, 2000).

53. This explanatory insight is interestingly anticipated in the seventh proposition of Immanuel Kant's essay "Idee zu einer allgemeinen Geschichte in weltbürgerlicher Absicht" (1784), in Preussische Akademieausgabe, vol. VIII (Berlin: de Gruyter, 1923), 24: "The problem of establishing a perfect civil constitution is subordinate to the problem of law-governed external relations among states and cannot be solved without the latter [problem]" (my translation).

CHAPTER 2

Agents of Justice

ONORA O'NEILL

Cosmopolitan Principles and State Institutions

Many of the best-known conceptions of justice are avowedly cosmopolitan.[1] They propose basic principles of justice that are to hold without restriction. Whether we look back to Stoic cosmopolitanism, to mediaeval Natural Law theory, to Kantian world citizenship, or to twentieth century theory and practice—Rawls and the UN Universal Declaration of Human Rights of 1948, for example—the scope of principles of justice is said to be universal or cosmopolitan, encompassing all humans. As is well known, such principles have been compromised in various ways, for example, by the exclusion or partial exclusion of slaves, women, laborers or the heathen from the scope of justice; these exclusions have been a focus of much debate, and recent cosmopolitan conceptions of justice have condemned them.

However, there are other less evident exclusions created by the commonplace assumption that cosmopolitan principles are to be instituted in and through a system of states. Many recent challenges have argued that the exclusions that borders create are further injustices, and that they should be addressed by abolishing borders, or at least by reducing the obstacles they present to movements of people, goods, or capital. Some conclude that justice requires the construction of a world state[2]; others that borders should be (more) open to the movement of peoples (Carens, 1987); others that powerful regional and global institutions can mitigate

37

or redress inequalities that states and borders create (Pogge, 1994; Held, 2000). I am at least partly skeptical about those attempts to realize cosmopolitan principles through cosmopolitan or global institutions that do not show what is to prevent global governance from degenerating into global tyranny and global injustice. Big may not always be beautiful, and institutional cosmopolitanism may not always be the best route to universal justice. In this chapter, I begin to explore a more realistic, and also (I hope) a more robust view of the plurality of agents of justice that might play some part in institutionalizing cosmopolitan principles of justice.

A plausible initial view of agents of justice might distinguish primary *agents of justice* with capacities to determine how principles of justice are to be institutionalized within a certain domain from *other, secondary agents of justice*. Primary agents of justice may construct other agents or agencies with specific competencies: They may assign powers to and build capacities in individual agents, or they may build institutions—agencies—with certain powers and capacities to act. Sometimes they may, so to speak, build from scratch; more often they reassign or adjust tasks and responsibilities among existing agents and agencies, and control and limit the ways in which they may act without incurring sanctions. Primary agents of justice typically have some means of coercion, by which they at least partially control the action of other agents and agencies, which can therefore at most be secondary agents of justice. Typically secondary agents of justice are thought to contribute to justice mainly by meeting the demands of primary agents, most evidently by conforming to any legal requirements they establish.

There is no fundamental reason why a primary agent of justice should not be an individual, for example a prince or leader, and in some traditional societies that has been the case. Equally there is no fundamental reason why a primary agent of justice should not be a group with little formal structure, for example a group of elders or chieftains, or even a constitutional convention, and in other instances this has been the case. However, in modern societies, institutions with a considerable measure of formal structure, and pre-eminently among them states, have been seen as the primary agents of justice. All too often, they have also been agents of injustice.

A low-key view of the matter might be simply this: It is hard to institutionalize principles of justice, and although states quite often do not do very well as primary agents of justice, they are the best primary agents available, and so indispensable for justice. Institutions with a monopoly of the legitimate use of coercion within a given, bounded territory often behave unjustly, both to those who inhabit the territory and to outsiders, but we have not found a better way of institutionalizing justice. On such views the remedy for state injustice is not the dismantling of states and of the exclusions their borders create, but a degree of reform and democratization coupled with international (that is, interstatal) agreements.

This very general response seems to me to take no account of the fact that states may fail as primary agents of justice for a number of different reasons. Sometimes they have the power to act as primary agents of justice, but use that power not to achieve justice, but for other ends. When these ends include a great deal of injustice we may speak of *rogue states,* and these are common enough. But on other occasions states fail because they are too weak to act as primary agents of justice: Although they are spoken of as states, even as sovereign states, this is no more than a courtesy title for structures that are often no more than *dependent states* or *quasi-states.*

These two types of failure pose quite different problems for other agents of justice. Powerful rogue states confront all other agents and agencies with terrible problems. Compliance with their requirements contributes to injustice rather than to justice; non-compliance leads to danger and destruction. These problems and conflicts formed a staple of 20th-century political philosophy, in which discussions of the circumstances that justify or require revolution and resistance against established states, or non-compliance and conscientious objection with state requirements, have been major themes. But when failure of supposed primary agents of justice arises not from abuse, but from lack of state power, the problems faced by other agents and agencies are quite different. In such cases it is often left indeterminate what the law requires, and the costs of complying with such laws as exist are increased, if only because others do not even aim to comply. Unsurprisingly, many of the stratagems to which agents and agencies turn when states are weak are themselves unjust. Where agents and agencies cannot rely on an impartially enforced legal code they may find that in order to go about their daily business they are drawn into bribery and nepotism, into buying protection and making corrupt deals, and so ride roughshod over requirements of justice. If the agents and agencies that could be, in better circumstances, secondary agents of justice are reduced to these sorts of action in weak states, why should we even continue to think of them as agents of justice?

Cosmopolitan Rhetoric and State Action in the Universal Declaration

These issues are often obscured because much of the cosmopolitan rhetoric of contemporary discussions of justice says little about the agents and agencies on which the burdens of justice are to fall. Nowhere is this more evident than in the text of the Universal Declaration of Human Rights of

1948. In this brief and celebrated text, nations, peoples, states, societies, and are variously gestured to as agents against whom individuals may have rights. Little is said about any differences between these varying types of agents, or about their capacities and vulnerabilities, and there is no systematic allocation of obligations of different sorts to agents and agencies of specific types. If we inhabited a world in which all states were strictly nation-states, and in which no nation spread across more than one state, or formed more than one society, the failure to distinguish these terms and the entities to which these terms refer might matter rather less. But that is not our world. Few states are nation-states; many nations spread across a number of states; the individuation of societies, peoples, and countries is notoriously complex. It may seem a scandal that the Universal Declaration is so cavalier about identifying agents of justice.[3]

Even if it is cavalier, I think that it is fairly easy to understand why the framers of the Universal Declaration felt no need for precision. The Declaration approaches justice by proclaiming rights. It proclaims what is to be received, what entitlements everyone is to have, but it says very little about which agents and agencies must do what if these rights are to be secured. Like other charters and declarations of rights, the Universal Declaration looks at justice from a recipient's perspective: Its focus is on recipience and rights rather than on action and obligations. Hence it is about rights and rights holders that the Declaration is forthrightly cosmopolitan. It identifies the relevant recipients clearly: Rights are ascribed to "all human beings" (Art. 1), and more explicitly to "everyone . . . without distinction of any kind, such as race, colour, sex, language, religion, political or other opinion, national or social origin, property, birth or other status" (Art. 2). Rights are explicitly to be independent of an individual's political status: "no distinction shall be made on the basis of the political, jurisdictional or international status of the country or territory to which a person belongs, whether it be independent, trust, non-self-governing or under any other limitation of sovereignty" (Art. 2). Human rights are to reach into all jurisdictions, however diverse.

So far, so cosmopolitan: The universalist aspirations are unequivocal. However, since nothing is said about the allocation of obligations to meet these aspirations, we do not yet know whether these universal rights are matched and secured by universal obligations or by obligations held by some, but not by all, agents and agencies. This is a more complex matter than may appear. Whereas traditional liberty rights for all have to be matched by universal obligations to respect those rights (if any agent or agency is exempt from that obligation, the right is compromised), other universal rights cannot be secured by assigning identical obligations to all agents and agencies. Universal rights to goods and services, to status and participation, cannot be delivered by universal action. For these rights the allocation of obligations matters, and some means of designing and enforcing effective allocations is required if any ascription of rights is to have practical import.

The Universal Declaration in fact resolves this problem by taking a non-universalist view of the allocation of obligations. For example, Arts. 13–15 reveal clearly that the primary agents of justice are to be states (referred to in several different ways). In these articles the Declaration obliquely acknowledges that different agents are to be responsible for securing a given right for different persons, depending on the state of which they are members. The import of these articles is probably clearest if they are taken in reverse order.

The two clauses of Art. 15 read:

Everyone has a right to a nationality.
No one shall be arbitrarily deprived of his nationality nor denied the
    right to change his nationality.

Evidently the term "nationality" is not here being used in the sense that is more common today, to indicate a specific ethnic or cultural identity. If the Declaration used "having a nationality" to mean "having an ethnic or cultural identity" it would not need to prohibit deprivation of nationality, or assert rights to change of one's nationality; it would need rather to speak of rights to express, foster, or maintain one's nationality. "Having a nationality" as it is understood in the Declaration is a matter of being a member of one or another state[4]: Such membership is indeed something of which people may be deprived, and which they can change, and which some people—stateless people—lack.

A right to a nationality, in the sense of being a member of some state, is pivotal to the Declaration's implicit conception of the agents of justice. It is by this move that a plurality of bounded states—explicitly anti-cosmopolitan institutions—are installed as the primary agents of justice, who are to deliver universal rights. This becomes explicit in Arts. 13 and 14, which make the following contrasting claims:

Art. 13
Everyone has the right to freedom of movement and residence within
    the borders of each state.
Everyone has the right to leave any country, including his own, and to
    return to his country.

Art. 14

Everyone has the right to seek and enjoy in other countries asylum from persecution.

This right many not be invoked in the case of prosecutions genuinely arising from non-political crimes or from acts contrary to the purposes and principles of the United Nations.

The rights proclaimed in Arts. 13 and 14 make it clear that the Declaration assumes a plurality of bounded states and exclusive citizenship. It is only in a world with this structure that it makes sense to distinguish the rights of freedom of movement, of exit and of reentry that an individual is to enjoy in whichever state recognizes him or her as a member, from the quite different right to asylum that a persecuted individual may have in states of which he or she is not a member. Rights, it appears, may legitimately be differentiated at boundaries: My rights in my own state will not and need not be the same as my rights in another state. In a world without bounded states, these distinctions would make no sense. Here it becomes quite explicit that the Declaration views states as the primary agents of justice: A cosmopolitan view of rights is to be spliced with a statist view of obligations. The statism of the Declaration should not surprise us. Its preamble addresses Member States who "have pledged themselves to achieve, in co-operation with the United Nations, the promotion of universal respect for and observance of human rights and fundamental freedoms." Yet since states cannot implement justice, let alone global justice, without constructing and coordinating many other agents and agencies, it is a matter of deep regret that the Declaration is so opaque about allocating the obligations of justice. The reason for regret is that in the end obligations rather than rights are the active aspects of justice: A proclamation of rights will be indeterminate and ineffective unless obligations to respect and secure those rights are assigned to specific, identifiable agents and agencies that are able to discharge those obligations (O'Neill, 1996, 2000).

If the significant obligations that secure rights and justice are to be assigned primarily to states, much would have been gained by making this wholly explicit. In particular it would have exposed the problems created by rogue states and weak states, and the predicaments created for other agents and agencies when states fail to support justice. Such explicitness might also have forestalled the emergence of the free-floating rhetoric of rights that now dominates much public discussion of justice, focuses on recipience, and blandly overlooks the need for a robust and realistic account of agents of justice who are to carry the counterpart obligations. This rhetoric has (in my view) become a prominent and persistently damaging feature of discussions of justice since the promulgation of the Universal Declaration.

Cosmopolitan Rhetoric and State Action: Rawls' Conception of Justice

It is not only in the Universal Declaration of Human Rights and the attendant culture of the Human Rights Movement that we find cosmopolitan thinking about justice linked to statist accounts of the primary agents of justice. This combination is also standard in more theoretical and philosophical writing that assigns priority to universal rights: As in declarations of rights, so in theories of rights, giving priority to the perspective of recipience distracts attention from the need to determine which agents of justice are assigned which tasks. More surprisingly, statist views of the primary agents of justice can also be found in theoretical and philosophical writing on justice that does *not* prioritize rights.

A notable example of hidden statism without an exclusive focus on rights is John Rawls' political philosophy. This is more surprising because Rawls hardly ever refers to states, and then often with some hostility. He claims throughout his writings that the context of justice is a "bounded society," a perpetually continuing scheme of cooperation, which persons enter only by birth and leave only by death, and which is self-sufficient.[5] In his later writing he increasingly relies on a *political* conception of bounded societies, seeing them as domains within which citizens engage in public reason, which he defines as "citizens' reasoning in the public forum about constitutional essentials and basic questions of justice" (Rawls, 1993, 10, 212; 1999, 132–3). He consequently views *peoples* rather than states as the primary agents of justice. Yet his account of peoples is surprisingly state-like:

> Liberal peoples do, however, have their fundamental interests as permitted by their conceptions of right and justice. They seek to protect their territory, to ensure the security and safety of their citizens, and to preserve their free political institutions and the liberties and free culture of their civil society. (Rawls, 1999, 29)[6]

Rawls, however, maintains that in speaking of a bounded society and its citizens he is *not* speaking of a territorial state. This is surely puzzling: If nobody is to enter except by birth or leave except by death, the boundaries of the polity must be policed; the use of force must be coordinated, indeed monopolized in the territory in question. If there is a monopoly of the use of legitimate force for a bounded territory, we are surely talking of entities that fit the classical Weberian definition of a state.

The reason why Rawls so emphatically denies that states are the primary agents of justice appears to me to be that he has in mind one specific and highly contentious conception of the state. In *Law of Peoples,* he explicitly rejects the realist conception of state that has been of great influence in international relations. He sees states as "anxiously concerned with their power—their capacity (military, economic, diplomatic)—to influence others and always guided by their basic interests" (Rawls, 1999, 28). He points out that:

> What distinguishes peoples from states—and this is crucial—is that just peoples are fully prepared to grant the very same proper respect and recognition to other peoples as equal. (Rawls, 1999, 35)

In Rawls' view, states cannot be adequate agents of justice because they necessarily act out of self-interest; they are rational, but cannot be reasonable.

However, this supposedly realist conception of the state is only one among various possibilities. Rawls' choice of *peoples* rather than *states* as the agents whose deliberations are basic to justice beyond boundaries is, I think, motivated in large part by an inaccurate assumption that states *must* fit the "realist" paradigm, hence are unfit to be primary (or other) agents of justice. Yet states *as we have actually known them* do not fit that paradigm.[7] The conception of states and governments as having limited powers, and as bound by numerous fundamental principles in addition to rational self-interest, is part and parcel of the liberal tradition of political philosophy and central to contemporary international politics. States *as they have really existed and still exist* never had and never have unlimited sovereignty, internal or external, and have never been exclusively motivated by self-interest.[8] States *as they actually exist today* are committed by numerous treaty obligations to a limited conception of sovereignty, to restrictions on the ways in which they may treat other states, and by demands that they respect human rights. Peoples *as they once lived* before the emergence of state structures probably did not have bounded territories; those peoples who developed the means to negotiate with other peoples, to keep outsiders out and to make agreements, did so by forming states and governments by which to secure bounded territories.

The motive of self-interest ascribed to states or other agencies in would-be realist thinking is so open to multiple interpretations that I do not believe that we are likely to get far in trying to determine whether agents or agencies—whether states or companies or individuals—are or are not always motivated by self-interest, or *necessarily* motivated by self-interest, however interpreted. I suspect that ascriptions of self-interest often have a plausible ring only because they are open both to a tautologous and to an empirical interpretation. If the empirical interpretation of self interested motivation fails for agents and agencies of any sort (as, according to Vasquez, it fails for states) the tautologous interpretation lingers in the background sustaining an unfalsifiable version of "realism" by which the action of states (or companies or individuals) is taken to define and reveal their motivation and their interests.

Once we have shed the assumption that all states (or other agents and agencies) must conform to this "realist" model, we can turn in a more open-minded way to consider the capacities for action that agents and agencies of various sorts, including states, actually have. In particular, we may then be in a position to say something about predicaments that arise when some states are too weak to act as primary agents of justice.

States as Agents of Justice: Capabilities and Motivation

Once we set aside the "realist" paradigm of state agency, many questions open up. Perhaps states are agents of a more versatile sort than "realists" assert, and capable of a wider range of motivation than self-interest (as has been argued by various "idealist" theorists of international relations). Perhaps states are not the only agents of significance in building justice: Various non-state actors may also contribute significantly to the construction of justice. Perhaps a system of states can develop capacities for action that individual states lack.

These are very large questions, and the literature on international relations has dealt in part with many of them. However, for the present I want to take a quite restricted focus, with the thought that it may be useful to work towards an account of agents of justice *by attending specifically to their powers rather than to their supposed motives.*

A focus on the powers of states may *seem* to return us to classical discussions of sovereignty. That is not my intention. An analysis of *state power* is not an account of *state powers*; nor is an analysis of the *power* of other agents and agencies an account of their *powers*. The powers of all agents and agencies, including states, are multiple, varied, and often highly specific. These specificities are worth attending to, since it is these capacities that are constitutive of agency, and without agency any account of obligations (and hence any account of rights or of justice) will be no more than gesture.

Amartya Sen has introduced the useful notion of a *capability* into development economics; it can also be helpful in discussing the powers of states, and of other agents and agencies.[9] Agents' capabilities are not to be identified with their individual capacities, or with their aggregate power. An agent or agency, considered in the abstract, may have various capacities or abilities to act. For example, a person may have the capacity to work as an agricultural laborer, or an ability to organize family resources to last from harvest to harvest; a development agency may have the capacity to distribute resources to the needy in a given area. However, faced with a social and economic structure that provides no work for agricultural laborers or no resources for a given family to subsist on or for an agency to distribute, these capacities lie barren. From the point of view of achieving justice—however we conceptualize it—agents and agencies must dispose not only of capacities that they could deploy if circumstances were favorable, but of *capabilities*, that is to say of *specific, effectively resourced capacities that they can deploy in actual circumstances*. Capabilities are to capacities or abilities as effective demand is to demand: It is the specific capabilities of agents and agencies in specific situations, rather than their abstract capacities or their aggregate power that are relevant to determining which obligations of justice they can hold and discharge—and which they will be unable to discharge (Sen, 1999). The value of focusing on capabilities is that this foregrounds an explicit concern with the action and with the results that agents or agencies can achieve in actual circumstances, so provides a *seriously realistic starting point for normative reasoning*, including normative claims about rights.

A focus on capabilities quickly reveals how defective weak states may be as agents of justice, and makes vivid why it is important also to think about other possible agents of justice in weak states. Weak states may simply lack the resources, human, material, and organizational, to do very much to secure or improve justice within their boundaries. They may lack capabilities to regulate or influence the action of certain other agents or agencies, or to affect what goes on in certain regions of the state, or to achieve greater justice. They may fail to represent the interests of their citizens adequately in international fora, and agree to damaging or unsupportable treaties or loans. They may lack the capabilities to end or prevent rebellions and forms of feudalism, insurgency and secession, banditry and lawlessness, or to levy taxes or enforce such law as they enact in the face of powerful clans or corrupt factions. Often when we speak of such entities as "states" the term is used in a merely formal sense, as a largely honorific appellation, and it is widely acknowledged that they lack capabilities that would be indispensable in any primary agent of justice.

Sometimes the lack of capabilities of states arises because other agents and agencies within or beyond the state have usurped those capabilities. The weakness of the Colombian state reflects the military and enforcement capabilities acquired by Colombian drug cartels; the weakness of a number of African states reflects the military capabilities achieved by secessionist and insurgent groups and movements within those states. However, even in cases where certain non-state agents have acquired selected state-like capabilities, which they use to wreak injustice, they do not enjoy the range of capabilities held by states that succeed in being primary agents of justice. When weak states lack capabilities to be primary agents of justice, there is usually no other agent or agency that has acquired these missing capabilities. The fact that a state is incapable of securing the rule of law, or the collection of taxes, or the provision of welfare within its terrain is no guarantee that any other agent or agency has gathered together these missing capabilities. An unpropitious bundling or dispersal of capabilities may simply leave both a weak state and all those agencies that are active within and around it incapable of securing (a greater measure of) justice.

When states fail as agents of justice, the problem is not therefore simply a general lack of power. It is rather a lack of a specific range of capabilities that are needed for the delivery of justice, and specifically for the coordination, let alone enforcement, of action and obligations by other agents and agencies. Unfortunately, weak states often retain considerable capabilities for injustice even when wholly unable to advance justice. In these circumstances other agents and agencies may become important agents of justice.

Non-State Actors as Agents of Justice

The odd phrase "non-state actor" as currently used in international relations is revealing. It identifies certain types of agent and agency *by reference to what they are not*. In an area of inquiry in which states have classically been thought of as the primary agents (not only of justice), the phrase "non-state actor" has been invented to refer to a range of agencies that are neither states nor the creations of states (Risse-Kappen, 1995). Etymology might suggest that all agents and agencies other than states—from individual human agents to international bodies, to companies and non-governmental institutions—should count as non-state actors. In fact the term is usually used more selectively, to refer to institutions that are neither states, nor international in the sense of being interstatal or intergovernmental, nor directly subordinate to individual states or governments, but which interact across borders with states or state institutions. Some non-state actors may acquire capabilities that make them significant agents of justice—and of injustice.

Examples of non-state actors in this relatively restricted sense include (at least) those international non-governmental organizations (INGOs) that operate across borders, transnational or multinational companies or corporations (TNCs/MNCs), and numerous transnational social, political, and epistemic movements that operate across borders (sometimes known as "global social movements" or GSMs).[10] Here I shall refer to a few features of certain INGOs, TNCs, and GSMs, but say nothing about other types of non-state actors.

Nobody would doubt that some non-state actors aspire to be and sometimes become agents of justice; others may become agents of injustice. However, their mode of operation in weak states is quite different from the standard activities of secondary agents of justice. Non-state actors do not generally contribute to justice by complying with state requirements: In weak states those requirements may be ill defined, and where adequately defined compliance may contribute to injustice. Sometimes INGOs seek to contribute to justice in weak states by helping or badgering them into instituting aspects of justice that a state with more capabilities might have instituted without such assistance or goading. INGOs may do this by mobilizing external powers (other states, international bodies, public opinion, GSMs), by advocacy work that assists weak states in negotiations with others, by mobilizing First World consumer power, or by campaigning for and funding specific reforms that contribute to justice in a weak or unjust state. The typical mission and raison d'être of INGOs is to contribute to specific transformations of states, governments, and polities, quite often to a single issue or objective. Although INGOs cannot themselves become primary agents of justice, they can contribute to justice in specific ways in specific domains. Even when they cannot do much to make states more just, they may be able to help prevent weak states from becoming wholly dysfunctional or more radically unjust. Their difficulties and successes in doing so are not different in kind from the long and distinguished tradition of reform movements and lobbies within states, whose ambitions for justice do not extend beyond improvements within (certain aspects of) that particular polity or state.

Some non-state actors, in particular INGOs, may contribute to justice precisely *because* the states in which they operate are relatively weak, *because* they can act opportunistically and secure an unusual degree of access to some key players, and *because* they are not restricted by some of the constraints that non-state actors in states with greater and better coordinated capabilities might face. Their successes and failures as agents of justice are therefore analogous *neither* to the achievements and failure of stronger states with the capabilities to be primary agents of justice, *nor* to those of secondary agents of justice within stronger states.

Other non-state actors are not defined by their reforming aims, and it may seem that they are less likely to be able to contribute to justice in weak states. For example, TNCs are often thought of as having constitutive aims that prevent them from being agents of justice at all, except insofar as they are secondary agents of justice in states that have enacted reasonably just laws. If this were correct, TNCs could not contribute to justice in weak states where laws are ill defined or ill enforced, and the very notion of compliance with law may be indeterminate in many respects. Companies, we are often reminded, have shareholders; their constitutive aim is to improve the bottom line. How then could they be concerned about justice, except insofar as justice requires conformity to law?

This view of TNCs seems to me sociologically simplistic. Major TNCs are economically and socially complex institutions of considerable power; their specific capabilities and constitutive aims are typically diverse and multiple. To be sure, they have to worry about their shareholders (even institutions that lack shareholders still need to balance their books and worry about the bottom line). Yet a supposition that companies must be concerned *only* about maximizing profits seems to me on a par with the "realist" supposition that states can *only* act out of self-interest. The notion of the *responsible company* or *responsible corporation* is no more incoherent than the notion of the liberal state; equally the notion of the *rogue company* or *rogue corporation* is no more incoherent than that of the rogue state. If these notions *seem* incoherent it may be because claims that some company pursues only economic self interest (understood as shareholder interest) are shielded from empirical refutation by inferring interests from whatever is done: *Whatever* corporate behavior actually takes place is defined as pursuit of perceived shareholder interest.

Much popular and professional literature on TNCs wholly disavows this trivializing conception of the pursuit of self-interest, and accepts that TNC action can be judged for its contribution to justice—or to injustice. For example, TNCs have often been criticized for using their considerable ranges of capabilities to get away with injustice: for dumping hazardous wastes in states too weak to achieve effective environmental protection; for avoiding taxation by placing headquarters in banana republics; for avoiding safety legislation by registering vessels under "flags of convenience"; or by placing dangerous production processes in areas without effective worker protection legislation. If the critics who point to these failings *really* believed that TNCs cannot but profit maximize, these objections would be pointless: In fact they assume (more accurately) that major TNCs can choose among a range of policies and actions. Yet surprisingly little is said—outside corporate promotional literature—about the action of companies that insist on decent environmental standards although no law requires them to do so, or on decent standards of employment practice or of safety at work even where they could get away with less. In some cases TNCs operating in weak states with endemic corruption may go further to advance justice, for example, by refusing complicity with certain sorts of corruption or by insisting on widening the benefits of investment and production in ways that local legislation does not require and that local elites resist.

These commonplace facts suggest to me that it is more important to consider the capabilities rather than the (supposed) motivation of TNCs. Many TNCs are evidently capable of throwing their considerable weight in the direction either of greater justice, or of the status quo, or of greater injustice. In many cases it may be a moot point whether their motivation in supporting greater justice is a concern for justice, a concern to avoid the reputational disadvantages of condoning or inflicting injustice, or a concern for the bottom line simpliciter. However, unclarity about the motivation of TNCs does not matter much, given that we have few practical reasons for trying to assess the quality of TNC motivation. What does matter is what TNCs can and cannot do, the capabilities that they can and cannot develop.

If these thoughts are plausible, it is plain that TNCs can have and can develop ranges of capabilities to contribute both to greater justice and to greater injustice. Shareholder interests are of course important to all TNCs, but they underdetermine both what a given TNC can and what it will do. Fostering justice in specific ways is an entirely possible corporate aim; so unfortunately is contributing to injustice. Although TNCs may be ill constructed to substitute for the full range of contributions that states can (but often fail to) make to justice, there are many contributions that they can make especially when states are weak. Corporate power can be great enough to provide the constellation of individuals and groups with influence in weaker states with powerful, even compelling, reasons to show greater respect for human rights, to improve environmental and employment standards, to accept more open patterns of public discourse, or to reduce forms of social and religious discrimination. Corporate power can be used to support and strengthen reasonably just states. Equally, TNCs can accept the status quo, fall in with local elites and with patterns of injustice, and use their powers to keep things as they are—or indeed to make them more unjust.

In the end, it seems to me, any firm distinction between primary and secondary agents has a place only where there are powerful and relatively just states, which successfully discipline and regulate other agents and agencies within their boundaries. But once we look at the realities of life where states are weak, any simple division between primary and secondary agents of justice blurs. Justice has to be built by a diversity of agents and agencies that possess and lack varying ranges of capabilities, and can contribute to justice—or to injustice—in more diverse ways than is generally acknowledged in those approaches that have built on supposedly realist, but in fact highly ideologized, views of the motivations of potential agents of justice.

Notes

1. Some relativists, communitarians, and nationalists are avowedly anti-cosmopolitan, but often with less startling conclusions than the conceptual resources of their starting points might permit.

2. There are many versions of the thought that supra-statal or global governance should replace states, often and perhaps inaccurately seen as a Kantian position (Lutz-Bachmann 1997; Habermas 1995; Mertens 1996).
3. I suspect that in the middle of the twentieth century it was usual to assume that all *states* were *nation-states*, and then to refer to them simply as *nations* (Morgenthau, 1948; for the influence of this book, see Vasquez, 1983, 1988).
4. Evidently the framers of the Declaration could not speak of *citizenship*, since they were working in a world in which there were numerous colonies, trust territories, and dependent territories whose inhabitants were not all of them citizens. Even today, when there are fewer such territories, the term *citizenship* would be inappropriate, since there are many members of states who do not enjoy full citizenship status, including minors and resident aliens, whose rights are nevertheless important.
5. This formulation is to be found from the first pages of John Rawls, *A Theory of Justice* (Rawls, 1971). In later work his emphasis on bounded societies continues, but their liberal democracy and the citizenship of their members are increasingly emphasized; these shifts are corollaries of his shift to "political" justification. For some further textual details see (O'Neill, 1998).
6. Note also the following passage: "The point of the institution of property is that, unless a definite agent is given responsibility for maintaining an asset . . . that asset tends to deteriorate. In this case the asset is the people's territory and its capacity to support them in perpetuity; and the agent is the people themselves as politically organized" (Rawls, 1999, 39).
7. Theorists of international relations acknowledge that many of the states we see around us fall far short of the realist paradigm of statehood: they speak of quasi-states and dependent states. Rawls acknowledges that realism provides a poor account of state action —yet leaves realists in possession of the concept of the state (Rawls, 1999, 46).
8. A recent comment runs "From the days of E.H. Carr . . . on, realists have claimed that their theories are empirically accurate, robust and fruitful, empirically sound guides to practice, and explanatorily powerful. . . . But what has been found is that the realist paradigm has not done well on any of these criteria" (Vasquez, 1988, 372). Although a "revealed" (ascriptive, interpretive) view of self-interest may seemingly rescue the claim that states act only out of self-interest from this and other empirical defects, this is a Pyrrhic victory. As with analogous moves in discussions of individual motivation, a "realist" insistence that state action *must* be self-interested survives only by offering a trivializing and unfalsifiable interpretation of motivation.
9. For present purposes I do not intend to discuss the links which Sen draws between capabilities and their actualization in an agent's functionings, or his arguments to identify which functionings, hence which capabilities, are valuable (Sen, 1993, 1999; Nussbaum, 2000). The usefulness of a focus on capabilities does not depend on basing it on one rather than another theory of value, or one rather than another account of justice, rights, or obligations.
10. For discussion of ways in which global social movements may act transnationally, see Robert O'Brien et al., *Contesting Global Governance: Multilateral Economic Institutions and Global Social Movements* (Cambridge: Cambridge University Press, 2000).

References

Bohman, James, and Lutz-Bachmann, Matthias, eds. (1997). *Perpetual Peace: Essays on Kant's Cosmopolitan Ideal*, Cambridge, Mass.: MIT Press, 59–76.

Carens, Joseph. (1987). "Aliens and Citizens: the Case for Open Borders," *The Review of Politics*, 49, 251–73.

Habermas, Jürgen. (1995). "Kants Idee des Ewigen Frieden aus dem historischen Abstand," *Kritische Justiz*, 28, 293–318; trans. as "Kant's Idea of Perpetual Peace, with the Benefit of Two Hundred Year's Hindsight" in James Bohman and Matthias Lutz-Bachmann, eds. (1997) 113–53.

Held, David. (2000). "Regulating Globalisation? The Reinvention of Politics," *International Sociology*, 15, 394–408.

Jackson, Robert H. (1990). *Quasi-States: Sovereignty, International Relations and the Third World*. Cambridge: Cambridge University Press.

Lutz-Bachmann, Matthias. (1997). "Kant's Idea of Peace and a World Republic," in James Bohman and Matthias Lutz-Bachmann, eds. *Perpetual Peace: Essays on Kant's Cosmopolitan Ideal*, Cambridge, Mass.: MIT Press, 59–76.

Mann, Michael. (1997). "Has Globalisation Ended the Rise and Rise of the Nation-State?," *Review of International Political Economy*, 4, 472–96.

Mertens, Thomas. (1996). "Cosmopolitanism and Citizenship: Kant against Habermas," *European Journal of Philosophy*, 4, 328–47.

Migdal, Joel S. (1988). *Strong Societies and Weak States: State Society Relations and State Capabilities in the Third World*, Princeton, N.J.: Princeton University Press.

Morgenthau, Hans J. (1948, revised 1978). *Politics among Nations: The Struggle for Power and Peace*, New York: Knopf.

Nussbaum, Martha C. (2000). *Women and Human Development: The Capabilities Approach*, Cambridge: Cambridge University Press.

O'Brien, Robert, Goetz, Anne-Marie, Scholte, Jan Aart, et al. (2000). *Contesting Global Governance: Multilateral Economic Institutions and Global Social Movements*, Cambridge: Cambridge University Press.

O'Neill, Onora. (1996). *Towards Justice and Virtue: A Constructive Account of Practical Reasoning*, Cambridge: Cambridge University Press.

O'Neill, Onora. (1998). "Political Liberalism and Public Reason: A Critical Notice of John Rawls, Political Liberalism," *The Philosophical Review*, 106, 411–28.

O'Neill, Onora. (1999). "Women's Rights: Whose Obligations?" in Jeffries, Alison, ed. (1999) *Women's Voices, Women's Rights: Oxford Amnesty Lectures*; reprinted in O'Neill, Onora, *Bounds of Justice* (2000).

O'Neill, Onora. (2000). *Bounds of Justice*, Cambridge: Cambridge University Press.

Pogge, Thomas. (1994). "An Egalitarian Law of Peoples," *Philosophy and Public Affairs*, 23, 195–224.

Rawls, John. (1971). *A Theory of Justice*, Cambridge, Mass.: Harvard University Press.

Rawls, John. (1993). *Political Liberalism*, New York: Columbia University Press.

Rawls, John. (1999). *The Law of Peoples*, Cambridge, Mass: Harvard University Press.

Risse-Kappen, Thomas, ed. (1995). "Bringing Transnational Relations Back" in *Non-State Actors, Domestic Structures and International Institutions*, Cambridge: Cambridge University Press.

Sen, Amartya. (1993). "Capability and Well Being" in Martha C. Nussbaum and Amartya Sen, eds. *The Quality of Life*, Oxford: Clarendon Press, 30–53.

Sen, Amartya. (1999). *Development as Freedom*, Oxford: Oxford University Press.

Strange, Susan. (1996). *The Retreat of the State: The Diffusion of Power in the World Economy*, Cambridge: Cambridge University Press.

Vasquez, John A. (1983). *The Power of Power Politics: A Critique*, New Brunswick, N.J.: Rutgers University Press.

Vasquez, John A. (1988). *The Power of Power Politics: From Classical Realism to Neo-Traditionalism* (extended and revised version of Vasquez, 1983), Cambridge: Cambridge University Press.

CHAPTER 3

Open and Closed Impartiality[1]

AMARTYA SEN

The role of impartiality in the evaluation of social judgments and societal arrangements is well recognized in moral and political philosophy. Here, I want to discuss a basic distinction between two quite different ways of invoking impartiality. The procedures involve disparate interpretations of the demands of impartiality, and can correspondingly have rather dissimilar substantive implications. The two approaches will be called *closed* and *open* impartiality, respectively. The distinction turns on whether or not the exercise of impartial assessment is confined (or more accurately, attempted to be confined) to a fixed group: I shall call it the *focal group*.

With *closed impartiality*, the procedure of making impartial judgments invokes only the members of the focal group itself. For example, the Rawlsian method of "justice as fairness" uses the device of an "original contract" between the citizens of a given polity.[2] No outsider is involved in such a contractarian procedure, or is a party to the original contract (neither directly nor through representatives). For the members of the focal group, the "veil of ignorance" requires them to be ignorant of their exact identity *within* the focal group, and this can be an effective procedure for overcoming individual partialities within the focal group. But even under the veil of ignorance, a person does know that she belongs to the focal group (and is not someone outside it), and there is no insistence at all that perspectives from outside the focal group be invoked. As a device of structured political analysis, the procedure is not geared to addressing the need to overcome group prejudices. In contrast, in the case of *open impartiality*, the procedure of making impartial judgments can (and in some cases, must) invoke judgments inter alia from outside the focal group. For example, in Adam Smith's[3] use of the device of "the impartial spectator," the requirement of impartiality requires the invoking of disinterested judgments of "any fair and impartial spectator," not necessarily (indeed sometimes ideally not) belonging to the focal group. Both approaches demand impartiality, but through different procedures, which can substantially influence the reach as well as the results of the respective methods.

The contrast applies to individual decisions as well as group choices. In the individual context, open impartiality is aimed at removing the biasing influences of one's objectives or interests or prejudices, not only in contrast with those of others in some group of which one is a member (there can, of course, be many such groups related, for example, to nationality, class, profession, and so on), but also of non-members of each group. Open impartiality is a demand that the viewpoints of others, whether or not belonging to some group of which one is specifically a member, receive adequate attention.

Smith's strategy in invoking impartial spectators makes room for taking note of perspectives that are not overwhelmed by the biases of one's own groups. The partialities of group-based thinking are to be identified, with an attempt to override them. Given the powerful influence, which can be implicit and not always clearly perceived, of one's situation and group affiliations, it is necessary to examine the perspectives of differently situated spectators—from far and near—to overcome partiality in general.[4] In contrast, the "veil of ignorance" as applied within a given society or polity provides a procedure for a more limited—*intra*societal or *intra*polity—impartiality (with the further presumption of seeing an individual primarily as a member of some uniquely defined group, such as a nation or a "people"). Whereas impartiality, broadly conceived, requires the removal of different types of biasing influences, each model of closed impartiality is devised to address one possible source of bias—in the form of interpersonal variations within a particular group.

The Main Themes

I shall examine some of the differences between the two approaches to impartiality and their implications. Among other things, I shall argue that closed impartiality has some very specific limitations. The difficulties from which closed impartiality suffers include the following themes.

Procedural Parochialism

Closed impartiality is devised to eliminate partiality toward the vested interests or personal objectives of individuals in the focal group, but it is not designed to address the limitations of partiality toward the shared prejudices or biases of the focal group itself.

Procedural parochialism may or may not, in fact, be seen as a problem. In some approaches to social judgments, there is no particular interest in avoiding group leanings—indeed, sometimes quite the contrary. To illustrate, some versions of communitarianism may even celebrate the "local" nature of such priorities. The same may apply to other forms of local justice. To take an extreme case, when the Taliban rulers of Afghanistan insisted that Osama bin Laden should be tried only by a group of Islamic clerics, all committed to the Shariah, the need for some kind of impartiality (against offering personal favors or partial treatment to bin Laden) was not denied—at least not in principle.[5] Rather, what was being proposed was that the impartial judgments should come from a closed group of people who all accepted a particular religious and ethical code. There is, thus, no tension in such cases between closed impartiality and the underlying affiliative norms.

In other cases, however, when a procedure of closed impartiality is combined, in one way or another, with universalist intentions, procedural parochialism may well be seen as a difficulty. This, I shall argue, is the case with Rawlsian "justice as fairness." Despite the thoroughly non-parochial intentions of the general Rawlsian approach, the use of closed impartiality involved in the "original position" (with its program of impartial assessment confined only to members of the focal group under a "veil of ignorance" regarding individual interests and goals) does not, in fact, include any procedural guarantee against being swayed by local group prejudices.

Inclusionary Incoherence

Inconsistencies can potentially arise in the exercise of "closing" the group when the decisions to be taken by any focal group can influence the size or composition of the group itself.

For example, when the size or composition of the population of a country (or a polity) is itself influenced—directly or indirectly—by the decisions taken in the original position (in particular, the choice of the basic social structure), the focal group would vary with decisions that are meant to be taken by the focal group itself. Structural arrangements, such as "the Difference Principle," cannot but influence the pattern of social—and biological—intercourse and thus generate different populations. This is not to deny the possible existence of a "fixed point" (with suitable assumptions regarding continuity) such that the decisions of a given focal group lead exactly back to the same focal group. But the problem of possible inconsistency cannot be ruled out in general when decisions to be taken by a focal group influence the composition of the focal group itself.

Exclusionary Neglect

Closed impartiality can exclude the voice of people who do not belong to the focal group, but whose lives are affected by the decisions of the focal group. The problem is not adequately resolved by multistaged formulations of closed impartiality, as in Rawls' "the law of peoples."

This problem will not arise if decisions taken by the focal group (for example, in the original position) do not have any effect on anyone outside the focal group. That would be quite extraordinary unless people live in a world of completely separated communities. This issue can be particularly problematic for "justice as fairness" in dealing with justice across borders, since the basic social structure chosen for a society can have an influence on the lives not only of members of that society, but also of others (who are not accommodated in the original position for that society). There can be much vexation without representation.

As it happens, the first two problems (namely, procedural parochialism and inclusionary incoherence) have hardly received any systematic attention at all—not even an adequate identification. The third problem (exclusionary neglect), in contrast, has received much attention already, in one way or another.[6] John Rawls[7] himself has addressed this issue, specifically in the context of justice across borders through his proposal of "the law of peoples," which invokes a second original position between representatives of different polities (or "peoples"). In this context, we have to see clearly why the demands of "global justice" may substantially differ from those of "international justice."[8] I shall argue that the Smithian device of the impartial spectator has insights to offer on this difficult subject.

In the second section, Smith's defense of open impartiality is briefly examined. In the third, I consider Rawls' critique of Smith. The fourth section investigates the complementarity between Smithian and Rawlsian reasoning, and draws on Rawls' analysis of objectivity in moral and political philosophy, and the particular role of a "public framework of thought," which can take us beyond the restricted structure of "justice as fairness." In the three final sections, the three identified problems of closed impartiality are scrutinized.

Adam Smith and the Impartial Spectator

The Smithian device of the "impartial spectator" differs substantially from the closed impartiality of "justice as fairness." The basic idea is pithily put by Smith in *The Theory of Moral Sentiments*, as the requirement, when judging one's own conduct, to "examine it as we imagine an impartial spectator would examine it," or as he elaborated in a later edition of the same book: "to examine our own conduct as we imagine any other fair and impartial spectator would examine it."[9]

The insistence on impartiality in modern moral and political philosophy does, of course, have strongly Kantian influence. Even though Smith's exposition of this idea is less remembered, there are substantial points of similarity between the Kantian and Smithian approaches. In fact, Smith's analysis of "the impartial spectator" has some claim to being the pioneering idea in this general enterprise of interpreting impartiality and of formulating the demands of fairness, which so engaged the world of European enlightenment. Smith's ideas were not only influential among such "enlightenment thinkers" as Condorcet (who was also a pioneering social choice theorist),[10] but Immanuel Kant, too, knew *The Theory of Moral Sentiments* (originally published in 1759), and commented on it in a letter to Markus Herz in 1771 (somewhat earlier than his *Groundwork*, 1785, and *Critique of Practical Reason*, 1788).[11]

There is, however, something of a parting of the way between the Smithian approach of "the impartial spectator" and the contractarian approach, of which Rawlsian "justice as fairness" is the pre-eminent application. The need to invoke how things would look to "any other fair and impartial spectator" is a requirement that can bring in judgments that would be made by disinterested people from other societies as well. The judgmental basis of Smith's concept of fairness is, in this sense, more universal than that of a polity-prioritized theory of justice, with closed impartiality. The institutionally constructive character of the Rawlsian system also restricts the extent to which "outsiders" can be accommodated within the exercise of impartial assessment.

Even though Smith often refers to the impartial spectator as "the man within the breast," one of the main motivations of Smith's intellectual strategy is to question the soundness of reasoning alienated from the way things look to others—far as well as near. He puts the issue thus:

> In solitude, we are apt to feel too strongly whatever relates to ourselves. . . . The conversation of a friend brings us to a better, that of a stranger to a still better temper. The man within the breast, the abstract and ideal spectator of our sentiments and conduct, requires often to be awakened and put in mind of his duty, by the presence of the real spectator; and it is always from that spectator, from whom we can expect the least sympathy and indulgence, that

we are likely to learn the most complete lesson of self-command.
(TMS, III.3.38, pp. 153–4)

This way of invoking impartiality, including "real spectators" (distinct from social contractors), has a very different reach from the impartiality in the closed form of contractarian reasoning.

Smith requires the impartial spectator to go beyond reasoning that may—perhaps imperceptibly—be constrained by local conventions of thought, and to examine deliberately, as a procedure, what the accepted conventions would look like from the perspective of a "real spectator" at a distance. This issue, as will be discussed presently, is particularly relevant to the challenge of "procedural parochialism." Smith's justification of such a procedure of open impartiality is spelled out thus:

> We can never survey our own sentiments and motives, we can never form any judgment concerning them; unless we remove our-selves, as it were, from our own natural station, and endeavour to view them as at a certain distance from us. But we can do this in no other way than by endeavouring to view them with the eyes of other people, or as other people are likely to view them. (TMS, III, 1, 2, p. 110)

Smithian reasoning, thus, not only admits, but also requires, the use of impartial spectators at a distance, and the procedure of impartiality to be used is open and broad, rather than closed and restricted.

On Rawls' Interpretation of Smith

The foregoing argument indicates that there can be substantial differences between the open impartiality of the impartial spectator and the closed impartiality of the social contract. But can the impartial spectator really be the basis of a viable approach to moral or political assessment without being, directly or indirectly, parasitic on some version of closed impartial-ity, such as contractarianism? As it happens, this issue has been addressed by Rawls himself in the *Theory of Justice*, when he comments on the general device of the impartial spectator (TJ, 183–92). Rawls interprets the impartial spectator conception as one particular example of "the ideal observer" approach (TJ, 184). Seen in this way, the idea allows some free-dom, as Rawls rightly notes, about how we may proceed from there to make the conception more specific. He argues that interpreted in this way, "there is no conflict so far between this definition and justice as fairness" (TJ, 184). Indeed, it "may well be the case that an ideally rational and impartial spectator would approve of a social system if and only if it satisfies the principles of justice which would be adopted in the contract scheme" (TJ, 184–5).

This is certainly a possible interpretation of an "ideal observer," but it is definitely not, as we have already seen, Smith's conception of "the impartial spectator." It is indeed the case that the spectator can take note of what may be expected had there been such a contract, but Smith requires the impartial spectator to go beyond that and at least see what the issues would look like with "the eyes of other people"—from the perspective of "real spectators" far and near.

Indeed, Rawls too goes on to note that "while it is possible to supplement the impartial spectator definition with the contract point of view, there are other ways of giving it a deductive basis" (TJ, 185). Rawls then proceeds, however, by looking at David Hume's, rather than Smith's, writings. This, not surprisingly, leads Rawls to consider the alternative of making the impartial spectator rely on "satisfactions" generated by sympathetic consideration of the experiences of others: "the strength of his approval is determined by the balance of satisfactions to which he had sympathetically responded" (TJ, 186). This, in turn, takes Rawls to the interpretation that the impartial spectator may really be a "classical utilitarian" in disguise. Once that extremely odd diagnosis is made, Rawls' response is, of course, quite predictable—and predictably forceful. He points out that already in the first chapter of the *Theory of Justice*, he has discussed why "there is a sense in which classical utilitarianism fails to take seriously the distinction between persons" (TJ, 187).

Indeed, in discussing the history of classical utilitarianism, Rawls lists Smith among its early proponents, along with Hume (TJ, 22–3, footnote 9). This, of course, is just a wrong diagnosis, since Smith had firmly rejected the utilitarian proposal of basing ideas of the good and the right on pleasure and pain, and had also spurned the view that the reasoning needed for complex moral judgments can be reduced simply to counting pleasure and pain. Indeed, more generally, Smith was critical even of looking for some one thing as a simpliciter of our diverse concerns and priorities:

> By running up all the different virtues to this one species of propriety, Epicurus indulged a propensity, which is natural to all men, but which philosophers in particular are apt to cultivate with a peculiar fondness, as the great means of displaying their ingenuity, the propensity to account for all appearances from as few principles as possible. And he, no doubt, indulged this propensity still further, when he referred all the primary objects of natural desire and aversion to the pleasures and pains of the body. (TMS, VII.ii.2.14, p. 299)

Thus, the Rawlsian interpretation of Smith and of his use of the "impartial spectator" is altogether mistaken.[12] More importantly, the impartial-spectator approach need not, in fact, be based either on Rawlsian contractarianism or on Benthamite classical utilitarianism—the only two options Rawls considers. Rather, the kind of diverse moral and political concerns that he himself discusses so illuminatingly are precisely the ones that the impartial spectator too has to grapple with, but without the additional (and in the Smithian perspective, inescapably arbitrary) insistence on closed impartiality. In the approach of the impartial spectator, the need for the discipline of ethical and political reasoning firmly remains, and also the requirement of impartiality stays paramount, and it is only the "closing" of that impartiality that is absent.[13] The impartial spectator can work and enlighten without being either a social contractor or a camouflaged utilitarian.

Open Impartiality and Rawlsian Reasoning

Even though the argument for giving more room to open impartiality is not a specific critique of Rawlsian justice as fairness, it is inter alia a demand for going well beyond that highly successful framework of moral and political investigation. I should emphasize, however, that the exploration of open impartiality can inter alia draw on the discipline of reasoning that we have learned from Rawls' own work.[14] For example, in the "open" conception of impartiality, there is an appeal to objectivity in some form, for which Rawls' discussion of the nature of objectivity in moral and political arguments is particularly relevant.

Smith's use of the impartial spectator relates to contractarian reasoning in a somewhat similar way to that in which models of fair *arbitration* (which can be done by anyone) relate to those of fair *negotiation* (in which participation is confined to the members of the group in the original contract). In Smithian analysis, the relevant judgments can come from outside the perspectives of the negotiating protagonists; indeed, they can come from, as Smith puts it, any "fair and impartial spectator."

There are, in fact, significant similarities between parts of Rawls' own reasoning and the exercise of fair arbitration involved in open impartiality. Despite the "contractarian" form of Rawlsian theory of justice, the social contract is not the only device that Rawls invokes in developing his theory.[15] Indeed, much of the reflective exercise happens even before the hypothetical contract is supposed to occur. The "veil of ignorance" can be seen as a meta-ethical demand of impartiality, which is meant to constrain any person's moral and political reflections whether or not a contract is ultimately invoked. Furthermore, while the form of that exercise of impartiality remains "closed" in the sense already discussed, it is clear that Rawls' intentions include inter alia the elimination of the hold of arbitrary influences related to past history (as well as individual advantages). In seeing "the original position" as "a device of representation," Rawls attempts to address various types of arbitrariness that may influence our actual thinking, which have to be subjected to ethical discipline to arrive at an impartial point of view:

> The original position, with the formal features I have called "the veil of ignorance," is this point of view. . . . These contingent advantages and accidental influences from the past should not affect an agreement on the principles that are to regulate the institutions of the basic structure itself from the present into the future. (TJ, 23)

Indeed, given the use of the discipline of the "veil of ignorance," the parties (that is individuals under this veil) would already agree with each other when the point comes to negotiate a contract. In fact, noting this, Rawls does ask whether a contract is at all needed given the precontract agreement. He explains that despite the agreement that would precede the contract, the original contract does have a significant role because the act of contracting—even in its hypothetical form—is itself important, and because the contemplation of the act of contracting—with a "binding vote"—may influence the precontractual deliberations that occur:

> Why, then, the need for an agreement when there are no differences to negotiate? The answer is that reaching a unanimous agreement without a binding vote is not the same thing as everyone's arriving at the same choice, or forming the same intention. That it is an undertaking that people are giving may similarly affect everyone's deliberations so that the agreement that results is different from the choice everyone would have otherwise made.[16]

Thus, the original contract remains important for Rawls, and yet a substantial part of Rawlsian reasoning concerns precontractarian reflections, and in some ways runs on parallel lines to Smith's procedure involving fair arbitration. What distinguishes the Rawlsian method, even in this part, from the Smithian approach is the "closed" nature of the participatory exercise that Rawls invokes through restricting the "veil of ignorance" to the members of a given focal group.

Rawls' remarks on objectivity are particularly relevant to the Smithian approach. The issue of objectivity, which is closely related to open impartiality, shares something with the often-repeated demand that justice should not only be done, but also be "seen to be done."[17] The rationale of the demand lies not just in the instrumental argument that disbelief in the fairness of judgments made by the legal establishment can make it harder to *implement* legally arrived decisions. But it also appeals, more foundationally, to the sense that, if impartial spectators—near and far—with the best of effort cannot see that a judgment is just, then even its *correctness* could be in some doubt.

In pursuing these demands of public comprehension and observability, we can get considerable guidance from the Rawlsian exposition of objectivity in ethics and political philosophy, particularly from his focus on the demand for "a public framework of thought": ". . . we look at our society and our place in it objectively: we share a common standpoint along with others and do not make our judgments from a personal slant."[18] Judgments of justice cannot be an entirely private affair—unfathomable to others—and the Rawlsian invoking of "a public framework of thought," which does not in itself demand a "contract," is a critically important move.

That move is further consolidated by Rawls' argument, particularly in *Political Liberalism*, that the relevant standard of the objectivity of ethical principles is basically congruent with their defensibility within a public framework of thought (there is no further test):

> To say that a political conviction is objective is to say that there are reasons, specified by a reasonable and mutually recognizable political conception (satisfying those essentials), sufficient to convince all reasonable persons that it is reasonable. (PL, 119)

This thesis links closely also with Thomas Scanlon's[19] argument that "thinking about right and wrong is, at the most basic level, thinking about what could be justified to others on grounds that they, if appropriately motivated, could not reasonably reject" (Ibid., p. 5).

The accord that is sought need not, of course, be anywhere near total.[20] The concurrence need not go beyond a partial ordering with limited articulation, which can nevertheless make firm and useful statements. The agreements arrived at need not demand that some proposal is uniquely just, but perhaps only that it is plausibly just, or at least not manifestly unjust. Indeed, the demands of reasoned practice can, in one way or another, live with a good deal of incompleteness or unresolved conflicts.[21] In particular, the acknowledgment of some incompleteness does not indicate that all is lost.[22] The agreement to emerge from "a public framework of thought" can be of a correspondingly permissive kind.

It might, however, be thought that a serious difficulty can arise from elsewhere, related to a different issue, in trying to extend the Rawlsian "public framework of thought" beyond the borders of a country, or a polity.

Can comprehension and thought cross geographical borders? While some are evidently tempted by the belief that we cannot follow each other across the borders of a given community, a particular nation, or a specific culture (a temptation that has been fueled particularly by the popularity of some versions of communitarian separatism), there is no particular reason to presume that interactive communication and public engagement can be sought only within such boundaries (or within the confines of those who can be seen as "one people"). Smith saw the possibility that the impartial spectator could draw on the understanding of people who are far as well as those who are near.

This was indeed a significant theme in the intellectual concerns of Enlightenment writers. While commenting on the importance of increased communication in expanding the reach of our sense of justice, Hume[23] noted:

> ... again suppose that several distinct societies maintain a kind of intercourse for mutual convenience and advantage, the boundaries of justice still grow larger, in proportion to the largeness of men's views, and the force of their mutual connexions. (Ibid., p. 25)

The possibility of communication and cognizance across the borders should be no more absurd today than it was in Smith's eighteenth century world. Indeed, right at this time, as the world is engaged in discussions and debates about the unacceptability—and the roots—of global terrorism, it is hard to think that we cannot understand each other across the borders of our polity.[24] Rather, it is the firmly "open" outlook, which Smith's "impartial spectator" invokes, that may be in some need of reassertion today. It can make a difference to our understanding of the demands of impartiality in moral and political philosophy in the interconnected world in which we live.

Procedural Parochialism

That the veil of ignorance, as defined by Rawls, does not, as a procedure, provide a bar against catering to local group interest is easy to see. Its extensive implications will be discussed presently. But the limitation of the closed framework of impartiality can go much further, since there is no procedural barricade here against susceptibility to local prejudices either. The Rawlsian exercise involves institutional reasoning among people "who are born into that society in which they lead their lives" (PL, 23). What is a matter of concern here is the absence of some procedural insistence on forceful scrutiny of local values that may, on further scrutiny, turn out to be preconceptions and biases that are common in a focal group.

The contrast with Smith's procedure involving the "impartial spectator" is particularly relevant here. Smith noted, in a chapter titled "On the Influence of Custom and Fashion upon the Sentiments of Moral Approbation and Disapprobation," that "the different situations of different ages and countries are apt . . . to give different characters to the generality of those who live in them, and their sentiments concerning the particular degree of each quality, that is either blamable or praise-worthy, vary, according to that degree which is usual in their own country, and in their own times" (TMS, V.2.7, p. 204).[25] Indeed, it may well emerge that what is taken to be perfectly natural and normal in a society cannot survive a broad-based and less limited scrutiny.[26] Smith gives various examples of parochial thought, swayed by the hold of local mores:

> . . . the murder of new-born infants was a practice allowed of in almost all the states of Greece, even among the polite and civilized Athenians; and whenever the circumstances of the parent rendered it inconvenient to bring up the child, to abandon it to hunger, or to wild beasts, was regarded without blame or censure. . . . Uninterrupted custom had by this time so thoroughly authorized the practice, that not only the loose maxims of the world tolerated this barbarous prerogative, but even the doctrine of philosophers, which ought to have been more just and accurate, was led away by the established custom, and upon this, as upon many other occasions, instead of censuring, supported the horrible abuse, by far-fetched considerations of public utility. Aristotle talks of it as of what the magistrates ought upon many occasions to encourage. Plato is of the same opinion, and, with all that love of mankind which seems to animate all his writings, no where marks this practice with disapprobation. (TMS, V.2.15, p. 210)

Smith's insistence that we must inter alia view our sentiments from "a certain distance from us" is, thus, motivated by the object of scrutinizing not only the influence of vested interest, but also the impact of entrenched tradition and custom. While Smith's example of infanticide remains sadly relevant in some societies even today, many of his other examples have relevance to other contemporary societies. This applies, for example, to Smith's insistence that "the eyes of the rest of mankind" must be invoked to understand whether "a punishment appears equitable."[27] Scrutiny from a "distance" may be useful for practices as different as the stoning of adulterous women in Taliban's Afghanistan; selective abortion of female fetuses in China, Korea, and parts of India;[28] and the use of capital punishment (with or without opportunity for celebratory public jubilation) in the United States. An impartial assessment requires not only the avoidance of the impact of individual vested interests, but also an exacting scrutiny of parochial moral and social sentiments, which may influence the ideas and outcomes in locally separated "original positions."

In the part of Rawlsian analysis that relates to the importance of a "public framework of thought," and the need to "look at our society and our place in it objectively" (TJ, 516–7) there is, in fact, much in common with Smithian reasoning. And yet the procedure of segregated "original positions," operating in devised isolation, is not conducive to guaranteeing an adequately objective scrutiny of social conventions and parochial sentiments which may influence what rules are chosen in the original position. When Rawls says, "our moral principles and convictions are objective to the extent that they have been arrived at and tested by assuming [a] general standpoint," he is attempting to unlock the door for an open scrutiny. Yet later on in the same sentence, the door is partially bolted by the procedural form of the requirement: ". . . and by assessing the arguments for them by the restrictions expressed by the conception of the original position" (TJ, 517).

Rawls insists on the closed nature of the "original position":

> . . . I assume that the basic structure is that of a closed society: that is, we are to regard it as self-contained and as having no relations with other societies. . . . That a society is closed is a considerable abstraction, justified only because it enables us to focus on certain main questions free from distracting details. (PL, 12)

Rawls goes on to note one limitation of this approach: "At some point a political conception of justice must address the just relations between peoples, or the law of peoples, as I shall say." That issue is indeed addressed by Rawls' later work (*The Law of Peoples*), and will be examined later on in this essay. But the "just relations between peoples" is an altogether different issue from the need for an open scrutiny, through a non-parochial procedure, of the values and practices of any given society or polity. The closed formulation of the program of Rawlsian "original position" extracts a heavy price in the absence of any procedural guarantee that local values will be subjected to an open scrutiny, and this loss is more than that of a "distracting detail."

The Rawlsian "veil of ignorance" in the "original position" is a very effective device in making people see beyond their personal vested interests and goals. And yet it may do little to ensure an open scrutiny of local and possibly parochial values. There is something to learn from Smith's skepticism about the possibility of going beyond local presuppositions— or even implicit bigotry—"unless we remove ourselves, as it were, from our own natural station, and endeavor to view them as at a certain distance from us." The Smithian procedure includes, as a result, the insistence that the exercise of impartiality must be open (rather than locally closed), since "we can do this in no other way than by endeavoring to view them with the eyes of other people, or as other people are likely to view them (TMS, III, 1, 2, p. 110). Even as the Rawlsian "veil of ignorance" addresses effectively the need to remove the influence of vested interests and personal slants of the diverse individuals within the focal group, it abstains from invoking the scrutiny of (in Smith's language) "the eyes of the rest of mankind." Something more than an "identity blackout" *within* the confines of the local focal group would be needed to address this problem. It is in this sense that the procedural device of closed impartiality in "justice as fairness" can be seen as parochial (despite Rawls' ecumenical intentions).

Inclusionary Incoherence and Focal Group Plasticity

The fact that the members of the focal group have a status in the contractarian exercise that nonmembers do not enjoy creates problems even when we confine our attention to one society—or one "people"—only. The size and composition of the population may alter with public policies (whether or not they are dedicated "population policies") and the populations can vary even with the "basic structure" of the society. Any rearrangement of economic, political, or social institutions, such as the "basic structure of the society" (including such rules as the "difference principle"), would tend to influence the size and composition of the group that would be born, through changes in marriages, mating, cohabitation, and other parameters of reproduction.[29] The focal group that would be involved in the choice of the "basic structure" would be influenced by that choice itself, and this makes the "closing" of the group for closed impartiality a potentially incoherent exercise.[30]

To illustrate this problem of group plasticity, suppose there are two institutional structures A and B that would yield, respectively, five million and six million people. Who, we have to ask, are included in the original position (OP) in which social decisions are made that would inter alia choose between A and B and thus influence the size and composition of the respective population groups? Suppose we take the larger group of six million people as the focal group who are included in the OP, and suppose also that it turns out that the institutional structure chosen in the corresponding OP is A, leading to an actual population of five million people. But, then, the focal group was wrongly specified. (We may also ask: How did the nonexistent—indeed *never* existent—extra one million people participate in the OP?) If, on the other hand, the focal group is taken to be the smaller number of five million people, what if the institutional structure chosen in the corresponding OP is *B*, leading to an actual population of six million people? Again, the focal group would turn out to be wrongly specified. Also, the additional one million people, then, did not participate in the original position, which would have decided the institutional structures that would extensively influence their lives (indeed not just *whether* they are to be born or not, but also *other* features of their actual lives). If the decisions taken in the OP influence the size and composition of the population, and if the population size and composition influence the nature of the OP, then there is no way of guaranteeing that the focal group associated with the OP is coherently characterized.

The foregoing difficulty applies even when we consider the so-called "cosmopolitan" or "global" version of the Rawlsian "justice as fairness," including all the people in the world in one large contractual exercise. The population plasticity problem is not dependent on societal specification, and would apply no matter whether we consider one "people" among many peoples or all the people put together.

When the Rawlsian system is applied to one particular "people" in a larger world, however, then there are further problems. In fact, the dependence of births and deaths on the basic social structure has some parallel also in the influence of that structure on the movements of people from one country to another. This general concern has some similarity with one of Hume's[31] grounds for skepticism of the conceptual relevance as well as historical force of "the original contract":

> The face of the earth is continually changing, by the increase in small kingdoms into great empires, by the dissolution of great empires into smaller kingdoms, by the planting of colonies, by the migration of tribes. . . . Where is the mutual agreement or voluntary association so much talked of? (Ibid., p. 279)

But the point at issue, in the present context, is not only—indeed not primarily—that the size and composition of the population is continually changing, but that these changes are not independent of the basic social structures that are meant to be arrived at, in contractual reasoning, precisely in the original position itself.

We must, however, examine further whether the dependence of focal groups on the basic social structure is really a problem for Rawlsian justice as fairness. Does the focal group actually have to determine the basic social structure through the corresponding OP? The answer, of course, is straightforwardly "yes," if the parties to the OP are meant to be exactly the focal group (namely, all—and only—the members of the polity or society).

But sometimes Rawls speaks of "the original position" as "simply a device of representation."[32] It might, thus, be tempting to argue that we do not have to assume that everyone in the society or polity—no more and no less—has to be a party to the original contract, and it could be argued that, therefore, the dependence of the focal groups on the decisions taken in the OP need not be a problem.

I do not think that this is an adequate rebuttal of the problem of inclusionary incoherence for two distinct reasons. First, Rawls' use of the idea of "representation" does not, in fact, amount to marshaling a wholly new set of people (or phantoms) as parties to the OP, different from the actual people in that polity. Rather, it is the *same* people under the "veil of ignorance" who are seen as "representing" themselves (but from behind "the veil"). Rawls explains this in the following way:

> This is expressed figuratively by saying that the parties are behind a veil of ignorance. In sum, the original position is simply a device of representation.[33] (Ibid., p. 401)

Indeed, Rawls' justification of the need for a contract, which invokes (as was noted earlier) "the undertaking that people are giving,"[34] indicates concrete participation (albeit under the veil of ignorance) of the people involved in the original contract.

Second, even if the representatives were to be different people (or imagined phantoms), they would have to represent the focal group of people (for example, through the veil of ignorance of possibly being any member of the focal group). So the variability of the focal group would be reflected in the variability of the people whom the representatives represent in the original position.[35]

This would not be much of a problem (1) *if* the size of the population did not make any difference to the way the basic structure of the society may be organized (complete scale invariance), and (2) *if* every group of individuals were exactly like every other in terms of their priorities and values (complete value invariance). Neither is easy to assume without further restrictions in the structure of any substantive theory of justice.[36] Group plasticity, thus, does remain a problem for the exercise of closed impartiality, applied to a *given* focal group of individuals.

We must, however, also ask whether the Smithian approach of the impartial spectator is not similarly troubled by incongruity arising from group plasticity, and if not, why not. It is not similarly troubled precisely for the reason that the impartial spectator does not come from a given focal group. Indeed, Smith's "abstract and ideal spectator" is a "spectator" and not a "participant" in any exercise like a group-based contract. There is no contracting group, and there is no insistence even that the evaluators (or arbitrators) must be congruent with the affected group. Even though there remains the very difficult problem of how an impartial spectator would go about deciding on such issues as variable population size (an ethical issue of profound complexity),[37] the problem of incoherence and incongruity in "inclusionary closure" in the contractarian exercise does not have an immediate analogue in the case of the impartial spectator.

Exclusionary Neglect and Global Justice

I turn now to the problem of exclusionary neglect. Since the decisions taken about the basic structure of a society S (and what results from it) can affect the lives of people in other societies, such as T, there is a clear asymmetry in the exercise of closed impartiality involving only the citizens of S, with no role being given to people in T. It is not hard to see a lacuna there. Indeed, problems created by this asymmetric formulation of justice have rightly received reasoned attention.[38]

Rawls himself has addressed this asymmetry by invoking another "original position," this time involving representatives of different "peoples."[39] With some oversimplification—not central in the present context—the two "original positions" can be seen as being respectively *intranational* (between individuals in a nation) and *international* (between representatives of different nations). Each exercise is one of closed impartiality, but the two together cover the entire world population.[40]

The idea of one global exercise of open impartiality, treating everyone symmetrically, may appear to be deeply "unrealistic" in the way the world is organized today. Certainly, there is an institutional lacuna here. We can nevertheless invoke the insights and instructions generated by a cross-border "public framework of thought," as Smith (among many others) have done. I shall not pursue further this issue here beyond noting that the ethical relevance and practical influence of global discussions are not totally conditional on the existence of a well-organized planetary forum for gigantic institutional agreements.[41]

More immediately, even in the politically divisive world in which we live, we have to give fuller recognition to the fact that different persons across borders need not operate only through international (or "inter-people") relations. The world is divisive all right, but it is diversely divisive, and the partitioning of the global population into distinct "nations" or "peoples" is not the only line of division.[42] Nor does the national partitioning have any pre-eminent priority over other categorizations (as implicitly presumed in "the law of peoples").[43]

Interpersonal relations across country borders go far beyond international interactions in many different ways. The "original position" of nations or "peoples" would be peculiarly restricted in dealing with many of the cross-border effects of human action. If the effects of the operation of transnational corporations are to be assessed or scrutinized, they have to be seen as what they are, namely, corporations that operate without borders, taking business decisions about registration, tax homes, and similar contingent matters according to the convenience of business. They can hardly be fitted into the model of one "people" impacting on another.

Similarly, the ties that bind human beings in relations of duty and concern across borders need not operate *through* the collectivities of the respective nations. To illustrate, a feminist activist in America who wants to do something to remedy particular features of women's disadvantage in, say, Sudan would tend to draw on a sense of affinity that need not work through the sympathies of the American nation for the predicament of the Sudanese nation. Her identity as a fellow woman, or as a person (male or female) moved by feminist concerns, may be more important in a particular context than her citizenship, and the feminist perspective may well be introduced in an exercise of "open impartiality" without its being "subsequent" to national identities. Other identities, which may be particularly invoked in other exercises of "open impartiality," may involve class, language, literature, profession, and so on, and can provide different and competing perspectives to the priority of nation-based politics.

Even the identity of being a human being—perhaps our most basic identity—may have the effect, when fully seized, of broadening our viewpoint correspondingly. The imperatives that we may associate with our humanity may not be mediated by our membership of smaller collectivities such as specific "peoples" or "nations." Indeed, the normative demands of being guided by "humanity" or "humaneness" can build on our membership of the wide category of human beings—irrespective of our particular nationalities, or sects, or tribal affiliations (traditional or modern).[44]

Behavioral correlates of global commerce, global culture, global politics, global philanthropy, even global protests (like those, recently, on the streets of Seattle or Washington or Melbourne or Prague or Quebec or Genoa) draw on direct relations between human beings—with their own standards, and their respective inclusions and priorities related to a variety of classifications. These ethics can, of course, be supported, scrutinized, or criticized in different ways, even by invoking other intergroup relations, but the intergroup relations need not be confined to—or even be led by—international relations (or by "the law of peoples"). They may involve very many diverse groups, with identities that vary from seeing oneself as a businessman or a worker, as a woman or a man, as a libertarian or a conservative or a socialist, as being poor or rich, or as a member of one professional group or another (of, say, doctors or lawyers).[45] Collectivities of many different types may be invoked. International justice—even in the finely tuned form of "the law of peoples"—is simply not adequate for global justice.

This issue has a bearing also on contemporary discussions on human rights. The notion of human rights builds on our shared humanity. These rights are not derived from the citizenship of any country, or the membership of any nation, but are presumed to be claims or entitlements of every human being. It differs, thus, from constitutionally created rights guaranteed for specified people (such as American or French citizens). For example, the human right of a person not to be tortured or subjected to terrorist attacks is affirmed independently of the country of which this person is a citizen, and also quite irrespective of what the government of that country—or any other—wants to provide or support.

In overcoming the limitations of "exclusionary neglect" use can be made of the idea of open impartiality embedded in a universalist approach—of the kind that relates closely to Smith's concept of the impartial spectator. That broad framework of impartiality makes it particularly clear why considerations of basic human rights, including the importance of safeguarding elementary civil and political liberties, need not be contingent on citizenship and nationality, and may not be institutionally dependent on a nationally derived social contract. Also, there is no need to presume a world government, or even to invoke a hypothetical global social contract. The "imperfect obligations" associated with the recognition of these human rights can be seen as falling broadly on anyone who is in a position to help.[46]

The liberating role of open impartiality allows different types of unprejudiced and unbiased perspectives to be brought into consideration, and encourages us to benefit from the insights that come from differently situated impartial spectators. In scrutinizing these insights together, there may well be some common understanding that emerges forcefully, but there is no need to presume that all the differences arising from distinct perspectives can be settled similarly. As was discussed earlier, systematic guidance to reasoned decisions can come from incomplete orderings that reflect unresolved conflicts. Indeed, as the recent literature in "social choice theory," allowing relaxed forms of outcomes (such as partial social orderings), has made clear, social judgments are not rendered useless or hopelessly problematic just because the evaluative process leaves many pairs unranked and many conflicts unsettled.[47]

For the emergence of a shared and useful understanding of many substantive issues of rights and duties (and also of rights and wrongs), there is no need to insist that we must have agreed complete orderings or universally accepted full partitionings of the just from the unjust. For example, a common resolve to fight for the abolition of famines, or genocide, or terrorism, or slavery, or untouchability, or illiteracy, or epidemics, and so on, does not require that there be a similarly extensive agreement on the appropriate formulae for inheritance rights, or income-tax schedules, or levels of minimal wages, or term limits, or copyright laws. The basic relevance of the distinct perspectives—some congruent, some divergent—of the people of the world (diversely diverse as they are) is part of the understanding that open impartiality tends to generate. There is nothing particularly defeatist in this recognition.

A Concluding Remark

This chapter has been concerned with contrasting two ways of approaching the demands of impartiality in moral and political philosophy. The procedure of closed impartiality, particularly exemplified by contractarian devices applied to closed groups, can involve a strictly partial approach to impartiality. It suffers, as a result, from a number of distinct problems, of which "exclusionary neglect" is one. This particular deficiency has already received some attention, but it can be further investigated through the Smithian device of "impartial spectators," which radically differs from the procedure of two-stage contractarianism as in "the law of peoples" (for example, intranational and international), and also from grand proposals of a single, gigantic global contract.

The closed impartiality enshrined in the contractarian approach can suffer from other serious problems as well, including "procedural parochialism" and "inclusionary incoherence." Since these limitations have not yet received much examination at all, they demand greater—and clearer—recognition, and a substantial part of this article was devoted to them, particularly to procedural parochialism. In tackling each of these problems, the alternative of open impartiality has some merit, which is not shared by closed impartiality with its parochial formulation. The impartial spectator does indeed have something to tell us—even more vocally today than in the world that Smith knew.

Notes

1. This chapter draws on my Wessons Lectures ("Democracy and Social Justice") at Stanford University, Ethics Program, given on January 15–16, 2001. I have greatly benefited from discussions with Akeel Bilgrami and Thomas Scanlon, and also from the comments of Kenneth Arrow, G.A. Cohen, John Deigh, Nick Denyer, Barbara Fried, Isaac Levi, Mozaffar Qizilbash, Emma Rothschild, Debra Satz, Kotaro Suzumura, and Bernard Williams.
2. John Rawls, *A Theory of Justice* (Cambridge: Harvard, 1971)—hereafter TJ; and *Political Liberalism* (New York: Columbia, 1993)—hereafter PL.

3. *The Theory of Moral Sentiments* (1759; revised edition, 1790; republished, New York: Oxford, 1976); hereafter TMS.

4. See TMS, Book III. As will be discussed, the Smithian procedure substantially differs also from the procedure, often suggested as a "corrective" to the Rawlsian scheme, of invoking one gigantic contractarian exercise involving all the people of the world, sometimes called the "cosmopolitan" or "global" version of justice as fairness—on this, see Thomas W. Pogge, *Realizing Rawls* (Ithaca, NY: Cornell, 1989).

5. The reference here is only to the principles of justice that the Taliban rulers were invoking—not to their practice.

6. See, for example, Charles R. Beitz, *Political Theory and International Relations* (Princeton, NJ: Princeton University Press, 1979); also Thomas Pogge, *Realizing Rawls* (Ithaca: Cornell University Press, 1989), and Brian Barry, *Theories of Justice, Volume I* (Berkeley: California University Press, 1989).

7. *The Law of Peoples* (Cambridge: Harvard, 1999).

8. I have tried to identify these issues in "Global Justice: Beyond International Equity," in Inga Kaul, I. Grunberg and M.A. Stern, eds., *Global Public Goods: International Cooperation in the 21st Century* (New York: Oxford, 1999), pp. 116–25, and also in "Justice across Borders," in *Global Justice and Transnational Politics*, Pablo De Greiff and Ciaran Cronin, eds. (Cambridge: MIT, 2002), pp. 37–51, originally presented as a lecture for the Centennial Year Celebrations of the De Paul University in Chicago in September 1998.

9. TMS, III, 1, 2; the extended version occurs in the sixth edition. On the points of emphasis, see the discussion in D.D. Raphael, "The Impartial Spectator," in Andrew S. Skinner and Thomas Wilson, eds., *Essays on Adam Smith* (New York: Oxford, 1975), pp. 88–90. On the centrality of these issues in the Enlightenment perspectives, particularly in the works of Smith and Condorcet, see Emma Rothschild, *Economic Sentiments: Smith, Condorcet and the Enlightenment* (Cambridge: Harvard, 2001).

10. On the importance of Condorcet's role in social choice theory, see Kenneth Arrow, *Individual Values and Social Choice* (New York: Wiley, 1951; extended edition, 1963). I discuss the contribution of Condorcet and his influence on modern social choice theory (initiated by Arrow), in my Nobel lecture, "The Possibility of Social Choice," *American Economic Review,* XCIX (June 1999): pp. 349–78.

11. See Raphael and Macfie, "Introduction," in Smith, TMS (republished edition, 1976), p. 31. It is, I suppose, immaterial that Kant chose to refer to the proud Scotsman as "the Englishman Smith."

12. Given Rawls' command over the history of ideas and his extraordinary generosity in presenting the views of others, it is uncharacteristic that he pays so little attention to the writings of Smith, especially TMS. In Rawls' far-reaching *Lectures on the History of Moral Philosophy,* (Barbara Herman, ed. (Cambridge: Harvard, 2000), Smith does get five mentions, but these passing references are confined to (1) Smith's being a Protestant, (2) a friend of Hume, (3) an amusing user of words, (4) a successful economist, and (5) the author of the *Wealth of Nations* published in the same year (1776) in which Hume died. In general, it is interesting to see how little attention the Professor of Moral Philosophy at Glasgow, so influential in economics and in philosophical thinking of his time (including Kant's), gets from contemporary moral philosophers.

13. I have argued elsewhere—"Consequential Evaluation and Practical Reason," *The Journal of Philosophy,* XCVII, 9 (September 2000): pp. 477–502—that there is a case for paying more attention to the Kantian idea of "imperfect obligations" (relatively neglected in contemporary moral and political philosophy) which involves broader reasoning, with some similarities with Smith's impartial spectator, instead of seeing the Kantian perspective as being mainly confined to the framework of "perfect obligations or to contractarian constructions.

14. I must also take this opportunity of recording my deep personal debt to Rawls, since my own understanding of moral and political philosophy (and also of welfare economics) has been deeply influenced by what I have learned from him, as is acknowledged in my *Collective Choice and Social Welfare* (San Francisco: Holden-Day, 1970; republished, Amsterdam: North-Holland, 1979); *On Economic Inequality* (New York: Oxford, 1973; expanded edition, 1997); *On Ethics and Economics* (New York: Blackwell, 1987); *Inequality Re-examined* (Cambridge: Harvard, 1992).

15. This is, in fact, a particularly good moment to re-examine the extraordinary reach of Rawlsian reasoning, since we have been lucky enough to have had a veritable feast of recent contributions from Rawls over the last three years, which have consolidated and extended his earlier writings. See Rawls, *Collected Papers*, Samuel Freeman, ed. (Cambridge: Harvard, 1999); *The Law of Peoples* (1999); *Lectures on the History of Moral Philosophy* (2000); *A Theory of Justice* (Cambridge: Harvard, revised edition, 2000); *Justice as Fairness: A Restatement*, Erin Kelly, ed. (Cambridge: Harvard, 2001).

16. Rawls, "Reply to Alexander and Musgrave," in *Collected Papers*, pp. 232–53, here p. 249; see also Tony Laden, "Games, Fairness and Rawls' *A Theory of Justice*," *Philosophy and Public Affairs*, XX (1991): pp. 189–222.

17. This is one of the major themes explored in my Wessons Lectures at Stanford University, "Democracy and Social Justice" (January 2001).

18. TJ, 516–7; more extensively, see TJ, 513–20, and PL, 110–6.

19. *What We Owe to Each Other* (Cambridge: Harvard, 1998); see also his "Contractualism and Utilitarianism," in Amartya Sen and Bernard Williams, eds., *Utilitarianism and Beyond* (New York: Cambridge University Press, 1982), pp. 103–28.

20. As Rawls puts it, "given the many obstacles to agreement in political judgement even among reasonable persons, we will not reach agreement all the time, or perhaps even much of the time" (PL, 118).

21. I have discussed the relevance of incompleteness and partial orderings in *Collective Choice and Social Welfare*; *On Economic Inequality*; "Internal Consistency of Choice," *Econometrica*, LXI (1993): pp. 495–521; "Maximization and the Act of Choice," *Econometrica*, LXV (1997): pp. 745–75; "Consequential Evaluation and Practical Reason." For a different but related approach to incompleteness, see Isaac Levi, *Hard Choices* (New York: Cambridge University Press, 1986), and *The Covenant of Reason: Rationality and the Commitments of Thought* (New York: Cambridge University Press, 1997).

22. Indeed, even when an incompleteness is not just tentative (resolvable on the basis of further discussion and scrutiny), but in fact claimed to be "assertive" (expressing the view that the alternatives *cannot* be ordered or classified on the basis of a congruence of nonrejectable principles), that too can be an affirmative claim (not an expression of defeat). These questions are further examined in "Justice and Assertive Incompleteness," the second Rosenthal Lecture at the Northwestern University Law School (1998), and "Incompleteness and Reasoned Choice," mimeographed essay written for a festschrift for Isaac Levi (2002).

23. *An Enquiry Concerning the Principles of Morals* (1777; republished, La Salle, IL: Open Court, 1966).

24. Elsewhere, I have tried to discuss the role of crosscultural interactions in the history of cultures (including the emergence of "Western civilization" and "Western science")—"Civilized Imprisonments," in *The New Republic* (June 10, 2002): 28–33.

25. Smith noted that the "effects of custom and fashion ... upon moral sentiments of mankind" frequently reflect the variability of circumstances that demand different priorities, so that we cannot, in general, "complain that the moral sentiments of men are very grossly perverted" (p. 209). But he also pointed out that, sometimes, local values are in very great need of a more open scrutiny.

26. The critical role of comparative reference and scrutiny supplements the ethical inclusiveness of a nonparochial approach, on which see Martha Nussbaum with Respondents, *For Love of Country* (Boston: Beacon, 1996).

27. Smith, *Lectures on Jurisprudence*, R.L. Meek, D.D. Raphael, and P.G. Stein, eds. (New York: Oxford, 1978; reprinted, Indianapolis: Liberty, 1982), p.104.

28. On this, see my "The Many Faces of Gender Inequality," *The New Republic* (September 17, 2001): 4–14.

29. On this, see Derek Parfit, *Reasons and Persons* (New York: Oxford, 1984).

30. This issue has been discussed in my "Normative Evaluation and Legal Analogues," presented at a conference on "Norms and the Law," at the School of Law of Washington University in St. Louis (March 2001).

31. "On the Original Contract," republished in Hume, *Selected Essays*, Stephen Copley and Andrew Edgar, eds. (New York: Oxford, 1996), pp. 274–91.

32. "Justice as Fairness: Political Not Metaphysical," in *Collected Papers*, p. 401.

33. As Rawls puts it elsewhere (PL, 23): "Justice as fairness recasts the doctrine of the social contract . . . the fair terms of social cooperation are conceived as agreed to by those engaged in it, that is, by free and equal citizens who are born into the society in which they lead their lives."

34. "Reply to Alexander and Musgrave," *Collected Papers*, p. 249.

35. To forestall a possible line of response, I should emphasize that this is not a similar problem at all to the difficulty of representing members of the future generation (seen as a *fixed group*). There is, to be sure, a problem there too (for example, about how much can be assumed about the future generations' reasoning since they are not here yet), but it is nevertheless a different issue. There is a distinction between (i) the problem of what can be presumed about the agreement of the future generations (seen as a fixed group) to be represented and (ii) the impossibility of having a fixed group to be represented, in choosing the basic structure of the society when the set of actual persons must *vary* depending on the choice of that structure.

36. It is important also to avoid a misunderstanding, which I have already encountered in trying to present this chapter, that takes the form of arguing that differing populations cannot make any difference to the Rawlsian original position, since every individual is exactly like any other under the "veil of ignorance." The point to note is that even though the "veil of ignorance" makes *different individuals within a given group* ignorant of their respective interests and values (making everyone much the same in the *as if* deliberative exercise for a given group), it does not, by itself, have any implication whatever in making *different groups of individuals* have exactly the same configuration of interests and the same cluster of values. More generally, to make the exercise of closed impartiality fully independent of the size and composition of the focal group, the substantive reach of that exercise has to be severely impoverished.

37. The complexity would have been even greater if it were necessary that these judgments must take the form of *complete* orderings, but, as has been already discussed, this is not needed for a useful public framework of thought, nor for the making of public choices based on "maximality" (on which see my "Maximization and the Act of Choice," *Econometrica*, LXV (1997): 745–75).

38. See, for example, Beitz, *Political Theory and International Relations*, and Pogge, ed., *Global Justice* (Malden, MA: Blackwell, 2001).

39. "The Law of Peoples," in Stephen Shute and Susan Hurley, eds., *On Human Rights* (New York: Basic, 1993), pp. 41–82 and *The Law of Peoples*.

40. This does not, of course, eliminate the asymmetry between different groups of affected people, since the different polities are diversely endowed in assets and opportunities, and there would be a clear contrast between covering the world population through a sequence of prioritized impartialities, as opposed to covering it through one comprehensive exercise of impartiality (as in the "cosmopolitan" version of the Rawlsian original position).

41. On this, see my "Consequential Reasoning and Practical Reason."

42. It is interesting that the priority of one specific partitioning of the global population has been proposed in disparate political discussions, giving the pride of place, respectively, to various *different* single categorizations. The categorization underlying the so-called "clash of civilizations" is an example of a rival partitioning (see Samuel P. Huntington, *The Clash of Civilizations and the Remaking of the World Order* [New York: Simon and Schuster, 1996]), since national or polity-based categories do not coincide with categories of culture or civilization. The coexistence of these rival claims in itself illustrates why none of these putatively foundational partitionings can easily drown the competing relevance of the others.

43. There is a related issue of the tyranny that is imposed by the privileging of an alleged "cultural" or "racial" identity over other identities and over nonidentity based concerns; on this, see K. Anthony Appiah and Amy Gutman, *Color Consciousness: The Political Morality of Race* (Princeton, NJ: University Press, 1996), and Susan Moller Okin, with respondents, *Is Multiculturalism Bad for Women?* (Princeton, NJ: University Press, 1999). I also discuss this issue in my *Reason before Identity* (New York: Oxford, 1998) and "Other People," Annual British Academy Lecture 2000; shorter version published in *The New Republic* (December 18, 2000): 23–30.

44. There is a related issue, which is not central to the present discussion, but which can be important in seeing the form and reach of identity-based normative arguments. When used in the form of an identity-based reasoning that draws on reciprocity or mutual relations, consideration may be taken to be owed to others precisely on the ground that they are

"fellow members" of some relevant category—broad or narrow. That line of reasoning can, however, be distinguished from those arguments that make no use of the *shared membership* of the subject and the object, but nevertheless invoke ethical norms (of, say, "humanity") that may be expected to guide the behavior of any human being. The identity of the protagonist may be important even when no special importance is attached to the sharing of that identity by others. I have tried to identify this distinction in "Other People" and discussed it further in my lectures on "The Future of Identity" at the Pardee Center at Boston University (2001–2002).

45. Similarly, dedicated activists working for global nongovernment organizations (NGOs) (such as OXFAM, Amnesty International, Medecins sans Frontieres, Human Rights Watch, and others) explicitly focus on affiliations and associations that cut across national boundaries.

46. Arguments in defense of this perspective have been presented in my "Consequential Evaluation and Practical Reason."

47. See Kenneth Arrow, Amartya Sen, and Kotaro Suzumura, eds., *Social Choice Re-examined* (Amsterdam: Elsevier, 1997).

PART II

Allocating Responsibilities

CHAPTER 4

Realizing Rights as Enforceable Claims

SUSAN JAMES

In cultures where the air echoes with demands for rights, some philosophers have begun to protest about the din.[1] Rights claims, it is often suggested, are potentially powerful tools of reform, but can be damaged if they are used carelessly. When governments or international organizations grant rights to education, free speech, or annual holidays to people who have no likelihood of gaining these things, their efforts are merely rhetorical gestures that display a lack of political and philosophical understanding. Still worse, such empty beneficence is insulting to disadvantaged individuals or communities, and can be "a bitter mockery to the poor and needy."[2] This powerful critique of contemporary mores is founded on the conviction that rights are best understood as practical entitlements that make a difference to the lives of those who hold them. Drawing on Hohfeld's analysis of legal rights as claims which depend for their existence on correlative obligations,[3] it assumes that one possesses a right if one is able to claim it (for example, by successfully demanding that other agents fulfill their obligations, or by simply taking advantage of the fact that they are already doing so) or else have it claimed in one's name.[4] However, if we take seriously the view that rights are practical claims that make a difference to the lives of those who hold them, it is not immediately clear how we should understand them. What does it take for a right to be claimable in practice? I shall argue that, in order to provide a satisfying account of rights as practical claims, we need to conceive of them as constituted by complex sets of conditions that jointly create and sustain them. I shall then go on to consider how this account bears on our understanding of the types of problems that rights can resolve. I shall suggest that, rather than reaching for rights to deal with every kind of difficulty, we need to distinguish circumstances where they can be efficacious from those where appeals to them are indeed little more than rhetorical gestures.

It is widely agreed that a large class of legal rights depends on juridical and social institutions that create and allocate obligations, and that when these institutions work efficiently and reliably we are able to claim our rights with relative ease, even if the procedures for doing so are lengthy and complicated. When institutions are precarious, inefficient, or corrupt, our ability to claim our rights is less secure. But what does it take to extinguish rights altogether? When do they become unclaimable and thus no rights at all? Onora O'Neill suggests that a right is only claimable when we can identify agents who are under an obligation to ensure that an entitlement is met. "Unless obligation-holders are identifiable by right-holders, claims to have rights amount only to rhetoric: nothing can be claimed, waived or enforced if it is indeterminate where the claim should be lodged, for whom it may be waived or on whom it could be enforced."[5] If we accept this proposal, a right cannot be claimed, and therefore does not exist, when we are unable to find anyone on whom to pin the correlative obligations. Elaborating this condition, O'Neill distinguishes between special rights held against particular agents and universal liberty rights held against everyone. A special right can only be claimed, she argues, if particular, identifiable agents are obliged to realize it. For example, one only has a right to health care if there are nurses, doctors, midwives, and so on, who are obliged to provide treatment or advice; and their obligations in turn depend on institutions through which duties are distributed and enforced. Special rights are therefore only claimable when they are guaranteed by social institutions. By contrast, universal liberty rights can in principle be claimed even if no institutions exist. The mere knowledge that everyone has an obligation to respect my right to have unrestricted access to public space, for instance, is enough to allow me to identify the agents against whom my right is held. And that in turn is enough to enable me to claim my right.[6]

This account is designed to accommodate a distinction between claiming and enforcing a right. One can claim a right to healthcare as long as one can identify the agents who are obliged to supply it, and who are therefore at fault if treatment is not delivered. However, one may still be unable to enforce the right. Even if one can pinpoint agents who have a responsibility to provide one with healthcare, it may be impossible to make them live up to their obligations. In addition, O'Neill offers a way to reconcile the requirement that rights must be claimable with the fact that some are harder to exercise than others. While exercising a right to sue for libel is usually rather difficult, it is comparatively easy for the inhabitants of the Scottish Highlands to exercise their right to breathe relatively clean air. So much so, in fact, that the problem is to see how they can avoid exercising this right. A dedicated exponent of the Choice Theory might infer that the first type of right is claimable while the second is not[7]; but according to O'Neill, this conclusion should be resisted. Claimability, in her sense of the term, does not require that an agent who holds a right should possess the power to choose whether or not to exercise it. It just gives them or their representatives the more limited power to identify those who are responsible for delivering it.

This account of what is involved in being able to claim, and thus possess, a right allows that a right exists when the agents who have a duty to realize it will not, or cannot, fulfill their obligations. For example, a welfare right to medical treatment is claimable as long as legal and social institutions distribute duties to nurses, doctors, and so on, even if medical staff illegally refuse to treat certain sectors of the population, or the drugs needed for treatment are permanently unavailable. Equally, an agent can claim a universal liberty right, such as a right of access to public space, in circumstances where other people are barring her way, where she is not powerful enough to defy them, and where there is no relevant institution to which to appeal for help.

Such a weak analysis of what it takes to make a right claimable sits strangely with O'Neill's aspiration to ensure that rights are more than empty gestures that mock the poor and needy. Is it not a mockery, one might wonder, to argue that rights are claimable in circumstances where the agents responsible for guaranteeing them lack the power or will to fulfill their obligations? Is it not empty rhetoric to offer people rights that are claimable but unenforceable, and thus in practice unobtainable? To put the point differently, why is it better to be offered a right that is claimable but unenforceable than to be offered one that is not even claimable? O'Neill replies that claimability guarantees the existence of a minimal procedure for demanding the enforcement of a right, and in some circumstances this is certainly an advantage. By protesting or appealing to a higher authority, it may be possible to enforce the obligations on which a right depends. In other circumstances, however, the fact that identifiable agents have a responsibility to guarantee one's right may be no help at all. Where the state is bankrupt, the police force corrupt, the judiciary too cowed to act, or the pharmacy empty, claimability is not a route to enforceability and makes no practical difference. In situations like these, will it not be little short of insulting to reassure agents that their rights are claimable?

To satisfy O'Neill's own sense of what rights ought to be able to achieve, it therefore seems that we need a stronger notion of claimability and a more exacting account of what it takes to possess a right. This line of thought has recently been taken up by Raymond Geuss, who agrees that the existence of a right depends on the existence of a specifiable mechanism for enforcing it, but adds that the mechanism must be "backed up by an effective method of implementation."[8] Since effectiveness comes in degrees, effective enforceability is a threshold concept. The question of what counts as implementing a claim effectively will have to be assessed on a case-by-case basis, and any decision will of course be contestable. Nevertheless, Geuss's view implies—and here he and O'Neill diverge—that when the mechanism for enforcing the obligations that correlate with a right cannot be effectively implemented, no right exists. This stringent requirement excludes some of the rights that O'Neill recognizes. First of all, it limits the number of special rights we possess. If the mechanism for supplying a given right must be an effective one, the existence of officials who are formally responsible for providing medical treatment, but are also intransigent or impotent, will not be enough to generate a right. Some further condition must be met, such as that these officials can be induced to cooperate, or that they command the necessary resources to do their job. Secondly, Geuss's account restricts our universal liberty rights. Whereas O'Neill holds that these can exist in the absence of institutions, his view implies that they are created only when and where effective institutional mechanisms for enforcing them are in place. In fact, going even further, Geuss is skeptical about the existence of universal rights of any kind. Since these will depend on the ability of institutions to enforce a claim the whole world over, they will at best be rare.

To appreciate the strengths of this position, we need to understand what it aims to achieve. Central to its motivation is a plea for conceptual and ontological clarity. If rights are best understood as practical claims that can make a difference to the lives of those who hold them, they must be claims against specifiable individual or collective agents who are under an obligation to realize them, and are capable of doing so effectively. Unless this condition is met, the fact that one possesses a particular right will not be enough to ensure that one can exercise one's claim, and thus will not be enough to ensure that it can make a practical difference to one's life. In Geuss's view, the significance of this condition often goes unrecognized, both in politics and in philosophy. For instance, when an international conference of physicians declares a universal right to healthcare, the language of claims is misleadingly employed to articulate what are in effect moral beliefs. What the conference is really doing, Geuss proposes, is expressing its conviction that it *ought* to be possible for anyone to claim certain benefits that are currently unclaimable by part of the population. However, we cannot create claims simply by naming them. The mere fact that the physicians believe that a state of affairs would be morally valuable is not enough to generate a practical claim, and is thus not enough to generate a right.

By introducing a conception of claimability that is more demanding than O'Neill's, Geuss blocks off the possibility that an agent can possess a right when the obligations on which it depends cannot be enforced. He thus rules out the troubling conclusion that the rights of the poor and needy may be useless to them in practice. However, by placing so much weight on the notion of effective enforceability, he also excludes a familiar conception of a moral right, which plays a vastly important role in philosophical and political debate. If, on his account, one does not have an effectively enforceable claim to a thing, one does not have a right to it, moral or otherwise. Furthermore (though this is not an implication Geuss pursues), people who have been treated badly will in many cases not have had their rights violated. This may seem an unduly high price to pay. Surely, one might protest, we should continue to appeal to moral rights in order to draw attention to injustices, and to identify claims to which we believe people are morally entitled, regardless of their circumstances. What is wrong with saying, for example, that victims of famine have a right to food? And do we not need to be able to say that torturers violate the rights of their victims?

Responding to the first part of this objection, Geuss agrees that we need to be able to voice our moral aspirations, to say what we think the world ought to be like and what sorts of relationships it ought to contain. But he doubts whether these aspirations are most lucidly expressed in the language of rights. One reason for this is that contemporary rights talk obscures the difference between claims and moral judgments.[9] Someone who says (in a jurisdiction where there is no provision for it) that gays have a right to same-sex marriage voices their belief that gays ought to be in a position to enforce this claim, and thus that other agents ought to be placed under obligations which would make the claim realizable. But until we have a situation where these conditions are in place, no claim exists, and all we have is a moral judgment. To describe this situation as one where the right exists is to present the process of creating it as a *fait accompli*, when in fact the work remains to be done. Papering over the gap between aspirations and practical claims can thus encourage complacency. For example, it allows organizations or nation states to bask in the benefits of endorsing rights, without pausing to consider what it would take to make them effectively enforceable.

If one accepts that statements about unenforceable moral rights are statements about the moral beliefs of those who make them, then refusing to use the language of rights to articulate these moral aspirations has a further advantage. By presenting our aspirations as beliefs or wishes rather than claims, we draw attention to the fact that they are not self-justifying, but need to be argued for. In some cases, the reasons we offer in favor of the view that society ought to recognize a certain claim are instrumental ones designed to realize values such as convenience or speed. Often, however, our reasons include strongly normative considerations which themselves form part of a broader moral outlook. Aspirational judgments of the form "X ought to have a right to Y" are regularly embedded in what I am calling moral outlooks, and conflicting outlooks are likely to generate conflicting judgments about the claims people ought to be able to realize. To assess, and perhaps resolve, such differences we need to focus on the outlooks (including our own) from which conflicting views arise. Once again, however, the language of moral rights tends to obscure this process. By presenting contestable moral judgments as freestanding moral claims, it invests them with an unearned moral authority, and draws attention away from the need to assess the grounds on which they are based. One consequence is that powerful defenders of a particular set of rights can easily overlook the disagreements and disputes surrounding it. (One might think here of defenders of a right to free speech or free trade.) It becomes easier to think of an aspiration as a stable and established claim, and harder to recognize it as a judgment which may be challenged by a range of conflicting outlooks, as well as defended in a variety of ways (for instance, by appeal to identity, need, care, capability, recognition, history, justice, virtue, or the good). The assumption that certain rights already belong to individuals can short-circuit discussion of the claims that different groups of people would like to be able to realize, and of the terms in which they would prefer to articulate them.

There are, however, several objections to the view I am proposing, all concerned with the ways in which appeals to moral rights are used. First, we rely on moral rights to call attention to what we regard as urgent claims. Arguably, "I have a *right* to food" compels a response and demands action in a way that "I ought to be given food" does not. If so, giving up the idea that we possess certain rights regardless of our circumstances would be giving up a means of indicating when something exceptionally important is at stake. It is true that we sometimes use the language of rights to draw attention to needs or values that we believe should be taken especially seriously. However, the success of this strategy does not stem simply from the fact that we appeal to a right, but rather from features of the particular right asserted, from the circumstances of the assertion, or from the position of the agent who makes it. For example, "I have a right to food" is compelling when uttered by someone suffering from hunger, or by someone whose food supply is in danger, but not when uttered by a peckish child at the end of an afternoon walk. Our responses to such statements are shaped by our assessments of the character and urgency of the demands they contain; in short, they are shaped by our understanding of the grounds on which these demands are based, grounds that are themselves embedded in moral outlooks. In themselves, then, assertions of moral right do not function as trumps, in Ronald Dworkin's phrase, and in replacing them by assertions of moral belief we do not lose the ability to discriminate between vital and trivial values. We distinguish these by assessing the reasons that underpin judgments about the claims that agents ought to be able to enforce.

A second argument for holding on to the idea that people possess moral rights regardless of their circumstances links it with a particular conception of equality. As the bearers of moral rights, human beings are equal. To remove the rights is therefore to take a retrograde step towards inegalitarianism. Once again, however, there is another way to look at the matter. Giving up the view that people are already equal by virtue of the fact that they possess moral rights does not prevent us from believing that everyone ought to be in an equally good position to enforce certain fundamental claims effectively, and thus from retaining an aspiration to a rights-based notion of equality. It therefore does not force us to take an inegalitarian stance. By urging us to attend to the different levels of power exercised by privileged and unprivileged groups and individuals, and to see the differences in their ability to enforce claims as differences in their rights, it seeks to shift the focus of our concern with equality from an aspiration, to the social conditions that the aspiration tacitly presupposes.

This shift has the advantages I have discussed, but is nevertheless sometimes said to be disempowering. According to some theorists—and also some activists—the ability to appeal to moral rights is an important emancipatory tool. For instance, if one has no access to healthcare, it is more affirming to be able to conceive of oneself as a bearer of rights who already possesses a legitimate claim than simply as someone who ought to be in a position to enforce their claim effectively.[10] The symbolic resonance of the language of rights is enormously important and needs to be taken into account, but this argument nevertheless seems to me to be equivocal. First, if one is not in a position to enforce a claim to healthcare, it may be more frustrating than empowering to fall back on a right that is impervious to one's circumstances. And secondly, as Marx pointed out, there may be something pacifying about a theory of moral rights that yields a formal conception of equality, while directing attention away from the differences between rich and poor, fortunate and unfortunate.

A final criticism of the suggestion that one should view rights as effectively enforceable claims points out that it undermines another familiar tool of protest. If, for example, one only has a right not to be tortured when someone can effectively enforce this claim, there will be many cases where we cannot say that a torture victim's rights have been violated.[11] Instead, we shall have to content ourselves with the less metaphorically charged assertion that the victim ought to have had a right to effective protection. However, this is not to say that it is impossible to make relevant discriminations. Understood as effectively enforceable claims, rights are not vested in individuals, but in complex arrangements of agents and institutions, so that no single factor determines what rights an individual possesses, and the very existence of a right can be a matter of degree. In situations where institutions are corrupt or poorly endowed, rights will usually be unstable. It would then be anachronistic to say that an individual who was unable to enforce a claim had had their right violated, and more apposite to ask whether they had a right at all. However, where institutions run smoothly and efficiently, so that individuals have well-founded expectations about the claims they will be able to enforce, we may be able to identify a failure to realize a claim as an aberration akin to a violation.

Although the claim that rights only exist when they are effectively enforceable is unfamiliar, it has a number of significant advantages and survives a range of criticisms. It remains possible, of course, that the conventional notion of a moral right could be adapted to suit our current purposes. A community of philosophers might decide that an agent only has a moral right to a thing when there is agreement that the agent ought to have an effectively enforceable claim to it, thus making the notion of a moral right parasitic on the practical notion of an effectively enforceable claim. Being philosophers, we can assume that they would use their language carefully, thus avoiding the confusions just outlined. This proposal offers a way to rescue a conception of a right to which many people find themselves profoundly attached. But it introduces a suspicion that such a measure would be little more than a panacea, a refusal to come to terms with the arguments in favor of understanding moral rights as contestable moral beliefs.

Judgments about the claims that people ought to be able to enforce, together with the moral outlooks in which they are embedded, provide justifications of existing rights, as well as reasons for reform. In many cases, groups do their best to persuade others of their moral convictions, and, where they are able, encourage governments to devise institutions and obligations that will turn their aspirations into rights. As a result, the rights guaranteed by a society's institutions are likely to reflect and alter the moral beliefs of its most powerful members. This is one form of interdependence between moral beliefs and rights, but there is also another. The process of deciding whether a claim is effectively enforceable, and thus whether a right exists, brings our moral beliefs into play, since our assessments of effective enforceability reflect our judgments about the relative importance and urgency of individual claims. Where a right is viewed as valuable in itself, or as a vital condition of other valuable practices, it will only be judged to exist when it is relatively easy to enforce effectively. In other cases, however, we may accept that, although claiming a right involves a great expenditure of effort, it is nevertheless real enough. We may even believe that some rights *should* be difficult to claim, and thus believe that they are effectively enforceable even when they involve complex and specialized procedures.

A similar argument applies to the relative urgency of claims. A group only has an effectively enforceable claim to food if they have the means to acquire food supplies before they begin to suffer from malnutrition. After all, the main reason for creating such a right is to avoid famine and starvation. By contrast, a long drawn out procedure for reclaiming property may be judged to be effectively enforceable, on the grounds that the claim is not urgent and the slowness of the procedure therefore does no serious moral harm. When we assess whether or not a claim is effectively enforceable, we measure it in the light of our (contestable) moral beliefs about its value. In this way, these beliefs enter into our interpretation of the condition that a right must be effectively enforceable, and into debates about what it takes to realize a particular right.

So far, I have sketched a defense of the view that rights depend on the existence of specifiable mechanisms for enforcing them, backed up by effective methods of implementation. However, if we accept this view, it remains to examine what it takes to create rights. A first and straightforward point is that the obligations from which rights flow only emerge within elaborate and interlocking sets of institutions. If the act of promising, for example, is to generate rights, a set of conventions will have to be taught, reinforced, and sanctioned. A more formally regulated right, such as a right to healthcare, will flow from a spreading net of obligations vested in government ministries, local health authorities, private insurance companies, hospital trusts, doctors' surgeries, medical schools, and so on, institutions which themselves depend on established rights-generating practices such as contract or representation. Although the rights that a society can provide will vary with the nature and design of its institutions, some such network will be a precondition of any effectively enforceable claims at all.

A second condition lies in the fact that institutional networks have to be brought alive by individual agents who take on various sets of responsibilities, and in doing so contribute to the creation of rights. To exercise their powers effectively, these agents must understand what they are obliged to do and must know how to carry out their duties. Satisfying this requirement is partly a matter of designing effective procedures and sanctions, skills that can be fostered or undermined from within institutions as well as from without. For instance, a health authority may or may not take the trouble to train and support its managers adequately, and its efforts may be helped or hindered by government spending policy or by changes in the law. However, institutional design is not the whole story, since the effectiveness of an institution also depends on the attitudes of the agents who contribute to it. To be effective, individual agents must, for example, be disposed to attend to the demands and abilities of their clients, to interpret their claims with some imagination, and to assess them fairly. This range of attributes cannot be taken for granted and presupposes, among other things, the prevalence of certain emotional dispositions, such as a reasonable level of benevolence towards the people that an institution is meant to serve, a respect for the sanctions attached to incompetence, sufficient determination to enable one to do one's job, and some satisfaction in one's successes. It also presupposes a reasonable moral consensus. People who do not share the values embodied in the obligations imposed on them may drag their feet or actively resist, thus disrupting the mechanisms from which a right flows.

The creation of institutions that work well enough to implement and enforce the obligations from which rights flow is therefore an elaborate and continuous process that must continually adapt to changing circumstances; without it, rights understood as effectively enforceable claims will not exist. But there is also a third factor to be taken into account: the fact that agents must be capable of claiming their rights. To exercise a right to sue for damages, for example, an agent will need money, information about procedures and entitlements, enough authority to lodge and negotiate her claim, and access to specialists of various kinds. As before, these resources presuppose institutions (for instance, firms of solicitors, courts of law, or libraries) and certain emotional dispositions on the part of the agent (for instance, self-confidence, determination, indignation, or solidarity).

This tripartite distinction between institutions, agents who fulfill obligations, and agents who claim rights is a rough and ready one that could be further subdivided. Nevertheless, it serves to concentrate attention on the complexity of the conditions that underpin rights when these are understood as effectively enforceable claims. Not only must all three elements be in place, they must also work together more or less harmoniously in order to avoid the many types of dislocation that can make it impossible to enforce claims effectively. This analysis of what a right requires departs not only from the idea that moral rights are vested in individuals, but also from a view that locates the rights guaranteed by particular societies in legal institutions, and consequently refers to them as "legal rights." It is true that the rules, processes, and sanctions of the law are often components of an enforceable right, and that legal institutions are often what we turn to in order to try to enforce a claim. (When a tenant refuses to pay rent, the landlord contacts a lawyer; a woman whose house has been burgled calls the police.) For some purposes, it may be helpful to view a right through a narrow lens that focuses sharply on the legal sanctions by which it is upheld. In other contexts, however, it is more productive to take account of the fact that these are only part of the story, and that there could in principle be rights in the absence of obligations backed up by the law. To appreciate what makes a claim effectively enforceable, we need to conceive of rights in the broader and more Foucauldian fashion I have outlined, as dependent on branching and variable sets of conditions, and upheld by interlocking institutions and practices.

A strength of this approach is that it encourages us to examine what claiming a particular right would involve, and allows us to consider whether demanding a right is likely to be effective as a means of solving a social or political problem. In circumstances where there are well-defined procedures for generating rights, the answer may be obvious. For example, it may be well within the reach of a particular society to generate new rights by introducing minor modifications into tax law. In other situations, however, the preconditions of a right may themselves have to be created or altered before the right itself can emerge. Because, as we have already seen, these preconditions are numerous and difficult to coordinate, they in turn can be met only in certain types of circumstances. They will usually depend on the existence of an overarching and effective source of political authority, or a hierarchy of authorities with well-defined and accepted jurisdictions. When this condition is not satisfied there may be areas where institutions do not operate effectively, and thus where fewer rights exist; or there may be competing authorities, liable to disrupt one another.

A further condition for the emergence of rights concerns the distribution of power between agents. In societies where some groups have little power, and where no one is capable of representing them, their ability to enforce their rights may be relatively limited, and this in turn will affect the kinds of rights it is possible to create and sustain. For instance, it may be impossible to generate rights that are held by all members of the society in question. In addition, effectively enforceable claims depend on the availability of certain resources, and on the existence of agents who are willing to play their part in the complex business of realizing them.

Although sanctions can be used to constrain them to fulfill their obligations, a right emerges most easily in a climate where it is commonly regarded as valuable.

If we now return to O'Neill's observation that promulgating unclaimable rights insults the poor and needy, we can see how our attitudes to unenforceable claims are shaped by our understanding of the obstacles standing in the way of their realization. In some cases, there is such a yawning gap between a formally guaranteed right and any serious attempt to realize it that the guarantee is no more than a mockery, liable to arouse feelings of anger and disgust. In other circumstances, however, one may view a claim that is far from effectively enforceable with hope. Although international protocols do not create rights, they may give grounds for optimism. And even before a piece of national legislation has been put into effect, it may constitute a positive step in the direction of a valuable new right. Alternatively, one may feel gloomy when an institution deteriorates or a prevailing attitude changes, so that a claim that has been effectively enforceable ceases to be so. And of course, since not all rights are valuable, we may view the creation of effectively enforceable claims with deep misgivings. We assess the meaning of the fact that a claim does or does not fall short of effective enforceability in the light of our moral judgments, together with our predictions about the direction and pace of change.

Conceiving of rights as effectively enforceable claims has an immediate bearing on our understanding of the circumstances in which it is useful to appeal to them, and has implications for the types of rights that can be created in democratic, multicultural societies. These points can be illustrated by examining Susan Okin's recent and influential call for more effective protection of young women who, on the one hand live in societies that formally guarantee universal moral rights, and on the other hand belong to cultural minorities whose practices violate these rights.[12] Okin protests that enforced marriage or disciplinary violence are incompatible with the rights that liberal societies extend to all citizens, and seems to take it for granted that the rights of minority women must be upheld. However, she does not consider the further question: What would it take to provide them with an effectively enforceable claim to be protected against the kinds of cultural practices she regards as oppressive?

A first requirement, according to the schema I have set out, is that institutions should allocate, sustain, and sanction the obligations out of which such a right emerges. The law and other institutions must grant women effective protection from violence and sexual coercion. A second requirement, and a particularly important one if claimants are inexperienced and relatively powerless, is that officials should meet their obligations. But when a society is morally and culturally heterogeneous, this condition may be extremely demanding. A young woman's right to seek protection is partly created by a general duty not to stand in her way. Yet where a community is convinced that the course of action to which she objects is for her good, it may be unrealistic to suppose that its members will stand back and let her do what she wants, and here the obligations of officials outside the community may become particularly burdensome. They may be called upon to enforce the young woman's claim in the face of opposition that strains their loyalties and courage, and so renders her right more precarious. Finally, rights to protection can only be effectively enforced if the obligations we have just been considering are balanced by the ability of claimants to demand their rights. Young women would need to be aware of their claims they were entitled to make, and would need to have opportunities to try to enforce them.

Because a woman who protests against a particular practice is usually not a lone voice, there will generally exist what James Scott calls a hidden transcript—an account of the practice seen from the point of view of those who are oppressed by it—to help her to articulate her plight.[13] Some members of her own community will support her, and there may be people outside it to whom she can turn for help. In these ways, her ability to claim a right of protection looks reasonably secure, but a lot will depend on the balance of power within the community. If those who support and impose the contested practice are in a position to coerce her and to impose heavy penalties if she resists, she will still have no effectively enforceable claim to protection, and thus no right to it.

What would have to change in order for a right to emerge? If we assume, with Okin, that the powers and moral beliefs of the liberal majority remain unaltered, the change would have to come from within the minority community itself. The community will have to change. The project of extending rights to its members will then become much easier to realize, and Okin's demand for a universal right to certain forms of protection will more readily be achieved.[14] If, however, we face the fact that there can be deeply entrenched and persistent moral and cultural clashes between—and also within—the constituent groups of a society, we shall have to acknowledge that her proposed solution may sometimes be beyond our reach. A society may find itself in a position where it cannot extend what are regarded as basic rights to some of its own members.

Okin's defense of an uncompromising liberalism is, among other things, an intervention in a discussion between feminist writers about the extent to which appeals to rights can improve the position of women in more or less patriarchal societies. Her aim is to stand up for universal civil and political rights; but one of the unintended benefits of her argument is to draw attention to the difficulty of extending such rights to the least powerful members of society. Western democracies are inclined to think of themselves as rights-creators *par excellence*, as societies where the political and material circumstances on which rights depend are present and in good working order. If, however, certain kinds of rights require a comparatively even distribution of power, and a moderate level of moral consensus, then the absence of these conditions will limit the rights that even such privileged polities can create. Okin's discussion of a situation where they do not obtain highlights the effect that this can have, even in societies that are accustomed to sustaining and generating effectively enforceable claims.[15]

If one responds to this difficulty as Okin does, by insisting on the rights that a constitution formally guarantees, there is a significant danger that one will fall foul of the requirement from which we began, that rights need to be more than formal entitlements if they are to provide practical benefits for those who hold them. By failing to confront the question, "What would it take to create such a right?", we may overlook the gap between moral convictions and claims, and underestimate the complexity of the conditions on which rights depend. A different response, and in my view a more constructive one, is to step back from the assumption that rights are a universal panacea able to cure a host of ills.[16] By taking account of the types of circumstances in which they can be realized, and working out how these bear on particular situations and problems, we can gain a richer understanding of when it is fruitful to appeal to rights, and when it is insufficient to invoke them.

Notes

1. I have benefited from points raised in discussions at the Aristotelian Society and at the Cambridge Moral Sciences Club, and am grateful for specific suggestions and criticisms made by Miranda Fricker, Anca Gheaus, Ross Harrison, Christopher Janaway, Matthew Kramer, Melissa Lane, Al Martinich, Anthony Price, Georgia Testa, and Quentin Skinner.
2. Onora O'Neill, *Towards Justice and Virtue. A Constructive Account of Practical Reasoning* (Cambridge, U.K.: Cambridge University Press, 1996), p. 133.
3. Wesley N. Hohfeld, *Fundamental Legal Conceptions as Applied in Judicial Reasoning* (New Haven: Yale University Press, 1919). Following Hohfeld, advocates of the view that rights are practical claims can distinguish rights from liberties and immunities. They can also allow that there are obligations with no matching claims.
4. Some philosophers anxious to defend a Choice Theory of rights argue that a right holder must be in a position to choose whether to enforce or waive their right. While I disagree with this view, it is not central to my argument. This concerns the question of what makes a right claimable at all, whether by the right holder or some other agent.
5. O'Neill, 1996, p. 129.
6. O'Neill, 1996, p. 132.
7. See, for example, Hillel Steiner, *An Essay on Rights* (Oxford: Blackwell, 1994).
8. Raymond Geuss, *History and Illusion in Politics* (Cambridge, U.K.: Cambridge University Press, 2001), p. 146.
9. This is at least partly explained by the fact that the vocabulary of rights grew up in a context where claims guaranteed by one form of law (natural or religious law) were pitted against

claims upheld by civil law. The supposed existence of natural or religious law made sense of the idea that claims and obligations existed, even when these were not upheld by civil codes. However, for people who do not believe that moral beliefs derive their validity from an extra-human law, this tradition poses a problem. We may defend our moral beliefs on various non-legal grounds, but it is misleading to think of them as claims.

10. Hannah Arendt, *The Origins of Totalitarianism* (New York: Harcourt Brace Jovanovich, 1973), p. 296.
11. See S. Meckled-Garcia in *The Proceedings of the Aristotelian Society,* forthcoming.
12. Susan Okin with respondents, *Is Multiculturalism Bad for Women?* Joshua Cohen, Matthew Howard, and Martha C. Nussbaum, eds. (Princeton, N.J.: Princeton University Press, 1999), pp. 9–24. For a response to Okin that contrasts interestingly with the one offered here, see Avigail Isenberg, "Diversity and Equality: Three Approaches to Culture and Sexual Difference," *Journal of Political Philosophy,* 11.1 (2003): 41–64.
13. James C. Scott, *Domination and the Arts of Resistance* (New Haven and London: Yale University Press, 1990), ch. 2.
14. *C.f.* Joseph Raz, in Okin (1999), p. 97–99.
15. The same problem is raised by the work of other liberal writers. See, for example, Martha C. Nussbaum, *Women and Human Development. The Capabilities Approach* (Cambridge, U.K.: Cambridge University Press, 2000.)
16. See Patricia Williams, *The Alchemy of Race and Rights* (Cambridge, Mass.; Harvard University Press, 1991). For an recent application of this view, see Brooke A. Ackerley, "Women's Human Rights Activists as Cross-Cultural Theorists," *International Feminist Journal of Politics,* 3.3 (2001): 311–46.

CHAPTER 5

Distributing Responsibilities[1]

DAVID MILLER

In this chapter, I examine a question that arises frequently in moral and political debate, but has not to my knowledge been examined in much depth by philosophers. Our world contains all too many instances of deprived or suffering people—people whose basic rights to security, subsistence, or health care are not being protected, and who as a result are in no position to live minimally decent lives. Nearly all of us believe that this is a situation that demands a remedy: Someone should provide the resources to end the suffering and deprivation.[2] The problem does not lie here, but in deciding which particular agent or agents should put the bad situation right. Very often there are many agents who could act in this way. The issue is how to identify one particular agent, or group of agents, as having a particular responsibility to remedy the situation. For unless we can do this, there is a danger that the suffering or deprivation will continue unabated, even though everyone agrees that it is morally intolerable, because no one is willing to accept the responsibility to step in and relieve it.

For an example of the problem I have in mind, consider the plight of Iraqi children in 2002 who are malnourished and lack access to proper medical care. No one doubts that their condition is a very bad one, nor is it difficult to grasp what would be needed to remedy it. But who has the responsibility for putting it right? Is it the United Nations, and more especially the Western powers, who on the one hand have contributed to the situation, or so it is alleged, by imposing economic sanctions on Iraq, and on the other are well placed to supply the necessary food and medical aid? Or is it Saddam Hussein and his henchmen, who have diverted a large percentage of Iraq's gross national product (GNP) to military expenditure, and who have deliberately (it is alleged) prevented aid from reaching poor families in an attempt to have the sanctions lifted? Or does responsibility lie with the Iraqi people as a whole, on the grounds that each nation has a duty to look after its own, which in this case might involve taking direct action to overthrow the current brutal regime?

I shall call this the problem of remedial responsibility. To be remedially responsible for a bad situation means to have a special obligation to put the bad situation right, in other words to be picked out, either individually or along with others, as having a responsibility towards the deprived or suffering party that is not shared equally among all agents. The problem is to find a principle, or set of principles, for assigning such responsibilities, which carries moral weight, so that we can say that agents who fail to discharge their remedial responsibilities act wrongly and may properly be sanctioned. (What form the sanctioning may take will vary from case to case, and it is not part of my brief here to pursue this question. I mention sanctions simply to underline the point that when we are arguing about where the responsibility for remedying a bad situation should fall, we mean our answer to have some teeth.) In other words, the problem is: What connects a particular agent A to a particular patient P in such a way that A is singled out as having a remedial responsibility towards P that others, in general, do not have? Note that the agents in question may be individual people, but, as the example I gave above illustrates, they may also be collectives of various kinds—governments, states, corporations, and even those amorphous entities called nations. Assigning responsibility to these collective bodies raises additional questions that I cannot address here.[3] Instead I shall assume that such assignments of collective responsibility are both meaningful and justifiable, and focus on the issue of how they should be distributed. In exploring this issue, I shall often refer to individual agents and patients, because we are likely to have better-formed judgments in these cases, but eventually our analysis should be applicable to collective cases too.

Because the problem of distributing responsibilities is so urgent, human societies have evolved mechanisms whereby they are formally assigned to individual people or to institutions. If we ask who is responsible for safeguarding this particular battered child, the answer is likely to be the social worker who has been assigned to the case. I am not concerned here with such formally assigned responsibilities, but with the underlying principles that should guide us when we are in a position to make formal assignments, and that we should appeal to directly when no formal assignments have been made. Very often, in fact, the problem arises precisely because of the lack of any institutional mechanism that can assign responsibilities formally—the international arena is replete with examples. We may believe that we should move towards a situation where for any group of deprived or suffering people there is some agency that has formally been assigned the responsibility to remedy their condition. But clearly that day is a very long way off, and meanwhile the best we can do is to lay out some principles for distributing responsibilities that we hope will command widespread agreement. That is the task of the present chapter.

Principles of Remedial Responsibility

Perhaps the most obvious solution to our problem is to say that agents should be held remedially responsible for situations when, and to the extent that, they were responsible for bringing those situations about. In other words, we look to the past to see how the deprivation and suffering that concerns us arose, and having established that, we are then able to assign remedial responsibility. In the case of the Iraqi children, for instance, we need to know why they are malnourished and sick: Who is responsible for bringing about this state of affairs?

Clearly, this answer invokes a different sense of "responsibility" from the one that directly concerns us. But which sense? Unfortunately, few concepts in moral and political philosophy are more slippery than that of responsibility, and it is a fair bet that real debates on issues such as the plight of Iraqi children become muddied as the protagonists slip from one meaning of responsibility to the next.[4] So we need to draw some distinctions, and in particular a distinction between *causal* and *moral* responsibility.

To say that an agent is causally responsible for some state of affairs is simply to highlight the causal role-played by the agent in the genesis of that state of affairs. Here I rely on what Hart and Honoré have called the commonsense understanding of causation, according to which when we say that C caused E, we are singling out C as one among a potentially large number of antecedent conditions for E's occurrence, distinguished from the other conditions by virtue of its abnormality (and also, in many cases, by virtue of its being a deliberate human action).[5] For an example of "bare" causal responsibility—causal responsibility that is not accompanied by moral responsibility—consider the case where I am walking along the pavement, taking ordinary care, but trip over a raised paving stone, knock down the person in front of me, and injure him. Then I am causally responsible for the injury, but not morally responsible, because I have done nothing that attracts moral praise or blame. My tripping is simply the unusual feature in the case that accounts for the unfortunate injury to the pedestrian.

Moral responsibility, on the other hand, involves an appraisal of the agent's conduct. In the cases that particularly concern us, the agent's role in bringing about the outcome must be such that it leaves the agent liable to moral blame. That in turn requires us to ask questions such as whether the agent intended the outcome, whether he foresaw it, whether his behavior violated some standard of reasonable care, and so forth. As the example above shows, moral responsibility is in one respect a narrower notion than causal responsibility, since there will be many cases in which someone's conduct is perfectly innocent but it just so happens that something he does is the main causal factor in injuring another. But in another respect it may be wider, for instance, if I negligently fail to take steps to prevent something from occurring. Suppose I take my son Jamie and his friend Nick to the park to play, and in the course of some rather boisterous game Jamie manages to break Nick's arm. Meanwhile I am sitting on the bench with my head buried in a newspaper and fail to notice what is going on. Then I may be morally responsible for Nick's arm getting broken, even though it is clearly Jamie who is causally responsible according to the criteria suggested above. (Whether Jamie is also morally responsible will depend on the details of the case—essentially whether it is reasonable to expect a boy of that age to foresee the likely outcome of the rough-and-tumble that is taking place.) I am morally responsible because I have failed in my duty to take care of the boys, something that I assumed when I offered to take them down to the park. I can properly be blamed for not preventing the broken arm.

Having clarified the distinction between causal and moral responsibility, we can now ask whether either of these yields an adequate principle for assigning remedial responsibility. The appeal of causal responsibility is straightforward. If A is the cause of P's deprived condition—and this appears to be something that can be established empirically—then what is more obvious than to hold A responsible for remedying it? If he was the sole cause, then remedial responsibility is his alone; if several agents together caused P's condition, then remedial responsibility should be distributed in proportion to causal responsibility. But on closer inspection, the causal principle faces a number of damaging objections.

The first is simply that there are many cases in which no identifiable A has caused P's condition, and yet we would be reluctant to say that no one has any remedial responsibility towards P. Prominent here are instances in which P's condition results from natural causes—P starves because of crop failure or is stricken with cancer. Of course it is always possible in such instances to specify forms of action that, had certain agents taken them, would have prevented the condition from emerging. The crop failure would not have occurred if company A had installed an irrigation system; the cancer would not have occurred if health authority B had decided to invest an extra £X million in preventative medicine. But there are an infinite number of such counterfactuals, and so they will not, in general, identify any particular agents as causally responsible for P's condition. When a particular counterfactual seems relevant, that is because the agent it describes has already been identified as bearing responsibility for P's condition. Thus if company A had contracted to install an irrigation system in P's neighborhood, it *then* becomes appropriate to single out A's inaction as the cause of the crop failure. But in the absence of any such agreement, or other special link between A and P, there is no reason to distinguish A's failure to install an irrigation system from B's failure to supply fertilizer, from C's failure to make available genetically modified seeds, and so on—the list containing all those actions the performance of any one of which would have prevented the crop failure.[6]

A second, related, difficulty arises when there are several agents whose actions can be plausibly linked to P's condition. Here there seems to be no merely empirical way of dividing up causal responsibility as a basis for assigning remedial responsibility.[7] Return to the case of the deprived Iraqi children. Suppose it is true, as seems plausible, that if the UN had not decided to impose economic sanctions, more money would have been available to fund health and social security in Iraq. Suppose it is also true that if Saddam had decided to cut military expenditure, enough would have been left, even with the sanctions, to prevent the destitution. Both the UN and Saddam can then be described as causally responsible for the sufferings of the children. But how should we apportion responsibility as between them? In answering this question, we cannot apparently avoid making moral appraisals of the relevant agents' conduct, especially examining how far their behavior was justified. If we think that Saddam's regime posed a serious threat to neighboring countries, and therefore that UN sanctions were justified, then we will single out Saddam's policy decisions as the cause of the children's suffering. If, by contrast, we see Iraq as a vulnerable regime surrounded by enemies, and therefore as justified in arming itself in self-defense, we shall lay causal responsibility at the door of the UN. Causal attributions are being determined by normative assumptions about justified behavior. But in that case we no longer have a causal principle in our original sense—the ethical question about who bears remedial responsibility for P's condition is no longer being answered just by looking empirically at who brought that condition about.

Finally, questions about justification appear to arise even in cases where there is only one agent who can plausibly be described as the cause of P's condition. For sometimes A may act in a way that is harmful to P, and yet bear no remedial responsibility for the harm he has caused, because we judge A's behavior to be legitimate. Suppose, for instance, that in a market setting A drives P out of business by offering a better service to customers, then provided he deals fairly we do not think that he bears any remedial responsibilities towards P. Or A may cast P into depression by marrying the love of his life. So it seems that the causal principle taken by itself cannot explain our remedial responsibilities. It falls down where no particular A can be identified as the cause of P's condition, and it also falls down where A is certainly causally responsible, in whole or in part, for the harm done to P, but A's behavior appears justifiable, and therefore does not bring remedial responsibilities in its train.

Yet it is interesting to notice that even innocent causation may place *some* special responsibility upon the agent. Return to the case where by simple mischance I stumble and knock down a pedestrian. Everyone in the vicinity is under some obligation to help him to his feet and make sure that he is not badly hurt; yet we believe that the responsibility is in the first place mine, so I have the primary obligation to act.[8] I did nothing wrong—indeed I could not help doing what I did—yet having done it, having been the cause of P falling to the ground, I seem to be linked to him more strongly than B who just happened to be passing by. (In the same way, it seems appropriate that I should apologize, or at least express regret for what has happened, even though I am not at all to blame for the event.[9]) This may seem mysterious; indeed some may find it disturbing that we can apparently incur responsibilities just by doing something as unintentional and innocent as walking along the street. I do not want to suggest that bare causation of this kind plays more than a minor part in distributing responsibilities. But the fact that it plays any part at all may help us in searching for the correct theory.

So let us now consider the alternative principle that A should be held remedially responsible for P's condition insofar as he is *morally responsible* for its occurrence, in the sense that carries with it ascriptions of fault and blame. This principle seems to capture nicely what is at stake in our original example: When we ask who is responsible for the plight of Iraqi children, we appear to be asking who is morally responsible for bringing about their condition of malnutrition and ill health, whether by acting wrongly (the UN and Saddam) or by failing to act as duty requires (the Iraqi people as a whole). We have seen already that moral responsibility is narrower than causal responsibility in some ways and wider in others, and it looks as though in both respects this enables it to fit better with our considered judgments about remedial responsibility. There are cases in which people are causally but not morally responsible for the outcome of their actions—for instance, those in which the chain of events connecting action and outcome is long and tortuous, so that the agent could not have reasonably foreseen the final result of her action—and here we are unlikely to hold them remedially responsible for the harm that may ensue. Equally, in cases where we judge people to be morally responsible for the occurrence of a harm, even though their causal role in bringing it about was merely a negative one—cases like the delinquent parent who is reading a newspaper when he should have been watching out for children—we *do* hold them remedially responsible. So at first glance it seems that the moral responsibility principle is going to perform better than the causal principle in explaining our remedial responsibilities.

But that is not to say that it explains everything. To begin with, it cannot explain why causation alone sometimes seems sufficient to generate remedial responsibilities—as in the example of the innocent pedestrian. Nor can it deal happily with cases of justified, but harmful, behavior. For instance, suppose that A must quickly find a certain drug to save Q's life, and the only way he can do this is to steal some from P, who needs the drug too, but less urgently. We think that that he should steal the drug from P, but that he then has a remedial responsibility to P to replace what he has taken.[10] But he is not morally responsible for harm suffered by P in the intervening period in the sense that leaves him liable to attributions to blame; provided he goes on to discharge his remedial responsibilities, his conduct is not faulty.

There is, however, an ambiguity in the meaning of moral responsibility that needs to be addressed at this point. As defined above, it is linked conceptually to liability to blame: To say of A that he is morally responsible for state S is to say that he has contributed to the bringing about of S in such a way as to incur blame. But one may sever this link and use a broader concept of moral responsibility according to which people are to be held morally responsible for the results of their actions, so long as these actions themselves satisfy certain conditions of intentionality, voluntariness, etc., without implying that they are blameable for what they did.[11] On this second view, A is morally responsible for the effects on P of stealing the drug, because he took the drug deliberately and freely, even though he was fully justified in acting as he did. The broader view, then, preserves the connection between moral responsibility and remedial responsibility in the drug case. But it runs into difficulties in cases where justified, but harmful, conduct appears not to bring remedial responsibilities with it—cases like that in which A engages in fair competition with P in a market setting. Suppose that A sets up a shop close to P's and by legitimate means attracts most of

P's customers; then A is morally responsible for P's loss of earnings, on the broader view. Even if A did not intend the precise outcome that occurred, he went into business deliberately, and could reasonably have foreseen as one result of his competitive behavior that P would be damaged. Yet we do not feel that he owes P anything by way of remedy so long as he has acted fairly.

So neither of the two concepts of moral responsibility we have considered—neither the narrow concept linked to blame, nor the wide, morally neutral, concept—gives us the link we are looking for between moral and remedial responsibilities. The narrow concept fails to explain why there are remedial responsibilities in the drug case; but the wider concept, which holds people responsible for the results of all their voluntary actions, whether blameworthy or not, implies that there are remedial responsibilities in the shopkeeper case too.[12] Neither concept appears to hit the target precisely.

The biggest problem with the moral responsibility principle, however—one that it shares with the causal principle—is that it looks too exclusively to the past in assigning remedial responsibilities. The question it asks is always "Who is responsible for bringing this bad situation about?" and never, for instance, "Who is best placed to put it right?" One obvious defect of the principle, therefore, is that it has nothing to say when the morally responsible agent proves to be incapable of discharging her remedial responsibilities—for instance when she is dead or incapacitated. Unless we want to say that remedial responsibilities disappear when we cannot find an agent who is both morally responsible for the situation in question and capable of remedying it, the principle remains incomplete.

Taking our cue from the last paragraph, consider next the principle of *capacity*, which holds that remedial responsibilities ought to be assigned according to the capacity of each agent to discharge them. The rationale for this is obvious enough. If we want bad situations put right, we should give the responsibility to those who are best placed to do the remedying. If there is a bather in trouble off the beach, and it makes most sense for one person to undertake the rescue, then we should choose the strongest swimmer. In other circumstances we may want to share responsibility among A, B, and C, in proportion to their respective capacities to rectify P's condition, as suggested by the slogan, "From each according to his abilities, to each according to his needs."

On closer inspection, however, the capacity principle seems to blend together two different factors that may not always point in the same direction. One has to do with the *effectiveness* of different agents in remedying the situation; the other has to do with the *costs* they must bear in the course of doing so. The strongest swimmer may also be fearful (so that although he is an effective rescuer, the rescue causes him considerable distress)—or perhaps he simply dislikes the kind of attention that goes along with a successful rescue. If A is slightly stronger than B, but A's costs are also much higher, is it obviously the right solution to hold A responsible for rescuing P? On the moral responsibility view, costs do not present ethical problems: If A has harmed P through some action of his, then he should remedy the harm regardless of the cost to himself; requiring that he should pay the cost here is justifiable in the light of what he has done.[13] But to apply the capacity principle, it seems, we have to begin by weighing effectiveness against cost to determine whose capacity is the greatest in the morally relevant sense.[14]

Another problem with the capacity principle is that, by focusing attention entirely on agents' present capacity to remedy some harm, it neglects to ask how variations in capacity have arisen. And so it is vulnerable to the grasshopper and ant objection: Assuming that the grasshoppers *could* have spent the summer gathering food for the winter rather than singing, we may wonder whether the ants, who now have the capacity to help the famished grasshoppers by virtue of their earlier diligence, have a remedial responsibility to do so. Perhaps the destitution of the grasshoppers imposes some residual responsibility on the ants, but not as much as if, say, the grasshoppers' store of food had been washed away by unexpected rain. The capacity view cannot explain why remedial responsibility is stronger in one case than in the other. This is the weakness that accompanies its strength: Its exclusive focus on the present necessarily blinds it to historical considerations.

Finally, we need to ask whether capacity alone—the simple physical ability to remedy P's bad condition—is sufficient to generate remedial responsibility in the absence of a stronger link between A and P. Return to the case of the drowning bather, and notice that we single out the strongest swimmer from among those already gathered on the beach. Perhaps, then, we appeal to capacity only after identifying a set of agents whose relationship to P is such that they already bear a special responsibility towards him; capacity is used to pick out one particular agent from the set.[15]

That thought suggests a fourth principle for distributing responsibilities, which we might call the communitarian principle, using "community" here in a fairly loose sense to capture special ties of various kinds such as those that exist within families, collegial groups of various kinds, nations, and so forth. The claim is that when people are linked together by such ties, whether arising from shared activities and commitments, common identities, common histories, or other such sources, they also (justifiably) see themselves as having special responsibilities to one another, responsibilities that are greater than those they have towards humanity at large; and this in particular imposes special responsibilities towards any member of the relevant community who is harmed or in need.

The great merit of the communitarian principle is that it can make sense of much of our existing practice when responsibilities have to be distributed without resort to artificial devices. Consider, for example, a group of hikers out on a trip in the mountains together, where one of the party falls and injures herself. Here we simply take it for granted that the responsibility for bringing aid to the injured member falls in the first place collectively on the whole group, rather than on, say, other climbers who happen to be in the vicinity at the time. By forming ourselves into a group to make the expedition, we create the kind of relationship that generates special responsibilities as a matter of course, and there is no need to invoke a hypothetical contract among the members, or to suppose that somehow members of such a group are better placed to understand their fellow-members' needs than non-members would be, in order to reach the conclusion that when one person gets injured, it is the group that bears the primary responsibility to remedy her condition.[16] But the communitarian principle does less well on two other counts.

First, and only too obviously, it cannot explain why remedial responsibilities sometimes exist in the absence of special relationships of the kind outlined above. But there are at least two cases in which their existence seems pretty clear-cut. One is the case in which A simply injures P without justification, particularly perhaps when the injury involves a violation of P's basic rights (to bodily integrity, say, or to subsistence). That A bears a remedial responsibility in such a case seems uncontroversial, and this is regardless of whether A and P are linked by some kind of communal bond. If I injure a complete stranger, someone not connected to me by nationality, religion, or any of the possible forms of communitarian tie, I still owe him a remedy for the injury I have caused.

Likewise, and only a little more controversially, A may be remedially responsible for P simply because he happens to be the only person currently in a position to do anything about P's condition. This assumes of course that P's condition is one of significant deprivation or injury. But if that is the case, then the general duty we all have to aid people who are seriously injured or deprived will devolve upon A simply because he is the only person able to discharge it, either because, for instance, he is the sole passer-by when the skater on the pond falls through the ice, or because he alone has the know-how to sort out P's condition. Once again these responsibilities appear to transcend any communal bonds that might exist between A and P.[17]

The second limitation of the communitarian principle is that it has nothing directly to say about how responsibilities are to be distributed *within* the community. It can accommodate the fact that one community may nest inside another, so that A can bear special responsibilities to everyone in C, but also more extensive responsibilities still to everyone in C1, a sub-set of C. But it cannot go beyond this in distributing responsibilities within C except by importing considerations that are not themselves of a communitarian character. Our belief that in some instances people with greater capacity to help P should bear more of the responsibility for doing so, as suggested by the capacity principle, cannot be generated from within the communitarian perspective alone. And since a full account of remedial responsibilities should aim to get beyond the group level and attribute responsibility to individuals, the communitarian principle taken by itself appears inadequate.[18]

Taking Stock

We seem to have reached an impasse. We have looked at four principles—causal responsibility, moral responsibility, capacity, and community—each of which seems *prima facie* plausible as a way of allocating remedial responsibilities, but none of which, on closer inspection, seem adequate by itself. So how should we proceed? There seem to be three main options. The first is to abandon the search for a general theory of remedial responsibilities. The grounds for doing this would be that my initial formulation of the problem (i.e., Here is a group of deprived or suffering people. Whose responsibility is it to put the situation right?) misleadingly amalgamates a range of quite different cases, in each of which a different principle applies. For example, that formulation glosses over the difference between the case in which P's deprivation or suffering is the result of human action and the case where it has purely natural causes. So instead of looking for a general theory to explain our remedial responsibilities, we need to disaggregate the cases first, and then perhaps construct specific accounts of responsibility to fit each of them in turn.

The second option is to mount a defense of one of the principles canvassed above, and then argue that all of our considered judgments about remedial responsibility can in fact be captured by that principle. This may involve conceding that there are cases in which people are deprived or suffering, but in which no one has a responsibility to help them. For instance, one might argue that agents have remedial responsibilities only when they are morally responsible for the deprivation and suffering in question. Someone who took that line would have to reject my original formulation in a different way: They would have to deny the premise that it is morally intolerable if (remediable) suffering and deprivation are allowed to continue, in other words that where they exist we are morally bound to hold *somebody* (some person or some collective agent) responsible for relieving them.

The third option is to construct a multi-principle theory that combines the four principles I have identified in some fashion. There are various ways in which this might be done, but broadly speaking we can distinguish theories that rank the principles in a certain way—recommend that they should be applied sequentially, for instance—and theories that are more straightforwardly pluralist, in the sense that they ask us to balance or weigh the various principles against one another when responsibilities have to be assigned.

The first option is really a counsel of despair. If our aim in developing a theory of remedial responsibility is eventually to be able to pin these responsibilities on to particular agents and then exert pressure on them to discharge their obligations, a unified theory is a much better tool than a string of sub-theories. But more importantly, few cases in real life will fall neatly into just one of the categories we might construct. The example with which I began illustrates this. When we think about who bears remedial responsibility for Iraqi children, we think about what certain agents have done, what other agents have failed to do, we think about who can claim to have acted with justification, and we also think about who is now best placed to help the children. It is not a simple case in which an identifiable A has unjustifiably injured an identifiable P, nor is it a simple case in which P's condition has purely natural causes. The same will hold in all but the most primitive cases of human deprivation and suffering. So it would be premature to abandon the search for a general theory of remedial responsibility.

The second option involves attempting to bring everything that we want to say about remedial responsibility under the auspices of one of the principles identified above. How might a theory of this kind be constructed? The most plausible candidates, I believe, are a backward-looking theory of moral responsibility and a forward-looking theory, some variant of the capacity view, which focuses on the effective relief of harm and deprivation. A theory of the first kind would hold that agents are only remedially responsible for situations when they are blameable for bringing them about, and a proponent of such a theory might be willing to accept that in cases where no such agent can be found, no remedial responsibilities exist (thus no one should be held remedially responsible for the victims of natural disasters, though no doubt it would be a morally worthy act to help them). Such a theory looks entirely to the past; the only question it asks is "Who has done this thing?"

A wholly backward-looking theory of this kind finds itself trapped in the following dilemma: Either it leaves victims intolerably exposed, in the sense that many injuries will go unremedied, or inadequately remedied, or else it imposes an intolerable burden on agents—this could mean any one of us—by making us responsible for potentially enormous costs resulting from our actions. To see this, consider a case in which some slight act of carelessness on my part results in injuries to Smith that require millions of pounds to compensate. In this instance, we can either narrow the concept of moral responsibility so that I am no longer responsible for everything that results from my careless action—in which case Smith's condition will largely go unremedied—or else we broaden it so that I become remedially responsible for Smith's condition, in which case we would seriously limit our freedom as actors. Every time we acted, we would face a small but significant risk of landing ourselves with crippling remedial responsibilities.[19] A purely backward-looking theory cannot satisfy our underlying interest in protection against harm and deprivation without burdening us with liabilities that would make everyday life (driving to work, walking down the street) a potentially hazardous business.

Forward-looking theories tell us to assign responsibility in whatever way will best achieve our aim of relieving victims, and thus to ignore the past except insofar as it tells us things about agents that are now relevant in deciding who is most appropriately placed to remedy P's plight. Such theories look at the issue from the side of the victim, and their corresponding weakness is that they assign no intrinsic weight to the value we attach to moral responsibility. Suppose A injures P in a simple and straightforward way. A forward-looking theory asks, "Who should now remedy P's condition?" and A will come into the frame only if we judge it most useful or beneficial to hold him responsible, either in the particular case, or because we think it a beneficial rule to assign remedial responsibility in such cases to the agent who brought about P's condition. But this does not take the past seriously enough: A has done this thing, he can now make amends, so why should we look any further in assigning responsibility? The roundabout reasoning that a forward-looking theory requires seems to violate a basic belief that, at least in simple cases, people should be held responsible for the harm that they do.[20]

It seems, therefore, that an acceptable theory of remedial responsibility must make room in some fashion for each of the principles identified above. But how is this to be done? Again, there are different ways of constructing a multi-principle theory. Let us consider some of the more plausible alternatives.

One possibility is that the relevant principles should be applied in sequence: We look to see whether there is any agent who can be held responsible for remedying P's condition under principle X, and if the answer is Yes that settles the matter; if the answer is No we proceed to principle Y, and so forth. The plausibility of such a theory will depend on the sequence chosen, so rather than review all of the variations let me focus on one likely candidate. This tells us to begin by applying the principle of moral responsibility. If we can find an agent who is responsible for P's plight, and also has the capacity to remedy it, then we should hold that agent remedially responsible for P. Failing that—if no morally responsible agent can be identified, or if the agent or agents who bear moral responsibility turn out to be incapable of supplying the remedy—we invoke another principle—causal responsibility, say, or community. Clearly there are different ways of completing the theory. But we need go no further, because I do not think that the first move is defensible.

The problem is that moral responsibility is a matter of degree, and degrees of moral responsibility for P's condition do not necessarily correlate with other relevant features, especially with the capacity to relieve P's suffering or deprivation. We can lose sight of this fact by thinking in terms of very simple cases, namely those in which A is solely responsible for injuring P, does so by virtue of a deliberate act, and as a result has the resources that could now be used to compensate for the injury. But although such cases undoubtedly occur, we are more often confronted with ones in which A bears a lesser degree of moral responsibility, either by virtue of the character of his action—he acted negligently, for instance, rather than deliberately, or he acted with justification, harming P in pursuit of some greater good—or because responsibility has to be shared between a number of different agents. Moreover the fact that A played some part in bringing about P's condition does not entail that he derived any tangible benefit from doing so. So if we think about a case such as the Iraqi children, we might well conclude that each of the agents identified in the case—the United Nations, Saddam's clique, and the Iraqi people—bore some share of moral responsibility for the suffering of those children, though the nature of the responsibility would differ in each case. The United Nations might be accused of pursuing a justifiable end by unacceptable means, the suffering of the children being a foreseeable side effect of the sanctions policy. Saddam might be accused, more harshly, of deliberately allowing the suffering to occur for propaganda purposes. About the Iraqi people, it could be said that their causal role in bringing about the suffering was almost entirely negative, but that in the circumstances they could reasonably have been expected to oppose Saddam's regime more effectively. If those judgments are accepted, we would have to conclude, first, that no agent can be singled out as uniquely morally responsible for the situation we want to have remedied; and, second, that the agent bearing the largest share of responsibility (Saddam's clique) is also worst placed to bring the children the help that they need. It is probably wrong to say that the Iraqi government is incapable of finding the resources in question. But clearly it would be very much easier for the Western powers to do so. In these circumstances, is it right to let our judgments of remedial responsibility be determined entirely by our prior beliefs about how far different agents are morally responsible for creating the situation that needs a remedy?

This suggests that, rather than applying principles of responsibility in strict sequence, our approach should be more openly pluralist: We should simply look to see which principle or principles apply in a particular case, and if we find that more than one applies, we should weigh their respective strengths. But before reaching this conclusion, we should consider a second way of ordering the principles. This approach sees them not as competing with one another, but as addressing different aspects of the allocation of responsibility. Again I shall focus on one particular version of this approach.

The position I have in mind holds that we need to distinguish *immediate* responsibility for relieving harm and suffering from *final* responsibility.[21] Where people are in distress or in danger of further injury, we need to identify the agents best placed to help them in the short term. But these may not be the agents who should bear the costs of such action in the long term. So A may be immediately responsible for relieving P, because A is the agent in a position to offer aid directly, but final responsibility may be B's, in which case B may have to compensate A for the resources she has provided to B or for incidental costs arising from the relief effort.

Adopting such a view, we might conclude that *capacity*, and to some extent *community*, are relevant principles when immediate responsibilities are being distributed, because these are criteria that tell us who is best able to relieve P's condition quickly and effectively. *Moral responsibility, causal responsibility*, and perhaps *community* again are invoked when final responsibilities are the issue.[22] Now clearly there are cases where something like that picture seems to apply. If I negligently allow my child to fall into the river, but I cannot swim, then immediate responsibility for the rescue may fall on a passer-by who can, while I remain ultimately responsible for my child's welfare once he is pulled out, and for any damage suffered by the rescuer. But what makes the picture appropriate is precisely the immediacy of the harm: If the child is not saved, at once he will drown. It is that feature that makes capacity the overriding consideration in the short term. In many other cases, however, the deprivation or suffering that motivates our assigning of responsibility is relatively stable, in the sense that we have no reason to expect the situation to deteriorate suddenly, and here it seems that capacity becomes one relevant consideration to consider alongside the others. And even where harm is immediate, capacity may not trump the other principles in a straightforward way: Where several swimmers could rescue the drowning child, we may not simply pick the strongest, but, for instance, the person who caused him to fall in, or the negligent parent who should have taken more care to keep him away from the water's edge.

The Connection Theory

It appears that we must settle for a pluralist approach to distributing responsibilities. Attempts to eliminate all but one of the principles we have unearthed lead to unacceptable results. Attempts to impose a fixed order of application on those principles also lead us astray. But can a pluralist approach give us a satisfying theory of remedial responsibility? I shall sketch such a theory, which I propose to call the *connection* theory.[23]

This begins with the observation that all of us have a strong interest in the existence of mechanisms that protect us from harm and injury. More particularly, in the event that we find ourselves in a bad condition, which it is difficult or impossible for us to remedy through our own devices, we want there to be some way of assigning responsibilities such that an identifiable A (or perhaps A, B, and C taken together) becomes responsible for rectifying our situation. We want A to feel that he is responsible, and to act accordingly, and we want everyone else to make the same judgment and therefore to put pressure of various kinds on A if he fails to act. Responsibility that is widely dispersed is no good, because then everyone will attempt to hang back in the hope that someone else will step in first, no one will be particularly liable to censure if the bad condition is not remedied, and so on.

The interest of potential P's in having clearly defined responsibilities is evident, reflecting the fact that all of us are vulnerable to outside events that may seriously harm our interests or threaten our lives. But equally, it may not matter so much, from P's point of view, which particular A is held responsible. There may be many agents who are able to remedy P's condition; it matters considerably to P that one such agent, or one group of agents, should be singled out, for the reasons given above, but apart from that P may be indifferent which agent this happens to be. In these circumstances we will fix responsibility on the agent who is already connected to P in some way; if several agents are so connected, we will choose the one whose link to P is strongest, or else, depending on the circumstances, divide up responsibility according to relative strength of connection. (Whether one agent is singled out, or responsibility shared between several, may depend on whether P's condition is better remedied by a single agent taking action or several agents acting in concert.)

What kind of connection is relevant here? My proposal is that we should return to the principles explored in the second section of the chapter, and now see them as specifying forms of connection between A and P that may, in particular cases, be sufficient to establish A's responsibility for remedying P's condition. That is, A may be remedially responsible for P either because he is causally responsible for P's condition, or morally responsible for it, or has the (special) capacity to rectify it, or already has a communal relationship with P. Any of these relations—causal responsibility, moral responsibility, capacity, or community—may establish the kind of special link between A and P that enables us to single out A as the one who bears the responsibility for supplying the resources that will remedy P's condition.

In many cases there will be independent moral reasons for using a particular connection as a basis for assigning remedial responsibility. This applies most obviously where the connection consists in A's moral responsibility for P's injury. There are two independent reasons for holding A remedially responsible in this case: First, where A has unjustly benefited from the injury he has inflicted on P—he has stolen something of P's, or exploited him, for example—then if A is made to compensate P by returning what he has taken or in some other way undoing the damage he has inflicted, then this will help to cancel out A's unjust gain, and so restore justice as between them. Second, even if A has not benefited from his actions, he has wronged P, and should therefore make recompense to P as a way of acknowledging the wrong he has committed; remedying P's injury is an obvious way to do this. In the cases of capacity and community, too, we can provide a plausible rationale for basing remedial responsibilities on these forms of connection (these rationales will be quite different from the one just given in the case of moral responsibility). But causal responsibility, in the absence of the other forms of connection, seems not to have its own ethical rationale. If A is causally responsible for P's condition, but he is neither morally responsible for it (say he could not possibly have foreseen the results of his action) nor especially well placed to assist P, nor linked to P by special communal ties, there seems no independent reason to hold him remedially responsible for sorting P out. Yet we do seem to think that a bare causal connection is enough to generate special responsibilities, as the case of the innocent pedestrian who knocks down another shows. Perhaps it might be argued that in such cases holding the causal agent responsible will create incentives to take special care not to inflict accidental injury, thus the rationale is indirectly utilitarian.[24] But this interpretation seems forced: If the link between action and outcome is such that the agent could not be expected to anticipate the injury to P, then how is A supposed to alter his behavior? I suggest instead that causal responsibility as a source of remedial responsibility confirms the theory I am putting forward: We need some way of identifying an A to hold remedially responsible for P's condition, so in the absence of any other link between potential As and P we fix upon the purely physical link of causality. This, admittedly, can be trumped fairly readily once other forms of connection come into play; but the fact that we are prepared to rely on bare causal connection in the first place underlines the necessity of finding some non-arbitrary way of assigning responsibility to a particular agent.

The connection theory successfully offers practical guidance in cases where only one of its four constituent principles is satisfied. There is nothing paradoxical, according to the theory, in assigning remedial responsibility on the basis of causation, say, in one case and on the basis of communitarian relations in the next case. Our overriding interest is to identify an agent who can remedy the deprivation or suffering that concerns us, and in pursuit of that aim we fix on whoever is linked to P according to one of the theory's four criteria, about which there is widespread agreement. Where two or more of the principles apply, the theory tells us to look at the strength of the various connections. Thus if A is weakly linked to P by virtue of moral responsibility, whereas B is strongly linked to P by virtue of capacity (B is in far better position to remedy P's condition than any other agent), the theory instructs us to hold B remedially responsible. In some cases it may recommend dividing responsibility between two or more agents, where this makes practical sense, and the ties are of comparable strength. On the connection theory there is no algorithm that can tell us to apply principle 1 first and then move on to principle 2, and so forth—my reasons for rejecting such an algorithm have already been given. This means, of course, that when connections have to be weighed against each other, we can do no more than appeal to shared moral intuitions about which is the stronger.

The strength of the connection theory, as I see it, is that it treats the obligation to relieve deprivation and suffering as of overriding concern. By using multiple criteria, we ensure that there is always *some* agent who can be assigned responsibility for remedying P's condition. At the same time, it makes room for other moral considerations, such as the deeply held belief that where we can point the finger at a particular A as being morally responsible for the harm suffered by P, it is A himself who should remedy the harm wherever possible. Single-principle theories, I have suggested, will inevitably run up against such beliefs sooner or later. And although the connection theory is internally complex, this complexity may simply mirror the complexity of real-world cases in which remedial responsibility has to be assigned. If there were a simple answer to questions such as who is responsible for the current plight of Iraqi children, we would not argue about it politically in the way that we do. The connection theory does not offer a mechanical answer to questions of that kind, but it provides a way of thinking about them—highlighting their complexity—that may in the end prove to be more illuminating.

Notes

1. Earlier versions of this chapter were presented to the Nuffield Political Theory Workshop and to the All Souls Seminar in Political Philosophy. I should like to thank both audiences for their helpful comments. I should particularly like to thank Jerry Cohen, Richard Dagger, Cecile Fabre, and Bob Goodin, plus three anonymous referees for the *Journal of Political Philosophy*, for their extensive written comments on earlier drafts.
2. I say "nearly all" because there may be philosophers with libertarian instincts who hold that deprivation and suffering call for remedy only when they are the result of some agent violating the victims' rights. I examine this position briefly later in the chapter.
3. I have tackled some of them in a companion paper, "Holding Nations Responsible."
4. It is worth citing a story invented by Hart to illustrate the slipperiness of the concept:

   > "As captain of the ship, X was responsible for the safety of his passengers and crew. But on his last voyage he got drunk every night and was responsible for the loss of the ship with all [others] aboard. It was rumored that he was insane, but the doctors considered that he was responsible for his actions. Throughout the voyage he behaved quite irresponsibly, and various incidents in his career showed that he was not a responsible person. He always maintained that the exceptional winter storms were responsible for the loss of the ship, but in the legal proceedings brought against him he was found criminally responsible for his negligent conduct, and in separate civil proceedings he was held legally responsible for the loss of life and property. He is still alive and he is morally responsible for the deaths of many women and children." (H.L.A. Hart, *Punishment and Responsibility: Essays in the Philosophy of Law* (Oxford: Clarendon Press, 1968), p. 211.)

5. See H.L.A. Hart and T. Honoré, *Causation in the Law*, 2nd ed. (Oxford: Clarendon Press, 1985), ch. 2, for this account. Their analysis raises many questions, not least the problem that the distinction between causes and (mere) conditions depends upon the perspective from which we are looking at any given event, which in turn determines what will be regarded as normal background conditions and what will be regarded as an abnormal intervening circumstance. This in turn raises the possibility that causal judgments are in part influenced by moral considerations that determine the perspective from which our causal enquiry is launched. I return briefly to this point later in the chapter. Here, I assume that we have a workable notion of causal responsibility that is distinct from moral responsibility, as illustrated by the example given in the text, even if there are ineliminable practical concerns that lie behind our judgments of causal responsibility.
6. Why not then treat *all* of these as in equal measure responsible for P's condition? If we do this then we lose the distinctive purpose of responsibility assignments as I understand them, which is to identify one or more agents who are under some special obligation to relieve P's condition, and who therefore can properly be put under pressure to act. In other words, responsibility loses its practical force if it is diffused among all those agents of whom it is true that they *might* have acted in such a way that P's condition did not occur. I return later to the reasons we have for wanting specific assignments of responsibility, not diffuse ones.
7. This can apply even where A and P herself are the only agents involved, as pointed out in S. Perry, "The moral foundations of tort law," *Iowa Law Review*, 70 (1992), 449–514, 463–4.
8. Someone might argue here that we assign responsibility in this way because the person who knocked the pedestrian over is also likely to be the person best placed (by virtue of proximity) to take care of him afterwards. However, if we think of the accident occurring in a crowded street, it seems that any advantage of this kind will be negligible, whereas our sense that it is the person who caused the fall who bears the primary responsibility is quite strong.
9. Cf. T. Honoré, "Responsibility and luck," *Law Quarterly Review*, 104 (1988), 530–53, 544–5.
10. A parallel case, involving a backpacker caught in a blizzard who breaks into an unoccupied hut and uses up what he finds there to keep himself alive, was introduced by Joel Feinberg in

"Voluntary euthanasia and the inalienable right to life," *Philosophy and Public Affairs*, 7 (1978), 93–102, and has subsequently been widely discussed—see, for instance, J.J. Thomson, "Rights and compensation" in *Rights, Restitution and Risk* (Cambridge, Mass.: Harvard University Press, 1986) and L. Lomasky, "Compensation and the bounds of rights," *Nomos XXXIII: Compensatory Justice*, ed. J.W. Chapman, (New York: New York University Press, 1991).

11. It not necessary here to spell this broader, non-appraisive concept of moral responsibility out in detail, except to say that it still remains distinct from causal responsibility: On the broader concept, A is morally responsible for the outcome of all the actions he deliberately performs, but not, for instance, for accidentally knocking down a pedestrian as a result of stumbling himself.

12. Can the moral responsibility principle be saved by adding in further conditions that differentiate the two cases? One difference between them is that P has a right to the drug that is stolen in the first case, but no right to his customers' patronage in the second case. This suggests the following: A is remedially responsible for P's condition if and only if he is morally responsible for a rights-violation that led to that condition. However, on closer inspection this turns out to be too restrictive. Suppose, for instance, that A publishes an unfair review of P's book, damaging his career. We may think that he has a responsibility to offset the damage (supposing there is some way he can do this) without believing that P has a right that has been infringed by the publication of the review. The wrongness of A's action together with the harm suffered by P seem sufficient in this case to generate a remedial responsibility without the invocation of a rights-violation.

13. This claim requires some fine-tuning. Even if A is unquestionably at fault in acting as he did, he may be liable only for the effects of his action that a reasonable person would have foreseen, not for consequences that arise in peculiar ways or through the intervention of other actors. For discussion of this principle in the context of tort law, see Hart and Honoré, *Causation in the Law*, ch. 9, and A. Ripstein, *Equality, Responsibility and the Law* (Cambridge: Cambridge University Press, 1999), ch. 4.

14. We could of course simply define capacity as effectiveness, in which case we would have to allow in, as a separate and competing principle, the principle that remedial responsibilities should be assigned to the agents who would bear the least costs in discharging them.

15. Unfortunately there is not sufficient space here to consider a close cousin of the capacity principle, the vulnerability principle defended in R.E. Goodin, *Protecting the Vulnerable: A Reanalysis of Our Social Responsibilities* (Chicago: University of Chicago Press, 1985). Goodin's central proposal is that protective responsibilities should be assigned in proportion to vulnerabilities: the more vulnerable P is to A, the greater A's responsibility to protect P from harm. I see this as a cousin of the capacity principle since, in general, the greater an agent's capacity to act, the greater her potential impact on others, and therefore the more vulnerable those others are to her decisions. However P's vulnerability, considered simply by itself, seems to correlate with a responsibility on A's part to avoid causing harm to P, rather than a wider remedial responsibility to rectify P's suffering or deprivation. Suppose that P is the young author of a book on a topic on which I am recognized to be the leading authority, and I am asked to review the book. P is highly vulnerable to my actions: A damaging review will blight his career; a favorable one may launch it. I have a responsibility here not to harm P willfully or carelessly. If I think the book is a bad one I should say so, but I should take care, for instance, not to indulge my prejudices, precisely because the author is relatively junior, and therefore more vulnerable to my judgment than an established figure would be. So I have a limited responsibility to avoid causing P harm. But I seem to have no special responsibility to protect P from the harm that others may inflict—other reviewers less scrupulous than myself, for instance—and in the event that P is damaged, whether by my own (fair) review, or by other hands, I bear no remedial responsibilities. (If I review the book unfairly, and P's career suffers as a result, then I do have remedial responsibilities, but these are better explained by the moral responsibility principle discussed earlier than by the vulnerability principle; it is the faultiness of my conduct, not the simple fact of P's vulnerability, that creates such responsibilities.)

16. The best non-reductionist account of such special responsibilities known to me is to be found in S. Scheffler, "Relationships and responsibilities," *Philosophy and Public Affairs*, 26 (1997), 189–209.

17. One may of course think that where communal bonds also exist, this *strengthens* A's obligation, so that if A has to decide which of two endangered skaters to rescue first, he should

give precedence to the one who lives in his neighborhood or belongs to his church. Similarly a medical specialist may give priority to treating critically ill patients in his own nation while also acknowledging some responsibility towards similar patients elsewhere.

18. In some cases, of course, responsibility does just rest with the group as a whole until it is assigned by some mechanism to individuals, as in the case of the mountaineering group who share responsibility equally for their injured comrade until, say, they draw straws to decide who should go back and call out the Mountain Rescue team. There is nothing to distinguish one member from another in the assigning of responsibility. But this will not be true in general.

19. Insurance provides a mechanism for offsetting this objection, and, as Honoré points out in relation to tort law "some form of insurance is essential if a system of corrective justice is to operate fairly in modern conditions": T. Honoré, "The morality of tort law," *Philosophical Foundations of Tort Law*, ed. D.G. Owen (Oxford: Clarendon Press, 1995), p. 90. But it is of course only contingent that such a mechanism exists—so a ground-level theory of remedial responsibility cannot presuppose that it does (that is, we cannot argue that it is essentially fair to hold people remedially responsible for compensating all of the harm that may eventuate from their actions on the grounds that, if insurance mechanisms exist, they can choose to protect themselves from incurring excessive burdens).

20. Some considerations in support of this basic belief are advanced in Honoré, "Responsibility and luck."

21. I am grateful to an anonymous referee for the *Journal of Political Philosophy* for suggesting this position.

22. Community might appear in both places because, on the one hand, it can serve to identify agents who are physically proximate to P and therefore likely well placed to help him, and on the other hand, it picks out a group of agents who have a special concern for P's welfare.

23. In thinking about the general shape of this theory, I have drawn inspiration from Hume's theory of justice and property, as set out particularly in *A Treatise of Human Nature*, ed. L.A. Selby-Bigge, 2nd ed., revised by P.H. Nidditch (Oxford: Clarendon Press, 1978), Pt. III, Secs. 2–3, 6. Hume argued that we have a shared strong interest in the existence of rules that stably assign possessions to persons as their property. The specific rules employed, however, depended less on utilitarian considerations than on common mental dispositions that lead us to connect persons to material objects in particular ways. The connection theory of remedial responsibility proposed here has a similar general structure, though as readers have pointed out there are also significant disanalogies between the two theories.

24. Another suggestion might be that causal responsibility always carries traces of moral responsibility with it. How can we be sure that the pedestrian who was apparently taking good care to watch his step did not in fact have a momentary lapse of concentration and fail to notice the raised paving stone which he ought to have noticed? Or alternatively, perhaps we are all to some small degree morally responsible for *everything* that results from our action, no matter how remote the causal chain, or how careful we have been. In ways such as these, we can put a moral gloss on causal responsibility. But then again, might not this be a case of the tail wagging the dog? Might it not be that *because* we want to hold causal agents remedially responsible for the harm they bring about, in certain cases, we are driven to impute moral responsibility to them, in defiance of our more usual (and defensible) understanding of that idea?

CHAPTER 6

Institutional Responsibility for Moral Problems[1]

MICHAEL GREEN

This chapter does three things. First, it maintains that our understanding of moral responsibility is inadequate for regulating large-scale social and especially global problems. Second, it argues that we should turn our attention to attributing responsibility to institutional agents; specifically, it holds that doing so helps to resolve the problems noted in the first point. Institutional agents are different kinds of agents than individuals are, and these differences justify departures from the inadequate conception of responsibility. Finally, it discusses questions about the legitimacy of attributing responsibilities to institutional agents that go beyond the interests and aims of the people who create and maintain them.

Commonsense Conceptions of Responsibility

We participate in complex social, economic, and political processes that increasingly implicate us in serious problems on a global scale. We seem both to cause and to benefit from a range of problems just through daily activity of the most mundane sort. For example, many of us believe that everyday activities like driving or using electricity contribute to potentially catastrophic climate change. We buy goods from societies whose economic organization bears an unacceptably high resemblance to slavery. The powerful

117

countries in which many of us live are leading the world in establishing a kind of political order, but it is not one that we can be entirely comfortable with insofar as it is far from democratic and only selectively ordered. I will assume, without further argument, that these are pressing moral problems.

My argument rests on some additional assumptions about the nature of morality and moral responsibility. Specifically, I assume that an important role of morality is not merely to note, but to regulate, the harms that fall under human control. By regulating the harms, I mean that morality contains rules that effectively control the harms when they are followed. An essential element of regulation is what I will call a *complete attribution of responsibility*. A complete attribution of responsibility involves at least two things: first, drawing a connection between a harm or injustice and actions or omissions that led to it and second, requiring actions or omissions in order to avoid or mitigate the harm or injustice. The two steps are often, but not always linked: The agents connected to a harm are not necessarily the ones responsible for doing something about it. Finally, I am assuming that morality's regulation works through abstract rules that can be learned and followed in novel situations. So, I am claiming that an adequate understanding of morality would present abstract rules that give a complete attribution of responsibility for the problems I mentioned and that, if followed, would serve to regulate these problems.

Unfortunately, I do not believe that we have an adequate understanding of morality in the sense just defined. Specifically, I will argue that our commonsense conception of moral responsibility is not up to the task of providing a complete attribution of responsibility for the problems I mentioned and, thus, it is inadequate on its own. There is, however, no obvious alternative conception of responsibility that could serve to regulate these problems.

Commonsense morality, that is, the rough moral code that most of us follow, embodies what Samuel Scheffler calls a *restrictive* conception of responsibility.[2] To see this, consider three elements of our commonsense conception of responsibility: individualism, the distinction between positive and negative duties, and the importance of special obligations.

First, individuals are the primary bearers of responsibility. The principles of commonsense morality are directed to individuals and the vast bulk of our thinking about responsibility concerns individuals. To the extent that we attribute responsibility to collectives, we feel most comfortable in doing so by tracing collective actions back to individuals by looking for the intentions or organization of their members.

The second restrictive feature of commonsense morality is the thesis that negative duties are stricter than positive duties where negative duties, roughly, are those that prohibit doing specific things to others, whereas positive duties require action to prevent harm or to provide benefits to others. We commonly believe that it is worse to harm others ourselves than it is to fail to prevent harm from some other source. We are thought to bear positive duties mainly in very clearly defined, exceptional cases: I might bear positive duties to you because I have promised to do so, because we have a definite socially salient relationship, or because there is something obvious that I can do at little cost to prevent great harm. There are two sides to the claim that negative duties are stricter than positive duties. First, when the two kinds of duty are weighed against one another, it is not thought to be permissible to harm one person in order to prevent equivalent harms from befalling several others. Second, when the two kinds of duty are weighed against the interests of those who bear them, negative duties are thought to outweigh the pursuit of personal interests more often than positive ones.[3] The exact interplay between positive and negative duties in commonsense moral thought is complex, but this generalization seems accurate enough: The threshold of harm that triggers a moral duty is typically much lower in the case of actions than it is in the case of omissions.[4]

The third restrictive feature of commonsense morality is the weight given to special obligations. Special obligations are based on relationships such as those among families, friends, and colleagues. These responsibilities are thought to have more weight than my responsibilities to people in general. As with negative and positive duties, there are two sides to this. I am required to perform my special obligations even at the expense of providing greater benefits to those with whom I am not related in any special way. For example, my obligations to my brother may take priority over obligations to others, even though others need my help far more than he does. In addition, special obligations are thought to outweigh the pursuit of my personal interests more often than duties to those with whom I have no special relationship. I am expected to make greater sacrifices for those with whom I share special relationships than I am expected to make for strangers. Again, the interaction among these kinds of obligations is more complex than this presentation suggests, but a rough generalization is not out of order: The threshold at which the interests of others trigger moral duties for me is much lower for those with whom I share special relationships than it is for anonymous others.[5]

These elements make the commonsense conception of responsibility a restrictive one; in addition to setting out some responsibilities, they limit others. For example, an individual is responsible primarily for what he does. An individual does not bear responsibility for what others do and her responsibilities for what she does only in concert with others are unclear. Thus the individualism of the commonsense doctrine limits our responsibility for collectively produced harms.[6] Second, the greater strength of negative duties compared with positive ones is motivated by the thought that morality should leave me great discretion in how I lead my life, provided I avoid actions that harm others in fairly direct ways. Again, the upshot of the distinction is to limit my responsibilities by holding that I am responsible for preventing harms only in very clearly defined, and presumably unusual, cases. The greater weight of special obligations relative to general ones also works to limit the extent of my obligations to others. If I join a relationship that is thought to generate special obligations with B, my obligations to a stranger, C, will be reduced: When B and C's interests conflict, I am to give B's interests greater weight than C's. Insofar as the relationships that are thought to generate special obligations are deeply rewarding, I can enjoy the benefits of significant relationships and thereby reduce my responsibilities to people in general.[7]

To see how the commonsense doctrine is restrictive, compare it with the vision of our responsibilities presented by consequentialist moral theories. According to consequentialist views, morality requires us to act in ways that bring about better overall results than any available alternative would. As Scheffler notes, consequentialist views make a sharp departure from commonsense notions of responsibility in part because they have no fundamental place for either the distinction between action and omission or for special duties.[8] Acts that seem benign in themselves are permissible only if there is no available alternative course of action that would make the world better and the interests of those with whom one shares close personal relationships count no more than the interests of strangers. Consequentialism thus has a much less restrictive conception of responsibility than the commonsense doctrine employs. Insofar as we blithely go about our daily activities without worrying about all the potential lives we might otherwise save, we employ a more restricted conception of moral responsibility than consequentialism does, and many find consequentialism objectionable because it would drastically expand our responsibilities compared with commonsense doctrine.

While the restrictive, commonsense conception of responsibility has considerable intuitive appeal, it faces important limitations in accommodating some of the problems I described in the first step of this paper. Insofar as these are problems that an adequate theory of morality should be able to regulate, the commonsense conception is inadequate.

Consider the case of global climate change. This is best described as a case of uncoordinated collective harm. Individuals do not cause the harm of global warming; the most they can be responsible for having caused is a small fraction of the harm. In fact, I doubt that any individual, acting on his own, has caused any harm at all with regard to climate change, though some in institutionally defined positions of great political or economic power might have done so. The contributions each of us makes to climate change are so negligible that they do not amount to harming anyone; the effect of my driving to work makes no difference to anyone, therefore, it is not a harm to anyone. Attributions of responsibility for climate change to individuals thus fails the first condition of a complete attribution of responsibility: They do not connect behavior with harm. Of course, groups, like "all the people in the United States," do cause substantial climate change and thus, assuming that climate change is harmful, they harm others. But such groups do not meet the second criterion of a complete attribution of responsibility: Nothing can be required of an unorganized group of people since such groups cannot make decisions and take actions. In sum, climate change is clearly a morally significant issue, but it is difficult to see how one could make a complete attribution of responsibility for its regulation.[9]

As a second example, take global justice. Here we have what is best described as a coordinated collective omission. Global poverty and human rights deprivations are moral problems of the first order. However, for the richest countries in the world, they fall into the secondary class of omissions. The inhabitants of these countries are not so much causing these harms as failing to halt or ameliorate them.[10] In these cases, it is the connection between individuals and harm, the first condition of a complete attribution of responsibility, which is tenuous.

Finally, consider special obligations and the case of social justice. Most have acknowledged responsibilities to satisfy material needs and protect against human cruelty within our societies. However, few acknowledge such responsibilities to the rest of the world and most feel entitled, or even obligated, to act in ways that undermines the position of the most vulnerable. For example, we erect trade barriers that make it more difficult for the poorest people in the world to participate in our economic system in order to protect relatively well-off members of our society. When pressed about this gap in our responsibilities, a common response is that we have special obligations to the members of our societies; the interests of fellow members take priority over those of non-members. From a global perspective, the position appears to be that the rich take care of one another and claim they are duty bound to continue doing so, generally to the neglect of those who suffer from poverty and vicious attacks, and sometimes even at the expense of the poorest.

Despite its limitations, I do not believe that we can give up or replace the restrictive conception of responsibility. Scheffler's diagnosis strikes me as correct: The restrictive conception seems natural to us and will continue to do so because it fits into a conception of our powers as agents that seems natural. Scheffler notes three features of what he calls the phenomenology of agency, that is, how we conceptualize our powers as agents.[11] First, we give a priority to action over omission. I count my intentional acts as things that I do. Only a few of my many omissions are counted as things that I do and this happens only in specialized circumstances, where I am expected to act but do not. Second, we give priority to near over remote outcomes. I perceive my agency as extending only to the effects of my actions that are clear to me and within my control. The effects of my behavior that are near in time and space are more likely to count as things that I do than distant ones. Driving to work is something that I see myself as doing, while heating the earth is not: It is a side effect, at best, not something that I do. Third, there is a priority for individual over group behavior. Outcomes that I bring about myself are more prominent for me than those brought about through the combined behavior of many people. That is part of why I do not see myself as heating the earth; the earth is heated only as a result of many people's driving to work and, while I may be one of them, my contribution is subsumed by the group's behavior.

These phenomenological features of agency explain the appeal of the restrictive conception of responsibility. The limitations in the restricted conception of responsibility seem natural because they correspond to my understanding of myself as an agent. This means that we have reason to be skeptical about the availability of an alternative conception of individual responsibility that would regulate global harms. We think in the terms laid out by the restrictive conception and the restrictive conception is inadequate for regulating the problems we face. Since that is so, what rules could there be that could be easily learned and followed and that would regulate the harms under discussion?

A way of making the point is to contrast our society with the relatively small-scale, static societies in which our commonsense moral code developed. One need not engage in excessively wild armchair anthropology to see how the restrictive conception would be adequate to regulate the major kinds of harm that people could inflict on one another in such societies. The relevant rules can be learned and applied to novel situations and, if followed, they would serve to regulate the most important ways of harming one another. In such societies, there were few remote effects of behavior and no mass behavior. I do not mean to suggest that preindustrial life was a golden age of harmony, only that the main ways of harming others involved direct, individual action and that the restrictive conception of responsibility seems well suited to regulating those harms.

The case should not be overstated. It is clearly possible for people to adopt a more expansive understanding of their responsibilities and place in the world. The influence of environmental concerns on our daily behavior surely illustrates our ability to incorporate consideration of distant effects into our lives. Still, the limits on the information and power individuals possess are such that it is hard to imagine a purely individualistic solution to these problems. What rules should individuals follow in order to regulate global problems that would have roughly the same effectiveness as the rules of commonsense morality had in regulating the problems of small, static societies?[12]

The problem we face can be put this way: The social circumstances in which the restrictive conception made sense have changed, but some basic facts about our nature as agents have not. We now have the technical ability to cause vast harms far away. But we still conceive of our agency as sharply limited. Consequently, while the restrictive conception is inadequate to regulate harms in our social circumstances, we have difficulty conceptualizing an alternative. If that is so, then we should expect that the restrictive conception will continue to seem natural, even if we acknowledge its inadequacies for our world. One result of this is to reduce our confidence in our moral intuitions about responsibility without providing a clear alternative way of thinking about these problems.

Institutional Responsibility as an Alternative

First, let me recapitulate the argument so far. I have said that there are global problems that should be regulated by morality. Nonetheless, our restrictive conception of responsibility impedes this regulation. Abandoning the restrictive conception is not an attractive option, however, insofar as the restrictive conception makes sense in the light of our nature as agents and there are no obvious alternatives to it. I will argue that the way out of this dilemma is to attribute responsibility for global problems to a different kind of agent that I will call an institutional agent. Specifically, I will claim that the problematic features of the restrictive conception are less relevant to institutional agents than they are to individuals. I wish to be clear about the scope of my argument. I am not trying to address general skepticism about the possibility of institutional moral responsibility. I take for granted both that institutions can be agents of some kind and that they are subject to moral restraints. My argument concerns the scope of institutional responsibilities compared with individual responsibilities.

By institutional agents I mean organized agencies. For example, governments, corporations, labor unions, and international agencies are all institutional agents. As the name "institutional agent" suggests, I focus specifically on institutions that are agents: that is, entities that can make decisions and act on them. There are other institutional theories in political and moral philosophy that take a broader focus. John Rawls, for example, defines institutions as systems of rules that govern our interactions with one another; the rules governing property rights are an institution in his sense.[13] I make no claim to have the true view about what an institution is. I am focusing on agents because I am concerned with how morality might require actions in order to regulate problems.

My argument is that the case for a restrictive conception of responsibility is much weaker for institutional agents than it is for individuals because institutional agents do not face the same limitations as individual agents. The restricted conception makes sense given the kinds of agents we are, and since institutional agents are different in the relevant respects, it makes sense that their moral responsibilities have a different structure. For example, one way that institutional agents are different from individuals concerns information. Institutions are better than individuals at collecting and processing information about the distant or indirect consequences of their actions. They have multiple sources of information, can use a division of labor to gather and process it, and appoint special officers whose job is to look out for particular problems. Because this is so, institutional agents are more capable of taking the remote effects of their actions into account than individuals are. In addition, institutional agents are not hampered by our phenomenal distinction between action and omission. They can collect and use information about the consequences of their omissions to a greater extent than individuals can. A second difference concerns power. Institutional agents can alter mass behavior; simple rules can alter the average speed on the highways or the amount of water used to flush a toilet. Individuals, by contrast, can have significant influence on mass behavior only in the rarest of cases and even then usually by virtue of some institutional role, such as being the head of the state. As is well known, even groups of individuals with shared interests will often find it difficult to coordinate their behavior. Finally, institutional agents can spread the costs of regulating a problem. Governments spread costs through uniform taxation and regulation; firms do it by passing on costs to consumers.

I do not mean to imply that institutional agents are perfect or even that they are better than individual agents. Institutional changes can have unpredictable results and institutional agents can make decisions in ways that no sensible individual would. I only claim that institutional agents are different kinds of agents than individuals are. In some cases, these differences are such that institutional agents are better able to act on certain kinds of problems than individuals are.

Since institutions have different capacities as agents than individuals, there is less reason to apply the restrictive conception of responsibility to them. This is the key to seeing how we might move towards a more adequate attribution of responsibility for global problems. For example, since institutional agents are better able to understand and regulate the distant consequences of their actions than individuals are, it makes sense to make more expansive attributions of responsibility to them. For similar reasons, institutional agents are better able to perceive and act on their consequences of their omissions than individuals are. Thus, in order to assign institutional responsibility for regulating global injustice, for example, it is less important to show that the putatively responsible institution has caused poverty or human rights abuse than it is to show that it is capable of taking effective steps against them.

In the case of climate change, institutional responsibility can help to resolve a puzzle I mentioned earlier in this chapter: No individual is responsible for causing any harm, no unorganized group could be responsible for preventing it, but no organized group caused the harm either. Since the distinction between action and omission is less significant for institutional agents than it is for individuals, there is more room to hold governments responsible for taking steps to regulate the harm its citizens collectively cause, even though it does not cause the harm itself. What is at issue is whether there are the same restrictions on attributing responsibility for omissions to institutional agents as there are for attributing such responsibilities to individuals. If there are not, then there is greater scope for holding a government responsible for regulating harms such as those stemming from climate change, even if it is not itself a cause of those problems. In addition to making progress on this problem, this view about institutional responsibility would undermine some objections to international efforts to stop climate change. The United States, for example, refuses to ratify the Kyoto Protocol to the United Nations Framework Convention on Climate Change because it fails to include restrictions on the production of greenhouse gases by poor countries. To the extent that this position is motivated by moral considerations, as opposed to greed or sincere doubts about either the problem or the Kyoto Protocol's solution, it is based on the idea that everyone who causes a harm ought to contribute to its mitigation, even though the cost to poor countries of reduced growth is much greater than it is to the United States. By contrast, if we think that who causes a harm is less important than who has the ability to alleviate it without hardship, then this view will seem less plausible and it will seem more plausible to assert that the burden of preventing climate change should fall on the wealthier countries. I should say that my view about responsibility does not offer positive support for attributing responsibility on the basis of the ability to bear the burdens of doing so, it just undermines the rationale for the way of distributing responsibility currently employed by the United States.[14]

The significant feature of the institutional theory is that it gives a rationale for paying less attention to commonsense ideas about responsibility in some contexts, while also taking them seriously in others. It is unlike utilitarianism, for example, which rejects the restrictive conception even for individuals. Nonetheless, other institutional theories put greater weight on preserving commonsense doctrine than my view does: I will mention these differences, not so much because I object to them, but to clarify my own view.

One alternative is presented by Thomas Pogge. Pogge understands institutions along Rawls' lines, as systems of rules that govern our interactions with one another, and claims that we harm others by participating in institutions that predictably lead to more bad results than alternative practices would. For example, our scheme of intellectual property rights leads to more poverty than would an alternative scheme that allows poor countries to exploit Western intellectual property. Therefore, individuals who participate in our system of property rights are guilty of causing the harm of poverty and violating a negative duty not to harm others.[15] Pogge accepts the commonsense distinction between positive and negative duties, but tries to show that our institutional affiliations mean that negative duties have wider scope than we commonly believe they have.

A second kind of alternative institutional theory, articulated by Henry Shue, seeks to retain the primacy of individual responsibility. According to this view, institutions are significant because they enable us to realize individual responsibilities by, for example, lowering the costs of meeting them; it trades on the point I made earlier that institutions can spread the costs of addressing a problem. This view thus treats institutional action as a way for individuals to meet their moral duties without bearing excessive costs.[16]

I believe both of these views express important truths. However, I also find it clearer to say that there is a distinctive set of institutional responsibilities that are structurally different from individual responsibilities.

Pogge's view expands negative duties relative to the way they are commonly understood. The truth in this view is that our behavior affects others through complex social relations and practices and that we are thereby connected to distant harms in novel and troubling ways: We contribute to distant harms without having obvious control over our contributions. Nonetheless, the claim that participating in a practice like a system of property rights can be construed as a violation of negative duties, traditionally understood, strikes me as exaggerated. For most, participating in such a practice is much more like failing to prevent harm than it is like harming: We comply with inherited practices that we did not institute, do nothing directly to enforce, and have very little power to change. Pogge's strategy is to retain the importance of the commonsense distinction between negative and positive duties, while at the same time showing that the boundaries of the distinction are significantly different than they are commonly thought to be. The goal is to extend the force of negative duties in commonsense morality to a range of behavior that is currently considered acceptable or, at worst, a violation of the putatively less strict category of positive duties. But it is not clear that this is a stable position. There are two ways of responding to Pogge's assimilation of negative duties and putatively acceptable behavior. One is to conclude that the behavior in question is not as acceptable as it seems since it falls in with violations of negative duties and negative duties are very strict. The other is to conclude that negative duties are not necessarily as strict as they seem since they prohibit apparently acceptable behavior. Few of us have a fully articulate sense of why negative duties are stricter than positive ones, but the distinction is believed to be based on the close connection between those who violate negative duties and the consequent harms suffered by others. This connection is dissipated by expanding the scope of negative duties to include mere participation in institutional practices that, in turn, have effects on others. I do not mean to deny that institutional practices can be harmful and that those who participate in harmful institutional practices are implicated in the harms. I am only questioning the characterization of our implication in these harms as a violation of negative duties with the same force that negative duties, narrowly construed, are thought to have.

Shue's point that institutions lower the individual costs of meeting duties is true: Institutions enable individuals to meet their responsibilities at lower cost. But this alone is not sufficient to dismiss the claim that there are additional, uniquely institutional responsibilities, nor does Shue suggest it is. The motivation for that further claim stems from the thought that institutional responsibilities must be derived from individual responsibilities and thus that they are not genuinely distinct. Institutions do not really have responsibilities, one might say, they are just the means that individuals use to discharge their responsibilities.

However, the claim that institutional responsibilities are derived from individual responsibilities is ambiguous. One thing it might mean is that there would be no institutional responsibilities unless there were individual responsibilities; taken on their own, apart from individuals, institutions have no responsibilities. This strikes me as correct. Since institutions are created by, used by, and composed of individuals, I do not know how to imagine institutions on their own, apart from individuals. In any event, I grant the point that it is hard to see how institutions would have moral responsibilities on their own, considered separately from their relationship with individuals. But this does not show that institutions do not really have responsibilities. Institutional responsibilities involve requirements that institutions act in certain ways and these requirements are instituted in order to regulate serious moral problems. What more is needed to say that they "really" have responsibilities?

A second thing that one might mean in charging that institutional responsibilities are derived from individual responsibilities is that institutional agents only enable individuals to meet their responsibilities, but do not have any distinctive responsibilities of their own. I think I have given good reasons for rejecting that. Since institutions are different kinds of agents than individuals are, their responsibilities have different characteristics. One may hold that institutional responsibilities are distinct from individual responsibilities in this sense while granting that institutions cannot be responsible for any problem that is of no concern to individuals at all. I believe that this is our situation with respect to what I called global problems: We regard ourselves as connected to them in morally problematic ways, but we have difficulty thinking of how we might be responsible for their regulation. My aim has been to explain why we face this difficulty while presenting a constructive alternative for overcoming it. In other words, I do not wish to deny that we are implicated in global problems, though I do take seriously our difficulties in thinking about them.

There is more to be said about the precise relationship between individual and institutional responsibilities. One especially important set of issues concerns individual responsibilities for ensuring that institutions meet their responsibilities. It is hard to imagine how a system of institutional responsibility would work without such a role for individuals. But that opens questions about who bears what responsibilities for which institutional agents. These questions will have to be answered in a way that preserves the independence of institutional responsibilities for my position to be vindicated. However, rather than addressing these details of the view, I should first acknowledge some limitations to the argument even as it stands.

Some Limitations of the Argument

My argument has gone like this:

> Both individuals and institutional agents bear responsibilities: They are responsible for avoiding causing certain harms and sometimes for preventing or ameliorating harms even if they did not cause them.
> There is a rationale for restricting individual responsibility roughly along some familiar lines from commonsense morality.
> This rationale does not apply to the institutional agents.

Therefore, the responsibilities of institutional agents are not necessarily limited in the same way as individual responsibilities are.

Ideally, we would like to reach a stronger conclusion, namely: Institutional agents are responsible for global problems.

That conclusion, however, does not follow from the argument I have given.

The significance of the problems I mentioned pushes us towards the stronger conclusion. An important role of morality is to regulate the harms that fall under human control such that they are minimized if moral responsibilities are met. For that reason, one might think, an adequate account of morality would show that someone or something is responsible for regulating global problems: Any account of morality worth the name would have to have a credible account of how to regulate problems such as global warming and poverty. If institutional agents can be held responsible for regulating these problems, and individuals cannot, we have good reason to attribute responsibility for regulating global problems to institutional agents.

Unfortunately, it does not straightforwardly follow that institutional agents are responsible for global problems. One way of reaching such a conclusion would be to assume something along the lines of "can implies ought." Then we could move from the point that institutional agents can regulate global problems to the conclusion that they ought to do so. I believe that the role of morality is to regulate the major harms under human control and, as such, I think there is a justifiable tendency to move from can to ought in our moral thinking. No one would think twice about saying that the only strong swimmer in the band of people on the beach ought to save the drowning man in the surf. Similarly, when confronted with new social circumstances, it strikes me as perfectly sensible to seek to apply our fundamental moral beliefs in new ways in order to regulate new kinds of harms. Such a project has to be governed by the goal of actually succeeding in regulating the problems at hand. Nonetheless, it also seems to me to be possible that there could be significant kinds of harm and suffering that are both subject to human control and that no one is morally responsible for addressing. The suggestion that moral rules could regulate all significant harms and suffering subject to human control is a very strong one and I certainly have not shown, nor do I know how to show, that it is true. Therefore, I cannot appeal to the general proposition that can implies ought.

A more modest conclusion one might draw is that the responsibilities of institutional agents are always broader than those of individuals. This seems to follow from the fact that the responsibilities of institutional agents are not limited in the same way that individual responsibilities are. In order to draw this conclusion, however, one would have to assume that there are no reasons for limiting the responsibilities of institutional agents other than the ones I have been discussing. That is not necessarily the case: There may be additional limitations on the responsibilities that institutional agents can bear.[17]

For example, one might object to an expansive conception of institutional responsibility on the grounds that it is incompatible with maintaining institutional legitimacy. People create and maintain institutions for specific purposes and institutional agents act legitimately only insofar as they perform their appointed roles. Requiring institutional agents to do a never-ending list of good deeds would make it impossible for them to perform their intended roles. Therefore, one might think, institutional agents cannot legitimately accept greater responsibilities than they are authorized to accept by their members. This is the institutional version of special obligations: An institution might have distinctive obligations to serve its members that it does not have to the rest of the world and that have more weight than the obligations they would, in the absence of the special ties, bear to non-members.

One especially pressing instance of this general objection concerns governments. Suppose we believe something like this: A government can legitimately act only insofar as its citizens authorize it to act. This conclusion seems to follow: A government's responsibilities cannot exceed those of its citizens, unless they authorize it to assume additional responsibilities. There are two ways of taking this objection. One is a mistake; the other poses an interesting challenge.

The mistake is to infer from the claim that individuals are not responsible for regulating global problems the conclusion that the governments that represent them are not responsible for regulating them either. This has some plausibility. I have already said that we cannot attribute responsibility to individuals in these cases. So how, one might ask, could their organization into states make them responsible? Why should they go from bearing no responsibility to bearing quite a lot? The mistaken assumption here is that an incomplete attribution of responsibility is equivalent to being absolved of all responsibility. As I described it, our situation is that we are connected to global problems such that we are implicated in them. The problem is that we cannot be held responsible for regulating the harms. When we are organized, we can act to alleviate our morally uncomfortable position and thus we can be held responsible.

The more difficult version of the objection maintains that governments cannot legitimately act on their global responsibilities. If we assume, as it seems plausible to do, that a government is legitimate if and only if its actions could not reasonably be rejected by its citizens, then we have a problem. The citizens of a state could reasonably reject governmental actions that impose significant costs on them for the sake of non-citizens.[18] If so, a state's global responsibilities could conflict with the conditions of its legitimacy. In these cases a government would neglect its responsibilities if it does nothing, but it would act illegitimately if it meets its responsibilities.

There are three ways of responding to such a dilemma. First, one might conclude that my view of institutional responsibility is too broad: It attributes responsibility to governments where they are forbidden to act and thus the attribution of responsibility must be wrong. Second, one might say that while there are potential conflicts between our views of institutional responsibility and political legitimacy these do not threaten either view. We recognize that there can be conflicts between obligations to keep promises and obligations to comfort a friend, for example, without concluding that one or the other must be mistaken. Third, one might say that it is our views of political legitimacy that are mistaken. They give too much weight to the interests of citizens and not enough to the interests of non-citizens. Since the decisions of one state have extensive impact on the citizens of other states, why should the only test of the legitimacy of a state's actions be that they are accepted by its citizens?

The first response is the only one that threatens my view. It is too hasty. My view is that the responsibilities of institutional agents are broader than individual responsibilities in that several restrictions on individual responsibility do not apply to institutional agents. One can hold such a view and agree that the interests served by allowing people to create institutions for specific aims pose a constraint on an institution's outside responsibilities. What is at issue is not whether the members of an institution will utterly lose control of it, but rather the extent to which an institution can be required to serve the interests of non-members. So while some attributions of responsibilities may objectionably exceed a government's legitimate powers, it does not follow that they all do so.

One thing to note is that even if we are convinced that governments really are limited in the responsibilities they can take on, we are not necessarily driven to skepticism about responsibility for global problems. We may conclude instead that this shows the need for more powerful international institutions that could legitimately bear the responsibilities. If political institutions are needed to deal with global problems and current governments are inadequate, the conclusion we may be compelled to reach is that we need different political institutions.

Conclusions

I claim to have done three things. First, I have given a diagnosis of our difficulties in thinking about global problems. Second, I have offered a novel view of responsibility. It differs from the commonsense view in two ways. It applies specifically to institutions and not individuals and it has different features; for example, it attributes less significance to the distinction between causing harm and allowing harm to happen. Finally, while the argument shows that some of the hurdles to making a complete attribution of responsibility to institutional agents are lower than they are for individuals, it does not prove that institutional agents are responsible for global problems. Proving that would require showing that there are no other reasons for limiting institutional agents' responsibilities and that is something I have not done.

One feature of the argument worth noting is that it employs a distinction between institutional and individual responsibility and concludes that institutions have greater responsibilities than individuals. Distinctions between individual and institutional morality are usually drawn for the purpose of restricting the moral duties of states, especially in international relations. The assertion that the strictures of commonsense morality do not apply to the state is usually given as a rationale for holding the state to lesser standards: Thus it is sometimes said that the statesman must be ruthless in ways that we would not tolerate in a mere individual because of his role in safeguarding the state. By contrast, I am arguing that the differences between states and individuals support departing from commonsense morality by requiring institutions to bear greater responsibility for the interests of others. We have become accustomed to thinking of the state's role in this way on the social level: We expect the state to address a variety of social problems that defy individual solutions. I am urging that we take a similar attitude towards institutional action on the global level.

Notes

1. I would like to thank Daniel Brudney, Chad Flanders, Christopher Kutz, Andrei Marmour, Liam Murphy, Martha Nussbaum, Thomas Pogge, and Iris Young for their comments on this chapter.
2. Samuel Scheffler, "Individual Responsibility in a Global Age," in *Boundaries and Allegiances: Problems of Justice and Responsibility in Liberal Thought* (New York: Oxford University Press, 2001), p. 37.
3. Ibid., p. 36.
4. This has exceptions, of course. According to commonsense, I'm responsible for preventing the blind man from stumbling over the curb and for meeting you at lunch, even though failure in either case would not do much harm. By contrast, I can inflict great pain by tackling you in a football game or by breaking off our romance without doing anything morally wrong.
5. For a more thorough account of the relative weights of special and general obligations, see Samuel Scheffler, "Families, Nations, and Strangers," in *Boundaries and Allegiances: Problems of Justice and Responsibility in Liberal Thought* (New York: Oxford University Press, 2001).
6. I do not mean to deny that there could be an individualistic account of collective responsibility; one such account is given by Christopher Kutz, *Complicity: Ethics and Law for a*

Collective Age (Cambridge: Cambridge University Press, 2000). It does seem to me that such accounts are, at least, refinements of commonsense moral thinking.

7. For discussion, see Thomas W. Pogge, "Loopholes in Moralities," *Journal of Philosophy* 89, no. 2 (1992) and Samuel Scheffler, "The Conflict Between Justice and Responsibility," in *Boundaries and Allegiances: Problems of Justice and Responsibility in Liberal Thought* (New York: Oxford University Press, 2001).

8. Scheffler, "Individual Responsibility in a Global Age," 37–8.

9. Of course, the citizens of the United States are organized—they have a government. But the federal government does not *cause* global warming. I will argue below that the federal government should still be held responsible even though it is not a cause of the problem. For a different analysis of this kind of problem, see Derek Parfit, *Reasons and Persons* (Oxford: Clarendon Press, 1987) p. 67–86.

10. There is a respectable line of argument that the wealthy countries are responsible for having caused poverty and human rights violations through their past behavior. Perhaps that is so, notwithstanding special difficulties in the attribution of responsibility for historical injustice. I am assuming that poverty and human rights violations would raise questions about moral responsibility even if they persisted after all historical injustices were fully rectified.

11. Scheffler, "Individual Responsibility in a Global Age," 38–40.

12. This strikes me as an important limit on Christopher Kutz's solution to Scheffler's problem. See Kutz, *Complicity: Ethics and Law for a Collective Age*, 184–91.

13. John Rawls, *A Theory of Justice* (Cambridge, MA: Harvard University Press, 1971) p. 55.

14. In saying that the distinction between positive and negative duties is less significant for institutional agents than it is for individuals, I do not mean to imply that I have shown it has no significance at all. Our difficulty with conceiving of omissions as something that we do, except in special cases, explains part of the appeal of the commonsense distinction between causing and allowing harm, but it may not account for all of this distinction's appeal. Knowingly harming someone strikes many as worse than knowingly failing to stop someone from being harmed and, whatever the merits of this belief, I have not undermined it.

15. Thomas W. Pogge, "Cosmopolitanism and Sovereignty," *Ethics* 103 (1992): 52–54; Thomas W. Pogge, "How Should Human Rights be Conceived?," in *Jahrbuch für Recht und Ethik*, B. Sharon Byrd, Joachim Hruschka, and Jan C. Joerden, eds. (Berlin: Duncker & Humblot, 1995), p. 116.

"The most remarkable feature of this institutional understanding is that it goes beyond minimalist libertarianism without denying its central tenet: that human rights entail only negative duties. The normative force of another's human right for you is that you must not participate in, and thereby help to uphold and to impose upon her, social institutions under which she does not have secure access to the object of her human right. You would be violating this duty, if you lived in a society in which such access is not secure (in which blacks are enslaved, women disenfranchised or servants mistreated, for example) and just went about your own business. Even if you owned no slaves and employed no servants yourself, you would still share responsibility: by contributing your labor to the society's economy, your taxes to its governments and so forth" (Pogge, How should human rights be conceived?" p. 116).

"We are asked to be concerned about human rights violations not simply insofar as they exist at all, but only insofar as they are produced by social institutions in which we are significant participants. Our negative duty not to cooperate in the imposition of unjust practices, together with our continuing participation in an unjust institutional scheme, triggers obligations to promote feasible reforms of this scheme that would enhance the fulfillment of human rights" (Pogge, Cosmopolitanism and sovereignty, p. 52).

In a seminar at the University of Chicago in the Spring of 2001, Pogge explained his position in this way: Individuals do not impose unjust institutions on the poor, it is the governments of wealthy societies that do so by insisting on, among other things, rules of international trade. Individuals impose by supporting governments.

16. Henry Shue, "Mediating Duties," *Ethics* 98 (1988): 695–9.

17. This also poses a problem for Robert Goodin's account of institutional responsibility. See Robert E. Goodin, "The State as a Moral Agent," in *Utilitarianism as a Public Philosophy* (Cambridge and New York: Cambridge University Press, 1995), p. 31–7.

18. Thomas Nagel, *Equality and Partiality* (New York: Oxford University Press, 1991), p. 169–79.

CHAPTER 7

Applying the Contribution Principle[1]

CHRISTIAN BARRY

Introduction

This chapter examines a methodological problem related to the application of a principle that is given substantial (and sometimes decisive) weight in most people's assessments regarding what (if anything) is owed, and by whom, to those who suffer from acute deprivations—shortfalls persons suffer in their health, civic status, or standard of living relative to the ordinary needs and requirements of human beings. The principle, which I shall refer to as the "contribution principle," holds that *agents are responsible for addressing acute deprivations when they have contributed, or are contributing, to bringing them about.* In the real world, it is often difficult, if not impossible, to determine with much confidence whether and to what extents different individual and collective agents (a person, a development bank, or a national government, etc.) have contributed to acute deprivations. It is therefore unclear whether those who grant substantial weight to the contribution principle should take these agents to have responsibilities to remedy them, or how weighty they ought to hold these responsibilities to be. This problem can only be fruitfully addressed by examining the appropriateness of different standards—which I shall call *standards of application*—that might be appealed to for determining agents' responsibilities in contexts where it is difficult or impossible to determine whether and to which extents different agents have in fact contributed to, are contributing to, or will have contributed to acute deprivations. These standards include the burden of proof, the standard of proof, and the admissibility of evidence for assessing which agents have contributed (and how much they have contributed) to acute deprivation. People are generally aware of the importance of these standards in the context of legal and scientific inquiry, but they tend not to reflect upon their significance for assessing ethical responsibilities. As a result, people seem often to lazily import standards of application from criminal legal contexts into this domain, asserting, for example, that they lack ethical responsibilities to remedy acute deprivations unless their contribution to them can be proved "beyond a reasonable doubt." This is problematic, I will argue, because the standards that are arguably appropriate for applying criminal legal norms are extremely implausible when applied to norms for determining other ethical responsibilities. I will show how adopting more plausible standards for applying the contribution principle would very likely lead adherents of this principle to interpret their ethical responsibilities with respect to acute deprivations much more broadly than they appear to do at present.

Criteria for Assigning Responsibilities

A *criterion* for assigning responsibilities to address acute deprivation can be identified in terms of the answers it gives to two questions:

1. *What* does acute deprivation consist of?
2. *Under what conditions* are there responsibilities for addressing acute deprivation, and how should they be distributed among different agents?

Question 1 concerns the characterization of acute deprivation, Question 2 relates to the characterization of responsibilities to address them.

A comprehensive answer to Question 1 will require an account of:

a. The *subjects*—such as present and future individual persons, groups, communities, states, or nations—who can be acutely deprived, and to whom one can bear responsibilities;
b. The *aspects* of these subjects—such as their income, resource holdings, capabilities, functionings, levels of utility, or some weighted combination of the preceding—that are relevant for determining whether or not they suffer acute deprivations;
c. The *threshold level*—the levels of income, resource holdings, capability, functioning, utility, or some combination of the preceding—under which these subjects will count as acutely deprived; and any plausible account will also require an account of;

    d. The *aggregation function*—the weights attached to the *depth* and *incidence* of deprivation, and perhaps also to its distribution—for assessing the overall magnitude of acute deprivation, and for the purpose of setting priorities.

A comprehensive answer to Question 2 will require an account of:

    e. The *agents*—such as individual persons, collective agents such as nongovernmental organizations, corporations, and states, or more dispersed and loosely affiliated groups and collectivities—who can bear responsibilities to address acute deprivation;

    f. The *principles* for assigning responsibilities among these agents: *limiting principles*, which identify the agents that have responsibilities with respect to some particular deprivation, and *principles of allocation*, which determine the nature and extent of these agents' responsibilities to address it;

    g. The *standards* for applying these limiting and allocative principles in real world contexts where there is often reasonable disagreement about whether, for example, different agents are capable of alleviating or mitigating some deprivations, or about the extent to which they have contributed to them.[2]

Many recent debates concerning policy questions that are directly relevant to acute deprivations do not appear to be rooted in differences with respect to their characterization. They focus instead on (f) and (g), the principles for allocating responsibilities to different agents and the standards for applying them.[3]

The Contribution Principle

Although other principles are often invoked in debates concerning responsibilities for addressing acute deprivation, the contribution principle seems generally to be taken to have special significance. All participants in the debate concerning access to antiretroviral medicines for the treatment of those suffering from HIV/AIDS, for example, seem to agree that, were it to be shown that some actor has substantially contributed to these deprivations, it would be their responsibility (though perhaps not *solely* their responsibility) to try to remedy them. The pains that various actors such as pharmaceutical company executives, government ministers, and WTO officials and trade representatives have taken to show that they have *not* contributed to these problems, or that more substantial contributions have been made by others, further emphasizes the importance that is attached to this principle.[4]

In what follows, I will neither justify nor criticize the contribution principle. Rather, I will simply assume that it is justified and address questions related to the plausibility of different standards for applying it to the real world.

Talk of an agent's "contribution" to some or other problem admits of many different interpretations, with different implications for practice.[5] Since this chapter focuses on a question that will arise in applying the contribution principle under *any* plausible interpretation, however, I will bypass these difficult interpretive issues and, to fix ideas, simply stipulate the following definition: Agent A contributes to Agent B's deprivation *if and only if*:

> A's conduct was *causally relevant to it*;
> A's conduct did not merely allow a causal sequence that had antecedently put B under threat of acute deprivation to play out, but rather *initiated, facilitated, or sustained* it.[6]

Both (a) and (b) clearly require further analysis. I shall here interpret condition (a) to require that A's conduct was a necessary element in a set of actual antecedent conditions that was sufficient for its occurrence.[7] The key distinction in (b) is between causally relevant conditions that allow an antecedent sequence to play out and causally relevant conditions that initiate, facilitate, or sustain the sequence. A's causally relevant conduct merely allows a sequence to continue rather than initiating, facilitating, or sustaining it *if and only if*:

1. There is a high antecedent probability, independent of what A might do, that B will suffer acute deprivation.
2. B suffers acute deprivation.
3. Had B avoided suffering the acute deprivation, it would have been through A's assistance.[8]

Standards for Applying the Contribution Principle

In some cases, it will be relatively easy to determine whether or not some agent has contributed to acute deprivation. In many other cases, however, things will not be so clear. Indeed, it is often difficult (if not impossible) to tell conclusively (or even with great confidence) whether and to which extent some agent has contributed to particular acute deprivations, and there are very few claims regarding the contributions of different agents to acute deprivations that cannot be plausibly contested. The plausibility of different explanations of some hardships is often obscured by the fact that each side in a debate—regarding the contribution of the International Monetary Fund's (IMF) structural adjustment programs to poverty in developing countries, for example—tends to be *fully* convinced of the

On page 139 and continuing on the top of page 140, the word "changed" was errantly inserted after three headings. The headings should read:

The Burden of Proof:

The Standard of Proof:

The Constraints on Admissible Evidence:

Global Responsibilities: Who Must Deliver on Human Rights?
ISBN: 0-415-95126-7 (Hardcover) 0-415-95127-5 (Softcover)

implausibility of their opponent's position. Anyone who is tempted to give weight to the contribution principle in his or her practical deliberations, then, ought to address the following question:

(Q1) In cases where it is unclear whether or to what extent some agent (A) has contributed to the deprivation of another agent (B), how should (A) conceive of its responsibilities to (B)?

It is clear that how Q1 is answered will substantially affect the practical meaning of this principle, and the behavior of agents who are committed to it. To examine the considerations that are relevant to answering Q1, let us imagine the following case:

A relatively poor developing country (which we shall call G77), asserts that a wealthy developed country (which we shall call G1), has undertaken a policy that has contributed to acute deprivations among its citizens. Because of this, G77 argues, G1 has strong contribution-based reasons to undertake efforts to alleviate these problems and to avert further deprivations that their past conduct will otherwise cause in the future. To help fix ideas, let us suppose that Policy P refers to the policy of unilaterally deciding when and to what extent monetary policy should be tightened in response to domestic inflation or other national macroeconomic concerns. And let us further suppose that G77 claims that G1's decision to raise interest rates in response to fears about inflation in its domestic economy has contributed to its debt crisis, with severe consequences for its most vulnerable citizens. Let us call G77's assertion regarding G1's responsibility Claim D.[9] To evaluate Claim D we must determine whether G1's conduct was a *cause* of these deprivations, and whether its conduct initiated, facilitated, or sustained a causal sequence that led to the suffering of citizens in G77, rather than merely allowing an antecedent threat to play out.

We may lack confidence in our ability to make these determinations. Evidence of Policy P's overall causal impact on G77, for example, will perhaps be inconclusive. And even if we are confident that Policy P was a causally relevant condition for the deprivations of citizens in G77, it may be unclear whether these citizens were antecedently under threat, or whether they would have avoided these deprivations only if G1 had provided assistance to them.[10] Evaluating Claim D in contexts in which substantial factual uncertainties of this kind are present will require us to distinguish three different *standards of application* for the contribution principle:

The Burden of Proof Changed: Who has the *burden* of proof in this case? Must G77 (or some other agent) show that Policy P contributed to the deprivations in question? Or must G1 show that it has not done so?

The Standard of Proof Changed: What evidential *threshold* must be reached for it to *count* as proven that Policy P did or did not contribute to deprivations among G77's people?

The Constraints on Admissible Evidence Changed: What kinds of *evidence* will be taken to corroborate the thesis that Policy P has contributed to deprivations amongst G77's people?

How each of these standards is specified will often be quite consequential. The placement of the burden of proof will determine whether or not G1 is taken to bear responsibility in cases where we cannot determine with any confidence whether or not Claim D is (or is likely to be) true. If the burden is on G1, it will be held to have contribution-based responsibilities with respect to these deprivations if it cannot demonstrate that Claim D is false or unlikely. If the burden is on G77, substantial evidential uncertainties will make it impossible for it to establish that G1 has contribution-based responsibilities. Similarly, the higher the standard of proof, the harder it will be for G77 to establish Claim D, and the lower the standard of proof, the easier it will be for G77 to establish it. Likewise, the broader the range of evidence taken to corroborate Claim D, the easier it will be for whichever party bears the burden of proof to do so. The narrower the range of evidence that is admitted to establish this claim, the harder it will be for this party to do so.

Establishing Fair Standards of Application

Unfairly allocating the burden of proof, lowering or raising the standard of proof too far, or broadening or restricting the range of admissible evidence too much will lead to unjustified costs for G77 or G1. But how can we determine whether any particular way of specifying these standards is fair? The first thing to note is that there is no obviously correct answer to this question, nor is there any neutral or natural way of specifying these standards that can serve as a default. It clearly depends upon the context of the inquiry and the goals of the practice within which it is undertaken.

Take, for example, standards of application with respect to establishing whether some agent's conduct was a cause of someone's acute deprivation. The appropriateness of different standards of application for establishing a causal connection between some chemical substance and a medical condition may vary depending upon whether we are engaged in scientific inquiry, criminal or civil legal proceedings, or ethical reflection. It is not (as is sometimes supposed) that different conceptions of causation must be employed in these cases, but that the distinct aims of these inquiries and the point of the practices in which they are embedded may admit or require different specifications of the standards of application. In a criminal trial in which some agent A is being tried for having released a chemical that, it is alleged, has caused serious health problems among children at a neighboring school, most would insist that high evidential thresholds be employed for determining the causal links between the substance and the harm, and that the burden of proof be placed with the prosecution.

We might further insist on very strict constraints on admissible evidence, perhaps allowing only epidemiological studies to count as evidence of causation. In a civil trial in which some agent A is being tried for a similar offense, however, establishing a "preponderance of evidence" that the chemical released by A has contributed to the children's health problems would provide adequate grounds for attributing liability to him. And we might also allow a broader range of evidence, such as studies of the effects of the chemical on animals. And if the question is whether further such chemical releases should be legally authorized, it is not implausible that even slight evidence that these releases harm children should suffice to disallow them.[11]

When we engage in ethical reflection, meanwhile, the mere suspicion that one *may* have been involved in causing some harm often provides sufficient reason to act to address it. If, for example, A suspects that the chemical she has released *may* have causally contributed to children's health problems, she might reasonably take herself to have an ethical responsibility (although not a legal or enforceable one) to contribute towards meeting the costs of the treatment of their problems—or at least more reason to do so than she would have in the absence of her suspicion that she may have contributed to his condition. And this may be true where it is impossible to determine whether the "preponderance" standard is met, or even when we know that it has *not* been met.

That reasons for specifying standards of application one way or another would seem to depend on our purposes should not really surprise us. The same is true, after all, of standards for assessing reasons of all kinds, including reasons for belief. Robert Nozick, for example, has suggested that for everyday belief, the rule that "we should not believe some statement H if some alternative statement incompatible with H has a higher credibility value than H does" provides a sufficient standard of credibility. More stringent standards of credibility must be applied, however, in science, where "a statement may be required to reach a certain level of credibility, not simply to be more credible than any incompatible alternative."[12] Nozick also warns that once stringent standards for assessing reasons (such as those required in science) are known, they tend to be extended to other contexts where—due to the energy, time, and resources would have to be devoted to employing procedures that satisfy them—they are inappropriate. Further, he cautions against "concluding that someone is being irrational simply because his reasons do not meet the most stringent standards we can formulate. They may meet the standards appropriate to their context."[13] We must be similarly cautious about extending standards of application, which are appropriate in legal proceedings, to other areas of practical deliberation.

During the confirmation hearings of (now) Justice Clarence Thomas, in which evidence that he had sexually harassed Anita Hill was introduced, there were several instances in which commentators argued that, because the evidence was not sufficient to prove that he had committed these offenses "beyond a reasonable doubt," there were no grounds for opposing his confirmation. Were he involved in a criminal trial, such concerns may have been entirely appropriate, but it is highly questionable whether these standards were appropriate in the context of confirmation hearings for a prospective member of the highest federal court.[14] Recognizing the general point that different standards of application may be more or less appropriate depending on the context, however, does not immediately help us resolve our assessment of G1's responsibilities with respect to G77—especially if the truth (or likelihood) of Claim D cannot be shown with much confidence. For that, we must know more about the *kinds* of contextual features that are relevant for specifying standards of application, and a clearer sense of which of these features best characterize this type of case.

We can sharpen our discussion of these contextual features by representing different standards of application in terms of the relative importance that they attach to avoiding what are commonly called "Type 1" and "Type 2" errors.[15] In the case of Claim D, a Type 1 error would occur if G1 were falsely taken *to have* contributed to the deprivations amongst G77's citizens. A Type 2 error would occur were G1 to be falsely taken *not to have* contributed to these deprivations.

Different specifications of standards of application will result in different probabilities of these types of errors. In characterizing any such set of standards, then, some view must be taken of the relative costs of these types of errors. Stringent standards of proof and restrictions on admissible evidence in criminal proceedings, for example, reflect a strong aversion to Type 1 errors—expressing the conviction that falsely criminalizing the innocent is more costly than allowing many crimes to go unpunished. The "preponderance" standard in civil procedures also expresses an aversion to Type 1 errors—reflecting a willingness to err on the side of failing to allocate resources to those who have been injured by inordinately risky conduct or products—but it is much less stringent, and foreseeably engenders only a higher probability of Type 1 errors and a lower probability of Type 2 errors.

In order to identify some of the contextual features that are relevant to the case of G1 and G77, then, it may be worthwhile to consider some of the reasons that might plausibly be offered for requiring different standards of proof in criminal and civil legal contexts, and also the kinds of cases in civil law that have encouraged many tort theorists and even some courts to depart more radically from traditional tort procedures.[16] These standards seem to vary because of the overall social *costs* of different kinds of Type 1 and Type 2 errors.

Consider the attitudes towards Type 1 errors in tort and criminal law, respectively. One reason for the stringency of standards of proof in criminal law is connected to the potential costs that are imposed on the *agent* who is erroneously identified as a lawbreaker. In criminal trials, defendants are faced with the prospect of losing their rights, liberties, and perhaps even their lives. Moreover, by identifying them as "criminal offenders," society *expresses* an assessment of them and an attitude toward them—that their conduct is paradigmatically blameworthy—that can be seriously damaging to others and to their own sense of themselves.[17] Because of its strong expressive function, falsely accusing an agent of criminal offenses carries an additional cost, namely that the agencies that are acting in the name of justice act unjustly. In criminal cases, it is the state that brings the case against the defendant. We care that the state agencies that represent us not only bring about desirable end-states, but that they take special precaution not to unduly harm individuals through what they *do*, even when this may lead them to allow still greater harms that are brought about by others. Because of these costs, we do not typically want to imprison someone for exposing others to a chemical unless we were confident—on the basis of the soundest available evidence—that it contributed to the medical condition in question.

This is not the case with civil law. Its core evaluative concepts—"tortuous" or "wrongful"—do not carry the same stigma as "offense." As Bernard Williams has put it, "someone might say that in an absolutely ideal world all and only guilty criminals would be prosecuted, but there could be no world in which it was only successful plaintiffs whose cases were heard. Tort, by its nature, must be more like a system for the allocation of costs than the criminal law is"[18] Although the potential costs to the agent who is falsely held to have wronged another may be significant, they will involve only compensation, not the loss of a broader range of liberties.[19] If our concern is with making legally binding decisions for the allocation of costs for treating the children's medical conditions, a "preponderance of evidence" that the chemical released by A has contributed to the harms may make it reasonable to shift these costs (at least in part) to A.[20] The agency of the state is also involved in tort law, but in a way that can plausibly be seen as changing the potential costs of different types of error. The judiciary plays an adjudicative role, but private individuals and collective agents typically bring civil cases against defendants. Even when states are litigants in civil suits, they do not claim, as in the criminal case, to be vindicating the claims of law.

Further, in the context in which we are faced with a decision regarding the regulation, rather than the punishment of some activity, such as whether A should be legally permitted to continue to release the chemical in question, we may feel justified in relaxing the standards of proof and broadening the range of admissible evidence even further. Even if, on balance, we think the benefits of A's activities outweigh its costs, and that requiring A to pay compensation to those who may be adversely affected by them would be counterproductive, it may still be incumbent upon us to offset these costs.

Unlike criminal and civil proceedings, or even regulatory action, assessments of ethical responsibility do not single out agents for sanctions that are backed by the coercive force of the state or any other "official" agency. All that is at stake is ethical censure, and even this need not take the form of blaming A for his conduct, or seriously impugning her character. We may simply conclude that, because she has contributed to the deprivation, she is obliged to share the costs of alleviating it, or at least to desist from releasing the chemical. If we consider it socially necessary for A to continue to release this chemical without paying compensation, and we wish to uphold legal permissions for him to do so, then we must at the very least explore the possibility of developing mechanisms of shifting the costs from the children, perhaps by instituting a general social insurance scheme or some other means of cost spreading.

It is also important to note that some legal and political theorists have recently argued that in certain circumstances further lessening the standard of proof, broadening the range of admissible evidence, or even shifting the burden of proof have seemed to many to be appropriate in legal contexts too. Several authors have recommended, for example, that the burden of proof be shifted in civil law in contexts where the causal links between potentially risky chemicals and injuries are uncertain (uncertainty about general causation); in cases involving multiple defendants each of whom has produced substances that are harmful to humans, but where it is uncertain whose injuries have been caused by particular producers (identity uncertainty about specific causation); or in cases where it is known that a chemical causes a particular injury in a certain percentage of cases of that injury, but it is not possible to distinguish the cases caused by the chemical from those caused by other factors (probabilistic uncertainty about specific causation).[21] The view that the range of evidence that should be deemed admissible in these contexts should be substantially broadened has also been advocated.[22]

These proposals, to depart from traditional standards of application in civil law, reflect a recognition that the goals of this social institution—such as allocating resources to those who have been injured by exposure to risky chemicals, and requiring injurers to compensate those they have harmed—may be served better by different standards in these special contexts. Some have gone even further to suggest that, with respect to some domains, the goals of tort law may be better served by abolishing it altogether in favor of a social insurance, or some other scheme. As Arthur Ripstein puts it, "It may be that a widespread social insurance scheme would actually approximate corrective justice better at the micro level than does the current tort system. Regulatory regimes may do more to make sure that people internalize the costs of their choices."[23]

Another consideration that may be relevant to relative willingness to allow Type 1 and Type 2 errors is related to the costs to those *subjects* who go "uncompensated" due to Type 2 errors. If subjects who typically go uncompensated due to Type 2 errors are generally left very badly-off, and we believe that these errors occur very frequently, we may have reason to revise our standards of application. It is important to note that the magnitude of these costs will depend on other features of the social system, such as whether it provides a system of social insurance that will cover the costs of treatment for them. And it seems plausible that the appropriateness of different standards of application may vary depending on changes in these background features. As noted above, in cases where Type 2 errors can be avoided only by substantially increasing the risk of costly Type 1 errors, we may have reason to instead offset the costs to uncompensated subjects through social insurance or some other scheme of cost spreading.[24]

In evaluating the relevant standards of application for assessing Claim D, then, we must establish the relative importance of the overall social cost of Type 1 and Type 2 errors. If it is believed that the cost of Type 1 errors to G1 is substantially less than the potential cost of Type 2 errors to G77, for example, we ought to strongly consider adopting standards of application that are far more tolerant of Type 1 than of Type 2 errors in assessing Claim D, and vice versa.

But what are the relative costs of Type 1 and Type 2 errors in the case of G1 and G77? Consider first the cost of a Type 1 error to respondents such as G1 (e.g., if Claim D is falsely found to be true). This cost will depend on how well-off G1 is, how badly-off the claimants (e.g., the deprived parties in G77) are, and how much it will cost for G1 to alleviate their deprivations.[25] These costs may be monetary, involving the transfer of resources, but they might also involve the extension of special privileges and rights to G77—such as tariff-free access to G1's markets—or perhaps G1's efforts to increase the quantity of funds available to G77 at lower rates of interest.[26]

But what other costs might G1 bear? Claim D implies nothing about *legal* sanctions for G1, nor need it imply anything regarding G1's *blameworthiness* for adopting policy P. Claim D is relevant only for the purpose of determining who ought (morally) to bear the burden of the cost of addressing deprivations in G77, and whether different institutional reforms that effectively remedy them would place morally objectionable burdens on G1. We can judge G1 to have responsibilities to alleviate deprivations in G77 on the basis of the principle of contribution regardless of how well meaning and generally unobjectionable G1's reasons for adopting policy P, provided that their failing to take precautions not to unduly expose G77's citizens to hazardous risk was causally relevant to their deprivation. The costs of Type 1 errors to G1, while certainly not negligible, need not necessarily be terribly severe.

But what of the costs of Type 2 errors to the subjects that might wrongfully go uncompensated—in this case, the deprived parties in G77? Since, by hypothesis, G77 is a poor country, those who suffer from acute deprivations within its territorial domain will—due to resource and other constraints—likely remain very badly off (indeed, in life-threatening situations) if they go uncompensated. This, of course, depends on the assumption that the world that G1 and G77 inhabit does not possess *formal* mechanisms (such as a global system of social insurance), or informal arrangements (such as a generally known and complied with norm of providing assistance to the acutely deprived) that reliably meet the costs of addressing acute deprivations within G77.

Given the relative costs to G1 and G77 of Type 1 and Type 2 errors, I conclude that there is a strong prima facie case for specifying standards of application for applying the principle of contribution *that expresses a willingness to err in favor of the acutely deprived subjects*, whether they are the party alleging that they have been harmed, or the party against which such claims have been made. I shall call this norm the "*vulnerability presumption principle.*" While implausible as principle for specifying standards of application in a criminal (and most likely in most civil) legal contexts, or as a principle for assessing ethical responsibilities more generally, the vulnerability presumption principle seems clearly superior to stringent standards of proof and evidence with respect to the determination of ethical responsibilities to address acute deprivations.

The Vulnerability Presumption Principle: Three Objections

I anticipate that the vulnerability presumption principle will be subject to sharp criticism. And although I cannot here provide an exhaustive defense of this principle, or fully work out how it might inform our deliberations about practical dilemmas in the real world, it is worth briefly discussing three deep objections to the line of argument that I have presented in this section.

The first objection is that the plausibility of my assertions regarding the potential costs of Type 1 and Type 2 errors to G1 and G77 (and thus about the relevant standards for assessing Claim D) depend on artificially restricting attention to costs of these types of errors to G1 and G77 *in this particular case*. An honest accounting will focus on the overall long-term social costs of standards of application that engender different prevalence rates and distributions of these types of errors.[27] And such an accounting may well find that the costs to G1 and other well-off agents will be quite substantial, since the G77's of the world will constantly put forth to the effect that that they have contributed to deprivations within their territories. Indeed, this may have the perverse effect that badly-off countries disown their *own* responsibilities for these deprivations through wild assertions regarding the contributions of outsiders. It may be, for example, that countries will blame their debt crises on Policy P even when their own poorly conceived domestic policies are mostly to blame.

This objection articulates a valid concern, but it does not seem to me decisive because it downplays the ongoing costs of more stringent standards of application.

Maintaining very stringent standards of proof and constraints on evidence with respect to contribution will disadvantage not only G77 with respect to Claim D, but will also tend to systematically disadvantage *all* badly-off populations who have or may have been adversely affected by the conduct of powerful governments and other actors.[28] Indeed, even if less stringent standards of application lead to a rapid increase in claims regarding the contribution of powerful countries to the deprivations within the territories of the weak countries, this may have the desirable consequence that powerful countries will find it in their interest to promote the development of shared formal institutions or informal norms that prevent and reliably respond to acute deprivations, and allocate the burdens of alleviating them more equitably.[29] In the case of Policy P, for example, new issues of Special Drawing Rights, which function in part as a hard currency line of credit available to all member countries of the International Monetary Fund, or the development of a global economic security council whose role is to prevent and alleviate acute deprivations, would both reduce the incentives for weaker countries to advance claims against more powerful countries and diminish the plausibility of such claims.[30]

The second objection is that my discussion has treated ethical reflection on responsibilities for acute deprivations as if it were, like criminal or tort law, a practice with well-defined goals that can be served more or less well by specifying its standards of application in different ways. But ethical reflection, it may be argued, is not like these other practices in the relevant sense. The argument would be that ethical reflection provides a standpoint from which to evaluate these practices, but the practice of ethical reflection should not *itself* be subject to this kind of evaluation.

This objection also has some merit, since the "purpose" of the practice of ethical reflection and argument cannot be characterized in terms of a well-defined set of goals in the way that law might be. Yet, like law, ethics is concerned not only to evaluate, but also to provide conduct-guiding structures of values and norms that shape the behavior of individual and collective agents. And like law, ethical theories generally specify aims and objectives that their adherents ought to promote. It would seem odd indeed if these theories are exempt from being evaluated in terms of their success in promoting the aims and objectives that—by their own lights—matter.[31] If an ethical theory includes a conception of responsibility for alleviating acute deprivations, and this conception gives substantial weight to the principle of contribution, it is implausible that adherents of the theory would be unconcerned by the fact that they are employing standards of application that undermine one of its central aims—to encourage agents to take precautions to avoid contributing to acute deprivations, and to try to alleviate them when they have done so.

The third objection is that I have been tacitly appealing to some further principle that gives more weight to the less well-off and discounts the costs to the well-off in ranking the desirability of different outcomes. I have, it might thus be argued, emphasized the importance of what one might call the "security interests" of the badly-off at the expense of the "liberty interests" of the well-off, assuming that we are justified in, to borrow Judith Thomson's language, disrupting the plans of the well-off when doing so would enhance the security of the badly-off. However, this is not the case. If an ethical theory incorporates the contribution principle, it presumably does so because it holds that conduct that contributes to acute deprivations is seriously wrong—so wrong, in fact, that considerations, including cost to oneself and observance of one's special obligations, which are normally held to have great moral weight can be overridden.

The vulnerability presumption principle expresses the strong disvalue that any such theory attaches to contributing to acute deprivations. Moreover, an ethical theory that gives precedence to the contribution principle already gives substantial weight to peoples' so-called "liberty interests." Unlike what David Miller has called the "capacity" principle, which requires that those who can alleviate acute deprivations most easily must do so regardless of their connection to them, the principle of contribution sharply limits the conditions under which those who suffer hardships can disrupt others' plans and shift the costs of alleviating their deprivations onto them.

Conclusion

When the Commission on Macroeconomics and Health recently estimated the cost of developing a comprehensive program to reduce the ill health of the global poor, and called upon wealthy nations to contribute $22 billion toward the $57 billion additional annual cost of scaling up its program in 2007—suggesting that "lack of donor funds should not be the factor that limits the capacity to provide health services to the world's poorest people"—few rallied to its cause.[32] It may be that this kind of neglect can be explained by the fact that people often act for self-interested reasons, and tend, often unconsciously, to interpret and apply their moral values in ways that will not threaten their own interests. Their behavior can also be partly explained in terms of what Amartya Sen has called "correspondence irrationality," in that people often act "without thinking," reason lazily about what to do, and are prone to weakness of will.[33] Widespread commitment to the contribution principle, it may be argued, also helps to explain why few well-off agents feel themselves responsible for addressing acute deprivations.

Would a *conscientious* application of the contribution principle lead to the conclusion that these agents lacked such responsibilities? Many have thought so, because they assume the truth of the following conditional: If there is conclusive evidence that either well-off agents *have not* contributed to acute deprivations, or that *conclusive* evidence that they *have* contributed to acute deprivation is lacking, then the contribution principle entails that these agents lack weighty moral reasons to address such deprivations. Some have argued vigorously that, whether or not the conditional is true, the antecedent is false since there *is* conclusive evidence that well-off agents have contributed to acute deprivation—whether through unfair trade practices, by shaping the policies of international financial institutions, due to enthusiastic participation in the global arms trade, or via other means.[34]

This essay has shown, however, that the assumption that agents bear little responsibility with respect to acute deprivations unless there is fairly conclusive evidence suggesting otherwise cannot be sustained. To think otherwise, I have argued, requires a commitment to standards of application that, while not implausible in some legal contexts, cannot be defended in the context of determining ethical responsibilities for addressing acute deprivations. It is true that the contribution principle would entail that well-off agents would lack moral reasons to address acute deprivations *if* there were conclusive evidence that they did not contribute to such deprivations; but, given the political and economic structure of our world, and the limits on our knowledge, such conclusive evidence does not seem at all likely to be available. Thus many well-off agents who are committed to the contribution principle have reason to significantly revise their behavior.

Notes

1. I am indebted to Thomas Pogge and Sanjay Reddy for conversations that helped me to develop the ideas presented in this chapter, and to Bashar Haydar, Andrew Kuper, Jedediah Purdy, Lydia Tomitova, Katia Vogt, and Jeremy Waldron for their very helpful criticisms of an earlier version of it.

2. Any plausible answer to Question 2 will also require an account of *default principles* that specify whom, if anyone, bears responsibilities in cases where those whose responsibilities to act are greatest fail to do so.

3. For an argument that this is the case with respect to the debate concerning access to antiretroviral medicines for the treatment of HIV/AIDS, see Christian Barry and Kate Raworth, "Access to Medicines and the Rhetoric of Responsibility," *Ethics & International Affairs*, Vol. 16, No. 2 (2002): 57–70.

4. Responsibilities with respect to acute deprivation to which one contributes are often held to have three features. First, they are thought to be especially *weighty*: there are strong moral reasons to refrain from contributing to others' acute deprivation regardless of any further connections that we may have to them, that we cannot so easily appeal to considerations of *cost* to ourselves to excuse our failure to act on them. (Compare with Shelly Kagan: "Although ordinary morality insists on the existence of options to allow harm, it rejects options to do harm. Only the minimalist believes in the existence of options to do harm for the sake of promoting one's own interests." Shelly Kagan, "Précis of the Limits of Morality," *Philosophy and Phenomenological Research*, vol. 51 No. 4 (1991), pp. 897–901.) Second, they bind a *broad range of agents*: these reasons are applicable not only to individual persons, but also to collective agents such as corporations and states which are otherwise not held responsible for preventing acute deprivation. Third, they are *broad* in scope: they apply to these individual and collective agents with respect not only to what they *directly* do to others, but also to what they indirectly do to others through creating and maintaining shared social rules and practices that can themselves contribute to acute deprivation.

5. For an exemplary discussion, see Jonathan Bennett, *The Act Itself* (New York: Oxford University Press).

6. This type of interpretation is developed by Phillipa Foot, "Killing and Letting Die" in Bonnie Steinbock and Alistair Norcross, *Killing and Letting Die* (New York: Fordham University Press, 1994), pp. 280–9, Frances Kamm, "Killing and Letting Die: Methodological and Substantive Issues," *Pacific Philosophical Quarterly*, Vol. 64 (1983): 297–312, and Jeff McMahan, "Killing, Letting Die and Withdrawing Aid," *Ethics*, Vol. 103, No. 2 (January 1993): 250–79.

7. See Richard. W. Wright, "Causation in Tort Law, Causation in Tort Law," *California Law Review*, Vol. 73 (1985): 1737–1828, and Tony Honoré, *Responsibility and Fault* (Oxford: Hart Publishing, 1999), pp. 94–120, for discussion of the applications of this conception of causation in legal contexts.

8. This interpretation has a clear evaluative component, since assessments of whether the alternative to B's deprivation is that he would have avoided the deprivation through A's aid will depend on prior moral judgments regarding A's and B's entitlements. See Jeff McMahan, "A Challenge to CommonSense Morality," *Ethics* 108, no. 2 (1998): 394-418, for discussion.

9. The mechanisms by which Claim D could be true may be complex. It might be, for example, that the effect of the debt crisis on G77 was further mediated by other policies undertaken by G1 (such as demanding the repayment of loans that they and other agents had extended to G77), or also by institutional arrangements—such as rules governing the management of sovereign debt, that G1 has played some role in shaping.

10. Even when we are confident that some agent has contributed to acute deprivation, we may be uncertain about *how much* they have contributed. I cannot address this important issue here.

11. See Carl F. Cranor, "Some moral issues in risk assessment," *Ethics*, Vol. 101, No. 1 (1990): 123–43; and *Regulating Toxic Substances: A Philosophy of Science and the Law* (New York:

Oxford University Press, 1993) for interesting discussions of the standards relevant for determining the toxicity of substances in basic scientific research and governmental regulation.

12. Robert Nozick, *The Nature of Rationality* (Princeton, NJ: Princeton University Press, 1992), p. 85. See also the discussion of the tradeoff between risk of error and informational value in Isaac Levi, *The Enterprise of Knowledge* (Cambridge, MA: MIT Press, 1980), ch. 2.

13. *Op. cit.*, p. 85.

14. For discussion, see Ronald Dworkin, "Justice for Clarence Thomas," *New York Review of Books*, Vol. 38, No. 18 (November 7, 1991).

15. For formal description of types of errors, see R.S. Witte and J.S. Witte, *Statistics* (6th ed.) (Fort Worth: Harcourt, Brace, 2001).

16. Given the diverse goals that criminal and tort law have been taken to serve, the reasons for the differences in evidential standards are quite complex and have been the subject of substantial disagreement among legal theorists. For more thorough discussions of these themes, see Joel Feinberg, "The Expressive Function of Punishment," in *Doing and Deserving: Essays in the Theory of Responsibility* (Princeton, NJ: Princeton University Press, 1970), pp. 95–118; Arthur Ripstein, *Equality, Responsibility, and the Law* (New York: Cambridge University Press, 1999); and Tony Honoré, *Responsibility and Fault*.

17. Joel Feinberg argues that criminal punishment is expressive in two ways, it allows society to distance itself from the wrongful conduct, and it also allows it to claim to be vindicating the claim of law.

18. Bernard Williams, "What Has Philosophy to Learn from Tort Law," in David G. Owen, ed. *The Philosophical Foundations of Tort Law* (Oxford: Clarendon, 1995), p. 391. On tort law as a system for fair allocation of cost, see also Jules L. Coleman and Arthur Ripstein, "Mischief and Misfortune", *McGill Law Journal*, Vol. 91 (1995): 91–141.

19. The fact that those who live in societies that maintain a system of tort law can often insure at reasonable cost against the risks that they may impose on others may further lessen the potential personal costs of type 1 errors.

20. This idea is interestingly explored by McCarthy's discussion of the case of "curable cancer." See David McCarthy, "Liability and Risk," *Philosophy and Public Affairs*, Vol. 25, No. 3 (Summer, 1996): 238–62.

21. I have borrowed these terms for different types of uncertainty from Heidi Li Feldman, who provides a helpful discussion of these issues as they arise in the context of products liability. Feldman proposes that the burden of proof should be shifted or plaintiffs should receive proportionate 50 percent recovery if they can demonstrate "strong" uncertainty regarding causation. See Heidi Li Feldman, "Science and Uncertainty in Mass Exposure Litigation," *Texas Law Review*, Vol. 74, No. 1 (1995): 1–48.

22. See, for example, Carl Cranor (1991) *op cit.* and the essays in *Acceptable Evidence: Science and Values in Risk Management*, Deborah Mayo and Rachelle D. Hollander, eds. (New York: Oxford University Press, 1991). These proposed reforms are quite controversial. See, for example, Mark Geistfeld, "Scientific Uncertainty and Causation in Tort Law, *Vanderbilt Law Review*, Vol. 54, No. 2 (2001): 1011–37. Indeed, since the United States Supreme Court's decision in *Daubert v. Merrell Dow Pharmaceuticals*, courts have increasingly relied on epidemiological evidence in establishing causation. Similar debates concerning the admissibility of different types of evidence advanced in support of causal claims have taken place in debates concerning the permissibility of affirmative action. See Michelle Adams, "Causation and Responsibility in Tort and Affirmative Action," *Texas Law Review*, Vol. 79 (2001) and the references cited therein for discussion.

23. Ripstein, *Equality, Responsibility, and the Law*, p. 21.

24. Indeed, it may be, as Robert Goodin has argued, that when causes are complex and intertwined, it typically costs more than it is worth to try to disentangle them to establish personal responsibility, and that in such contexts, a no-fault system is superior to a fault system for allocating costs. See Robert E. Goodin, *Political Theory & Public Policy* (Princeton, NJ: Princeton University Press, 1982), especially ch. 8.

25. Other considerations that may also be relevant concern whether there are other parties on whom G77 can make similarly justified claims, and whether G77's own negligence played a substantial role in the deprivation of its citizens.

26. For a valuable discussion of measures to offset the deleterious effects of monetary decisions in powerful countries, and their relevance to global distributive justice, see Sanjay G. Reddy,

"Developing Just Monetary Arrangements," *Ethics & International Affairs*, Vol. 17, No. 1 (2003): 81–94. For an account of the effects of the United States' monetary policies in the 1970s, see Harold James, *International Monetary Cooperation Since Bretton Woods* (Washington, D.C.: International Monetary Fund, 1996).

27. This objection was put to me by Jedediah Purdy and Sanjay Reddy.

28. It is noteworthy that developing countries lack mechanisms by which they can formally complain and seek compensation that is caused by the grave negligence of international financial institutions and donor countries. This contrasts with the rights of individuals in the Anglo-Saxon legal system, in which they can even sue financial consultants for negligent advice. Kunibert Raffer has recently advocated an international arbitration panel to assess such claims. See his "Some Proposals to Adapt International Institutions to Developmental Needs" in *The Role of International Institutions in Globalisation: The Challenges for Reform*, J. Chen, ed. (Northampton: Edward Elgar, 2003), pp. 81–101.

29. As discussed above, the existence of reliable mechanisms for addressing acute deprivations reduces the cost of type 2 errors, thus weakening the case that standards of application should be relaxed.

30. For discussion of these reforms, see Reddy "Developing Just Monetary Arrangements"; George Soros, *George Soros on Globalization* (New York: Public Affairs, 2002) and "Commission on Global Governance," *Our Global Neighbourhood* (Oxford: Oxford University Press, 1995).

31. For discussion of this theme, see Derek Parfit, *Reasons and Persons* (Oxford: Oxford University Press, 1983) ch.1, and Thomas Pogge, "The Effects of Prevalent Moral Conceptions," *Social Research*, Vol. 57, No. 3 (Fall 1990).

32. WHO, Report of the Commission on Macroeconomics and Health Macroeconomics and Health: Investing in Health for Economic Development (Geneva: WHO, 2001), p. 4. See Gopal Sreenivasan, "International Justice and Health: A Proposal," *Ethics & International Affairs*, Vol. 16, No. 2 (2002): 81–89, for discussion. Other widely reported estimates of the cost of addressing acute deprivations include the so-called Zedillo High-Level Panel of 2001, which set the cost of the extra resources needed to achieve the Millennium Development Goals at US $65 billion per year. United Nations, "Report to the Secretary-General of the High-level Panel on Financing for Development: The Zedillo Report," New York, June 25, 2000. To get a sense of proportion regarding these expenditures, note that the total Overseas Development Assistance (ODA) currently provided by the high-income countries and multilateral organizations is now roughly US $50 billion a year.

33. Amartya Sen, "Uncertainty and Rationality," reprinted in *Rationality and Freedom* (Cambridge: Harvard University Press, 2002), especially pp. 22–3.

34. See, for example, Thomas Pogge, *World Poverty and Human Rights* (Oxford: Blackwell, 2002), Amartya Sen, "How to Judge Globalism," *American Prospect*, XIII no. 1 (2002), A2–A6, and Joseph Stiglitz, *Globalization and Its Discontents* (New York: Knopf, 2002).

PART III

Individual Responsibility for Poverty Relief

CHAPTER 8

Global Poverty Relief: More Than Charity[1]

ANDREW KUPER

The Politics of Global Poverty

Nothing is more politically important to think about, and act upon, than global poverty relief. Numbers can mask the human faces of poverty, but do bring out its scale: Today, any day, 30,000 children under the age of five will die from preventable illness and starvation. A further 163 million children who will survive this day are severely undernourished. Some 1.2 billion people will try to subsist on less than one dollar a day, while 2.4 billion will not have access to basic sanitation.[2]

It's reasonable to feel some despair. What can any one of us, the relatively rich, even begin to do to reduce this immense daily misery? How much would we have to sacrifice? Since the costs to ourselves may be significant, how much *ought* we to sacrifice? And as the terminology of a richer "we" and poorer "they" hides vast differences within groups, it helps to ask the more concrete and controlled question: Which of us must do what for whom?

In practice, the traditional "statist" answer to this last question has been brute and inadequate: "The state must look after some basic needs of its own citizens." International institutions are highly visible these days, but that should not deceive us into thinking things have changed all that much. Including support for bodies like the United Nations, the United States spends only .13 percent of its yearly resources on assisting poor and marginalized people in other countries. It is not alone. Almost every developed state lavishes over 99 percent of its gross national product (GNP) solely on "looking out for its own."[3] Since this parochialism of states is the dominant order of the day, we should hardly be surprised that few inroads have been made into relieving global poverty.

How can a better alternative world be achieved—politically, economically, militarily, socially? Some massive failures of development strategies in recent decades offer hard lessons about our limited grip on these vexing questions, and the difficulty of formulating feasible answers. Because these questions are vast and interlinked, and because the answers are matters of vision as well as prudence, the need for a systematic orientation of our practical thinking and action has never been greater.

This chapter evaluates one important attempt to provide such an orientation—that of the moral philosopher most widely known outside academia, Peter Singer. Singer's commitment to social activism is admirable and—rare amongst philosophers—he is a pleasure to read. But I argue that his overall approach to poverty relief—he labels it "The Singer Solution to World Poverty"—is irremediably lacking as a theoretical orientation for action. I show how Singer's approach neglects the ways in which the scale of societies and their complex interdependence in today's world significantly reshape what is practically feasible and morally required of us. After criticizing the "Singer Solution," I argue that a different theoretical orientation for development and politics is needed—a "political philosophy," not a dangerously individualist "practical ethics." I show that this theoretical orientation enables us to identify a very different range of actions and actors necessary to reduce mass poverty.

Both Singer's approach and the alternative approach that I develop here fall within a school of moral thought that can be labeled "cosmopolitan." Cosmopolitans broadly agree that the interests of all persons (Singer would say animals) must count equally in moral deliberation, and that geographical location and citizenship make no intrinsic difference to the rights and obligations of those individuals. In one sense, then, what follows is a debate between friends. But in another sense, the divide is more serious: Singer yokes cosmopolitanism (individual-centric morality as the basis of justice) to individualist social explanation and moral directives. Both of the latter are implausible routes to understanding the justice or injustice of structures of governance and society, and the rightness or wrongness of the actions of individuals operating within those structures. Worse, both routes, taken as bases for action, are likely to be perilous to the poor, hurting those whom cosmopolitans generally wish to help.

I attempt to rescue cosmopolitanism as a plausible and practical guide to social action by linking it to better forms of explanation and recommendation that are likely actually to help the poor. Hume may have been right, on the whole, that "truth springs from argument among friends";[4] but, with so much at stake, I must rather try to rescue others from the charmingly simple persuasions of my friend.

The Singer Solution to World Poverty

Singer is famous for his extremely demanding view about what we, the relatively rich, *ought* to do and sacrifice to help the poor. His article "Famine, Affluence and Morality," written in 1972, stated this view with the help of a resonant analogy: Singer asked readers to imagine that, on the way to giving a lecture, he walks past a shallow pond, and witnesses a child in danger of drowning.[5] He can easily wade in and rescue the child, but he may dirty or even ruin his clothes, and fail to make the lecture. Singer rightly points out that it would be morally monstrous to allow these minor considerations to count against taking action to save the child's life. Then Singer generalizes from this ethical case to the situation of relatively wealthy people, especially in developed countries, vis-à-vis people starving or dying of preventable diseases in developing countries. We do nothing or almost nothing, while thousands die. Yet it is seriously wrong to fail to give aid when the costs to oneself are not of "moral significance" or even of "comparable moral importance."

When we think about it, Singer points out, very few things are as morally important as saving life. On his account, this is demonstrated both by eliciting our intuitions (with thought experiments) and by utilitarian reasoning (moral action involves minimizing suffering and maximizing well-being). Either mode of reasoning makes most of our material acquisitions (say, another jacket) and new experiences (say, enjoying an opera or a concert) seem like luxuries of little or no moral significance. In a more recent article Singer concludes: "The formula is simple: whatever money you're spending on luxuries, not necessities, should be given away."[6] Who should give how much exactly? The average American household should give away any annual income over $30,000.[7] Singer acknowledges that widespread and deep altruism from such relatively rich people is profoundly unlikely. But he still insists that "we should at least know that we are failing to live a morally decent life"—above all because this knowledge is likely to motivate us to donate more than we do at present.[8] Singer is even willing to be sparing in his blame: Given the present "standard . . . of normal behavior" of American citizens, he "wouldn't go out of [his] way to chastise" those who donate only 10 percent of their income.[9]

So we know *who* ought to do *what*; but for *whom*? Whom should the rich select as recipients of this (obligatory) charity? Only two considerations count for Singer: the relative extent of poor people's need, and "the degree of certainty that . . . our assistance will get to the right person, and will really help that person."[10] Singer is clearly a cosmopolitan, emphatically rejecting shared membership in a nation or a state as grounds for choosing to give to one person rather than another. He insists that "in important respects, the tie of nationality is more like the tie of race than it is like the tie of family or friend."[11] His reasoning, in short, is that "human life would not be as good" without intimate ties, and any attempt to eradicate them would require abhorrent levels of coercion. National or patriotic ties, on the other hand, neither are necessary to the well-being of all of us nor are they intransigent. Thus these ties cannot be justified from "an impartial perspective."[12] Citizens and governments that accord priority to compatriots, while people in foreign lands are in far more urgent and desperate need, are committing a sin that comes close to discriminating on the basis of race.

We now have before us Singer's answer to our question, who must do what for whom? Three main points about his argument are vital:

1. It relies on (a) analogies between individual cases—actually, thought experiments—and more complex real-world situations and/or (b) on utilitarian positions about maximizing happiness and minimizing pain. These analogies and positions aim to reveal that there is no moral equivalence between our penchant for luxuries and the survival needs of poor people.
2. It denies that (a) shared citizenship and (b) distance per se make any difference to the nature and extent of our obligations to help others: "It makes no moral difference whether the person I help is a neighbor's child ten yards from me or a Bengali whose name I shall never know, ten thousand miles away."[13]
3. It results in a simple measure of sacrifice and a definite injunction to act: Donate a large portion of your income—(a) at least 10 percent, or (b) to really avoid wrongdoing, every cent not devoted to purchasing necessities. Singer even passes along the toll-free numbers of UNICEF (1-800-378-5437) and Oxfam (1-800-793-2687) so that "you, too, have the information you need to save a child's life."[14]

This is an emotive and appealing argument. But if Singer's exhortations make you want to act immediately in the ways he recommends, you *should not* do so. First, be wary, for he tells us something we so want to hear: that there is a simple way to appease our consciences, that there is a royal road to poverty relief. Sadly, as much as we wish it, this is not the case. By exploring a complex of mistakes in Singer's arguments, and by elucidating recent hard lessons from the theory and practice of development and politics, I now show that his approach is likely to seriously harm the poor. We must be careful not to make ourselves feel better in ways that damage the capabilities and well-being of the vulnerable. I show that a very different kind of approach to relieving mass poverty is called for. It is more analytically demanding (it resists any comforting illusion of a royal road), but it would in fact help the poor. Although Singer rightly endorses a morality that shows global concern, and rightly criticizes the parochialism of states, there are more coherent theoretical foundations for the effective practice of cosmopolitan development.

Why Charity Is Never Enough

Arguments from analogy may be rhetorically effective, but do not stand up even as initial forms of philosophical reasoning about how we ought to act at a distance and over time. They are acontextual. I will mention the kind of *moral* acontextualism that preoccupies Singer's leading critics, but only as a prelude to arguing that both Singer and his critics suffer from a more serious kind of *political* acontextualism.

Singer's critics also like using thought experiments: What if, every day, as Singer walks past the pond, fifty children were close to drowning? Every day, he takes his self-imposed obligation seriously, and spends the day rescuing them, abandoning his lectures. Princeton gets wind of this and does not share his ethical orientation. Now, it is one thing to expect someone to save a drowning child and give up one lecture, but it is quite another—if there are tens or thousands drowning (or starving, or ill) every day—to expect him to devote himself to being a lifeguard instead of a teacher. And since there is always so much misery and danger in the world, it seems that moral people will have to give up almost any job that doesn't directly or maximally involve saving lives. Yet there are many values other than survival: Can it really be morally required to give up vital sources of meaning such as the work we do, the social commitments we have, and the knowledge and excellences we pursue? Some of these life projects are so central to our existence that it is a sheer "overload of obligation" to expect people to give them up. As Bernard Williams famously argued, people should not be regarded as levers for utility or survival maximization[15]: We ought also to care about love, work, wisdom, art, truth, and much more that is relevant to our dignity and significance as beings. In short, Singer demands that we deal with poverty by impoverishing our human lives.

I don't intend to discuss these kinds of criticism much further. It is quite evident that we cannot achieve a plausible weighting of values if we use reasoning that removes from view, or underrepresents, all values other than survival. In his more recent writings—partly in light of this criticism—Singer wisely tempers his claims. He allows that we can justify spending more on our families and the necessities of their existence; all he asks is that we give away everything beyond that, or donate at least 10 percent of our income. So all we have to do is give up expensive shopping, eating, and traveling. Is this too much to ask?

Unlike Singer and his panoply of Williams-type critics, I just don't think this is the central question. We need to see our way through the debate between them, because it is couched in terms of an unhelpful binary opposition of "self-ish" against "self-less." The whole debate is too narcissistic in its preoccupation with conscience and sacrifice. As a consequence, the recommendations from both sides are the opposite of helpful.

Let's take as a pressing case the HIV/AIDS pandemic ravaging my own country of origin, South Africa, and the desire to help prevent ever-increasing infection. This example is less artificial than those Singer favors. Does his conception of the nature and extent of sacrifice make a difference or provide a plausible route to alleviating this misery?

I could take most of my money and give it to an AIDS organization. But the effect of my contribution would be dwarfed and perhaps overridden by President Mbeki's bizarre and injudicious remarks that HIV does not cause AIDS. So perhaps then I want to contribute to political accountability and economic reforms. But here I find that South Africa is locked into a complex global economic and political order dominated by strongly neoliberal presumptions. The problem is not simply that structural adjustment and Mbeki may eradicate any positive effect of my donation (doing no good). The problem is not even simply that—as in Zimbabwe—I may increase the power and hold of a kleptocratic elite (doing harm). Rather, given the structure of the world as it is, the most serious problem for Singer is that we may do better for South Africans by buying furniture and clothes from ethical manufacturers and manufacturers in developing countries than by donation. Adequate employment opportunities, for instance, are the leading determinant of people's ability to provide for themselves and their families.[16] After all, more than 50 percent of the world's manufacturing jobs are now located outside the OECD region—a twelvefold increase in four decades.[17] As for tourism, a labor-intensive industry, it generated $476 billion worldwide last year, but sub-Saharan Africa received only 2.5 percent of the total number of visitors.[18] Think what a tremendous difference it might make to poor people in the region if that number could be brought closer to 10 or 15 percent.

These kinds of considerations should make us extremely wary of Singer's perfunctory and categorical claims—that we should give up indulgences such as expensive clothes, restaurants, beach resorts, and house redecoration.[19] Indeed, in the South African case, manufacturing exports, tourism, and other service industries are among the few successful mechanisms that have kept people from falling further into grinding poverty. If many citizens of developed countries gave up their luxuries, three central planks of the country's development strategy would collapse. (For all that Mbeki is wrong to question the link between HIV and AIDS, he is not mistaken in pointing out that poverty renders people systematically more vulnerable to most diseases.) Among other disastrous consequences would be the crippling of governmental and NGO abilities to curb the rate of HIV/AIDS infection and help those suffering from the disease.

So, when Singer says that luxuries are "unnecessary," he is right that rich individuals can survive without them, but wrong to think that poor people can—that is, that their well-being is independent of the market in luxury goods. None of this means that industries and market practices cannot and should not be constrained and reoriented so that they are less rapacious and much more socially beneficial. On the contrary, it tells us that this kind of constraint and reorientation is a priority. But, to bring positive change about, we have to consider more carefully the direct and indirect, cumulative and complex effects of multiple human interactions.

This real case, then, reveals that we need to adopt a very different way of thinking. Where we do not share our everyday lives with people, we interact with them through a complex and differentiated web of political and economic relations. This has great relevance to the plausibility of Singer's argument. *Distance matters because scale matters*—in several ways. The scale of contemporary societies makes more people more vulnerable in more ways to my action and inaction, and to the interactions of multiple other individuals and collectives. That is, my impact at a distance brings more people within the ambit of my moral concern—at the very least, by making me aware of their existence, their capacities, and their need. So scale changes *whom* I ought to prioritize when addressing mass poverty: not so much the poor rather than my family, as large numbers of people enmeshed in social systems rather than isolated individuals. We cooperate and succeed (or fail) not merely through direct interaction, but through social rules and institutions. Effective poverty relief will thus require above all extensive cooperation with other agents—indeed it will require the creation or reform of agencies to reduce poverty. Thus we also need to reconsider *how* to alleviate the plight of the needy, with a particular eye on *who* (which agencies) it is that can best help.

Here's the rub: It is not enough to say that all persons have equal moral claims on us; we need to ask how best to organize ourselves politically and economically to meet those claims. Which combinations of rules and institutions of governance are most effective? What roles ought we to play as individuals in respect of the primary agents of aid and justice? Analogies to ethical decisions by an individual in a hermetically sealed case actually obscure all these problems and questions. For while it is true that we often act as individuals, the causal relevance or impact of our actions depends on the positions we occupy within complex social systems.

Philosophers may want me to put the point a little more technically: Singer conflates issues of practical reason—our obligations to the vulnerable—with issues of judgment—the obligations of the relatively rich to the poor in the particular case of the world in which we live. If we are to make judgments of how to act in this world, we should not confuse abstract with practical requirements. From the fact that we have an abstract obligation of aid or charity, it does not follow that we are practically obliged to donate to the poor. How we address poverty is a matter of judgment: understanding the relevant features of a social system or situation; considering which principles are relevant, whether they present competing demands in practice, and how other agents are likely to act; and finally, adjudicating on a contextual course of action. Nothing in the principle of aid or charity determines that the right action in any or all contexts is donation. All-too-quick recommendations are not just a leap from principle to action; they are symptomatic of an implicitly apolitical outlook that does not take the real demands of contextual judgment seriously.

Singer might say that analogies are merely designed to show that we do have an extensive obligation of charity. But this is no answer. His analogies and other arguments abstract from the causal dynamics of poverty and opportunity, and from the mediated and indirect nature of social relations at a global scale. This leads to a serious underestimation of the complexities of the remedies and the diversity of roles available to us. Indeed, it leads to a failure to see that, in making judgments about poverty relief, knowledge of institutions and awareness of roles must frame thinking about individuals. Even aggressively laissez-faire capitalists maintain that their actions are best for the poor. That is, what is at stake most of the time is not how much we should sacrifice, but whether and which uses of resources and what kinds of agencies make a positive difference, and how.

Political Judgment in Context

Lest I seem to sound like a neoliberal apologist, or a defeatist, it is helpful to see how much more informative is the theoretical orientation of Karl Marx. Marx understood that the first step in approaching political struggle and producing change is a structural analysis of the dynamic causes of impoverishment and immiseration. A theory that does not include a contextual and institutional analysis (in the broadest sense) is condemned to recommending brief symptomatic relief, or even damaging and counterproductive action. This is not a peculiarly Marxist point, and one does not have to sympathize with Marxists to think that telling the bourgeoisie to be more charitable as individual actors is unlikely to produce deep changes.

There is, ironically, a quasi-Calvinist strand to the individualist approach to development: an insistence that one can never do enough, never be as moral as one ought to be; and an emphasis on individual conscience rather than effective collective moral norms and political institutions. Yet the well-documented failure of relief efforts in recent decades is a powerful indicator that a structure-sensitive approach to development is indispensable to any wise, humane program or philosophy of right action. Consider, most starkly, the perpetuation and intensification of the Rwandan conflict and the human misery aggravated by aid agencies that sustained refugee camps. In spite of the camps becoming bases for militiamen and incubators for cholera, the prospect of international NGO aid encouraged people not to return to their homes even when it was safer to do so, thus intensifying and prolonging the conflict. Consider also the "food relief" of the 1970s that so damaged the situation of developing world farmers and their dependents. It is hardly an unfamiliar thought that things can always get worse: Consider Shakespeare's King Lear on the Heath, or Titus Andronicus. Development experts will be highly aware of countless more-recent examples that we can only wish were fictional.

Marx understood all too well the possibility of this kind of inversion of the invisible hand: The well-intentioned agent focusing on his or her lone action may well do more harm than good. In retrospect, Singer would acknowledge that his 1972 claim that "expert observers and supervisors . . . can direct our aid to a refugee in Bengal as we could get it to someone in our own block"[20] is grievously optimistic. Yet Singer remains fond of saying, in one way or another, "We must do something." Given the complex interdependence and economic and political perversities that characterize our shared world, the injunction "first do no harm" deserves at least equal consideration. Or, since we may sometimes have to do some harm to do significant good—courses of action are rarely cost-free—perhaps the most relevant injunction of all is "proceed carefully."

Of course, well-intentioned institutional reform can also do horrible things; moreover, donations can be used to reform the existing institutional order. But there is an important asymmetry here. International and other NGOs can never be the primary agents of justice and aid over the long run.[21] I shall merely list some of the major reasons: their funding is too capricious; their position is too dependent on the will or whim of others (often rulers) whose interests necessarily diverge from those of NGOs; NGOs are far from democratically elected or accountable; and they cannot produce large-scale growth and redistribution. We need NGOs, but we need good government and better markets even more. This is a direct result of our interest in sustainability: The primary agents of justice and aid must, especially in the long run, possess the ultimate power to act as such, and it must be possible to hold them properly accountable for those actions.

I am not proposing conservatism, inertia, or any other individual abro-gation of responsibility. What I am suggesting is that if Singer, the reader, and I are concerned to do something to assist the most marginalized and desperate in our world, we must not rest content with a purportedly "practical ethics" that is misleading and potentially dangerous because of its methodological individualism and limited scope—temporal and spatial. The last thing we can afford to be is ahistorical, acontextual, and non-institutional in our approach to global poverty relief. We need a polit-ical philosophy.

What Can Political Philosophy Contribute?

There are three broad components necessary for such a political philosophy: a *political economy* that charts the causal dynamics of the global economy and indicates the extent to which these could be controlled[22]; a *theory of jus-tice* that supplies a metric for evaluating goals and derives a set of principles with which to approach the problems of development; and a *political sociol-ogy* that encompasses and distinguishes the respective roles of individuals and various institutions in advancing these moral ends. In considering South African realities and Marxist thought, I have said something about the first; I now examine dimensions of the remaining two by contrasting John Rawls' approach to global justice with that of Singer.

Rawls' groundbreaking *A Theory of Justice* (1971) begins with the recog-nition that society is a scheme of cooperation for mutual advantage. The primary determinant of how well each of us fares is a set of basic social insti-tutions and laws that embody certain principles of justice. In *The Law of Peo-ples* (1999), Rawls extends this idea to international society.[23] He asks, in short, what basic laws and institutions form fair bases for cooperation between "peoples"—or what I have elsewhere called "thin states."[24] Each of these thin states is a national political structure, one that is non-aggressive toward others and takes members' interests into account—at least as mem-bers of ethnic, religious, and other groups. Rawls then develops a conception of justice appropriate to an ideal Society of Peoples or "thin state system."

When it comes to distributive issues related to poverty relief, Rawls argues that decent and liberal peoples do have an obligation to assist burdened societies (that is, developing countries unable to maintain a well-ordered regime). Nevertheless, as Singer points out, Rawls emphasizes that "a change of culture"—by which Rawls means the political system as well as ethos[25]—is most crucial to ensuring that the lives of individuals within such societies go better.

Singer is deeply critical of this approach. He writes that Rawls' "emphasis on the need for a change of culture leaves untouched the plight of individuals who are dying of starvation, malnutrition, or easily preventable diseases *right now*, in countries that presently lack the capacity to provide for the needs of all their citizens."[26]

In one respect, Singer and I are entirely in agreement: By placing states (along with the ethnic and religious groups they contain) at the center of his ideals of justification and justice, Rawls erroneously prioritizes group identities and national citizenship over individual moral claims.[27] Rawls also fails to take account of the extent to which people's life chances within a state, and the political cultures of that state, are affected by structures and events beyond its borders and control.[28] But Singer is asserting more than this. He thinks that it is unhelpful and irresponsible, while thousands are dying and institutions are slow to reform, to focus on an ideal theory of justice—a compelling conception of the basic institutions of a just society. This fierce accusation is surely mistaken. As I now want to show, ideal theory *serves as a valuable orienteering mechanism for action right now*. As such, along with a focus broadly on political culture, it better serves the poor than does the "Singer solution."

An ideal conception of justice is very far from the atrociously non-ideal conditions in developing countries; but, for judging potential courses of action, such a metric and set of principles is indispensable, for seven reasons:

1. By having the appropriate ideal ends in view, we can distinguish courses of action and institutional change that get us closer to or further from these aims; we are not condemned to a reactive development strategy. And where we are forced by adverse conditions to make difficult or tragic choices, we will not unwittingly make suboptimal compromises.[29]
2. By focusing on the social system, and on the ways in which others are vulnerable to us, we take account of the context and consequences of individual agency. Actors who consider their location and capacities relative to other role-players are more effective in coordinating collective action, and better at channeling their individual efforts to produce cumulative benefits.[30]

3. A structure-sensitive focus leads us to emphasize actions' indirect and long-term consequences for a social system's capacities to provide for the needy. This emphasis is the cornerstone of sustainable development rather than ad hoc interventions.

4. We will not uncritically support simple equality, since we can recognize that some inequalities can be justified—on the grounds that they improve the lot of the most needy or of all of us.[31] (Some attention to incentives, for example, is surely realistic.) Singer, on the other hand, has no criteria for distinguishing fair from unfair asymmetric distributions.

5. A systemic account constantly directs our attention to the need for an explanatory and predictive political economy, one that sets realistic limits to our ideal theories. This makes for relevant and realistic, not naïve, idealism.

6. A more complex causal story also reminds us to avoid a Singerian tendency to treat active individuals in developing countries almost wholly as recipients or moral patients.[32] Poor people are neither powerless nor ignorant in respect of important problems and opportunities for action; they need to be addressed as agents, capable of independent action as well as cooperative endeavor.

7. It becomes possible to identify the primary agents of justice and aid.[33] We ask: Which persons and institutions are capable of, and bear definite responsibility for, dealing with which individual and collective predicaments and opportunities? The "we" that Singer addresses are single and fairly undifferentiated wealthy individuals. The "we" that Rawls addresses are all individuals understood as organized into cooperative groups and societies. This is the beginning of a proper political sociology—even if it needs to be adjusted and developed far further and on the whole far less developed than that of Marx and Lenin.

Things do not all go Rawls' way. His sociology, for instance, is unjustifiably organicist and statist. He chooses to recognize the wrong collectives—ethnic, religious, and national groups—as the authoritative sources of value and valuation.[34] Those who think that the state, let alone the nation, is a guarantor of order and rights would do well to recognize that, from the time that a state system was effectively inaugurated in the Treaty of Westphalia of 1648, 150 million people have been killed by their own governments. Marxists can hardly feel comfortably superior either, given some famously misguided notions about the privileged agent of political struggle, the proletariat (or its vanguard). Further, Marx did not accept that piecemeal institutional reforms could make a lasting difference to the lives of the poor. In his view, reforms serve as ultimately insignificant attempts by the ruling class to stave off revolution. Thus Marx lacked a differentiated account of the many possible agents of justice. None of these many mistakes should lead us to deny the centrality of sociological insight.[35] On the contrary, it should encourage us to carefully and critically identify complexes of agencies that do and might operate successfully in the face of global transformations.

Of course, an important thinker cannot be blamed for all that he or she has not done. What we may legitimately demand, however, is that he or she attempts to recognize and specify the limits of his or her own account. When a philosopher is as public and exhortatory as Singer, this kind of circumspection is a pressing requirement, lest his philosophy be taken as an unmediated basis for (possibly disastrous) action. Note that it is not a good reply to say that the economy will continue regardless of my or Singer's individual action: Singer intends that his philosophy be a basis for ethical and political movements (for example, animal rights) that do change the way a large number of people live, produce, and consume. As Singer once wrote: "I think that if you try to cover up the cracks in the ethic, you're likely to get a major crash in the long run."[36]

No Royal Road to Poverty Relief

What might Singer reply along these several dimensions? In various places, he seems to have made four powerful and relevant points.[37] First, he accepts that not much weight should be placed on arguments from analogy, but maintains that these are useful devices for eliciting people's intuitions and focusing their thinking. Second, he is clear that, in considering how to act under conditions of complex interdependence, what is right for each individual to do "will depend on the story you believe," on which political-economic explanations and predictions you accept. Third, there is a very low probability of bringing about structural change, whereas there is a high probability of doing direct good through well-targeted donation. Fourth, he argues that there is no trade-off between private giving and governments' taking responsibility: If citizens give more, then governments will too, because governments tend to value what their citizens value; further, even if there is a trade-off, more good will be done by individual giving than harm done by the reduction in government aid; and, finally, the argument "governments bear primary responsibility" is generally an excuse for not giving.

I will consider these responses in turn. Singer's analogies do focus the mind, but they focus it on only one thing or the wrong thing. As a result, they are likely to mislead in at least equal measure, and their use is justified if and only if there is a responsible filling out and adjustment of the analysis and injunctions that seem to flow from such one-dimensional examples. "It will depend on the story you believe" does not meet these criteria. On this ultrawide specification, one seems compelled to acknowledge that the sincere extreme neoliberal agent is deeply moral in his or her character and conduct, since he or she believes that conspicuous consumption and massive differentials in income are the most effective ways to alleviate the plight of the poor. Singer's metric for improvement—without a related set of political principles—leaves us with few grounds on which to dispute this narrow neoliberal interpretation. This presents us with a further large problem: An agent with this view is by no means unusual; in fact, given the dominance of Chicago-style economics and neoliberal business attitudes, that agent is probably the norm. Marxist and Rawlsian theories locate agents' outlooks against a background system of justice or injustice, and so contain the resources to make a critical judgment of this pervasive kind of case (Marx's theory of "false consciousness" and ideology is as relevant and disputable as ever). Singer's arguments—whether analogical, utilitarian, or vaguely intentionalist—are bereft of the necessary critical purchase.

As for Singer's remaining points, it may be true that well-targeted donations do significant good and do not reduce the amount of governmental aid or the extent to which governments and individuals take responsibility for development. Moreover, making people "aware of the shameful record of the U.S." is certainly worthwhile.[38] But an articulated philosophy is not going to recommend suboptimal (if not counterproductive) courses of action, and so we need to know from Singer which kinds of production and consumption, investment and savings, we should abandon and which are necessary and most beneficial to global development and poverty relief. We have seen that the brute everything-in-excess-of-$30,000 donation rule should *not* apply.

Finally, let's address Singer's remaining point that governments' policies mirror the private policies of their citizens. Well, sometimes they do, but sometimes they are in direct contrast. In the United States, after all, the absence of taxation and state intervention to assist the needy at home is constantly justified on the basis that voluntary donation and other forms of charity are preferable. We need to know from Singer which courses of action, if widely adopted, will provoke which kinds of response from which agents. Should we become activists or active import consumers or both? Which campaigns for increased private aid will encourage more governmental foreign aid, and which will provoke a reactive decline? Should we lobby governments to place democratizing conditions on loans, or will that express and entrench existing power structures? These questions must be asked and answered responsibly. There is a great difference between making relatively wealthy people conscious of widespread suffering, on the one hand, and helping individuals and manifold massive institutions to become effective agents of justice and aid on the other.

Multiple questions do not constitute excuses for failing to make the world a better place. Rather, they are an acknowledgment that "moral experts"—to adopt a term from one of Singer's first articles—concerned with effective praxis have an obligation to provide a tougher, more nuanced and accurate picture of the temporal, spatial, and causal considerations that operate at great scale. Singer himself once wrote: "Caring about doing what is right is, of course, essential, but it is not enough, as the numerous historical examples of well-meaning but misguided men indicate."[39]

Conclusion: Cosmopolitan Paths to Poverty Relief

If my arguments are correct, the amount of donating and the extent of sacrifice are not the central issue; the real set of issues is how to redeploy resources and energy to roles and institutions within an extremely complex division of labor. Here are four limited suggestions:

Consumption. Instead of giving up quality clothes and holidays, we may find ourselves buying clothes from ethical manufacturers and taking holidays in places that badly need the tourist dollar. The South African government's new "Brand SA" initiative makes exactly this kind of argument to elicit trade and tourism.

Production. The granting of mining and drilling concessions to corporations could be tied to obligations to manage medical and social needs arising out of HIV/AIDS in the regions in which companies wish to operate. This would be akin to extending the well-established principles of ecotourism to the heart of the big business of resource extraction. The World Bank has begun to take this kind of approach.

Activism. Instead on relying solely on states to fund international organizations, or solely on individuals to fund NGOs, people can lobby for taxes on capital flows that give the UN and similar bodies a minimal independent revenue base. And they can take to the streets when a large corporation turns out to be violating labor standards or rights anywhere in the world.

Aid. One of the paradigmatic instances of effective intervention is the provision of microcredit and technology that enable access to wider opportunities for work, exchange, collective action, and the acquisition of skills. Some International Labour Organization and Grameen Bank projects are successful examples of this approach. Success in each case has been heavily dependent on systematic analyses as to the effects of incentives and of local norms and institutions, and on government help too.

Sensitive support of this kind can enable the poor to help themselves, and to engage in markets in ways that can also benefit themselves and others—including at times the relatively well-off. Yet innovation and transfer of such cost-lowering technology, for instance, require a social system that encourages some people to be entrepreneurs and engineers rather than lifeguards and development workers. Unfortunately, I doubt whether such entrepreneurs and engineers would play their roles if there were no selfish rewards (again, incentives can't responsibly be ignored).[40] But I am less skeptical of the possibility that they might become ethical consumers and investors, or be prepared to accept "social clauses" to profitable contracts.

Advocating a donation to Oxfam might conceivably in some contexts be the best means to noble ends, but this is by no means a foregone conclusion and universal remedy. Often, instead of telling individuals to dispense piecemeal charity—generally in the face of some new disequilibrium in the social system—we contribute better by creating, reforming, or participating in lifestyles and institutions that tend to generate resilient and ongoing inclusion in the benefits of cooperation.

The suggestions above derive from a cosmopolitan morality, insofar as our concern is with the capabilities, rights, and obligations of all individuals, not first with citizens of our own states while the distant poor come a distant second. But these suggestions are also political, in the good sense, taking account of the scale of societies and the complex interdependence of our shared world. Of course, none of these suggestions should lead us to rush headlong into action—microcredit, for instance, only works and is only appropriate in some situations.[41] We need to subject cosmopolitan proposals to detailed scrutiny, because the details of context and consequences matter for the poor.

I have repeatedly asked what difference philosophical theories make to the project of global poverty relief. It should by now be clear that an analysis from the broader perspective of political philosophy—as opposed to the simple individualist lens of a purportedly "practical ethics"—enables us to begin to distinguish peremptory directives from considered, politically aware, and sustainable strategies. But there remains the deep disjuncture between the perspective of a system of global justice and the sedimented power structures of the current global order. Part of what a clearly articulated theory reveals is that some individuals giving away income may do little to remedy this schism. While charity may produce improvements, it may at worst cause harm or at least the relevant resources might be better used in another way. No doubt there are good reasons to support organizations that produce sustainable changes in the background framework of social institutions. But a systemic and long-term approach involves far more than targeting donations better. It requires a nuanced awareness that politics is ineradicably about scale and connectedness, and thus the coordinated action of multiple interdependent roles. We must play those roles not with an eye to making us, the relatively wealthy or developed country citizens, feel better, but with a view to which complexes of agencies and actions will generate the most sustainable positive momentum. This means that the language of sacrifice must generally give way to a deeper and better language: the language of social and economic cooperation conditioned by the interests of the globally disadvantaged.

For all their deficiencies, both Rawls and Marx have in place large parts of a political philosophy. Singer does not. It is badly needed if he wishes to provide guidance for engendering lasting improvements to the lives of the needy. Singer and political philosophy might benefit significantly from his turning his mind and formidable pen to this range of difficult questions. As Wittgenstein put it, with characteristically wry acuity: "If someone tells me he has bought the outfit of a tightrope walker I am not impressed until I see what he has done with it."[42]

Notes

1. I am grateful to Onora O'Neill, Christian Barry, Michael Pitman, Simon Stacey, Zeev Emmerich, and Laurance and Jos Kuper for their astute comments on earlier drafts. Thomas Pogge kindly arranged the face-to-face debate that resulted in this critical exchange with Peter Singer, whom I thank for his candid responses.
2. These figures are from the United Nations *Human Development Report 2001* (New York and Oxford: Oxford University Press, 2001), pp. 9–13.
3. World Bank, *World Development Indicator 2000*, table 6.8 (provides definitions and measures of the limited extent of development assistance), available at www.worldbank.org/data/wdi2000/pdfs/tab6_8.pdf.
4. Cited in Dennis Leyden, *Thinking Critically in Economics*, second Web edition, at www.uncg.edu/eco/dpleyden/ctworkbook/hbook_1discussions(2e).htm.
5. Singer, "Famine, Affluence and Morality" (1972), reprinted in his *Writings on an Ethical Life* (New York: Ecco Press, 2000), pp. 105–17.
6. Singer, "The Singer Solution to World Poverty" (1999), reprinted in *Writings on an Ethical Life*, pp. 118–24, p. 123.
7. Ibid. The amount is in 1999 dollars.
8. Ibid., p. 124.
9. Ibid., p. 122.
10 Singer, "Outsiders: Our Obligations to Those Beyond Our Borders," (forthcoming), pp. 1–14, p. 3.
11. Ibid., p. 7.
12. Ibid.; see also "The Good Life," in *How Are We to Live?* (1993), reprinted in *Writings on an Ethical Life*, pp. 264–72, p. 267.
13. Singer, "Outsiders," p. 3.
14. Singer, "The Singer Solution to World Poverty," p. 120.
15. Bernard Williams, "Persons, Character and Morality," in his *Moral Luck* (Cambridge: Cambridge University Press, 1982), pp. 1–19.

16. Amartya Sen, *Development as Freedom* (New York: Knopf, 1999), pp. 111–45 and 160–88; for case studies, see Amartya Sen, Jean Drèze, and Athar Hussain, eds., *Hunger and Public Action* (Oxford: Clarendon Press, 1995).

17. John Keane, "Who's in Charge Here? The Need for a Rule of Law to Regulate the Emerging Global Civil Society," *The Times Literary Supplement*, May 18, 2001.

18. Audrey D'Angelo, "SA Loses Out While Global Tourism Expands," *The Saturday Star*, May 26, 2001.

19. Singer, "The Singer Solution to World Poverty," p. 123.

20. Singer, "Famine, Affluence, and Morality," p. 108.

21. Onora O'Neill, "Agents of Justice," *Metaphilosophy* 32 (January 2001): 180–95.

22. John Dunn has repeatedly stressed the centrality of these questions to political understanding. See his *The Cunning of Unreason* (London: HarperCollins, 2000).

23. John Rawls, *The Law of Peoples* (Cambridge, MA: Harvard University Press, 1999).

24. Kuper, "Rawlsian Global Justice: Beyond *The Law of Peoples* to a Cosmopolitan Law of Persons," *Political Theory* 28 (October 2000): pp. 640–74.

25. Rawls, *The Law of Peoples*, pp. 57–85.

26. Singer, "Outsiders," p. 12 (italics in original).

27. Kuper, "Global Justice," pp. 645–53.

28. See some of the excellent essays by Thomas Pogge collected in *World Poverty and Human Rights* (Cambridge: Polity Press, 2002).

29. Kuper, "Global Justice," pp. 658–67.

30. For an empirical study of this kind of informed efficacy, from the perspective of the media as agents, see Andrew Kuper and Jocelyn Kuper, "Serving a New Democracy: Must the Media 'Speak Softly'?" *The International Journal of Public Opinion Research* 13, no. 4 (2001): 355–76.

31. Rawls, *A Theory of Justice* (Oxford: Oxford University Press, 1972), pp. 60–108 and 258–84.

32. My thanks to Sanjay Reddy for insisting on this point.

33. O'Neill, "Agents of Justice." O'Neill has long argued, eloquently and persuasively, that we need to know the corresponding and specific agent of obligation if we are to have a clear conception of the content of rights and the plausibility of claiming them.

34. Many of the problems of our world are problems not simply of distribution among states but of a state-centric system. A nesting of political structures that attempts to concentrate power around unitary, territorially differentiated loci of control is inescapably prone to conflict and misallocation. Such a system not only divorces the location of issues from the location of capability to resolve issues, but also encourages action to amplify a friend–foe dichotomy in politics. On these topics, see Kuper, "Global Justice," and David Held, Anthony McGrew, David Goldblatt, and Jonathan Perraton, eds., *Global Transformations: Politics, Economics and Culture* (Cambridge: Polity Press, 1999).

35. See the discussion of this point in Quentin Skinner, Partha Dasgupta, Raymond Geuss, Andrew Kuper, Melissa Lane, Peter Laslett, and Onora O'Neill, "Political Philosophy: The View from Cambridge," *The Journal of Political Philosophy* 10, no. 1, Tenth Anniversary Issue (2002): 1–19.

36. Singer, "What's Wrong with Killing?" from *Practical Ethics* (1993), reprinted in *Writings on an Ethical Life*, pp. 125–45, p. 125.

37. Singer, "Famine, Affluence, and Morality," pp. 114–16; "Outsiders," pp. 3, 5–10; "The Singer Solution to World Poverty," pp. 122–24; and *Practical Ethics* (Cambridge: Cambridge University Press, 1993), pp. 218–63.

38. Singer, "Outsiders," p. 14.

39. Singer, "Moral Experts" (1972), reprinted in *Writings on an Ethical Life*, pp. 3–6, p. 4.

40. The need to take incentives seriously was one reason Rawls settled on "maximin" rather than "maximize" as a distributive principle.

41. The ILO Social Finance Unit itself insists on this point; see www.ilo.org/public/english/employment/finance.

42. Cited in Ray Monk, *Ludwig Wittgenstein: The Duty of Genius* (London: Vintage, 1991), p. 464.

CHAPTER 9

Poverty, Facts, and Political Philosophies: A Debate with Andrew Kuper[1]

PETER SINGER

Andrew Kuper begins his critique of my views on poverty by accepting the crux of my moral argument: The interests of all persons ought to count equally, and geographic location and citizenship make no intrinsic difference to the rights and obligations of individuals. Kuper also sets out some key facts about global poverty, for example, that 30,000 children die every day from preventable illness and starvation, while most people in developed nations have plenty of disposable income that they spend on luxuries and items that satisfy mere wants, not basic needs. Yet after summarizing an essay I wrote for the *New York Times Sunday Magazine* in which I argued that the average American family should donate a large portion of their income to organizations like UNICEF and Oxfam, Kuper writes: "But if Singer's exhortations make you want to act immediately in the ways he recommends, you should not do so." Why not? Because the approach I advocate "would seriously harm the poor."

These are strong words. It is startling to be told that a substantial transfer of resources from comfortably off American families to UNICEF or Oxfam would harm the poor. What about those 30,000 children dying from preventable illness and starvation? In its 2001 fund raising material, the U.S. Committee for UNICEF says that a donation of $17 will provide immunization "to protect a child for life against the six leading child-killing and maiming diseases: measles, polio, diphtheria, whooping cough, tetanus, and tuberculosis," while a donation of $25 will provide "over 400 packets of oral rehydration salts to help save the lives of children suffering from diarrheal dehydration." Perhaps these figures do not include administrative costs, or the costs of delivery, but even so, wouldn't more resources for immunization and oral rehydration salts benefit the poor, rather than harm them? What about the projects Oxfam funds, like providing equipment and expertise so that Ethiopian villagers can dig wells to get safe drinking water near their village? Since getting water in Ethiopia is women's work, this saves village women up to four hours a day. How can Kuper show that such projects "seriously harm the poor"?

Instead of discussing the work of the specific organizations I recommend, Kuper takes as his example the HIV/AIDS pandemic in South Africa, and asks whether it would help to give most of one's money to an AIDS organization. Here I have to say, first, that since I have never recommended doing that, what Kuper says about this example does nothing at all to support his claim that what I recommend would seriously harm the poor. Putting that aside, however, Kuper does not give any grounds for believing that giving most of one's money to an AIDS organization would "seriously harm the poor." All he says is that the effect of his contribution "would be dwarfed and perhaps overridden" by President Mbeki's views about AIDS. If something that helps the poor is dwarfed by a more powerful factor that harms the poor, that does not mean that it would have been better if the source of benefit had never existed. Some of the poor, at least, will still be better off. And while it is plausible that the benefits to South Africans brought about by the money Kuper could donate to an AIDS organization would be dwarfed by the failure of the Mbeki government to address the issue effectively, it is not so plausible to imagine that these benefits would be "overridden," that is, totally negated, by Mbeki's attitude. At least, Kuper would need to explain why this would be the case.

Instead of doing so, Kuper switches the example yet again, suggesting that we might want to contribute instead to "political accountability and economic reforms." Rather than examine this suggestion in detail, however, Kuper then asserts that in Zimbabwe, "I may increase the power and hold of a kleptocratic elite." The passage leaves it unclear whether it is my donation to an AIDS organization that may do this, or my contribution to an organization promoting political accountability and economic reforms. Presumably, however, there are ways of giving money to organizations working in Zimbabwe that do not increase the power and hold of the "kleptocratic elite." If this assumption can be shown to be incorrect, then I would agree with Kuper that we should not give to organizations working in Zimbabwe. But does Kuper imagine that his reference to the difficulties of working in a country ruled by a corrupt elite will be news to agencies like Oxfam? Does he think that, over the fifty years they have been working in Africa and elsewhere, Oxfam has never noticed this problem? Is he unaware of the extensive, detailed discussions these agencies have, both in-house and with outside experts, about how to overcome these difficulties, or, if they cannot be overcome, when to pull out of a country in which they are unable to help the people they are seeking to help?[2]

Bounding on over this complex terrain, Kuper hits on another idea: that "we may do better for South Africans by buying furniture and clothes from ethical manufacturers and manufacturers in developing countries than by donation." I agree that we should support "fair trade" schemes that buy goods produced in poor countries and ensure that the workers who produce them get as much as possible of the purchase price. Whether $100 spent in this way does more good than $100 given to Oxfam is a factual question. Oxfam, like other agencies, is itself involved in helping to set up fair trading schemes, both at the marketing end in rich nations, and in making microloans to workers so that they can buy the tools or raw materials needed to set themselves up in manufacturing goods to sell through such schemes. (Kuper later expresses support for such microcredit schemes, but minimizes the role played by agencies like Oxfam in supporting them.) There are, however, some very poor people who cannot be helped through fair trading. Rural villagers may live too far from transport to get their goods to international markets, or they may lack the raw materials to produce goods that anyone in rich nations wants to buy. It is therefore my belief that generally the donation will do more good than the purchase of goods of equivalent value. Should I be given evidence that this view is wrong, I will be happy to recommend that, instead of donating to aid agencies, Americans should spend a substantial part of their income on buying products from ethical manufacturers in developing countries, or on tourism to developing country resorts that have ethical labor practices. To do so would not require any change in my underlying ethical position. It would still be true to say that people in rich nations ought to be using a substantial amount of our income in the way that will most effectively help the world's poorest people.

This response is one I have made previously. Kuper refers to it as "It will depend on the story you believe."[3] He counters:

> On this ultrawide specification, one seems compelled to acknowl-
> edge that the sincere extreme neoliberal agent is deeply moral in his
> or her character and conduct, since he or she believes that conspicu-
> ous consumption and massive differentials in income are the most
> effective ways to alleviate the plight of the poor. Singer's metric for

improvement—without a related set of political principles—leaves us with few grounds on which to dispute this narrow neoliberal interpretation.

Here at last there is a fundamental disagreement between Kuper and me. Not over the neoliberal view of the most effective way to alleviate the plight of the poor—we agree that it is wrong—but over how we can know that it is wrong. I believe that it is wrong because I do not think that the evidence supports it. Of course, whether the evidence does support the neoliberal view is a large question, and not one that can be adequately addressed here. Nevertheless, it is on the evidence of the impact of neoliberal policies, unsupported by either government or private aid, on the plight of the world's poor, that I would rest my case against the neoliberal. Kuper, on the other hand, appears to seek some kind of political philosophy that would make the case against the neoliberal immune to refutation on the basis of evidence. If that is what he wants, I think it is misguided. To want some kind of guarantee, independently of how the facts may turn out, that the neoliberal is wrong, is to have a kind of faith that is independent of the evidence. Do we want to hold our political philosophies in the way that many theists hold their faith, persisting in believing in God independently of any evidence or sound argument for such a belief, and in the face of substantial evidence—the problem of evil—that there cannot be a God with the attributes they claim God has? There have, unfortunately, been adherents of political philosophies who have taken this attitude to their ideology. The results have not been encouraging. I prefer to remain open to believing in whatever the balance of evidence supports.

For completeness, I shall mention a few other things that Kuper says with an air of dissenting from my views, when there is really no disagreement between us. Thus, he says that we ought to help "large numbers of people enmeshed in social systems rather than isolated individuals." I have never said that our aid should be directed to isolated individuals. In a similar vein he writes: "Effective poverty relief will thus require above all extensive cooperation with other agents—indeed it will require the creation or reform of agencies to reduce poverty." That is exactly what Oxfam and UNICEF already do. He points out that sometimes aid has had unwanted negative consequences, and tells us that "perhaps the most relevant injunction of all is 'proceed carefully'"—again a recommendation that does not tell anyone in the field anything they did not already know. Drawing on Rawls, he says that some inequalities can be justified on the grounds that they improve the lot of the most needy, or of all of us. I have never denied that.

Given the paucity of argument Kuper offers to support his claim that giving to organizations like Oxfam "would seriously harm the poor," I find it troubling that he tells people that they "should not" donate substantial sums to these organizations. He must know that most people are only too happy to find an excuse for not giving money away. By providing them with just such an excuse, the major impact of his chapter, should it be widely read, would be to maintain the status quo in which most residents of developed nations do virtually nothing to relieve the extreme poverty in which 1.2 billion people live. Kuper, I am sure, does not want that. He would therefore do better to direct his criticisms to the real obstacles to relieving poverty, and not to those people who are already thinking much as he does about how the world needs to change.

REPLY TO SINGER

Andrew Kuper

The main thrust of my argument was that ad hoc suggestions of charity cannot replace a systematic and theoretically informed approach to poverty relief. Charitable donation sometimes helps—and sometimes harms—but is no general solution to global poverty, and can be positively dangerous when presented as such. We need to consider, and often choose, other routes to helping the poor—including ethical tourism and fair trade in luxury goods. We will not be able to invest in such feasible routes if we give away all our extra income, as Singer recommends. Sticking to donation above all, when a combination of other strategies is necessary, is highly likely to harm the poor.

Singer doesn't really engage my argument. Instead, he caricatures our "fundamental disagreement": Apparently, Singer rejects various policies because he takes into account the "facts"; whereas Kuper is the one seeking a "faith," a "political philosophy . . . immune to refutation on the basis of evidence." Anyone who has read my contribution must find this puzzling. The chapter explains at length which kinds of background theories help us to discern and responsibly consider the relevant facts. I show that Singer selects and uses facts uncritically precisely because he has no political economy, no political sociology, and no theory of justice. We are seriously misled if we do not draw adequately on the wisdom and tools of these bodies of knowledge. Some facts are just the tip of the iceberg.

Take any one of his examples: He tells us that a $17 donation from you or me will save the lives of children who suffer from the six leading child-killing and maiming diseases. In light of this "fact," Singer thinks it wrong to express concern about throwing money at the problem of poverty. But is donation really a general solution? If brute amounts of money were the issue, the World Bank or United Nations could stop the awful yearly deaths of 11 million children tomorrow. After all, $187 million is a small sum by World Bank and UN standards. The Bank and UN must be foolish or evil if saving children is so easy. Alas, the problem of poverty is just more complicated than that.

Children starve, suffer, and die because of political and economic arrangements. Above all, they starve, suffer, and die because of the unaccountability of people with the power to rule, exploit, and exclude the poor. This has been demonstrated time after time by luminaries of genuine poverty relief such as Amartya Sen, who happens to be the president of Oxfam. Sen insists that unless attention is paid to transforming these deep institutional factors, aid agencies will have only limited victories in a losing battle against the sources of poverty. It is for these reasons that I wrote, "We need NGOs, but we need good government and better markets even more. This is a direct result of our interest in sustainability."

One can't help asking why Singer knows better. I can find only one, very limited argument in his "Response" that might defend his contrary position:

> There are, however, some very poor people who cannot be helped through fair trading. Rural villagers may live too far from transport to get their goods to international markets, or they may lack the raw materials to produce goods that anyone in rich nations wants to buy. It is therefore my belief that generally the donation will do more good than the purchase of goods of equivalent value.

Singer doesn't ask why these rural people are excluded from the economy; he just takes it as a fact. Yet building roads and transport networks is a paradigmatically political decision. And when a government decides to assist some producers but not others, it is strongly influenced by the relative political power and economic clout of those groups. So "fair trading" isn't just about existing producers, it also requires a concerted push to level the playing field and include all in the game. NGOs like Oxfam have an important role, but they lack the ongoing capacity to build roads, generate large-scale growth, and regulate markets—and they suffer intrinsic problems of accountability. We can't just "leave it to Oxfam." So we need institutional reform above all: through activism, through consumption and production decisions, and yes, sometimes through donation to NGOs. Which of these strategies is most effective in various contexts is not determined merely by noble intentions or high emotion. It is determined by careful analysis—underpinned by rich and responsible political theories—of what actually works.

From this perspective, we can immediately see the basic logical flaw in Singer's argument. He claims, "X may be better than Y *depending* on Z factors (donation X may be better than fair trade Y depending upon a lack of transport, and so forth)," but then immediately concludes "X is therefore *generally* better than Y." He has said almost nothing about these factors and their underlying causes. Are the factors prevalent, persistent, and the main sources of poverty in most contexts? Why, for instance, does Singer assume that charity is generally best for those masses of the urban poor who are part (often an exploited part) of the world economy? Again, I am not against charity in all instances. But to answer these questions, we need not brute assertion of facts, nor vain hopes—reiterated by Singer in his "Response"—that no counterevidence will be presented. We need deeper theories that promote thorough empirical analysis, leading to strategies that deal in complexity rather than denial.

Finally, Singer asks why I am directing criticism at him, since we both want change. The answer is that his individualist language of selfishness versus sacrifice, and his rigid refusal to seriously explore alternatives other than charity, weaken our realistic case for reform. It would be far better if he focused on how to create political and economic institutions that include the poor in the ongoing benefits of social cooperation. Singer is an eloquent and influential advocate. I will not give up hope of provoking him to think more about sustainable poverty relief, about how we can move reliably from high principle to *effective* action.

Reply To Kuper

Peter Singer

The one central point in all my writing on this topic, from "Famine, Affluence and Morality" onward, has been that the failure of people in the rich nations to make any significant sacrifices in order to assist people who are dying from poverty-related causes is ethically indefensible. It is not simply the absence of charity, let alone of moral saintliness: It is wrong, and one cannot claim to be a morally decent person unless one is doing far more than the typical comfortably off person does.

Nothing Kuper has said, either in his original chapter or his reply to my response, contradicts this central claim. His arguments go to the details of how best we can assist people in desperate poverty. Perhaps instead of giving money to Oxfam, he suggests, we should buy goods from suppliers who ensure a fair return to laborers in developing countries. Perhaps we should stop going to Florida and Paris, and instead go on environmentally sustainable and non-exploitative trips to developing countries. Perhaps we should support movements against corruption, or for better terms of trade for developing countries. I'd be very happy if people would do any or all of these things, and if they have nothing left over to give to Oxfam, that wouldn't trouble me either. I don't claim to have any expertise in assessing whether these options are better or worse than giving to Oxfam. If someone can convincingly show me that one of them is clearly better than giving to Oxfam, then that's what I'll do in future.

Now Kuper writes:

> I show that Singer selects and uses facts uncritically precisely because he has no political economy, no political sociology, and no theory of justice. We are seriously misled if we do not draw adequately on the wisdom and tools of these bodies of knowledge.

I'm not sure why Kuper says that I have no theory of justice. It's no great secret that I'm a preference utilitarian, and so he could have inferred that I believe that goods ought to be distributed so as to maximize the satisfaction of preferences in the long run. But in writing about the obligation to assist the world's poorest people, I want to reach people who are not utilitarians, so I don't rely on utilitarian premises for that argument. I make a simple argument that challenges people to justify spending money on luxuries when that money could be used to save lives. Since there is no consensus about which is the right theory of justice, it still seems a better strategy than relying on one particular theory.

As for political economy and political sociology, it should be obvious why the central claim I sketched above doesn't require these, beyond the grounds for believing that there is *something* we can do to help people in extreme poverty. But in any case, I'm skeptical about the extent to which these fields offer a relevant "body of knowledge." Kuper writes: "One does not have to sympathize with Marxists to think that telling the bourgeoisie to be more charitable as individual actors is unlikely to produce deep changes." But what does Marx tell us about how to produce "deep changes"? Join with the proletariat in the class struggle, and the coming proletarian revolution will bring about a better world. No "body of knowledge" there, just a prediction that has proved sadly in error.

Giving to Oxfam is doing something that helps relieve desperate poverty. Maybe it won't change the structure of things. But until I'm shown how to do that, I'll settle for making some people better off. If giving more money to Oxfam were liable to "seriously harm the poor," as Kuper suggested in his first critique, isn't it odd that Amartya Sen, who Kuper now describes as one of the "luminaries of genuine poverty relief," should have accepted the position of president of Oxfam—a position that presumably commits him to doing exactly what I have sought to do in my writing, namely, persuading more people to donate more money to Oxfam?

When we can't make deep structural changes, it is still better to help some people than to help none. When Oskar Schindler protected Jews who would otherwise have been murdered, he had no impact on the structure of the Nazi genocide, but he did what he could, and he was right to do so. One can only wish that more Germans had done the same. Fortunately, without risking our lives, we have more options than Schindler. We should do our best to find out what will produce the best outcome, whether it is giving money, buying fair trade products, voting, joining an organization, or all of those things. Then we should do it.

Notes

1. I am grateful to Paula Casal for helpful comments on a draft of this response.
2. For an example of Oxfam's politically aware thinking that is already seventeen years old, see Diana Melrose, *Nicaragua: The Threat of a Good Example?* (Oxford: Oxfam, 1985).
3. See, for example, my response to the claim that giving aid would only worsen the population crisis and lead to a greater disaster in the future, in Singer, *Practical Ethics*, 2nd ed. (Cambridge: Cambridge University Press, 1993), pp. 235–41. Fortunately the factual claims on which that objection was based have proven erroneous.

PART **IV**

Accountability of Actors in the Global Economy

CHAPTER 10

Globalization, Corporate Practice, and Cosmopolitan Social Standards[1]

DAVID HELD

The struggle over the accountability of the global economic order has become increasingly intense. Violence in Seattle, Prague, Genoa, and elsewhere has marked a new level of conflict about globalization, democracy, and social justice. The issues that have been raised are clearly fundamental, concerned as they are with the nature of free markets, the relation between corporate and public agendas, and with the type and scope of political intervention in economic life. These matters are complex and extremely challenging, although they are not new to political debate and political theory. What is new is the way the issues are framed, disseminated, and fought over—in transnational and global contexts.

According to neo-liberal doctrines dominant since the late 1970s, questions about distributive justice and corporate roles can be answered only with reference to the broadly unhindered activities of individuals, interacting and coordinating their activities in the market place. Socially or politically imposed restrictions on the market system are coercive and, accordingly, unjust. The "framework for utopia" is the space for maximum markets and minimum states (Nozick, 1974).

For many social thinkers, who emphasize the importance of membership in and belonging to particular communities, this is a wholly untenable position (Walzer, 1983; Miller, 1988; MacIntyre, 1981, 1988). For markets, like other social goods, depend on trust and cooperative relations tied to public cultures and the provision of public goods, such as education, training, and a stable social order. What matters most for these social thinkers is the preservation and nurturing of the social standards inherent in community and locality. Corporations should not take their social cues from wide-ranging, unregulated markets, but from the traditions, cultures, and linguistic communities in which they find themselves.

In this chapter, I want to suggest another view—a view, I believe, more appropriate to our increasingly regional and global order. I will do this by developing an argument in five parts, ranging from an initial section on globalization to a final part on how markets and business activities can be "reframed." My position, in brief, will be that economic affairs and corporate practice are better served in the long-run by grasping a number of cosmopolitan social standards that are emerging in the contemporary world, and that create the possibility of a new framework of economic action and regulation. I take "social standards" here to mean, in the first instance, a set of universal requirements that all actors, economic and political, must uphold and sustain; and I take "cosmopolitanism" to denote, again in the first instance, those standards that can, in principle, apply to each person, each individual, who is equally worthy of concern and respect. The nature and scope of these standards needs to be clarified and developed in order to create the basis for greater global economic accountability and social justice.

Globalization

Globalization has become the "big idea" of our times, even though it is frequently employed in such a way that lacks precise definition. Moreover, it is so often used in political debate that it is in danger of becoming devoid of analytical value. Nonetheless, if the term is properly formulated, it does capture important elements of change in the contemporary world that can be usefully specified further.

Globalization can best be understood if it is conceived as a spatial phenomenon, lying on a continuum with "the local" at one end and "the global" at the other. It implies a shift in the spatial form of human organization and activity to transcontinental or interregional patterns of activity, interaction, and the exercise of power (Held, McGrew, Goldblatt, and Perraton, 1999). Today globalization embraces at least four distinct types of change. First, it involves a stretching of social, political, and economic activities across political frontiers, regions, and continents. But if these are something other than occasional or random, then something else is suggested: intensification. Thus, second, globalization is marked by the growing magnitude of networks and flows of trade, investment, finance, culture, and so on. Third, globalization can be linked to a speeding up of global interactions and processes, as the evolution of worldwide systems of transport and communication increases the velocity of the diffusion of ideas, goods, information, capital, and people. And, fourth, it involves the deepening impact of global interactions and processes such that the effects of distant events can be highly significant elsewhere and even the most local developments can come to have enormous global consequences. In this particular sense, the boundaries between domestic matters and global affairs become fuzzy. In short, globalization can be thought of as the widening, intensifying, speeding up, and growing impact of worldwide interconnectedness.

Globalization is made up of the accumulation of links across the world's major regions and across many domains of activity. It can be related to many factors including the rapid expansion of the world economy: world trade has grown enormously; the world's financial systems are now more integrated than ever before with nearly $2 trillion changing hands daily in the foreign exchange markets; and multinational companies are centrally involved in national and international economic transactions (Goldblatt, Held, McGrew, and Perraton, 1997). In addition, a denser pattern of interconnectedness also prevails as a result of changes in migration patterns, communications, the environment, and many other factors. Although these developments fall far short of creating an integrated world order, they have significant political and democratic consequences.

The world is no longer comprised of relatively "discrete civilisations" or "discrete political communities" (Fernández-Armesto, 1995, ch. 1); rather, it is a world of "overlapping communities of fate," where the fate of nations is significantly entwined. Political communities are enmeshed and entrenched in complex structures of overlapping forces, processes, and movements. During the period in which nation-state was being forged—and the territorially bound conception of democracy was consolidated—the idea of a close mesh between geography, political power, and democracy could be assumed. It seemed compelling that political power, sovereignty, democracy, and citizenship are simply and appropriately bounded by a delimited territorial space. These links were by and large taken for granted, and generally unexplicated in modern political theory (Held, 1995). Globalization raises issues concerning the proper scope of democracy, or democratic jurisdiction, given that the relation between decision makers and decision takers is not necessarily symmetrical or congruent with respect to the territory.

Globalization and Democracy: Five Disjunctures

The changing relation between globalization and the modern nation-state can be characterized by five disjunctures. All indicate an increase in the extensiveness, intensity, velocity, and impact of globalization. And all suggest important questions about the evolving character of the democratic political community in particular.

First, the idea of a self-determining national collectivity—which delimits and shapes a community of fate—can no longer be simply located within the borders of a single nation-state. Many of the most fundamental, economic, social, cultural, and environmental forces and processes that determine the nature of the political good and political outcomes, now lie—in terms of their operation and dynamics—beyond the reach of individual polities. The current concern about genetic engineering and its possible regulation is a case in point.

Second, it can no longer be presupposed that the locus of effective political power is synonymous with national governments and the nation-state; national states and national governments are now embedded in complex networks of political power at regional and global levels (see Keohane, 1995, 2001; Rosenau, 1997, 1998). In other words, political power is shared and negotiated among diverse forces and agencies at many levels, from the local to the global. The link between effective government, self-government, and a bounded territory is being broken.

Third, while significant concentrations of power are found, of course, in many states, these are frequently embedded in, and articulated with, new and changing forms of political authority. The power and operations of national government are altering, although not all in one direction. The entitlement of states to rule within circumscribed territories—their sovereignty—is not on the edge of collapse, but the practical nature of this entitlement—the actual capacity of states to rule—is changing its shape (Held, McGrew, Goldblatt, and Perraton, 1999, the Conclusion). A new regime of government and governance is emerging that is displacing traditional conceptions of state power as an indivisible, territorially exclusive form of public power.

Fourth, the nurturing and enhancement of the public good increasingly requires coordinated multilateral action (e.g., to ensure security or to prevent global recession). At the same time, the resolution of transboundary issues (e.g., responsibility for carbon omissions) may often impose significant domestic adjustments. In this respect, political and social agents are witnessing a shift in the operation and dynamics of state power and political authority. This has become most apparent, as states have become locked into regional and global regimes and associations. The context of national politics has been transformed by the diffusion of political authority and the growth of multilayered governance (see Nye and Donahue, 2000).

Fifth, the distinctions between domestic and foreign affairs, internal political issues, and external questions are no longer clear-cut. Governments face issues, such as the international drugs trade, AIDS, BSE (Bovine Spongiform Encephalopathy), the use of non-renewable resources, the management of nuclear waste, the spread of weapons of mass destruction, and global warming, which cannot meaningfully be categorized in these terms. Moreover, issues like the location and investment strategy of multinational corporations (MNCs), the regulation of global financial markets, the threats to the tax base of individual countries in the context of a global division of labor, and the absence of capital controls all pose questions about the continued value of some of the central instruments of national economic policy. In fact, in nearly all major areas of policy, the enmeshment of national political communities in regional and global flows and processes involves them in intensive transboundary coordination and regulation.

In the context of these complex transformations, the meaning of accountability and democracy at the national level is altering. In circumstances where transnational actors and forces cut across the boundaries of national communities in diverse ways, where powerful international organizations and agencies make decisions for vast groups of people across diverse borders, and where the capacities of large companies can dwarf many a state, the questions of who should be accountable to whom, and on what basis, do not easily resolve themselves. The mesh between geography, political power, and democracy is challenged by the intensification of regional and global relations.

Cosmopolitanism: Ideas and Trajectories

The problems and dilemmas of contemporary national politics, just described, can be referred to, following Jeremy Waldron, as the "circumstances of cosmopolitanism" (2000, pp. 236–9); that is, the background conditions and presuppositions that inform and motivate the case for a cosmopolitan framework of accountability and regulation. Not only are we "unavoidably side by side" (as Kant put it), but also the degrees of mutual interconnectedness and vulnerability are rapidly growing. The new circumstances of cosmopolitanism give us little choice but to consider the possibility of a common framework of standards and political action, given shape and form by a common framework of institutional arrangements (Held, 1995, part III).

How should cosmopolitanism be understood in this context? There are three broad accounts of cosmopolitanism that are important to bear in mind and that contribute to its contemporary meaning. The first was explored by the Stoics who were the first to refer explicitly to themselves as cosmopolitans, seeking to replace the central role of the *polis* in ancient political thought with that of the *cosmos* in which humankind could live in harmony (Horstmann, 1976). The root idea of classical cosmopolitanism involves the notion that each person is "a citizen of the world" and owes allegiances, first and foremost, "to the worldwide community of human beings" (Nussbaum, 1996, p. 4). While there are many difficulties with this classical formulation (for instance, its link to a teleological view of nature: see Nussbaum, 1997), the main point of the Stoics contained a most significant idea: "that they were, in the first instance, human beings living in a world of human beings and only incidentally members of polities" (Barry, 1999, p. 36). The boundaries of polities were understood to be historically arbitrary, and most often the result of coercion and violence. Borders obscured the common circumstances of humankind and, thus, could not have the moral significance frequently ascribed to them (Pogge, 1994b, p. 198). The individual belongs to the wider world of humanity; moral worth cannot be specified by the yardstick of a single political community.

The second conception of cosmopolitanism was introduced in the eighteenth century when the term *weltbürger* (world citizen) became one of the key terms of the Enlightenment. The most important contribution to this body of thought can be found in Kant's writings (above all, 1970, pp. 41–53, 54–60, and 93–130). Kant linked the idea of cosmopolitanism to an innovative conception of "the public use of reason," and explored the ways in which this conception of reason can generate a critical vantage point from which to scrutinize civil society (see Schmidt, 1998, pp. 419–27). Building on a definition of enlightenment as the escape from dogma and unvindicated authority, Kant measured its advance in terms of the removal of constraints on "the public use of reason" (see O'Neill, 1990). Individuals can step out of their entrenched positions in civil society and enter a sphere of reason free of "dictatorial authority"—which Kant associated (rather uncritically) with the world of writers, readers, and intellectuals—and can, from this vantage point, examine the one-sidedness, partiality, and limits of everyday knowledge, understanding, and regulations. In this context, individuals can learn to think of themselves as participants in a cosmopolitan dialogue—a critical process of communication—in which they can come to an understanding with others about the nature and appropriateness of the demands made upon them (cf. Arendt, 1961, pp. 220–1). The third conception of cosmopolitanism is more recent and is expounded in the work of Beitz, Pogge, and Barry, among others (see, in particular, Beitz, 1979, 1994, 1998; Pogge, 1989, 1994a; and Barry, 1998a and 1999, although they by no means agree on many matters: see,

for instance, Miller, 1998). In certain respects, this work seems to expli-
cate, and offer a compelling elucidation of, the classical conception of
belonging to the human community first and foremost, and the Kantian
conception of subjecting all beliefs, relations, and practices to the test of
whether or not they allow open-ended interaction, uncoerced agreement,
and impartial judgment. This third conception of cosmopolitanism
involves three key elements. The first is that the ultimate units of moral
concern are individual human beings, not states or other particular forms
of human association. Humankind belongs to a single moral realm in
which each person is regarded as equally worthy of respect and consideration (Beitz, 1994; 1998; Pogge, 1994a). This element can be referred to as
the principle of individualist moral egalitarianism or, simply, egalitarian
individualism. To think of people as having equal moral value is to make a
general claim about the basic units of the world comprising persons as free
and equal beings (see Kuper, 2000). This broad position runs counter to
the view of moral particularists that belonging to a given community limits and determines the moral worth of individuals and the nature of their
autonomy. It does so because, to paraphrase (and adapt) Bruce Ackerman,
there is no nation without a woman who insists on equal liberties, no society without a man who denies the need for deference, and no country
without a person who does not yearn for a predictable pattern of meals to
help sustain his or her life projects (see Ackerman, 1994, pp. 382–3). The
principle of egalitarian individualism is the basis for articulating the equal
worth and liberty of all humans, wherever they were born or brought up.
Its concern is with the irreducible moral status of each and every person—the acknowledgment of which links directly to the possibility of self-
determination and the capacity to make independent choices. The second
element emphasizes that the status of equal worth should be acknowledged by everyone. It is an attribute of every living person, and the basis
on which each person ought to constitute their relations with others
(Pogge, 1994a, p. 89f). Each person has an equal stake in this universal
ethical realm and is, accordingly, required to respect all other people's status as a basic unit of moral interest (Pogge, 1994a, p. 90). This second element of contemporary cosmopolitanism can be called the principle of
reciprocal recognition. To be satisfactorily entrenched in everyday life it
necessitates that all people enjoy an equality of status with respect to the
basic decision-making institutions of their communities. Agreed judgement about rules, laws, and policies should ideally follow from the "force
of the better argument" and public debate—not from the intrusive outcome of non-discursive elements and forces (Habermas, 1973; Held, 1995,
ch.7). If people are marginalized or fall outside of this framework, they
suffer disadvantage not primarily because they have less than others in this

instance, but because they can participate less in the processes and institutions that shape their lives. It is their "impaired agency" that becomes the focus of concern (Doyal and Gough, 1991, pp. 95–6; see Raz, 1986, pp. 227–40).

The third element stresses that equality of status and reciprocal recognition requires that each person should enjoy the impartial treatment of their claims—that is, treatment based on principles upon which all could act. Accordingly, cosmopolitanism is a moral frame of reference for specifying rules and principles that can be universally shared; and, concomitantly, it rejects as unjust all those practices, rules, and institutions anchored in principles not all could adopt (O'Neill, 1991). At issue is the establishment of principles and rules that nobody, motivated to establish an uncoerced and informed agreement, could reasonably reject (see Barry, 1989; cf. Scanlon, 1998).

To test the generalizability of claims and interests involves "reasoning from the point of view of others" (Benhabib, 1992, pp. 9–10, 121–47). Attempts to focus on this "social point of view" find their most rigorous explication in Rawls' original position, Habermas's ideal speech situation, and Barry's formulation of impartialist reasoning (see Rawls, 1971; Habermas, 1973, 1996; Barry, 1989, 1995). These formulations have in common a concern to conceptualize an impartial moral standpoint from which to assess routine forms of practical reasoning. The concern is not overambitious. As one commentator aptly explained:

> All the impartiality thesis says is that, if and when one raises questions regarding fundamental moral standards, the court of appeal that one addresses is a court in which no particular individual, group, or country has *special* standing. Before the court, declaring "I like it," "it serves my country," and the like, is not decisive; principles must be defensible to anyone looking at the matter apart from his or her special attachments, from a larger, human perspective." (Hill, 1987, p. 132, quoted in Barry, 1995, pp. 226–7)

This social open-ended, moral perspective is a device for focusing our thoughts, and a basis for testing the intersubjective validity of our conceptions of the good. It offers a way of exploring principles, norms, and rules that might reasonably command agreement (cf. Nussbaum, 1997, pp. 29–36).

Impartialist reasoning is a frame of reference for specifying rules and principles that can be universally shared. In order to meet this standard, a number of particular tests can be pursued, including an assessment of whether all points of view have been taken into consideration; whether there are individuals in a position to impose on others in such a manner as would be unacceptable to the latter, or to the originator of the action (or inaction), if the roles were reversed; and whether all parties would be equally prepared to accept the outcome as fair and reasonable irrespective of the social positions they might occupy now or in the future (see Barry, 1989, pp. 372 and 362–3).

Impartialist reasoning will not produce a simple deductive proof of the ideal set of principles and conditions that can overcome the deficiencies of the global economy or global political order; nor can it produce a deductive proof of the best or only moral principles that should guide institutional formation. Rather, it should be thought of as a heuristic device to test candidate principles of moral worth, democracy, and justice and their forms of justification (see Kelly, 1998, pp. 1–8). These tests are concerned with a process of reasonable rejectability, in a theoretical dialogue that is always open to fresh challenge and new questions and, hence, in a hermeneutic sense, can never be complete (Gadamer, 1975). But to acknowledge this is not to say that the theoretical conversation is "toothless" either with respect to principles or the conditions of their entrenchment.

One "biting" principle is the principle of the avoidance of serious harm and the amelioration of urgent need. This is a principle for allocating priority to the most vital cases of need and, where possible, trumping other, less urgent, public priorities until such a time as all human beings enjoy the status of equal moral value, reciprocal recognition, and have the means to participate in their respective political communities and in the overlapping communities of fate that shape their needs and welfare. A social provision that falls short of this can be referred to as a situation of manifest "harm" in that the recognition of, and potential for, active agency will not have been achieved for all individuals or groups; that is to say, some people would not have adequate access to effectively resourced capacities that they might make use of in particular circumstances (see Sen, 1999). This practical and participative conception of agency denotes, in principle, an "attainable" target—because the measure of optimum participation, and the related conception of harm, can be conceived directly in terms of the "highest standard" presently achieved in a political community (see Doyal and Gough, 1991, p. 169). But attainable participative levels are not the same thing as the most pressing levels of vulnerability, defined by the most urgent need. It is only too clear that within many, if not all, countries, certain needs, particularly concerning health, education, and welfare, are not universally met (Held and McGrew, 2000, chs. 31, 32, and 37). The "harm" that follows from a failure to meet such needs can be denoted as "serious harm," marked as it often is by immediate, life-and-death consequences. Accordingly, if the requirements specified by the principle of the avoidance of serious harm are to be met, public policy ought to be focused, in the first instance, on the prevention of such conditions; that is, on the eradication of severe harm inflicted on people "against their will" and "without their consent" (Barry, 1998b, pp. 231, 207).[2]

I take cosmopolitanism ultimately to connote the ethical and political space that sets out the terms of reference for the recognition of people's equal moral worth, their active agency, and what is required for their autonomy and development (see Held, 2002b).[3] It builds on principles that all could reasonably assent to in defending basic ideas that emphasize equal dignity, equal respect, the priority of vital need, and so on. On the other hand, this cosmopolitan point of view must also recognize that the meaning of these cannot be specified once and for all. That is to say, the connotation of these basic ideas cannot be separated from the hermeneutic complexity of traditions with their temporal and cultural structures. The meaning of cosmopolitan regulative principles cannot be elucidated independently of an ongoing discussion in public life (Habermas, 1996). Accordingly, there can be no adequate specification of equal liberty, rights, and vital interests without a corresponding institutionalization of "the public use of reason" in uncoerced national and transnational forms of public dialogue and debate (McCarthy, 1999). The institutionalization of cosmopolitan principles requires the entrenchment of accessible and open public fora.

Cosmopolitan Realities

After 200 years of nationalism, sustained nation-state formation and intensive geopolitics, cosmopolitan principles and political positions could be thought of as out of place. Yet, in certain respects, cosmopolitanism defines a set of norms and legal frameworks in the here and now—and not in some remote future. Cosmopolitanism is already embedded in rule systems and institutions that have transformed the sovereign states system in a number of important respects.

The principles of egalitarian individualism, reciprocal recognition, and impartialist reasoning find direct expression in significant post–Second World War legal and institutional initiatives and in some of the new regulatory forms of regional and global governance (Held, 2002a). To begin with, the 1948 UN Declaration of Human Rights and subsequent 1966 Covenants of Rights raised the principle of egalitarian individualism to a universal reference point: The requirements that each person be treated with equal concern and respect, irrespective of the state in which they were born or brought up, is the central plank of the human rights worldview (see UN, 1988). In addition, the formal recognition in the UN Declaration of all people as persons with "equal and inalienable rights," and as "the foundation of freedom, justice and peace in the world," marked a turning point in the development of cosmopolitan legal thinking (UN, preamble). Single persons are recognized as subjects of international law and, in principle, the ultimate source of political authority (see Crawford and Marks, 1998; Weller, 1997). Moreover, the diverse range of rights found in the International Bill and regarded as integral to human dignity and autonomy—from protection against slavery, torture, and other degrading practices to education and participation in cultural, economic, and political life (irrespective of race, gender, or religious affiliation)—constitute the basis of a cosmopolitan orientation to politics and human welfare. Human rights entitlements can trump, in principle, the particular claims of national polities; they set down universal standards against which the strengths and limitations of individual political communities can be judged.

The human rights commitment to the equal worth of all human beings finds reinforcement in the acknowledgment of the necessity of a minimum of civilized conduct and of specific limits to violence found in the laws of war and weapons diffusion; in the commitment to the principles of the Nuremberg and Tokyo war crimes tribunals (1945–6, 1946–8), the Torture Convention (1984), and the statutes of the International Criminal Court (1998), which outlaw genocide, war crimes, and crimes against humanity; in the growing recognition of democracy as the fundamental standard of political legitimacy that finds entrenchment in the International Bill of Human Rights and regional treaties; in the development of new codes of conduct for IGOs and INGOs, concerning the transparency and accountability of their activities; and in the unprecedented flurry of regional and global initiatives, regimes, institutions, networks, and treaties seeking to tackle global warming, ozone depletion, the pollution of oceans and rivers, and nuclear risks, among many other factors (see Held, 2002a for a survey).

Cosmopolitan ideas are, in short, at the center of significant post–Second World War legal and political developments. The idea that human well-being is not defined by geographical or cultural location, that national or ethnic or gendered boundaries should not determine the limits of rights or responsibilities for the satisfaction of basic human needs, and that all human beings require equal respect and concern are notions embedded in aspects of contemporary regional and global legal and political thinking, and in some forms of transnational governance (Beitz, 1994, p. 127; see Held, McGrew, Goldblatt, and Perraton, 1999, ch.1 and the Conclusion). There has been a significant shift in emphasis, as one observer has noted, "in the character and goals of international society: away from minimalist goals of coexistence towards the creation of rules and institutions that embody notions of shared responsibilities, that impinge heavily on the domestic organization of states, that invest individuals and groups within states with rights and duties, and that seek to embody some notion of the planetary good" (Hurrell, 1995, p. 139). Yet, while there may be cosmopolitan elements to existing international law, these have, of course, by no means generated a new deep-rooted structure of cosmopolitan accountability and regulation. The principle of egalitarian individualism may be widely recognized, but it scarcely structures much political and economic policy, north, south, east, or west. The principle of universal recognition informs the notions of human rights and other legal initiatives such as "common heritage of humankind" (embedded in the Law of the Sea [1982]), but it is not at the heart of the politics of sovereign states or corporate colossi; the principle of impartial moral reasoning might be appealed to justify limits on reasons of state and the actions of IGOs, but it is, at best, only an incidental part of the institutional dynamics that have created such chronic political problems as the externalities (or border spill-over effects) generated by many national economic and energy policies, overlapping communities of fate in areas as diverse as security and the environment, and the global polarization of power, wealth, and income.

This should not be a surprise. In the first instance, the global legal and political initiatives of 1948 onward, referred to above, do not just curtail sovereignty; they clearly support and underpin it in many ways. From the UN Charter to the Rio Declaration on the environment, international agreements have often served to entrench, and accommodate themselves to, the sovereign international power structure. The division of the globe into powerful nation-states, with distinctive sets of geopolitical interests, has often been built into the articles and statutes of IGOs (see Held, 1995, chs. 5 and 6). The "sovereign rights of states" are frequently affirmed alongside more cosmopolitan leanings. Moreover, while a case can be made that cosmopolitan principles are part of "the working creed" of officials in some United Nations agencies, such as UNICEF, UNESCO, and the WHO, and NGOs, such as Amnesty International, Save the Children, and Greenpeace, they can scarcely be said to be constitutive of the conceptual world of most modern politicians, democratic or otherwise (Barry, 1999, pp. 34–35; cf. Held and McGrew, 2000, pp. 31–9).

Second, the cosmopolitan reach of contemporary regional and global law rarely comes with a commitment to establish institutions with the resources and clout to make declared cosmopolitan intentions and objectives effective. The susceptibility of the UN to the agendas of the most powerful states, the partiality of many of its enforcement operations (or the lack of them altogether), the underfunding of its organizations, its continued dependency on financial support from a few major states, and the weaknesses of the policing of many environmental regimes (regional and global) are all indicative of the disjuncture between cosmopolitan aspirations and their partial and one-sided application.

Finally, the focus of cosmopolitan political initiatives since 1945 has been on the domain of the political. These efforts have only had a tangential impact on the regulation of economic power and market mechanisms. The emphasis has been on checking the abuse of political power, not economic power. Cosmopolitan international politics has developed few, if any, systematic means to address forms of economic domination. Its conceptual resources and leading ideas do not suggest or push toward the pursuit of self-determination and autonomy in the economic domain; they do not seek the entrenchment of democratic rights and obligations outside of the sphere of the political. Issues concerning corporate power, corporate governance, and flourishing economic inequalities have to be brought back into the centre of cosmopolitan practice if this lacuna—at the heart of the struggle over globalization today—is to be addressed. Cosmopolitan theory, with its emphasis on illegitimate and unacceptable structures of power and vital need, has to be reconnected to cosmopolitan institution building.

Addressing the Institutional Deficit: Reframing the Market

The impact of developing cosmopolitan standards is highly differentiated and uneven across the world's regions. This creates moral and competitive problems for socioeconomic agents and institutions of economic governance, and generates a conundrum: how to uphold cosmopolitan standards and values without eroding sound economic practice and legitimate corporate interests. Outside of a cosmopolitan framework there is, I think, no escape from this conundrum.

Onora O'Neill has argued recently that in the context of political turbulence (i.e., against the background of rogue states or imploding polities), corporations can find that they are "the primary agents of justice"; that is, the primary agents with responsibility for maintaining and sustaining cosmopolitan standards and virtues (2000, pp. 21–2). She holds that both states and companies can be judged by the principles and standards they claim to uphold; and that such a judgment today must be made in relation to the principles and standards that are already developing as the universal basis of action—as a result of the spread of democratic values, human rights agreements, environmental regimes, and so on. This already provides a tough matrix of social requirements even before the cosmopolitan thinker presses it further.

There is much in this position to affirm: the particular culture and practices of companies matter; the difference between a responsible or rogue corporation with respect, for example, to pollution is of great significance; and the involvement of companies in the infrastructural development of local communities can be of marked import. Nonetheless, corporations can find themselves extremely vulnerable to shifting competitive circumstances if they bear the burdens and costs of certain environmental or social standards alone. In my view, business men and business women object less to political regulation and social reform *per se* than to the intrusion of regulatory mechanisms that upset "the rules of the game" in some particular place or country only. Stringent environmental conditions, tough equal opportunities requirements, high labor standards, more accommodating working hours, for example, are particularly objectionable to companies if they handicap those companies' competitive edge in relation to enterprises from areas not subject to similar constraints. Under such circumstances, companies will be all too tempted to do what they can to resist such standards or depart for more "hospitable shores"; and this will be perfectly rational from their economic point of view.

Accordingly, if economic interaction is to be entrenched in a set of mechanisms and procedures that allow markets to flourish in the long run within the constraints of cosmopolitan principles and processes, the rules of the game have to be transformed systematically, at regional and global levels (e.g., at the level of the EU and the WTO). This target for political and economic change provides a potentially fruitful focus, I believe, for both corporate interests and social movements concerned with widespread poverty, social standards, and environmental degradation. What are the institutional and procedural implications of these considerations? The requirements of the cosmopolitan framework of accountability and regulation are many and various; there are legal, political, economic, and cultural preconditions. But I only have the space here to focus on the economic (see Held, 2002a and b).

The market system is highly indeterminate—often generating costly or damaging externalities with regard to health, welfare, income distribution, or the environment. The "anti-globalization" protestors are at their clearest and most articulate on these issues. These challenges can only be adequately addressed, and market economies can only function in a manner fully commensurate with cosmopolitan principles and virtues, if the market system is reframed. This should not be taken, as it is all too often, as an argument for either abandoning or undermining the market system—not at all. The market system has distinct advantages, as Hayek has emphasized, over all known alternative economic systems as an effective mechanism to coordinate the knowledgeable decisions of producers and consumers over extended territories (1976). But it is an argument for restructuring—or "reframing," as I prefer to put it—the market itself. A bridge has to be built between international economic law and human rights law, between commercial law and environmental law, between state sovereignty and transnational law, and between cosmopolitan principles and cosmopolitan practices (see Chinkin, 1998). Precedents exist in, for instance, the Social Chapter of the Maastricht Agreement or in the attempt to attach labor and environmental conditions to the NAFTA regime, for the pursuit of this objective.

This position generates a rationale for a politics of intervention in economic life, not to control and regulate markets *per se*, but to provide the basis for reforming and regulating those forms of power that compromise, disrupt, or undermine fair and sustainable conditions for economic cooperation and competition—the necessary background conditions of the particular choices of human agents in a world of overlapping communities of fate. What is required is not only the firm enactment of existing human rights and environmental agreements and the clear articulation of these with the ethical codes of particular industries (where they exist or can be developed), but also the introduction of new terms of reference into the ground rules or basic laws of the free-market and trade system.

At stake, ultimately, are two interrelated sets of transformations. The first is the entrenchment of revised rules, codes, and procedures—concerning health, child labor, trade union activity, environmental protection, stakeholder consultation, and corporate governance, among other matters—in the articles of association and terms of reference of economic organizations and trading agencies. The key groups and associations of the economic domain will have to adopt, within their very *modus operandi*, a structure of rules, procedures, and practices compatible with cosmopolitan social requirements, if the latter are to prevail. The second set of transformations concerns the institutionalization of cosmopolitan principles as the basis of rightful public authority, at local, national, regional, and global levels. Recognizing the complex structures of an interconnected world, cosmopolitanism views certain issues as appropriate for delimited (spatially demarcated) political spheres (the city, state, or region), while it sees others—such as the environment, genetic engineering, the terms of trade, and financial stability—as requiring new, more extensive, regional and global institutions to address them (see Archibugi, Held, and Köhler, 1998, chs. 1, 10, and 14).

Only by introducing new rules, standards, and mechanisms of accountability throughout the global economic system, as a supplement and complement to collective agreements and measures in national and regional contexts, can an enduring settlement be created between business interests, regulatory capacity, and cosmopolitan concerns (cf. Lipietz, 1992, pp. 119–24). While the advocacy of such a position clearly raises enormous political, diplomatic, and technical difficulties, and would need a substantial period to pursue and, of course, implement, this is a challenge that cannot be avoided if people's equal interest in cosmopolitan principles and outcomes is to be adequately protected.

There are many possible objections to such a scheme and advocacy position. Among these are pressing cultural concerns that the standards and values being projected are those of Western origin and, concomitantly, mask sectional interests—to the advantage, for example, of entrenched corporate and labor interests in the developed world. This point is often made in relation to ILO standards vis-à-vis child labor, freedom to join trade unions, and equal pay for men and women for work of equal value. However, this concern is, in my judgment, misplaced and hits the wrong target.

In the first instance, dissent about the value of ideas such as equal consideration, equal liberty, and human rights is often related to the experience of Western imperialism and colonialization. The way in which these ideas have been traditionally understood in the West—that is, the way in which they have been tied to political and civil rights, above all, and not, for example, to the satisfaction of fundamental human need—has fueled the view that the language of liberty and democracy is the discourse of Western dominance, especially in those countries that were deeply affected by the reach of Western empires in the nineteenth and twentieth centuries. There are many good historical reasons why such language invokes skepticism. Understandable as they are, however, these reasons are insufficient to provide a well-justified critique: It is a mistake to throw out the language of equal worth and self-determination because of its contingent association with the historical configurations of Western power. The origins of principles should not be confused with their validity (Weale, 1998).

A distinction must be made between those political discourses that obscure or underpin particular interests and power systems and those that seek explicitly to test the generalizability of claims and interests, and to render power, whether it be political, economic, or cultural, accountable (see Section 10.3). The framework of cosmopolitan principles and values is sound, preoccupied, as it is, with the equal liberty and development possibilities of all human beings, but it cannot be implemented plausibly without addressing the most pressing cases of economic suffering and harm. Without this commitment, the advocacy of cosmopolitan standards can easily descend into high-mindedness, which fails to pursue the socioeconomic changes that are a necessary part of such an allegiance.

At a minimum, this means linking the progressive implementation of a cosmopolitan regulative framework with efforts to reduce the economic vulnerability of many developing countries by eliminating debt, reversing the outflow of net capital assets from the South to the North, and creating new economic facilities at organizations like the World Bank, the IMF, and the UN for development purposes (see Lipietz, 1992, pp. 116ff; Falk, 1995, ch. 6). In addition, if such measures were combined with a (Tobin) tax on the turnover of financial markets, and/or a consumption tax on energy usage and/or a shift of priorities from military expenditure to the alleviation of severe need, then the developmental context of Western and Northern nation-states could begin to be accommodated to those nations struggling for survival and minimum welfare (see Held, 1995, ch. 11; Giddens and Hutton, 2000, p. 213ff; and Held and McGrew, 2002, for a fuller account of these proposals).

Improbable? Unrealistic? Two points should be made in this regard. First, a cosmopolitan covenant is already in the making as political authority and new forms of governance are diffused "below," "above," and "alongside" the nation-state, and as new forms of international law, from the law of war to human rights law and environmental regimes, begin to set down universal standards. Second, these standards can be built upon, locking-in cosmopolitan principles into economic life, in developed and developing countries. To meet the requirements of impartialist reasoning, they have, of course, to be pressed much further. The intense battles about globalization are helping to create an environment in which questions about these matters can be pursued in the public domain. Entrenched geopolitical and economic interests are more likely to respond to a mix of pressure and argument, rather than to argument alone. But the risk of a severe backlash (championed already by the Bush administration) is clear. Certainly, the protestors need to come to understand the complexity of the issues they are seeking to address, the diversity of legitimate viewpoints (the difference, for example, between those who object to unbridled free trade and the positions of many developing countries seeking greater access to developed markets), and the extraordinary complexity of institutional solutions. Unless this happens, the gulf between confrontation and constructive engagement will not be bridged. In the end, whether cosmopolitan rules and regulations can be pursued successfully in the long term remains to be seen. But one thing is certain: The modern territorial state was not built in a generation, and one should not expect major and equally significant transformations—in this case to a multilevel, multilayered cosmopolitan polity—to take less time.

Notes

1. This chapter was first presented as a paper at the conference, *Globalisierung und Sozialstandards*, 30/31 March 2001, held at the *Internationales Führungszentrum der Siemens AG*, Feldafing, Starnberger See, and organized by the *Deutshes Netzwerk Wirtschaftsethik*.
2. Another way to put this point is to ask whether anyone would freely choose a "principle of justice", which determined that people (present and/or future generations) suffer serious

harm and disadvantage independently of their consent, such as, for instance, the 17 million children who die each year of diarrhea. In the face of impartialist reasoning, this principle is wholly unconvincing. The impartialist emphasis on the neccesity of taking account of the position of the other, of only regarding political outcomes as fair and reasonable if there are good reasons for holding that they would be equally acceptable to all parties, and of only treating the position of some socioeconomic groups as legitimate if they are acceptable to all people irrespective of where they come in the social hierarchy, does not provide grounds on which this principle could be accepted. And, yet, this is the principle of justice people are asked to accept, de facto, as a, if not the, principle of distribution in the global economic order. No wonder protest levels are so intense and growing.

3. Contemporary cosomopolitans, it should be acknowledged, are divided about the demands that cosmopolitanism lays upon the individual and, accordingly, upon the appropriate framing of the necessary backgound conditions for a "common" or "basic" structure of individual action and social activity. Among them there is agreement that in deciding how to act, or which rules or regulations ought to be established, the claims of each person affected should be weighed equally—"no matter where they live, which society they belong to, or how they are connected to us" (Miller, 1998, p. 165). The principle of egalitarian individualism is regarded as axiomatic. But the exact moral weight granted to this principle depends heavily upon the precise modes of interpretation of other principles (see Nussbaum, 1996; Barry, 1998b; Miller, 1998; Scheffler, 1999). I shall not pursue these issues here, although the position suggested below indicates one way of linking cosmopolitan universalism with the recognition of the irreducible plurality of forms of life (see Habermas, 1996).

References

Ackerman, B. (1994). Political liberalisms. *Journal of Philosophy* 91: 364–86.

Archibugi, D., Held, D., and Köhler, M. (eds.) (1998). *Re-imagining Political Community: Studies in Cosmopolitan Democracy.* Polity Press: Cambridge.

Arendt, H. (1961). The crisis in culture. In: *Between Past and Future: Six Exercises in Political Thought.* Meridian: New York, pp. 197–226.

Barry, B. (1989). *Theories of Justice.* Harvester Wheatsheaf: London.

Barry, B. (1995). *Justice as Impartiality.* Clarendon Press: Oxford.

Barry, B. (1998a). "International society from a cosmopolitan perspective." In: Mapel, D. and Nardin, T., (eds.). *International Society: Diverse Ethical Perspectives.* Princeton University Press: Princeton, pp. 144–63.

Barry, B. (1998b). Something in the disputation not unpleasant. In: Kelly, P. (ed.). *Impartiality, Neutrality and Justice: Re-thinking Brian Barry's Justice as Impartiality.* Edinburgh University Press: Edinburgh, pp. 186–257.

Barry, B. (1999). Statism and nationalism: a cosmopolitan critique. In: Shapiro, I. and Brilmayer, L. (eds.). *Global Justice.* New York University Press: New York, pp. 12–66.

Beitz, C. (1979). *Political Theory and international Relations.* Princeton University Press: Princeton.

Beitz, C. (1994). Cosmopolitan liberalism and the states system. In: Brown, C. (ed.). *Political Restructuring in Europe: Ethical Perspectives.* Routledge: London, pp. 123–36.

Beitz, C. (1998). Philosophy of international relations. In: *Routledge Encyclopedia of Philosophy.* Routledge: London, pp. 826–33.

Benhabib, S. (1992). *Situating the Self.* Polity Press: Cambridge. Brown, C. (ed.) (1994). *Political Restructuring in Europe: Ethical Perspectives.* Routledge: London.

Chinkin, C. (1998). International law and human rights. In: Evans, T. (ed.). *Human Rights Fifty Years On.* Manchester University Press: Manchester, pp. 105–29.

Cohen, J. (ed.) (1996). *For Love of Country: Debating the Limits of Patriotism.* Beacon Press: Boston.

Crawford, J. and Marks, S. (1998). "The global democracy deficit: an essay on international law and its limits." In: Archibugi, D., Held, D., and Köhler, M. (eds.) (1998). *Re-imagining Political Community: Studies in Cosmopolitan Democracy.* Polity Press: Cambridge, pp. 72–90.

Doyal, L. and Gough, I. (1991). *A Theory of Human Need.* Macmillan: London.

Falk, R. (1995). *On Humane Governance.* Polity Press: Cambridge.

Fernández-Armesto, F. (1995). *Millennium.* Bantam: London.

Gadamer, H.G. (1975). *Truth and Method.* Sheed and Ward: London.

Giddens, A. and Hutton, W. (2000). *On the Edge: Living with Global Capitalism.* Jonathan Cape: London.

Goldblatt, D., Held, D., McGrew, A., and Perraton, J. (1997). Economic globalization and the nation-state: shifting balances of power. *Alternatives* 22: 269–87.

Habermas, J. (1973). Wahrheitstheorien. In: Fahrenbach, H. (ed.). *Wirchlichkeit und Reflexion.* Neske: Pfüllingen, pp. 211–65.

Habermas, J. (1996). *Between Facts and Norms: Contributions to a Discourse Theory of Law and Democracy.* Polity Press: Cambridge.

Hayek, F. (1976). *The Road to Serfdom.* Routledge: London.

Held, D. (1995). *Democracy and the Global Order: From the Modern State to Cosmopolitan Governance.* Polity Press: Cambridge.

Held, D. (2002a). Law of states, law of peoples. *Legal Theory* 8: 2.

Held, D. (2002b). *Cosmopolitanism.* Polity Press: Cambridge.

Held, D. and McGrew, A. (eds.) (2000). *The Global Transformation Reader.* Polity Press: Cambridge.

Held, D. and McGrew, A. (eds.) (2002). *Governing Globalization: Power, Authority and Global Governance.* Polity Press: Cambridge.

Held, D., McGrew, A., Goldblatt, D., and Perraton, J. (1999). *Global Transformations: Politics, Economics and Culture.* Polity Press: Cambridge.

Hill, T. (1987). The Importance of autonomy. In: Kittay, E. and Meyers, D. (eds). *Women and Moral Theory.* Roman and Allanheld: Totowa, NJ, pp. 129–38.

Horstmann, A. (1976). Kosmopolit, Kosmopolitismus. In: *Historisches Worterbuch der Philosphie.* Band 4. Schwabe: Basel, pp. 1156–68.

Hurrell, A. (1995). International political theory and the global environment. In: Booth, K. and Smith, S. (eds). *International Relations Theory.* Polity Press: Cambridge, pp. 129–53.

Kant, I. (1970). *Kant's Political Writings.* Reiss, H. (ed.). Cambridge University Press: Cambridge.

Kelly, P. (ed.) (1998). *Impartiality, Neutrality and Justice: Re-reading Brian Barry's Justice as Impartiality.* Edinburgh University Press: Edinburgh.

Keohane, R.O. (1995). Hobbes' dilemma and institutional change in world politics: sovereignty in international society. In: Holm, H. and Sorenson, G. (eds). *Whose World Order?* Westview Press: Boulder, pp. 165–86.

Keohane, R.O. (2001). Governance in a partially globalized world. *American Political Science Review* 95: 1–13.

Kuper, A. (2000). Rawlsian global justice: beyond *The Law of Peoples* to a cosmopolitan law of persons. *Political Theory* 28: 640–74.

Lipietz, A. (1992). *Towards a New Economic Order.* Polity Press: Cambridge.

MacIntyre, A. (1981). *After Virtue.* Duckworth: London.

MacIntyre, A. (1988). *Whose Justice? Which Rationality?* Duckworth: London.

McCarthy, T. (1999). On reconciling cosmopolitan unity and national diversity. *Public Culture* 11: 175–208.

Miller, D. (1988). The ethical significance of nationality. *Ethics* 98: 647–62.

Miller, D. (1998). The limits of cosmopolitan justice. In: Mapel, D. and Nadin, T. (eds). *International Society: Diverse Ethical Perspectives.* Princeton University Press: Princeton, pp. 164–81.

Nozick, R. (1974). *Anarchy, State and Utopia.* Blackwell: Oxford.

Nussbaum, M.C. (1996). Patriotism and cosmopolitanism. In: Cohen, J. (ed.). *For Love of Country: Debating the Limits of Patriotism.* Beacon Press: Boston, pp. 3–17.

Nussbaum, M.C. (1997). Kant and cosmopolitanism. In: Bohman, J., Lutz-Bac mann, M. (eds.). *Perpetual Peace: Essays on Kant's Cosmopolitan Ideal.* The MIT Press: C nbridge, MA, pp. 25 7.

Nye, J.S. and Donahue, J.D. (2000). *Governance in a Globalizing World.* Brookings Institution Press: Washington, D.C.

O'Neill, O. (1990). Enlightenment as autonomy: Kant's vindication of reason. In: Jordanova, L. and Hulme, P. (eds.). *The Enlightenment and Its Shadows.* Routledge: London, pp. 184–99.

O'Neill, O. (1991). Transnational justice. In: Held, D. (ed.). *Political Theory Today.* Polity: Cambridge, pp. 276–304.

O'Neill, O. (2001). Agents of Justice. *Metaphilosophy* 32: 1/2, pp. 1–30.

Pogge, T. (1989). *Realizing Rawls.* Cornell University Press: Ithaca, N.Y.

Pogge, T. (1994a). Cosmopolitanism and sovereignty. In: Brown, C. (ed.) (1994). *Political Restructuring in Europe: Ethical Perspectives*. Routledge: London, pp. 89–122.

Pogge, T. (1994b). An egalitarian law of peoples. *Philosophy and Public Affairs* 23: 195–224.

Rawls, J. (1971). *A Theory of Justice*. Harvard University Press: Cambridge, Mass.

Raz, J. (1986). *The Morality of Freedom*. Oxford University Press: Oxford.

Rosenau, J. (1997). *Along the Domestic-Foreign Frontier*. Cambridge University Press: Cambridge.

Rosenau, J. (1998). Governance and democracy in a globalizing world. In: Archibugi, D., Held, D., and Köhler, M.(eds.). *Re-imagining Political Community*. Polity Press: Cambridge, pp. 28–57.

Scanlon, T.M. (1998). *What We Owe to Each Other*. Belknap: Cambridge, Mass.

Scheffler, S. (1999). Conceptions of cosmopolitanism. *Utilitas* 11: 255–76.

Schmidt, J. (1998). Civility, enlightenment and society: conceptual confusions and Kantian remedies. *American Political Science Review* 92: 419–27.

Sen, A. (1999). *Development as Freedom*. Oxford University Press: Oxford.

UN. (1988). *Human Rights: A Compilation of International Instruments*. United Nations: New York.

Waldron, J. (2000). What is cosmopolitan? *The Journal of Political Philosophy* 8: 227–43.

Walzer, M. (1983). *Spheres of Justice: A Defence of Pluralism and Equality*. Martin Robertson: Oxford.

Weale, A. (1998). From contracts to pluralism? In: Kelly, P. (ed.). *Impartiality, Neutrality and Justice: Re-Reading Brian Barry's Justice as Impartiality*. Edinburgh University Press: Edinburgh, pp. 9–34.

Weller, M. (1997). The reality of the emerging universal constitutional order: putting the pieces together. *Cambridge Review of International Studies*, X, Winter/Spring: 40–63.

CHAPTER 11

Corporate Codes of Conduct and the Success of Globalization

S. PRAKASH SETHI

The Blessings of Globalization

A strong argument can be made that globalization and the unrestricted flow of capital, goods, and services lead to the creation of wealth and prosperity among all participating nations. Comparative advantage allows both the industrially advanced nations and developing countries to maximize their gains from trade. Industrially advanced countries make better use of their technology and capital by exporting it to less-developed or poorer countries, which in turn make better use of their cheap and abundant labor by exporting their low-tech and labor-intensive products to the richer countries.[1] Globalization also leads to economic integration and convergence in economic policies around the world. Economic integration leads to economic growth through reform and harmonization in the countries' fiscal and monetary policies, tax systems, ownership patterns, and other regulatory arrangements.

But there are costs as well. There have been waves of globalization in the past: in the United States (1870–90 and circa 1970), Western Europe (1890–1913 and 1950–92), and Japan (1913–38). Most of these waves eventually petered out because of their adverse impact on the social infrastructure of the countries involved. These adverse impacts included greater income disparities and unequal sharing of the gains of globalization between countries and among different groups within countries, and the dislocation or dismantling of the "social safety net." In the current round of globalization, the distribution of gains from international trade and investment has been skewed strongly in favor of those who control capital and against those who contribute human labor. According to the World Bank, the disparity between rich and poor countries has grown ten times wider during the last thirty years. As Jeffrey Sachs and Andrew Warner point out:

> Long-held judgments about the development process, as well as the workhorse formal models of economic growth, suggest that the poorer countries should tend to grow more rapidly than richer countries and therefore should close the proportionate income gap over time. The main reason for expecting economic convergence is that the poorer countries can import capital and modern technologies from the wealthier countries, and thereby reap the "advantage of backwardness." Yet in recent decades, there has been no overall tendency for the poorer countries to catch up or converge with the richer countries.[2]

Large multinational corporations (MNCs) play an increasingly critical role in the growth and development of the economies of emerging nations. MNCs have become an engine of change through their injection of capital, technology, organizational skills, and a competitive environment. Foreign corporations not only bring with them new technologies and management systems, they also bring a different kind of corporate culture and assumptions about the relations between the national governments and the countries' economic and sociopolitical institutions.

An ancillary effect of globalization has been the blurring of political boundaries and diminution in the control of national governments in the domestic arena. Both the governments of industrially advanced countries and multinational corporations have sought to exploit these weaknesses for their own ends. The governments of the industrially advanced countries have used their influence essentially to protect the interests of their home country-based MNCs in expanding their business activities in developing countries.[3] MNCs and the governments of industrially advanced countries have asserted that the greater expansion of international trade and economic growth would lead to a fostering of democratic institutions and an improvement in the human rights records of developing countries where authoritarian and totalitarian regimes currently hold sway. Such assertions are made almost as truisms. Yet they are actually untenable claims. America's trade with China has risen sixfold in the last ten years and now stands at $85 billion. In the same period, U.S. investments there grew to $56 billion from $32 billion. Yet one would be hard-pressed to find commensurate gains in democratic institutions or enhancements of human rights in China.[4] MNCs have worked hard to ensure that products made for them in developing countries meet quality standards acceptable to consumers in the industrially advanced countries. MNCs have, however, been indifferent to, if not downright negligent of, the health and welfare of the workers who make those products. Consequently, MNCs have been involved in abusing and exploiting workers and in causing egregious harm to the environment.[5]

Multinational Corporations and Globalization—A Case of Neomercantilism

For the benefits of free trade to be distributed equitably according to standard trade theory, it is important that both capital and labor have maximum mobility, so that each can maximize the reward from its efforts. MNCs currently enjoy all of the advantages of moving capital between different sectors and nations in order to maximize their return on investment. Workers, however, lack such mobility. They cannot migrate easily, if at all, to countries with labor shortages; thus, workers are prevented from eliminating inefficiencies in the labor market.

The imbalance between the mobility of capital and goods and the immobility of labor are more characteristic of neomercantilism than of truly free markets. MNCs use both the fact and threat of capital mobility to extract maximum productivity gains from cheap and abundant labor. The control of overseas markets provides the MNCs with monopoly-like power, which they use on local manufacturers to extract the lowest prices possible and thus put extreme downward pressure on local wage rates. Local manufacturers, in their turn, cooperate among themselves by not competing for workers on the basis of higher wages—a situation that is easily maintained because of abundant labor.

The mobility of capital has "rendered an important segment of the local governments' tax base footloose," leaving governments with the unappetizing option of imposing disproportionately high taxes on income from labor, agricultural products from even poorer rural areas, household consumption, and taxes on local property.[6] Short of resources, host country governments have been unwilling and unable to exercise regulatory oversight, or to enforce the already rudimentary local labor and environmental protection laws—a practice that multinationals find quite agreeable.

Control of final product-distribution channels by MNCs leads to standardization in manufacturing processes, which emphasize the use of cheap labor over capital. This in turn leads to the harmonization of labor requirements and allows MNCs to shift production among suppliers in different countries in a seamless manner. It puts an added burden on manufacturers in one country to harmonize their production costs—in dollar terms, regardless of different local conditions—to compete with manufacturers in other countries. An inevitable outcome of this process is that workers in one poor country must compete with workers in other poor countries, further depressing marginal wage rates by vastly expanding the relevant labor pool.

An abundance of cheap labor leaves little incentive for MNCs to improve technology and thereby enhance labor productivity. MNCs further exacerbate this situation through outsourcing most, if not all, of their production needs to local entrepreneurs. Lacking in capital and technology, these entrepreneurs resort to further exploitation of labor through long working hours, often without payment of overtime, and under dangerous and unhealthy working conditions.

Unable to reduce supply through emigration, local workers compete with each other for available jobs and work for subsistence-level wages. These bare-minimum wages do not provide workers with savings that they might invest in education and training to upgrade their skills and increase their incomes. Most workers are unaware of even the minimal rights they have under local laws. These imbalances help to explain the fact that although the minimum wage rates are $5.15 per hour in the United States, they are less than $.30 per hour (in U.S. dollars) in most developing countries, despite productivity levels that are similar to, or even higher than, those in industrialized countries.[7]

Subsistence-level wage rates propel rural families to produce more children to work in the factories in order to sustain the family. This "creates a self-perpetuating cycle of poverty."[8] This situation is further exacerbated by the fact that most manufacturing operations—except in high-skill areas—employ primarily young workers in the sixteen-to-eighteen-year-old (and often even twelve-to-fourteen-year-old) age group and do not keep them beyond the ages of twenty-to-twenty-one years, when they are replaced by another cadre of sixteen-to-eighteen-year-old workers. The older workers are thrown out to join the armies of the destitute and unemployed.

MNCs' Responses to Criticism—A Sea of Red Herrings

MNCs' responses to public concern and criticism about their role in the current phase of globalization can be grouped in two categories: justifications for their conduct, and proposals for institutionalizing changes in their conduct.

They have justified their conduct on the basis of market and competitive factors and pointed to increased societal benefits through income growth and job creation in countries where they operate. They have chastised critics as unrealistic. Employment of fourteen-to-sixteen-year-olds, long working hours, and low wages are presented as the necessary price of progress, unfortunately inevitable in the early stages of economic takeoff, but leading to accelerated growth and prosperity. MNCs assert that increasing local wage rates would be counterproductive since it would force them to increase the retail prices of their products, reducing aggregate demand. It would also shift production to manufacturers that are less scrupulous with regard to treatment of workers. MNCs contend that they adhere to local laws and regulations in their own operations and insist that their suppliers also adhere to similar standards of compliance. They put the blame for poor working conditions largely on the shoulders of local manufacturers and local labor authorities. At the same time, they condone laxity in compliance as a necessary evil because developing countries cannot afford the luxury of enforcing labor and environmental standards similar to those that prevail in industrially advanced countries.[9]

The second aspect of MNCs' response to public criticism is more proactive. Recognizing that some allegations of poor and unfair working conditions may indeed be valid, MNCs have proposed additional action on their part as both desirable and feasible. Individual companies and industry groups have promulgated voluntary codes of conduct to govern their overseas operations and those of their local manufacturers and suppliers. These codes generally commit the MNCs and their local suppliers to comply with all the local laws regarding wages and working hours; prohibit employment of children, forced labor, or prison labor; protect workers from abuse, discrimination, and harassment; and prevent work under dangerous or unhealthy conditions. Some codes go even further, calling for working and living conditions better than those mandated by local laws and regulations; training and opportunities for skill enhancement; guarantees of workers' rights to free speech and freedom of association; formal procedures for resolving workers' complaints; and opportunities for workers to consult with management on issues that affect their wages, or working and living conditions.

An examination of MNCs' rationales and defenses for the prevailing state of affairs reveals the flaws in their logic. Evaluating the substance and adequacy of their proactive responses toward improving the lot of workers in developing countries shows that MNCs' pledges toward reforms through code adoption are more rhetorical than substantive.

Rationales

Sweatshops Are Good for You!

One of the most egregious, factually incorrect, and morally offensive arguments made by apologists for MNCs' overseas practices is that the "horrible conditions" described by critics can be considered horrible only when compared with the conditions prevailing in industrially advanced countries, for example, the United States.[10] When viewed in the context of the poorer countries, these sweatshop-like conditions are a distinct improvement over conditions that existed before and still prevail in businesses that produce primarily for domestic markets. Corporate critics are accused of "cultural imperialism" for insisting on a minimum age for workers, ridiculed for seeking a "living wage." Sometimes critics are branded as protectionist, their complaints portrayed as an attempt by organized labor in the United States to prevent companies from purchasing from low-wage countries. Defenders of MNC conduct assert that even in the United States, there were no minimum age limits until the latter part of the twentieth century, and that even now young adults regularly work in places like convenience stores and fast-food restaurants where minimum wages are far below any reasonable definition of "living wage."

But this logic is problematic. If a country's economic growth is to be accelerated and the cause of free trade furthered, why confine work hours to ten hours a day when young workers are healthy enough to work twelve-hour days? Why indulge in such luxuries as one day off a week? Workers can do more for their countries and their families by working twelve-hour days and seven-day weeks. And what about working conditions? Certainly costs could be reduced if one did not have to pay for proper air ventilation, or a clean facility, or personal safety equipment for workers.

The proponents of the status quo do not offer any cogent explanation as to why they consider the current conditions optimal. When pushed, they revert to the assertion that these countries and their workers cannot afford wages and working conditions that are similar to those currently prevailing in the United States. Ethan Kapstein, for example, states that "forcing the standards of industrialized nations on developing countries and the firms that operate in them could backfire by reducing investment and job creation."[11] And a recent article in the *New York Times Magazine* suggests that MNCs have contributed to raising workers' wages in China from $50 to $250 a month. But these claims are not backed by verifiable data.[12] No credible opponents of sweatshops have ever demanded that wages and working conditions in developing countries match those in the United States.

Reports about the effects of labor standards on the livelihoods of workers in developing countries are often produced without careful scrutiny of the sources on which they are based. In a Special Report on Globalization published in *Business Week,* for instance, it was reported that "soon after a bill was proposed in the U.S. Congress in 1993 to ban imports from countries where children work in factories, garment makers in Bangladesh fired 36,000 workers under age eighteen, most of them girls. . . . Few of the fired workers ended up in school. Instead, many took more dangerous jobs and became prostitutes."[13]

The source of this information was the association of the local owners of apparel factories in Bangladesh—who are among the most notorious sweatshop owners in the world.[14] Even the internal audits of foreign MNCs show that these owners hire younger workers, keep false records, maintain unsafe factories, and tolerate work conditions that border on slavery and human bondage. Yet the data provided by these employers are supposed to be taken at face value.

This Job Is Brought to You by Your Favorite Multinational Corporation

MNCs and their supporters never seem to tire of citing their contributions to job creation in developing countries. But these jobs were not created out of some sense of altruism; they are the result of coldhearted financial calculations. If MNCs were really serious about their role in bringing prosperity to these countries, they would pay wages that would allow workers to have some savings to invest in human capital. A decent wage would allow a worker's children to go to school, and perhaps train for a better job and hope for a better future. Can we really justify inhaling toxic fumes, eating insufficient and unhealthy food, and living in highly unsanitary and overcrowded conditions as the necessary price of development?

The issue for us, and for the MNCs, is not what poor workers with no bargaining leverage are willing to accept in order to keep their jobs, but what the MNCs should be willing to pay as a simple matter of fairness. The cost differences between $5.15 per hour in the United States and $.30 per hour in the developing world are so huge that MNCs could pay three or four times these wages and still make enormous profits compared to the alternative of manufacturing these products at home.

Paying Higher Wages Would Cause MNCs to Raise Prices and Lose Customers

U.S.-based multinationals have argued that the retail price of, say, a man's shirt or woman's blouse would go up by 5 to 10 percent if wages of workers in their factories in China, Indonesia, or other countries were to be raised by 5 to 10 percent. But even a cursory examination of data shows that paying wages marginally higher than current levels (which are often below the level putatively required by local laws) would not make MNCs unprofitable. Although these companies are loath to reveal cost or profit data about their overseas operations, most knowledgeable experts agree that in-country production costs rarely exceed 10 percent of the end-user price. Direct labor costs typically range between 2 percent and 5 percent of all costs incurred by the time the product is ready to leave the factory (i.e., of the product's ex-factory cost). A branded men's polo shirt might retail for between $30 and $50 in the United States, while the direct labor cost of manufacturing this shirt in a factory in a developing country is less than $1. Similarly, a well-known brand of sneakers may retail for $75 in the United States and represent less than $2 in direct labor costs. As even *Business Week* points out, "Workers' pay [is] pitiful considering the nearly 40% gross profit margins Nike and Reebok earn."[15]

This suggests that even multiplying wages by a factor of two or three, to $.60 to $.90 per hour, would not make a significant difference in the retail prices of these products. Nor should it affect the overall profitability of the company, unless this increase in wages is marked up by 100 percent at every level of the supply chain until it reaches the retail consumer.

Another untenable assumption in this argument is that all other elements of a company's cost structure are so finely tuned that no other efficiencies are possible to offset increased wage costs. MNC executives experienced in overseas operations acknowledge that field expenses often get bloated because of the high cost of maintaining expatriate managers and their families. These companies also become inefficient in terms of utilization of raw materials and of processing costs because labor is so cheap that it can pay for a lot of mistakes in other aspects of the business.[16]

Low wages may indeed be necessary for creating more employment and income growth, but industries do not have to exploit people under sweatshop conditions. The incremental cost of providing fair wages and decent working conditions is minimal and easily affordable when seen in the context of total wage costs, ex-factory cost of goods, or wholesale prices received by MNCs. If MNCs find these calculations inaccurate, they should provide relevant information for analysis and verification by mutually acceptable independent auditors.

Proactive MNC Responses: Believe What I Say, Don't Question What I Do

MNCs often promulgate voluntary codes of conduct to address the concerns of their critics. These codes have become de rigueur for MNCs that profess to be good corporate citizens and to conduct their operations in a professional and socially responsible manner. Unfortunately, most of these codes are viewed with skepticism, and even ridiculed, by knowledgeable observers, influential opinion leaders, the news media, and large segments of the population.[17]

In general, these codes offer too much by way of promise and deliver too little by way of substantive actions. They are presented as public statements of lofty intent and purpose, but lack specific content. Managers and employees within the firm are often uninformed about the codes, and do not take them seriously. Code compliance is not integrated into the organization's reward structure, operating procedures, or corporate culture. MNCs provide little verifiable evidence as to how these codes are being implemented, or how performance of the companies' overseas operations is monitored. In most cases, companies do not provide details of shortcomings found by their internal auditors, or of any actions taken against offending plant operators. MNCs almost invariably refuse to identify their overseas suppliers. Codes fail to provide any commitment or framework for communicating to external constituencies in terms that are reliable and believable. The entire process lacks credibility because it is shrouded in secrecy. Instead, the MNCs insist that people should have trust in the companies' statements as to their compliance efforts—a somewhat dubious proposition under the best of circumstances. To wit, why should the companies be so reluctant to open their performance to public scrutiny if they have nothing to hide and everything to gain where their good performance would engender public trust and enhance corporate reputation?

Corporations are often seen as being dragged into action only when public pressure becomes too intense to ignore. A review of MNC and trade association efforts in the sphere of codes of conduct over the last fifteen-plus years leads to one inescapable conclusion: MNCs, in general, do not see codes of conduct as an opportunity to improve their overseas performance with regard to labor, the environment, protection of human rights, or thwarting bribery and corruption. Nor do companies view them as a means of building public trust. Instead, codes are viewed as a necessary evil and an inconvenient nuisance, which should be handled with minimum cost and as little effort as possible.[18] Consequently, codes become a corporate liability and may even exacerbate the situation by revealing the absence of long-term strategies to address issues that are important to the public at large, and to communicate in a manner that is meaningful and believable.

Challenges in Effective Code Creation and Implementation

There are currently two approaches—group and individual—to codes of conduct. In the group approach, a number of companies in a particular region or industry develop a common set of guiding principles and implementation standards. This approach appears to be the preferred choice of companies when they are first confronted with pressure to implement a code of conduct; it offers group members a measure of protection in dealing with their critics. The second approach is for individual companies to develop their own codes of conduct. Individual company codes are created when a group approach does not succeed or is proceeding slowly. Individual codes are offered as a stopgap arrangement or as a complement to the groupwide approach.

A survey of current efforts in code development in the United States and Western Europe reveals a dismal picture. At the group level, codes are often used to retard progress, while at the individual company level codes seldom move beyond exercises in public relations and halfhearted efforts at improving conditions.

Group-Based or Industrywide Approach

The industry- or regionwide approach is based on the premise that companies in an industry or region face similar problems, competitive conditions, and external pressures; therefore, a coordinated approach should be more cost-effective. An industrywide approach creates a level playing field and generates cooperation among all member companies toward achieving their common goal.

But a group-based approach can all too easily serve as a disguise under which participating companies retard meaningful action in developing and implementing a code of conduct. It goes against the grain of market competition and the creativity it generates for solving unusual and apparently difficult problems. MNCs contend that too many codes would cause confusion in the minds of the public and make it difficult for local manufacturers to comply with codes from different foreign companies. This line of reasoning, however, is quite specious and self-serving. Companies all over the world compete with each other in providing products and services to customers. It is hard to imagine that a company that believes that it has a superior product would delay introducing it in the marketplace until competitors could offer similar products. Why should codes of conduct be any different? Different companies may develop codes whose viability would be determined in the marketplace. Once the superiority of a particular code has been established in terms of its content and implementation, other companies would adapt it to meet their own requirements.

The major flaw in this approach is that it suffers from the "free-rider" problem. Individual companies have little incentive to improve their performance because the recalcitrant companies are not interested in doing so in the first place, and the forward-looking companies have nothing to gain from doing so. Industrywide efforts depend on "voluntary compliance" and rarely incorporate any enforcement measures to ensure that all companies meet their commitments. An industrywide or group-based approach requires a consensus decision before any action can be taken. This situation plays into the hands of the companies that are least inclined to undertake substantive action and thus can postpone implementation through endless discussions, procrastination, and obfuscation. It forces industry performance standards to the lowest common denominator—the company with the weakest record sets the pace for the entire industry—and it inevitably leads to public ridicule and distrust.

The proof of this logic is evident from the fact that despite years of consultation and negotiation, none of the major industry groups generally associated with the sweatshops, human rights violations, and related issues have developed or implemented meaningful codes. Industry associations in toys, apparel, and mining and minerals, among a host of industries, have yet to create meaningful codes after years of negotiations and consultations.

A review of three initiatives that exemplify different formulations of the group-based approach—The Sullivan Principles in South Africa, the Global Compact sponsored by the United Nations, and the U.S.-based Fair Labor Association—suggests that these group-based efforts have not delivered their promised results. Instead, they may have helped companies postpone urgently needed reforms.

The Sullivan Principles in South Africa

The best and perhaps the most successful example of a "groupwide" approach is the case of the Sullivan Principles in South Africa. As opposed to other industry or areawide efforts currently under way, the Sullivan Principles, created in 1977, were developed independently of the companies that became its initial sponsors. It was the first voluntary code of ethical conduct to be applied under realistic operating conditions, involving a large number of corporations, recipient constituencies, and an institutional framework for project implementation, project monitoring, and performance evaluation. The principles had a large measure of moral authority to validate corporate actions, and where necessary, to exhort companies to undertake activities that they might not otherwise consider.

The Sullivan Principles created compliance standards and an independent external monitoring system. Although the signatory companies to the principles provided significant inputs in creating performance standards and measurement systems, the final decision was always made by the Principles Oversight Committee and the independent monitor.

Studies show that despite extensive planning and built-in checks and balances, the principles failed to deliver fully on either their promise or their potential. A major part of the blame for this failure lies with the companies, because they resisted all efforts to allow public disclosure of the performance of individual companies or even group performance on specific measures. The system was thus unable to exert pressure on individual companies. Company conduct coalesced around broad, comfortably achievable measures. Whether or not these were the most important measures was of secondary importance. The question of whether the level of performance was the best that could be achieved given the corporate resources and culpability was ignored.[19]

It is doubtful that the Sullivan Principles contributed significantly to the abolition of apartheid, or left a lasting legacy in terms of improving black economic empowerment. Nevertheless, the operations of the Sullivan Principles offer an excellent laboratory to examine the efficacy of various modes of corporate actions when confronted with hostile sociopolitical environments, conflicting economic and social goals, and even lack of full support from host country managers both as to the rationale for the principles and the manner in which they were applied to local subsidiaries.[20]

The Global Compact: Corporate Leadership in the World Economy

UN Secretary-General Kofi Annan challenged the top leadership of the global business community to enact a Global Compact between the United Nations and the private sector to promote human rights, improve labor conditions, and protect the environment.[21] The Global Compact (GC) was formally launched on July 26, 2000.[22] It contains nine principles derived from the Universal Declaration of Human Rights, the Declaration of the International Labor Organization on Fundamental Principles and Rights, the 1995 Copenhagen Social Summit, and the Rio Declaration of the 1992 UN Conference on Environment and Development (the Earth Summit).

GC emphasizes working at the local level, using a cooperative approach to encourage MNCs and the countries involved to create systems that improve conditions for workers. A number of companies from developing countries are participating in GC-sponsored meetings wherein learning is emphasized through exchange of ideas and experiences. It is, however, too early to predict the extent to which local companies will actually take corrective actions implementing the principles of GC in their plants. GC has also faced skepticism from MNCs, which tend to see UN-sponsored initiatives as the first step toward international regulation of business.

A more fundamental issue with GC, however, is its intended purpose. All the covenants underlying the GC principles are already in existence, but have not been fully implemented even by member nations. Regulations and enforcing mechanisms at the country level have been grossly lacking in large parts of the world where human rights violations and environmental protection problems are particularly acute. Why should the Global Compact make a major difference in the status quo?

The organizers of GC have anticipated these problems. GC is not designed as a code of conduct; rather, "it is meant to serve as a [frame] of reference to stimulate best practices and to bring about convergence around universally shared values."[23] GC documents state that "the success of the Global Compact will be measured by how effectively it provokes and stimulates action."[24] This sums up both the strength and the weakness of the Global Compact: To the extent that multinational corporations are *predisposed* to create a fair, safe, and coercion-free work environment, harnessing physical resources within the context of sustainable development, GC will enhance and support these activities in an environment of trust and mutual cooperation; conversely, if a large number of multinationals are not inclined to take substantive action in this direction, GC will fail to achieve its goals.

As the UN's Georg Kell explains, "One can readily appreciate why corporations would be attracted to the Global Compact. It offers one-stop shopping in three critical areas of greatest external pressure: human rights, environment, and labor standards, thereby reducing their transaction costs."[25] The downside of this approach is already apparent. The initial meetings of GC attracted corporations that were suffering from adverse publicity and were only too eager to gain respect by hanging on Kofi Annan's coattails. GC suffers from an ambiguity of goals, and inadequate linkages between purposes and means to accomplish them. If the primary purpose of GC is to encourage dialogue and share experiences among different groups for mutual learning, it is quite laudable in itself. In this case, a meaningful and measurable compliance with the Global Compact's principles will be *an intended, but second-order effect.* However, if GC is designed to increase meaningful and measurable compliance with the principles of GC as its primary goal, and the dialogue and shared experiences as means to achieving this goal, then the compact is setting itself up for failure. The compact has disavowed any effort toward setting standards by which compliance with its principles can be uniformly and objectively measured, and systems by which corporate compliance can be verified and made transparent. In the absence of these linkages, the Compact will suffer the fate of all such grand designs where process becomes all-consuming and the end result gets lost.

Fair Labor Association

Fair Labor Association (FLA) is the successor organization to former President Clinton's Apparel Industry Partnership (AIP), which was created in 1996. Despite more than three years of intensive negotiations between the companies and NGOs, the AIP had failed to make any discernible progress toward its goal of creating a viable system of monitoring overseas plants for worker abuses and human rights violations. As presently constituted, FLA is a nonprofit organization created in 1999 that includes thirteen apparel and footwear manufacturers and retailers as participating members. In addition, 160 colleges and universities are affiliated with FLA to ensure that companies producing goods as their licensees are operating in accordance with FLA principles and workplace code of conduct. A notable feature of FLA is the inclusion of various human rights and labor rights groups. The group's formation was not without controversy, as two of the nation's largest unions and one church-affiliated group that had participated in the discussions leading to FLA's formation decided not to join the group because of weak monitoring procedures.[26]

The FLA exemplifies the advantages of a group-based effort toward code creation and implementation. It has a board of directors that includes major constituent groups, which oversees FLA's operations, sets policy guidelines, and monitors corporate compliance. A common code, widely applied, offers economies of scale in terms of field audits. The combined purchasing power of the member companies also ensures that local manufacturers have greater incentive to comply with the code, because otherwise they risk being excluded from major foreign markets. The participating companies cover a vast segment of the developing country manufacturing sector with over 3,500 factories covering almost 3 million workers in more than seventy countries. The participation of local NGOs in conducting field audits helps to engage in-country community groups and thereby make effective use of their familiarity with local conditions.

Unfortunately, FLA is also encumbered with all the drawbacks associated with an industrywide approach. It has a bureaucratic and highly structured governance system whose overriding concern seems to be protecting the member companies from overzealous NGOs, aggressive members of the community, and the news media. Every element of FLA's work reflects political compromises designed to protect the vital interests and strategies of its most powerful members, the corporations. Both the governance structure and operating procedures guarantee that FLA's potential and mandate will remain largely unfulfilled. FLA promises more than it can deliver.

In general, the code is quite similar to the multitude of codes that have been promulgated by companies and industry groups that employ low-skilled or unskilled workers abroad, for example, apparel, toys, and shoes. The FLA monitoring standards call for auditing 30 percent of a participating company's vendors. These vendors are to be selected by the participating company, although FLA's board chairman has the final authority as to selection. This is a serious flaw in the system and undermines the credibility of the monitoring process. The problem with this process is that of information asymmetry: Since the companies will almost always have more information, they will choose vendors that are most likely to have complied with the code. And yet, the primary objective of FLA is to find vendors that are *not* in compliance with the FLA code and induce them to improve their performance.

Under FLA's procedures, there is no disclosure of the compliance record of individual plants. Instead a participating company—that is, brand—is certified as having complied with the code. The process seriously undermines the integrity of the entire FLA effort when we realize that: (a) vendors are not randomly selected and instead are nominated by the participating company; and (b) public disclosure is severely limited and reduced to FLA's assertion that the brand is in compliance with the code.

In the end, we are left with the distressing observation that after all the expense and efforts of a large number of well-intentioned groups and individuals, the current structure and operation of FLA is unlikely to make significant and observable improvement in the working and living conditions of the workers.

Individual Company or Go-It-Alone Approach

Advantages

The go-it-alone approach calls for a company to create a code of conduct that is unique to the needs of the company in terms of both content and implementation. The current situation with regard to international codes of conduct is similar to that of an emerging industry where there are no established products and markets; where customer needs and expectations are well defined—often in terms of dissatisfaction with current products; and where the customer is ready and willing to try out new products that offer better price-value than existing products. Therefore, an enterprising firm has an opportunity to garner greater market share, earn higher profits, build customer loyalty, and enhance corporate reputation by being first on the market with the right product.

A company can improve its bottom line by creating an international code of conduct that (a) is markedly different in quality, and (b) provides an information base, which allows its code to be evaluated in an objective and dependable manner. Such a code has the advantage of including only those issues that are relevant to the corporation, and that the corporation has greater ability to control through its actions and performance. This approach also avoids the "free-rider" problem: The company stands to gain or lose only from its own actions. It enhances public trust in the corporation, which can translate into a more hospitable sociopolitical environment.

MNCs' Reluctance to Pursue the Go-It-Alone Approach

Why are MNCs not vigorously following the go-it-alone approach, with its apparent advantages? A major problem, and one that is rarely discussed, is that when it comes to creating codes of conduct and complying with them, most companies have been entrapped in their own false promises. A good illustration of this is an imbroglio involving Nike: A public interest group in California charged in a civil complaint that Nike had committed consumer fraud by making false assertions, through its code of conduct, regarding its treatment of workers in overseas factories. In this instance, the court accepted Nike's contention that its statements were protected under the First Amendment guarantees of free speech, and dismissed the case.[27]

MNCs almost invariably assert that they follow their own codes of conduct, with their requirements that they abide by local labor laws with regard to wages, working hours, and working conditions. In reality these assertions are far from accurate. This author's experience examining sweatshop conditions around the world suggests that at best fewer than 10 percent of these plants are likely to be in full compliance with local laws.[28] And the gap has widened as the years have passed and the promises have become more specific. The problem facing the multinationals is not so much making good on their promises regarding current conditions or their commitments to do right in the future, but how to take care of years of labor law violations and the heavy financial burden—not to mention loss of public credibility—that would be imposed if the companies were required to pay workers for wages and benefits that were owed them for prior years.

There is another aspect to this problem in terms of MNCs' local suppliers. In the past, MNCs sought to abrogate their responsibility for the conduct of their overseas suppliers by arguing that these suppliers were independent entrepreneurs and that the companies had no control over these suppliers. However, it has been shown that foreign multinationals exert tremendous control over the operations of their suppliers because of their buying power. Further, MNCs have detailed information about their suppliers' cost structures and therefore know the extent to which local suppliers can comply with local labor laws within the price constraints imposed by the MNC buyers. Faced with public pressure, MNCs more recently have claimed that their overseas suppliers were also required to comply with the companies' codes of conduct—but MNCs have, in fact, done little or nothing to monitor or enforce local suppliers' compliance. These hollow claims have further widened the gap between promise and performance and increased the cumulative potential liability of MNCs.

These problems will not go away, and will only get worse if MNCs refuse to face the reality of their conduct. Already, the pressures of increased public scrutiny, adverse media attention, and consumer outrage have forced companies to take positive actions that have gone beyond cosmetic damage control and crisis management. Nike and other companies have been spurred to action following revelations of worker abuse, wages below legally minimum rates, and unhealthy and unsafe working conditions.[29]

Imperative for Multinational Codes of Conduct

Despite difficulties and problems, voluntary codes of conduct offer perhaps the best, if not the only, viable option for bridging the gap between the adverse side effects of the imperfect workings of free trade and the minimal necessary standards for wages and working conditions that must be afforded to workers in developing countries.

Once individual codes by more enlightened MNCs have been introduced and tested in the marketplace, there will be a natural tendency by other MNCs to implement their own codes that emulate the more popular features of successful codes. This process will lead to convergence among various codes and provide a baseline standardization of code characteristics, yet leave ample scope for customization to meet the specific needs of individual companies.

Corporations should not look upon these codes with fear and trepidation or as an instrument for creating further intrusion into corporate affairs. Instead, by setting clear and mutually agreed upon performance criteria—where current standards are weak or nonexistent—they assure themselves of external accountability within the limits of economic feasibility and competitive reality. MNC-sponsored and voluntarily implemented codes of conduct are here to stay. When properly developed and implemented, they can serve both corporate interests and public purposes, and strengthen free market institutions. They will also restore public faith in the market economy as the best avenue for enhancing human welfare, advancing regional economies, and strengthening democratic institutions.

The first step in developing a workable code of conduct is to define clearly its scope of action. This includes:

Definition—What aspects of corporate business activities are to be included in the code of conduct?

Measurement and Verification—How should corporate performance of these activities be measured and the accuracy of performance verified?

Accountability and Reporting—To whom should the corporation be accountable for its performance, and how should this performance be made public?

For a code of conduct to meet the expectations of the parties involved, it must:

Be economically viable for the corporation given the dynamics of competition, industry structure, and the economic and sociopolitical realities of the developing countries where operations are located;

Address substantive issues that are of importance to the workers themselves and the corporation's major stakeholders, and to the NGO community concerned with these issues, host country governments, and other affected groups;

Engage and consult important groups with a stake in the content and implementation of the code; and

Be specific as to performance standards that can be objectively measured.

The code must be translated into a quantifiable and standardized audit instrument that lends itself to objective and consistent measurement. Codes of conduct must be an integral part of the company's culture, organizational structure, and operational philosophy. The company's top management must be strongly and unequivocally committed to implementing the code. It must be integrated into the company's performance evaluation and reward structure. The company must be willing to expose its operations and code compliance to public verification if it expects to garner the "reputation effect" and thereby benefit from increased consumer patronage and public approval of its activities. Code implementation and monitoring cannot be a one-time phenomenon; it should be undertaken on a regular basis as an integral part of the company's operational philosophy.

Overcoming a Final Objection: The Cost of Independent External Monitoring

MNCs often—and fallaciously—argue that a comprehensive program of independent external monitoring of work conditions in developing country plants would be very expensive, and that its perceived benefits cannot justify its high cost. Some MNCs claim that the cause of improving worker conditions in poorer countries would be better served if moneys were instead devoted to worker training and other forms of assistance to local vendors.

The absurdity of these claims is revealed by running some calculations with plausible cost figures. A senior vice president of Gap Inc., Elliot Schrage, stated last year that "Gap spends $10,000 a year for the independent monitors at Charter, which is owned by Taiwanese investors, and thousands more for management time to arbitrate disputes and for its own company monitors to recheck the facts on the ground. For the company to duplicate these intensive efforts at each of the 4,000 independent factories it contracts with would have taken about 4.5 percent of its annual profit of $877 million last year."[30]

A survey of various monitoring groups certified by both FLA and Social Accountability International standards suggests that the cost of a single factory audit ranges between $3,000 and $8,000, depending on the size of the plant and the thoroughness of the audit; nonetheless, let's accept for the sake of argument that GAP spends $10,000 for independently monitoring a plant. Now let's assume that a typical plant employs about 5,000 workers, each of whom earns about $2 a day based on a wage rate of $.25 an hour for an eight-hour workday. Therefore, the $10,000 cost would be equal to one day's wages per year for the entire plant. Further assuming that employees work only five days a week, this cost represents .38 percent of the "normal" yearly wage costs of the plant. This cost estimate represents a liberal interpretation of the relation between employee wages and monitoring costs, since most employees work ten-to-eleven-hour days and six-day weeks. Some of these hours are worked on an overtime basis, and many plants operate for two or three shifts, both factors that would further depress the cost of an audit in relation to work hours. It is hard to imagine that an audit should cost more than .2 percent of the actual yearly wage costs of a typical plant.

Why is this cost not justifiable as "insurance" to ensure that workers are paid their legally mandated wages and benefits, and that they work in a relatively safe and healthy environment? Do the MNCs and their local vendors realize that they are looking at huge potential liability fifteen to twenty years down the line, similar to that confronted by tobacco companies or asbestos users?

We might also be justifiably skeptical of Schrage's estimate that the total cost of monitoring 4,000 factories at a cost of $39.5 million per year would represent about 4.5 percent of the company's annual profit in the year 2000. Let's assume that the audits are similar in character to financial audits that all publicly owned companies are required to do annually. Even under the most stringent standards, the audit process requires a careful sampling of only a small portion of all transactions, in order to assess the accuracy of all transactions. The process is highly scientific and statistically valid, with a high degree of confidence as to its accuracy—and it can be accomplished at a fraction of the cost of an audit involving all transactions.

Why not use a similar approach in the case of code-of-conduct audits? A carefully designed, objectively determined, and randomly selected sample of factories from the total universe of 4,000 factories would not need to be larger than 500 to 800 factories. All factories would stand an equal chance of being audited and thus have a strong incentive to comply with the company's code. In this case, the cost of audits would stand at a mere .04 percent of a typical plant's annual wage cost. Certainly this is a justifiable expense, particularly when considered in relation to what MNCs spend to ensure that products manufactured by overseas vendors meet their standards for quality, product safety, and delivery schedules.

Some Concluding Thoughts

Codes of conduct offer an invaluable opportunity for responsible corporations to create an individual and highly positive public identity for themselves. This "reputation effect" can directly improve their bottom lines through increased revenues, improved customer loyalty, expanded markets, a more productive workforce, and a supportive political and regulatory environment. From society's perspective, voluntary codes serve to achieve a larger public purpose in a flexible and pragmatic manner.

Public sentiment and perspective play a very important role in defining the parameters of discretion that a society will allow the leaders of its various social, political, and economic institutions. As in many previous instances involving social issues, critics of corporations currently have the lead in the fight for public opinion. The companies, fearing a lack of public trust, have refrained from a stance of proactive public debate and instead have limited themselves to disputing their critics' charges. This is, and will remain, a losing battle. By yielding the initiative to their critics, MNCs have allowed critics to shape the public debate in ways that highlight what MNCs have done wrong, instead of what they are doing right.

An increased level of trust between MNCs, host-country governments, concerned NGOs, the news media, and important segments of the public would allow MNC management greater discretion in running their business operations, and insulate them from the actions of other, less scrupulous firms in the marketplace. A voluntary approach to code formulation and implementation would minimize the need for further governmental regulation, which is invariably more expensive and less efficient.

Corporations can and should undertake meaningful audits, both to regain public trust and to meet their responsibility for public accountability for the social consequences, or second-order effects, of their normal business activities. Cost is not a defensible argument against the need for audits. With proper care and due diligence, social and human rights audits can be conducted in a highly responsible manner; corporations do not run any excessive risk of irresponsible disclosure or unwarranted charges of bad conduct.

NGOs can play an important and constructive role in a voluntary system of code creation and implementation. They bring a unique perspective, and can analyze issues and design remedies that enhance outcomes from the perspective of groups that are normally not involved in the corporate decision matrix. This system does not need to be inefficient in either economic or technological terms. However, it would call for the companies to analyze their traditional ways of doing business and develop new approaches that are both cost-effective and socially desirable.

The emerging global economic order of the 1990s has once again brought capitalism and its principal actor, the multinational corporation, to the apex of social institutions. Unlike the 1960s, when the multinational corporation was seen as a threat to national sovereignty and political freedom, the new world views the multinational corporation as an agent of positive change. Underneath the thin veneer of hope and expectation, however, lies the ever-present danger of the unaccountability of the corporate behemoth, and its potential for doing harm through abuse of its power. The paradox of economic globalism has inevitably created two societies, which are quite disparate in their needs and resources, as well as their aspirations. The current ethical problems stemming from the conflict between business and society do not concern obvious right and wrong, guilt or innocence, but rather the choice of one type of inequity over another, the virtue of frugality and the sin of accumulation, and the morality of principles versus the morality of situations. In an unjust world, the distinctions between the guilty and the innocent have become ambiguous. We are confronted with the realization that we live in an increasingly interdependent society where individual good is not possible outside the context of common good. It makes no sense to separate moral principles from institutional behavior, political power from economic influence, and environmental values from material rewards. To do so is to divorce the social system from its basic element, the human being, which does not behave in a fragmented manner.

Notes

1. Jagdish Bhagwati, *A Stream of Windows: Unsettling Reflections on Trade, Immigration, and Democracy* (Cambridge, MA: MIT Press, 1998); Robert Batterson and Murray Weidenbaum, *The Pros and Cons of Globalization* (St. Louis: Center for the Study of American Business, Washington University, January 2001), pp. 1–22; "Globalization and Its Critics," *Economist*, September 29, 2001: 1–30.

2. Jeffrey Sachs and Andrew Warner, "Economic Reform and Process of Global Integration," *Brookings Papers on Economic Activity*, no. 1 (1995): 1–118.

3. Fareed Zakaria, "Globalization Grows Up and Gets Political," *New York Times*, Op-Ed, December 31, 2000: 24.

4. S. Prakash Sethi, "Human Rights and Corporate Sense," *Far Eastern Economic Review* (October 19, 2001): 37.

5. "Global Capitalism: Can It Be Made to Work Better?" *Business Week*, November 6, 2000: 72–90; "Take a Break, Trade Bullies," *Business Week*, November 6, 2000: 100–1; Sethi, "Human Rights and Corporate Sense," p. 37.

6. Dani Rodrik, "Has Globalization Gone Too Far?" (Washington, D.C.: Institute for International Economics, 1997), p. 7.

7. This author's considerable experience observing manufacturing operations in many developing countries suggests that worker productivity in low-skilled and comparatively less capital-intensive manufacturing operations is considerably higher in developing countries. A large part of this productivity comes from long working hours and high production speeds. This also accounts for the fact that relatively young, sixteen-to-eighteen-year-old, workers perform most of these operations. The fact that such long hours and high manufacturing speeds lead to exhaustion, worker injury, and long-term health damage rarely enters into employers' consideration.

8. Daniel Cohen has made a similar argument with respect to the use of women as beasts of burden in Africa. See Daniel Cohen, *The Wealth of the World and the Poverty of Nations* (Cambridge, MA: MIT Press, 1998), p. 7.

9. Dennis Rondinelli and Jack Behrman, "The Promises and Pains of Globalization," *Global Focus* 12, no. 1 (2001): 6; Batterson and Weidenbaum, The Pros and Cons of Globalization; "Globalization and Its Critics," *Economist*; John M. Berry, "This Time, Boom Benefits the Poor," *Washington Post*, February 11, 2000: C5; Cohen, The Wealth of the World and the Poverty of Nations, p. 7; Ethan B. Kapstein, "The Corporate Ethics Crusade," *Foreign Affairs* 80, no. 5 (September–October 2001): 105–19; Barry Bearak, "Lives Held Cheap in Bangladesh Sweatshop" *New York Times*, April 15, 2001, Section 1: 1.

10. See, for example, "The Case for Globalization," *Economist*, September 23, 2000: 19–20; "Anti-Capitalist Protest—Angry and Effective," *Economist*, September 23, 2000: 85–7; Nicholas D. Kristof and Sheryl WuDunn, "Two Cheers for Sweatshops," *New York Times Magazine*, September 24, 2000, Section 6: 70; and Kapstein, "The Corporate Ethics Crusade," pp. 105–19.

11. Kapstein, "The Corporate Ethics Crusade," p. 106. See also "The Case for Globalization," *Economist*; and "Globalization and Its Critics," *Economist*.

12. Kristof and WuDunn, "Two Cheers for Sweatshops," p. 70.

13. "Global Capitalism: Can It Be Made to Work Better?" *Business Week*, p. 76.

14. Bearak, "Lives Held Cheap in Bangladesh Sweatshop," p. 1.

15. "Global Labor: A World of Sweatshops," *Business Week*, November 6, 2000: 52.

16. Ibid.

17. Illustrations of various corporate codes of conduct can be found on company Web sites, for example, Levi Strauss, Gap, Mattel, McDonald's, Wal-Mart, Walt Disney, Shell, Nike, Motorola, Texas Instruments, and Sara Lee, to name a few.

18. Steven Greenhouse, "Labor Groups Join Coalition to Eliminate Sweatshops," *New York Times*, August 8, 2001, Section B, p. 7; Leslie Kaufman and David Gonzalez, "Labor Standards Clash with Global Reality," *New York Times*, August 24, 2001, p. 1.

19. S. Prakash Sethi and Oliver F. Williams, "Creating and Implementing Global Codes of Conduct: An Assessment of the Sullivan Principles as a Role Model for Developing International Codes of Conduct—Lessons Learned and Unlearned," *Business and Society Review* 105, no. 2 (Summer 2000): 169–200. See also S. Prakash Sethi and Oliver F. Williams, *Economic*

Imperative and Ethical Values in Global Business: The South African Experience and International Codes Today (Boston: Kluwer Academic Publishers, 2000).

20. Sethi and Williams, *Economic Imperatives and Ethical Values in Global Business.* See also Sethi and Williams, "Creating and Implementing Global Codes of Conduct."

21. Georg Kell and John Gerard Ruggie, "Global Markets and Social Legitimacy: The Case of 'Global Compact,'" (paper presented at an international conference, Governing the Public Domain beyond the Era of the Washington Consensus? Redrawing the Line Between the State and the Market, York University, Toronto, Canada, November 4–6, 1999), p. 10. See also Sandrine Tesner and Georg Kell, *The United Nations and Business* (New York: St. Martin's Press, 2000); United Nations, *The Global Compact* (New York, 2000).

22. The author of this chapter worked as a consultant-adviser to the Executive Office of the Secretary-General on issues pertaining to the implementation strategies of the Global Compact.

23. Sandrine Tesner, "How to do Business with the United Nations: The 1997 Update," *UNA-USA*, 1997, p. 226. See also Tesner and Kell, *The United Nations and Business*, p. 53.

24. *The Global Compact*, published by the Global Compact Office, United Nations, January 2001. See www.unglobalcompact.org.

25. Kell and Ruggie, "Global Markets and Social Legitimacy," p. 11.

26. David M. Schilling, director, Global Corporate Accountability Programs, Interfaith Center on Corporate Responsibility, in a letter to Editor Desk of *New York Times*, November 18, 1998, Section A, p. 30. See also "Two More Unions Reject Agreement for Curtailing Sweatshops," *New York Times*, November 6, 1998, Section A, p. 15.

27. *Marc Kasky on Behalf of the General Public of the State of California v. Nike, Inc.*, San Francisco County Superior Court, September 25, 1998. See also "Corporation, Officers Cleared in Public Relations Misrepresentation Case," *Corporate Officers and Directors Liability Litigation Reporter* 15, no. 11 (April 3, 2000), p. 12.

28. See "Global Labor: A World of Sweatshops," *Business Week*, p. 52.

29. Ibid., p. 52. Tania Mason, "Nike Axes Sweatshop after BBC Investigation," *Marketing*, October 19, 2000, p. 5; Dexter Roberts and Aaron Bernstein, "A Life of Fines and Beating" *Business Week*, October 2, 2000, p. 122; Kaufman and Gonzalez, "Labor Standards Clash with Global Reality"; Normandy Madden, "View from Hong Kong," *Ad Age Global*, October 1, 2000, p. 25.

30. Leslie Kaufman and David Gonzalez, "Labor Standards Clash With Global Reality," *New York Times*, April 24, 2001, Section A, p. 1.

CHAPTER 12

The Moral Dimension of Corporate Accountability[1]

MELISSA LANE

Introduction

Calls for the greater accountability of corporations have filled the political landscape in recent years, from anti-globalization activists and academics alike. But is corporate accountability more than a placeholder for the millennial aspiration to popular control of capitalism? It is argued in this chapter that while corporate accountability to the law is essential, both legal and looser ideas of social accountability need to be bolstered by a robust understanding of what may be called either "corporate moral accountability" or "corporate moral responsibilities". Although I defend the validity of the former term, I eventually adopt the latter on grounds of familiarity. After distinguishing between legal, social, and moral accountability, I proceed to ask whether corporations *can* be subject to moral responsibilities, and whether they *should* be. I conclude by canvassing specific responsibilities that corporations might be held to bear.[2]

First, some general remarks on the sudden popularity of "accountability" as a concept in political life, and its place in the vocabulary of political thought. At least two currents converge in contemporary Anglo-American appeals to accountability. One is the legacy of the Thatcherite and Reaganite revolutions in government. The introduction of competition and private sources of supply into the public services at once undermined traditional chains of accountability directly to ministers while promising new forms of accountability. Particularly in Britain, where centralized parliamentary government continues to promote reforms along similar lines, clients have become customers to whom service-providers are accountable, while new agencies can be established to regulate and set standards for private suppliers. Yet accountability can slip through the cracks of these vaunted new mechanisms: The extent to which corporate confidentiality clauses can undermine accountability constitutes a dark underside of these developments.[3]

The other driver for accountability-talk in recent years has been the broad discourse of globalization. Despite endless academic rebuttals, popular and media discussion has been haunted by the idea of globalization undermining the power of the state. Power in these stories attaches instead either to multinational corporations, or to international bodies and regimes such as the World Bank, International Monetary Fund, and World Trade Organization. (Because the next chapter will discuss some of these international bodies and regimes, the focus here will be on corporations.) The globalization story speaks of "private" corporations undermining "public" power, as in this representative quotation from Benjamin Barber:

> International markets spin out of control not just because the economy has been globalized, but because, nation by nation by nation, we have conspired in the transfer of sovereignty from popular hands that are transparent and accountable to private hands that are neither.[4]

Such an exhaustive distinction between public power and private corporations, however, overlooks important senses in which corporations can be considered "public," more public certainly than ordinary "private" individuals. Many corporations are "public" corporations in the sense that they are open to public shareholding and trading. Moreover, they are constituted by the public power of the state that grants them incorporation, unlike private individuals who exist independently of state action. Incorporation itself exists to further general public purposes, invented as a literal privilege reserved for those bodies whose incorporation would serve the state or Crown or public interest. Because corporations are publicly created and often publicly owned, their power feels to many citizens like a quasi-public power rather than a purely private power. Accountability thus becomes envisaged as a bridle for the power of such entities, a new mechanism distinct from the traditional solution of national electoral control, but somehow still linked to the fundamental value of political legitimacy.

For these two reasons, and no doubt for others, accountability has come to occupy a central place in political discourse and debate, despite having been a rather marginal concept in political theory and the history of political thought. While various mechanisms of accountability have been observed in diverse regimes—beginning with the Athenian requirement that magistrates give an account of their actions at the end of their period of office[5]—political theorists have tended to see accountability as a rather technical instrument for achieving legitimacy. Those who have focused on it have largely confined their interest to the accountability of elected representatives to their electorate.[6] Indeed, the paradigm of election has mesmerized political theorists, to the extent of distracting them even from the question of the accountability of the executive to the legislature that has preoccupied their colleagues in political science. Yet accountability through election is the very context that the Thatcherite/Reaganite legacies and the effects of globalization purportedly conspire to marginalize. In the absence of an electorate and a clear theory of political legitimacy, those interested in extra-legal forms of corporate accountability find few resources in political theory on which to draw.

Legal, Social, and Moral Accountability

Can political theory now rise to the occasion by defining accountability as a concept? Several instructive attempts have been made to do so. Most identify a two-party relationship, A being accountable to B, and stress that A must be at least answerable to, and at most sanctionable by, B, for some set of actions.[7] Yet this two-party structure does not apply to the case of moral accountability. Again, political theorists tend to assume that accountability obtains only where some institutional mechanism exists to enforce it; yet this too is inapplicable to the idea of moral accountability. Similarly, most definitions assume that accountability runs from A to B just in case A has been authorized by B to act on her behalf. Yet this principal–agent structure, embedded as it is in economics, does not capture all the senses of accountability in the common law (where, for example, trustees are not agents for a principal in the same sense; explicit authorization is not always required; and an agent's act may create new accountabilities of the principal to third parties).[8]

As these points indicate, the attempt to define a single skeletal concept applicable to all contexts of accountability may be misguided. Rather than attempting to define one here, I shall instead rely on a working hypothesis that conceptions of accountability display family resemblances—one drawing on ideas of answerability, responsibility, and sometimes scrutiny and sanction—in the various contexts in which they arise. The two primary contexts that apply to corporate accountability are the legal and the moral, though they are both implicated also in a looser conception of social accountability. An evaluation of these contexts and the conceptions of accountability embedded within them provides the framework within which the unspecified demand for "corporate accountability" must be understood.

The notion of corporate accountability to the state, within the law, is straightforward. Law sets requirements for which corporations are held accountable by the courts, responding to initiatives by public prosecutors or private plaintiffs, and wielding a range of sanctions from fines to imprisonment of corporate officials. In adversarial legal systems, the emphasis is not on what the corporation voluntarily acknowledges, but rather on what prosecutors or plaintiffs can elicit in the course of the trial. Correspondingly, sanctions are ordinarily seen as effective because of the financial loss they impose and the compensation they recover, rather than because they evoke acknowledgement and reform on the part of the corporation. The emphasis in the legal context of accountability is on the ability of the court to require corporate accountability and to sanction it where necessary: This includes both financial and operational accountability (for health and safety, environmental impact, and so on), and also internal accountability in terms of the required structure of the board and its relationship to the management and to shareholders.[9] Thus this conception exemplifies the assumptions that accountability must involve requirement, specific mechanisms, and sanction.

Calls for reform of the legal treatment of corporate crime have focused in part on smarter sanctions, which can evoke and interact with corporate self-awareness and so the possibility of future behavioral change, in part on the need to impose in extremis the ultimate sanction of "corporate capital punishment" or dissolution.[10] The issue of globalization, for its part, has raised the question of the extent to which corporations can already be held accountable in one jurisdiction for crimes committed in another, and the extent to which laws can be developed to impose such accountability. More general demands for greater corporate accountability are translated into calls for further legal control of working conditions, minimum pay, environmental standards, and other such desiderata. So, for example, the passionate call for a "Framework Convention on Corporate Accountability" made by CorpWatch in January 2002 consists entirely of proposals for new legal requirements on corporations (including reporting requirements, consultation, extended liability, rights of legal redress and legal aid, and community rights to resources, veto rights over development, and rights to compensation). These would be backed by sanctions including suspending stock exchange listing, fines, and de-chartering or withdrawal of limited liability status.[11] As this example shows, despite existing limits to the scope of corporate accountability within the law, even trenchant critics of corporate activity continue to hold that law provides the most effective way in which corporations can genuinely be held accountable.

This contention is fundamentally correct. Accountability in its fullest sense can only be demanded of corporations by and through the law. But this conclusion should give activists calling for "greater corporate accountability" pause. For in an imperfect world, legal accountability of corporations leaves gaping holes not only in weak states, but also in mature democracies. First, the laws applying to corporations may be out of date, so that corporations can exploit new technical or social developments before law catches up to hold them accountable for doing so. Next, the laws passed are often shaped by the intervention of special interests (including corporations themselves), so that they do not demand accountability for certain wrongs that corporations do. Finally, even where laws exist to hold corporations accountable, the corporations may choose to risk non-compliance and may defeat any attempt at prosecution, in both cases relying on legal staff who often dwarf public prosecutors in the skills and resources they command.[12] For all these reasons, legal accountability alone—despite its virtues of clarity and sanction—all too often falls short of the expectations for control of corporations so prominent in popular discourse today.

For this reason, the call for "corporate accountability" sometimes appeals instead to a vaguer notion of informal social—rather than legal—accountability. Modeling itself on the legal, the demand for "corporate accountability" to the "public" implies that some actors in civil society (often the very non-governmental organizations—NGOs—making the demand) can stand in for the state in being entitled to hold corporations accountable on behalf of the public. Civil society processes of publicity, pressure, boycott, and so on are de facto treated as the appropriate institutional mechanisms to enforce that accountability. But civil society actors have neither authorized the corporations to exist (a state has done that) nor are they uncontroversially identifiable as being owed accountability (as is the state). While civil society pressure is not illegitimate per se, it does not contain within itself an objective account or arbiter of its own legitimacy. The danger of goalposts being moved, or fixed where they should never have been placed, is real.

Such social pressure risks falling into the trap of opposing static invocations of virtue, the NGOs proclaiming their virtue, the corporations defending theirs. Instead, what is needed is an objective criterion, not one that will settle the issue as a *deus ex machina*, but that can rather provide the interpretative terms and standards for the parties on both sides to debate. This is the role of moral accountability. Moral account-ability underpins calls for greater legal and social accountability alike by providing a standard of expectation and assessment, while in the mean-time opening the door to corporate initiative as well as activist pressure. It places the corporation and its critics on an equal footing in which both sides can seek to defend the principles they adopt and their judg-ment of the application of those principles in a given case.[13]

What then is moral accountability? Whereas law fits the common assumption that A is accountable to some distinct and identifiable B (the corporation is accountable to the law), morality does not. For morality holds both that A is accountable to herself (to her own judgment), and that A is accountable to moral agents generally—but not that there is someone identifiable, B, who stands in a uniquely privileged position. Moral accountability can apply to any agent capable of governing their conduct according to moral requirements, without this implying that the agent is a "moral agent" in the full sense of the term, one to be accorded rights and respect as well as responsibilities.

Accountability to oneself derives from religious assumptions that one is accountable to God for one's actions and one's beliefs.[14] But God being a normally silent, and in the last hundred years a largely disappearing part-ner for many, the onus of accountability is thrown back on the individual and her own judgment. One must take responsibility for one's beliefs and one's actions and for scrutinizing and judging them in accordance with what (one believes) the substantive canons of morality demand. Here, there is no two-place relation: Scrutiny is a reflexive matter, and A's own judgment of her responsibility is more fundamental than any external pressure or sanction.

Like accountability to oneself, accountability to moral agents generally is a feature of contemporary thought with a specific genealogy. The secu-larization of moral thought performed in different ways by Hume, Smith, Kant, Bentham, and their followers has made it almost axiomatic that morality is a matter of what one owes other people. While this standard is in the nature of a thought experiment for the deduction of moral princi-ples, such a stance for moral theory cannot wholly isolate itself from social pressures in which the moral and the social indeed intermingle. The need to ask oneself what one owes other people opens the door to the claims that some of those actual others might make, and so to an open-ended if imperfect engagement with real others and real scrutiny, which cannot be entirely rejected on pain of losing one's own internal standard of judg-ment. Sanction may accompany scrutiny, though it will do so not via any institutional mechanism but rather via the informal interactions of every-day life: One may be shunned, lambasted, embarrassed, or avoided if one is judged to have failed in something one was accountable to do. So there is no single B, no institutional mechanism, and no "obligation" on or "requirement" of A to account to B, yet a meaningful sense of accountability here persists.

Consider, for example, works by Robert E. Goodin[15] and Thomas Scanlon,[16] both of whom make accountability central to their accounts of basic moral demands. It is claimed that one is accountable to others for acting in such a way as to protect the interests of the vulnerable (Goodin) or for acting according to principles that others could not reasonably reject (Scanlon). In both of these characteristic modern moral systems, accountability inheres in relationships among (moral) equals without any need for explicit authorization or contracting to establish its basis or terms.

There is a sense in which such talk of moral accountability is merely a metaphor, a way of testing what morality requires rather than a specification of obligations owed to and enforceable by distinct other people. Morality does not require me to miss my plane in order to listen to the haranguing of a street preacher, for example. But it is also true that what moral accountability does require of me can only be settled by judging between claim and counterclaim. If I plug my ears and close my mind to all counterarguments to my own view of my moral duties, I cannot know that that view is justified. While in theory I could generate all possible counterarguments myself, in practice moral agents will be enmeshed in debate with others who advance claims that they might not have thought of themselves and that they owe to themselves and to others generally to consider. Moral accountability thus shades into social accountability again, but it does so now with a putative objective standard in mind for social actors to debate. If corporation Y should listen to what NGO Z says, and vice versa, this is not because of the identity of either, but because of the strength of the arguments put forward. This is a subtle distinction, but one that opens the door in the best case to cycles of argument rather than cycles of intimidation. Moral accountability in short seeks objective moral standards, but lives in the competing contestation of claims about what those actually are.

One common objection made, for example, by the pressure group Corpwatch is that moral accountability is merely "voluntary" (we might better say "optional," since voluntariness is a key feature of moral action in Kantian theory) in contrast with compulsory or mandatory legal accountability.[17] But this is to misunderstand the nature of moral demands. While they govern voluntary actions, moral demands are not equivalent to demands that one arbitrarily chooses or fails to choose to impose on oneself. Even in a Kantian view, while moral requirements are imposed on the will by itself, this is done in conformity with reason. Moral demands may require agents to establish binding commitments rather than to operate through "voluntary" (in the conventional sense) initiatives. To say that corporations have moral responsibilities does not imply that these enjoin only optional corporate actions, nor, as argued earlier, that legal accountability is either obsolete or secondary. Moral demands will not by definition have the compulsory mark of the legal. Nevertheless, they needn't be considered to be purely "optional," because they may require mandatory actions and they may also require that corporations work toward a legally binding regime on themselves and others.

Moral accountability, then, has a life of its own, independent of the existence of agent-authorization or accountability-compulsion. It is applicable to those whose conduct can and should be governed by moral requirements deriving from the ways in which people should be treated, not only to those natural persons who figure in the fundamental justifications for such requirements. Legal and moral accountability confront us with two sharply divergent conceptions of the term. The legal conception stresses institutional mechanisms, defined assessors, and sanction over sense of responsibility; the moral conception is devoid of the institutional and the well defined, and stresses responsibility over sanction. Having defended a conception of moral accountability, however, it is now prudent to replace that term with the term "moral responsibility." Because the legal conception of accountability with its attendant sanctions and mechanisms is so much closer to the popular everyday usage of the term, it is easiest to conform to popular usage by restricting the term "accountability" to the legal conception that to avoid fruitless controversies about the fact that the moral conceptions lack such sanctions and mechanisms.

The thesis of this chapter can now be stated as follows: Legal corporate accountability is the highest priority, but needs to be supplemented with corporate moral responsibilities. Compared with some elements of the "corporate social responsibility" (CSR) literature, the corporate moral responsibilities approach emphasizes moral constraints on what corporations ordinarily undertake, rather than additional optional positive actions that they may choose to take. It is more important that corporations not avoid paying taxes than that they give a small donation to charity. Compared with other discussions of CSR, the present approach does not simply involve social pressure, but explicitly identifies an underlying moral standard that can serve as common (or contestable) ground between corporations and their critics. The emphasis here is also on the prevention of harm caused by corporations, rather than as in David Miller's chapter on the rectification of harm however caused; the specific question of what responsibilities corporations have to rectify situations of injustice that they have *not* caused is addressed in the chapter by Onora O'Neill.

Yet it will be immediately objected that corporations cannot bear moral responsibility—for they are not full moral agents—and that they should not bear it, for they are entitled and should be expected simply to realize their profit-making purpose. The remainder of this chapter considers whether corporations *can* bear moral responsibilities; whether they *should* be held to do so; and *what, if anything,* it is for which they should be morally responsible.

Can Corporations Be Subject to Moral Responsibilities?

In the early years of the common law doctrine of equity, a breach of the terms on which land held in trust was sold could invalidate the sale only if the purchaser knew of the trust arrangement: for only then could he be bound in "conscience" to obey it. Corporations posed a problem for such a doctrine, for they were held to have no conscience and so to have no moral inhibition—hence to be subject to no legal prohibition—on breaking the terms of a trust. But the doctrine evolved, through a notion of "reasonable expected knowledge," to the evanescence of the conscience restriction altogether. So for practical purposes the law came to hold corporations, like anyone else, responsible in such circumstances. The historian Maitland summed up the situation thus: ". . . we read in our old books that a use cannot be enforced against a corporation because a corporation has no conscience . . . [but] we have rejected the logical consequence of a certain speculative theory of corporations to which we still do lip-service."[18]

While the practical import of the theory of corporations as having no conscience may, as Maitland observed, have fallen away in the common law, it survives today in philosophical and practical objections to the idea of corporate moral responsibility. Many claim that corporations are essentially amoral, moral duties having no purchase on them: The idea that they might observe moral standards in their conduct without legal or other external compulsion is simply a delusion. Such views implicitly agree with Maitland's "old books" on the common law, exemplified best in the comment by the eighteenth century Lord Chancellor Edward, First Baron Thurlow (1731–1806): "Did you ever expect a corporation to have a conscience, when it has no soul to be damned, and no body to be kicked?"[19]

Without soul or body of its own, a corporation is either a fiction; an artificial legal form conferred on a preexisting group; or an artifice all the way down. The artifice-all-the-way-down theory has attracted most support in recent years, usually articulated in the terms of the common law treating corporations as "artificial persons" as opposed to "natural" ones.[20] The moral responsibilities of such an artificial person may derive either from those of its representatives (for an artificial person must itself be represented by a natural person or persons if it is to be able to act) or from its own peculiar constitution.

Certain moral responsibilities do carry over to the artificial person from the natural ones who act in its name. Because all natural persons have the fundamental moral duty not to enslave others, no role can absolve them of that duty per se: Therefore, since no one could morally act for it to do so, no corporation can permissibly enslave people either. Conversely, not all moral duties of natural persons apply to corporations. Corporations have no duty of filial piety, for example, nor do their representatives qua representatives. Nor are corporations necessarily entitled to the protection of their rights, since rights in their case derive from positive legal stipulation rather than from fundamental moral features. Corporations are not "full moral agents" in the sense that they are equally and fundamentally entitled to moral protection and liable to moral responsibilities; in the case of artificial persons, moral protection and moral responsibility may not be commensurate and may well derive from utterly distinct roots. Even the recent judicial extension of Bill of Rights protections to American corporations has been an uneven, incomplete, and somewhat inconsistent march.

New moral responsibilities accrue to natural persons who represent corporations in their capacity as representatives. Because these representatives represent institutions of a certain kind—institutions that can, as specified in the chapter by Michael J. Green, make decisions and act on them, and whose capabilities to amass and analyze information and to effect changes in the material world may far exceed those of most ordinary people—they incur new moral responsibilities to do with their exercise of these new capabilities. Unlike the duty not to enslave, these new moral duties are role responsibilities that attach to natural persons in their capacity as representative of a corporation and so attach to the corporation itself.[21]

Another way of seeing why corporations should bear moral responsibilities even though they are not full moral agents can be illuminated by reversing the agency perspective that we have been considering. Assuming that most fundamental moral values will revolve around natural persons (whether their rights, or their welfare, or their moral worth), it is important to look at morality not only from the standpoint of the agent but also from that of the patient, the person affected by the actions of others. To that agent, the actions of a corporation look more like the actions of a natural person than they do the result of the forces of nature. To appeal to Rousseau's distinction in *Emile*, a person can legitimately resent the actions of a corporation in a way in which it would be mad to resent the effects of fire. This is because the actions of a corporation are recognizably constituted by human agency at various levels: the human agency authorizing the corporation's existence, buying shares in it, acting in its name, and so on. Although the corporation is not itself a natural person, it is the effect of human agency and, as argued earlier, understandable as the effect of public rather than private human agents in several meaningful senses. So from the perspective of the patient who may suffer from moral wrongdoing, the question of whether the harms were caused by a corporation or by a natural person is secondary to the fact that they are morally blameworthy and demand rectification.

Returning to the capacity of agents, we should not be distracted by the question of corporate motivation for moral behavior. The motivation for compliance with moral principles is, as Onora O'Neill argues in this volume, less important than the capacity for it. Motivation may draw on the motivation of the representatives who don't themselves wish to be associated with immoral action on behalf of the corporation; a corporate culture that prizes and so informs good corporate conduct of which representatives and employees can be proud; or a prudential assessment of the long-term requirements of the "license to operate" or the "business case" for moral action (and here informal social pressure can play a crucial role in changing the balance of corporate calculations). Reputation (both of the representatives as natural persons, and of the corporation as valued by those natural persons associated with it) and prudence, and the complex interplay between them, can go a long way to providing adequate motivation for moral responsibilities both for corporations and for natural persons alone.

Perhaps the best response to the vexed ontological debates about corporate agency, however, is Maitland's pragmatic one. As with the doctrine of equity, we have practical ways of going on which sidestep the perplexities of these debates. Corporations are not alone in raising deep questions about representation and artificial personhood. Similar problems arise in the case of the state. Yet we can hold states to have certain moral duties—for example, to abide by the principles of natural justice, or to provide compensation for historical injustices—without having to settle the vexed ontological question about whether they are moral agents and what moral features their artificial personality bestows upon them.

I have argued that corporations "can" bear moral responsibilities, in the sense that it is not impossible for them to do so. But there is another sense of "can" to be confronted. This is the question of whether an agent "can" be held to bear moral responsibilities while other agents of the same kind are shirking theirs. The problem here is one of contingent compliance.[22] There may be some moral duties that I bear subject to all (or enough) of those who also bear them doing their part, but that in the absence of such general compliance lose their purchase on me as well. Do I have a duty not to cheat on an examination determining my future if I know (and know that it is well known) that most others will cheat? Similarly, a CEO may demand to know how one could expect her company to refrain from making facilitation payments in a country where this is common and expected practice, so that she can expect her competitors to gain a competitive advantage if she refrains. The problem here is not whether corporations have the capacity to act, but whether they "can" so act while engaged in competition that could undermine and destroy their very existence.

I am skeptical about this argument both in the individual and the corporate case. Moral life can depend on someone being prepared to pierce the pretenses of a corrupting situation, as Václav Havel did in his essay "The power of the powerless," which described and enacted the refusal to adhere to the systemic lies of the Czechoslovak Communist regime as a condition for moral truth.[23] Was Havel's act supererogatory? Perhaps there was for him no moral way to behave in a non-superogatory fashion: His contemporaries were not justified by morality in colluding, whether or not they were required by morality to resist. Here there is at the minimum a moral duty to seek ways to make resistance possible, by persuading others—other individuals, or other corporations—to do so as well. In the case of corporations, this task is made easier by the fact that many are not "powerless" to begin with. Those corporations that are relatively powerful, at least, have the chance to change the terms of the game, finding ways to make moral action profitable by new technologies or by reputation effects on its employees, customers, suppliers, or host states. Business is adept at turning challenges into opportunities—why not moral challenges too? Contingent compliance should not be accepted as an excuse either from individuals or from corporations without evidence of creative efforts to break the deadlock.

Should Corporations Accept Higher Standards of Moral Responsibility Than the Law Demands?

I have argued that a suitable conception of moral responsibility can in practice apply to corporate agents. But this leads us to ask whether it *should* so apply. The question is best addressed by confronting two trenchant objections, each associated with a broader theory of the place of corporations in society. The first objection, associated with what I will call the "liberty theory," holds that the corporation's moral duty to its shareholders or owners excludes it from most other moral responsibilities. The second objection, buttressed by what I shall call the "efficiency theory," looks not to the interests and rights of individual shareholders but rather to the interests of society as a whole, arguing that the social good (itself a moral good, if you will) is not best served by having corporations accept higher standards of moral responsibility than the law demands.

Consider the first objection. This is that the duty to put shareholders' interest in a good return first is not only a legal duty, but also a moral one. As Milton Friedman put it in a classic intervention in 1970, "the social responsibility of business is to increase its profits."[24] On this view, this social responsibility (conceived as a moral duty) trumps most rival moral duties that might be offered as part of the content of corporate responsibility. It is the board's fiduciary duty to the shareholders that should, within the limits of the law, be the overriding determinant of business conduct.[25] The objection can root itself in a broader theory of corporations as founded in the exercise of associational liberty. Because people are free within the law to set up institutions directed at particular purposes, those institutions should be free to pursue those purposes and those alone. Moral suasion from outside is illegitimate, and the corporation need not adopt moral constraints on its actions other than those arising from the law.

This objection can be defused by two considerations. First, by pointing out that fiduciary duty is not interpreted in either boardroom or courtroom practice as a maximizing duty. Onora O'Neill has perceptively commented that to imagine that corporations think only of maximizing shareholder returns is similar to imagining that states think only of pursuing self-interest against other states; both claims can be made true by stipulation, but are experientially false on any ordinary understanding. Second, by noting that the liberty theory itself offers shareholders ample opportunity for exit, and that this protects them so long as the moral conditions shouldered by the corporation are publicly acknowledged by it. Should shareholders disagree with the moral constraints applied by the management (the guiding principles of which should be made public in advance), they can simply exit. The hazard to which they are thus exposed is no greater than that to which they are exposed by the market generally.[26] Liberty makes it easy for shareholders to escape, but it does not preclude the assumption of moral responsibilities: Indeed, part of the value of liberty is that it makes it possible for people to act as they should, while allowing others the freedom to decline to do so should they so choose.

Consider now the second objection. This appeals, as mentioned earlier, not to the interests of particular shareholders but rather to those of society as a whole, arguing that these interests are undermined by corporations accepting higher standards of moral responsibility than the law demands. This claim is based on a social theory oriented not to the protection of individual liberty, but to the maximal achievement of social efficiency measured by Pareto-optimality. Legal penalties in this view are understood as assigning costs to action, which rational agents should then include in their calculations alongside other costs and benefits. The law, then, is ideally the perfect mechanism for calibrating social efficiency, and corporations should not gum up the works by applying blanket moral injunctions instead of subtle cost–benefit analyses to their choice of action.

An oddity of this view is that it holds that law is not necessarily to be obeyed. Law should aim not ipso facto to eliminate prohibited action, but rather to make sure that those who do it value this more than those (as represented in the law) who value that it not be done.[27] So it is perfectly legitimate to work out how much it is worth to one to break the law, and then to do so if the expected value is high enough. As advocates of this view have argued: "Managers not only may but also should violate the [legal] rules when it is profitable to do so."

Efficiency theory does offer a plausible interpretation of certain minor legal offenses. If the real aim of the law were to eliminate undesirable parking, for example, it would impose penalties far higher than ordinary parking fines; as it is, many Manhattanites daily decide that it is cheaper and more convenient to risk a fine than to park elsewhere. Cigarette taxes are an even more egregious case. The British Chancellor of the Exchequer would be in serious difficulties if such taxes actually deterred smoking altogether, as he depends on the revenue that they are expected to generate.

But there are well-known difficulties with the assumption that the law always calculates its penalties so as to allow prohibited action (only) on the basis that the social costs are considered. Many of these difficulties, which take us from the realm of the ideal into that of the imperfect, apply in particular to laws affecting corporations. One problem, for example, is that the penalty needed to deter everyone from some prohibited activities would be so great as to drive corporations into bankruptcy—yet the social cost of such bankruptcy itself outweighs the cost of the prohibited activity. This is known as the "deterrence trap," as Fisse and Braithwaite explain: "the inability of corporations, especially highly leveraged corporations, to pay fines of the amount needed to reflect the gravity of the offence and the low risk of detection and conviction."[28] Only someone with an overly narrow view of efficiency could conclude that because it is too expensive to deter the biggest companies from polluting altogether (should they be inclined to break pollution law if it is not too costly for them to do so) it is socially efficient for them to decide and proceed to pollute.

This means that we cannot assume (as ideal efficiency theory does) that the law always sets its penalties exactly right to achieve the social effect that the legislature wants, even if that effect may include some people or groups breaking the law. Law does not provide an absolute standard of social efficiency, so that moral claims that go beyond the law cannot automatically be judged to create social inefficiencies by so doing. Conversely, efficiency theory would allow companies to break the law in certain circumstances, a result that is anathema to the liberty theory that puts its trust in the limits of the law.

The attempt to invoke the law as the only legitimate constraint on corporate action (so excluding morality) cannot rely on either efficiency or liberty for a full justification. It is further undermined by the point that corporations often profoundly affect the shape of laws themselves. Corporate political donations and influence mean that the limits of the law cannot necessarily be taken to mark out a neutral and rational domain of action for corporations, as both the liberty and efficiency theories assume. A given corporation may enjoy certain latitude for action due to its own lobbying or that of other firms in the same field. Now the liberty theory may be able to cope with this, by clinging to a strictly procedural account of lawmaking such that whoever wins, so long as they do so legally, the outcome is legitimate—though such strict proceduralism begins to look a little bit ostrich-like. Efficiency theory, however, collapses in the face of corporate lobbying.

The arguments that corporations should not accept moral responsibilities beyond the law, either out of duty to their shareholders or because of their place in the overall scheme of social efficiency, are not conclusive enough to bar such responsibilities prima facie. The points made in the previous section about moral patients, for whom the assumption of moral responsibilities by their possible violators is a matter of urgency, suggest that corporations may and should assume those moral responsibilities that they rightly bear. In the final section we will consider some candidates for the content of these responsibilities.

What Might Corporate Moral Responsibilities Include?

The first response to the question of what corporate moral responsibilities might include is that the question must be put to corporations themselves, though not by any means only to them. To ask anyone to shoulder a moral responsibility is to ask them to accept it responsibly,[29] that is, affirming what it requires of them whether or not they have actually worked this out for themselves, or simply approved a candidate version offered by others. This chapter has argued that corporations have the obligation to affirm their moral responsibilities and to make these public, and that doing so will involve their engaging with rival accounts of corporate moral responsibilities offered by others (such as philosophers and NGOs). But here lurks a difficulty. Such a process of judgment seems to require a richer account of agency than the one defended above: Now corporations have not only to be able to decide to regulate their conduct in accordance with moral norms, but also to take part in adjudicating the content of those norms themselves. Is this a dangerous, or an impossible, task?

It certainly gives rise to a final set of objections. For if corporations are asked to go beyond the law, they will inevitably go beyond social consensus as well, and end up taking sides on contested social issues. Corporations that reorganize their activities to accommodate a stringent definition of animal rights, for example, will face criticism from some that the animal-rights contribution to social well-being is far less important than that of the contribution of human rights, as well as commendation from others on the reverse grounds. And they may also contribute to changing the general balance of cultural views on this question. But do we want corporations to play such a crucial role in ethical debate?[30]

Moreover, is not corporate discretion to do and decide on the good, also corporate license to do and decide for the bad? By asking corporations to be responsive to social claims, without there being a fixed legal mechanism by which they could be held responsible for such responsiveness, one is opening the door for them to do all kinds of harmful things in the name of society.[31] Clever corporate managers will leap at the chance to install soft-drink machines in schools, for example, on the pretense that they are doing so to benefit society in the shape of children.

Both of these points raise serious difficulties for advocates of corporate moral responsibility. Yet neither constitutes grounds for rejecting such responsibilities outright. It is true that there will be inevitable disagreement in an imperfect world, both inside and outside corporations, as to what substantive and important social goals are, or conversely, what the avoidance of serious harm to society might mean. But the suggestion that corporations should only respond to broad social goals when the goal in question already commands a broad social consensus[32] overlooks the nature of the dynamic process of establishing moral standards and moral accountability itself. The very process of attempting to build a social consensus around some goal—for example, divestment from South Africa—will involve trying to sway companies and other institutions (including, in that instance, cities and other public bodies) to adopt it, an adoption that will then enhance the degree of perceived social consensus and so sway others, and so on.

As artificial persons set loose in a world of natural persons, walking among us in a common society, corporations will inevitably be called upon to respond as other natural agents do to issues of moral concern. This fact underscores the value of the pragmatic account of corporate moral agency given in the previous section. It would be artificial to exclude corporations from this process of seeking to change social values, a process that is always in motion and behind which the law inevitably lags. The attempt to draw a line on the basis of historical experience—as if one were to say, "it would have been legitimate for corporations to resist Nazi genocide, since that was clearly and uncontroversially wrong, but it is not legitimate for them to take a stand on child labor about which reasonable people disagree"—imputes a current consensus to the very much contested past (not all "reasonable people" thought it right to stand up to Nazi genocide at the time). It ignores the fact that in their own day, all such moral claims are likely to be disputed.

The problem of corporate discretion to do harm under cover of doing good is part of the broader problem of contestation. Moral debate is essentially open to contestation, and corporate self-interpretation of their moral duties will constitute only one voice in the moral dialogue. NGOs, activists, government, journalists, and the like are able to weigh in, to challenge the corporate self-identified moral standards, and to propose alternatives to which the corporation must respond. The value of a moral conception of corporate accountability, as opposed to a purely social one, is that it makes clear that the standards sought are those of objective morality rather than those of any particular group, even while inviting all interested groups to contribute to the moral dialogue about what those standards are. The search for objectivity enlivens debate because it means that no one group's views are inherently privileged above those of any other. Meanwhile, the fact that the corporation must take responsibility for its own moral standards, rather than simply reacting to external demands, is more likely to strengthen its commitment to embed those responsibilities within its organization.

As the argument above implies, it is not the role of this chapter to decree the content of corporate moral responsibility from on high. It is the task of all moral agents, including the corporation itself, to set about defining that content, and to acknowledge in so doing that others will have rival definitions of it to contest. If corporations cannot be insulated from moral pressures, their decision-making processes both at shareholder and management level will be made on the same basis as those made elsewhere in society, and will contribute to the formation of the social consensus that they cannot therefore be expected to presuppose. Yet that is cold comfort to corporations struggling with public pressure in all kinds of directions and on all kinds of issues, not to mention suspicious to activists who fear that all this high talk will come to naught. Are there any guidelines that can be derived from the discussion so far?

The foregoing suggests two principles: one substantive and one procedural. For the purposes of advising corporations as to which demands they might best accept (without ruling out of court a priori any demand that someone in society might try to press), it matters whether the demand does or does not relate to a generally agreed social goal. Human rights are an example of an agreed social goal, being recognized by every country in the world in some form (at a minimum via signing of some international treaty) and by international law, though in both cases the direct legal responsibility of corporations for human rights remains quite sharply limited. It is relatively uncontroversial from the standpoint of the social consensus on values for companies to acknowledge a moral duty (going beyond their legal duty) to respect human rights, though the question of whether such rights are best respected by divesting from, say, Myanmar remains hotly debated and socially divisive. A company could legitimately take a stand on that question, adding its voice to the determination of the particular issue, on the basis of its more general and socially consensual commitment to human rights. Contrast this with the case of animal rights, which do not command anything like a comparable consensus in national or international law. It is therefore more justifiable for a company to assume an extra-legal moral duty based on human than on animal rights, though it is open to animal rights activists to try to create a new consensus.

The procedural principle arising from the foregoing discussion is that of publicity. Corporations have a duty to make the results of their moral deliberations known, and to publicize the moral constraints under which they take themselves to be operating. This duty derives from the structure of moral accountability discussed in Section II. It was argued there (in effect) that all those to whom moral responsibilities apply have an imperfect obligation to participate in debate about the responsibilities that they take themselves to have and the way in which they have sought to carry them out. Here, social and moral accountability will come in practice to intertwine, as observers debate the principles adopted by a given company and the way in which those principles have been applied in practice. The duty of publicity further includes the duty not to obscure information that may help to verify or falsify the assertions publicly made. Such self-avowal of principles and practice may prove unexpectedly stringent for companies, since they can be checked. Paradoxically, negative duties, such as the duty to avoid corruption, may when publicized become far more demanding than the compliance with the positive duty of giving the occasional charitable contribution.

David Miller's account of responsibility in this volume can assist us in making further suggestions of a second-order kind. In the case of harms that a corporation may itself cause, the corporation is likely to bear causal, moral, and (because of its institutional powers) at least some capacity responsibility both for preventing and for rectifying those harms. I lay more emphasis on prevention than Miller does, because it is here that the assumption of additional moral responsibilities may make a real difference, before any clean-up operation by the law comes into play. Communitarian responsibility in these contexts is something that may be unfamiliar and initially uncomfortable for corporations, though corporations vary dramatically in their relationships with local communities: Those involved in textile manufacturing may deliberately hold themselves aloof from a temporary and cheap workforce, while those involved in extraction industries often have no choice but to involve themselves deeply with the communities on the site of the resource. The idea of communitarian responsibility, however, is something that corporations would do well to consider. Through their representatives, they are party to relationships as well as to contracts: And just as they can in practice recognize the claims of equity, so they may be expected to come to recognize the claims of community.

In the case of harms caused by other agents, such as social, political, or economic turmoil in a place where a corporation arrives, the capacity of the corporation to help rectify these harms may be considerable. But here we must consider the cautionary point made by Michael J. Green, that there may be overriding role responsibilities that trump the claims of capacity, as well as the distinction made by Onora O'Neill between primary and secondary agents of justice. Corporations cannot be primary agents of justice—they are not representative in the requisite sense—and they do have the responsibility to pursue if not to maximize their profit. Corporate capacity needs to be harnessed to public legitimacy, perhaps through partnerships with local, regional, national, or international governmental agencies, if externally caused wrongs are to be addressed in the appropriate way.

A final second-order candidate for the content of corporate moral responsibility is the sharp restriction—either by voluntary corporate action or compulsory state law—of the role of corporations in political debate and decision making.[33] In both of the political theories of the role of corporations discussed above—the liberty theory and the efficiency theory—it is assumed that the state of the law broadly represents the appropriate level of coercive regulation of corporations. Yet if corporations are actively engaged in lobbying and influential through political donations, the resulting distortion in the law—or even merely the suspicion thereof—threatens to undermine this fundamental assumption. If the law is not what it should be because of corporate interference, then it is not plausible to say that corporations are more or less adequately accountable to society by obeying the law.

Further moral responsibilities will depend on the particular moral theory that one adopts. Goodin's theory of the duty to protect the vulnerable, for example, could be applied to the case of those vulnerable to the harmful externalities of corporate activity, as well as to workers vulnerable to damaging conditions of work. The refusal to dictate a moral theory from on high is consonant with the broader thesis defended in this chapter, insofar as corporations are morally accountable not least for considering and defending their decisions about what morality requires of them, just as we are morally accountable for considering and defending our counter-claims on them in turn. The establishment of moral standards is not the same as their realization, but it is a first step, and while a world of corporate moral responsibility would not be a world without the need for legal accountability, it would be one in which less might fall through the inevitable legal cracks.

Notes

1. Precursors of this chapter were presented as a paper at the American Political Science Association Annual Meeting (2002) and in political theory seminars and workshops that autumn in Cambridge, Sussex, and Reading. Many people made helpful comments, including especially John Abraham, Andrew Chitty, Alan Cromartie, Monique Deveaux, Amanda Dickins, John Dryzek, Lawrence Hamilton, Serena Olsaretti, Emile Perreau-Saussine, Tom Sorell, Marc Stears, and John R. Wallach. Andrew Kuper and Andrea Sangiovanni additionally and kindly commented on a penultimate draft, for which Jo Maybin contributed valuable research assistance. I have also learned much from exchanges with Marion Fremont-Smith, Jill Horwitz, David Held, David Howarth, Onora O'Neill, Mark Philp, Anita Ramastrasy, Emma Rothschild, David Runciman, Adam Tooze, and Richard Tuck.

2. There is an enormous literature on these questions, much of it couched in terms of "corporate social responsibility" or "voluntary approaches to corporate responsibility" (my reasons for avoiding these terms will be explained in what follows). For an overview and an excellent bibliography, see the NGLS (Non-Governmental Liaison Service of the United Nations) Development Dossier, *Voluntary Approaches to Corporate Responsibility: Readings and a Resource Guide*, written by and available from the United Nations Research Institute for Social Development, May 2002. A major form taken by corporate moral responsibility is that of corporate codes of conduct, on which see the chapters by David Held and S. Prakash Sethi in this volume.

3. On corporate confidentiality, see George Monbiot, *Captive State: The Corporate Takeover of Britain* (London: Macmillan, 2000). Similar problems were experienced in the Australian state of Victoria after its wholesale introduction of privatization principles into the public services.

4. Benjamin R. Barber, "Globalizing Democracy," *American Prospect* 11:20 (11 September 2000); cited from www.americanprospect.com/print/V11/20/barber-b.html; also quoted in Elizabeth Markovits, "Economizing Debate: Rhetoric, Citizenship and the World Bank," paper presented at the 2002 Annual Meeting of the American Political Science Association and available on its website, p. 27.

5. See the overview given in Jon Elster, "Accountability in Athenian Politics," in Adam Przeworski, Susan C. Stokes, and Bernard Manin (eds.) *Democracy, Accountability, and Representation* (Cambridge: Cambridge University Press, 1999), pp. 253–78; for a more detailed general historical account, see Jennifer Tolbert Roberts, *Accountability in Athenian Government* (Madison: University of Wisconsin Press, 1982). It was Grote's emphasis on accountability in ancient Athens in his *History of Greece* that did so much to overturn the view of Athenian democracy as mob rule, and this probably did much to influence his friend John Stuart Mill's reflections on the subject of accountability, on which see Mark Philp, "Mill, Tocqueville and the Corruption of Democratic Accountability," paper presented at the 2002 Annual Meeting of the American Political Science Association and available on its website.

6. See the papers collected in Przeworski, Stokes, and Manin (eds.) *Democracy, Accountability, and Representation*, especially the clear statement of focus on electoral accountability in the "Introduction," by Bernard Manin, Adam Przeworksi, and Susan C. Stokes, pp. 1–26, at p. 10.

7. For example, the useful definition offered by Andreas Schedler, "Conceptualizing Accountability," in Andreas Schedler, Larry Diamond, and Marc F. Plattner (eds.) *The Self-Restraining State: Power and Accountability in New Democracies* (Boulder and London: Lynne Rienner Publishers, 1999), pp. 13–28, at p. 16: "A is accountable to B when A is obliged to inform B about A's (past or future) actions and decisions, to justify them, and to suffer punishment in the case of eventual misconduct." Schedler generally distinguishes between two basic elements of accountability: answerability and enforcement, while noting that they are not always conjoined (p. 17).

8. The striking contrast between conceptions of accountability in economics and in law was brought to my attention by Mark Philp. For the economic perspective, see the essays collected in J.W. Pratt and R.J. Zeckhauser (eds.) *Principals and Agents: The Structure of Business* (Boston: Harvard Business School Press, 1985). For the legal perspective, see F.M.B. Reynolds with Michele Graziadei, *Bowman and Reynolds on Agency*, 17th ed. (London: Sweet and Maxwell, 2001), Article 1.

9. See Ngaire Woods' discussion of kinds of accountability, including financial and internal, in this volume.

10. The call for "corporate capital punishment" made by Robert E. Goodin, *No Smoking: The Ethical Issues* (Chicago and London: University of Chicago Press, 1989), was taken up *inter alia* by Brent Fisse and John Braithwaite, *Corporations, Crime and Accountability* (Cambridge: Cambridge University Press, 1993).

11. "Greenwash + 10: The UN's Global Compact, Corporate Accountability and the Johannesburg Earth Summit," *Corpwatch* (January 2002), p. 12.

12. Chilling if extreme examples of corporate lawyering are given in Ralph Nader and Wesley J. Smith, *No Contest: Corporate Lawyers and the Perversion of Justice in America* (New York: Random House, 1996).

13. If such equality of footing seems to unduly advantage the rich and powerful corporations (though it is well to remember that not all corporations are rich and powerful), the requirement that they argue in moral terms may prove unexpectedly demanding for them.

14. Consider, for example, Thomas Reid's observation in his 1788 *Essay on the Active Powers of Man* (Edinburgh: John Bell; London: G.G.J. and J. Robinson, 1788), report as facsimile of first edition under same title (New York and London: Garland, 1977) that "it is of the highest importance to us, as moral and accountable creatures," to determine the principles under which we should act.

15. Robert E. Goodin, *Protecting the Vulnerable: A Reanalysis of Our Social Responsibilities* (Chicago and London: University of Chicago Press, 1985).

16. T.M. Scanlon, *What We Owe to Each Other* (Cambridge, Mass. and London: Belknap Press of Harvard University Press, 1998).

17. "'Greenwash + 10': [v]oluntary corporate responsibility, while potentially positive, can become an obstacle when used as a diversion from attempts to hold corporations accountable" (p. 1). The report also argues that Shell has damagingly adopted "responsibility without accountability" (p. 10), pointing to a risk that this chapter must take seriously.

18. F.W. Maitland, "The Unincorporate Body," in *Maitland: Selected Essays*, H.D. Hazeltine, G. Lapsley, and P.H. Winfield (eds.) (Cambridge: Cambridge University Press, 1936), pp. 128–40, at p. 133.

19. Quoted in Mark Bovens, *The Quest for Responsibility: Accountability and Citizenship in Complex Organizations* (Cambridge: Cambridge University Press, 1998), p. 53 n. 1 (where he attributes it to John C. Coffee, "'No Soul to Damn, No Body to Kick': An Unscandalized Inquiry into the Problem of Corporate Punishment," *Michigan Law Review* 79 (1981) 386–459, p. 386 n. 1); see also Bovens, p. 67.

20. The distinction between fiction and artifice is brought out, principally in the context of the state, by David Runciman, *Pluralism and the Personality of the State* (Cambridge: Cambridge University Press, 1997). An alternative image to that of the artificial person—that of the computer or intelligent machine—is defended by Meir Dan-Cohen, *Rights, Persons, and Organizations: A Legal Theory for Bureaucratic Society* (Berkeley, Los Angeles, and London: University of California Press, 1986), pp. 49–51, a reference I owe to Jill Horwitz. Further

bibliography for the nature of corporate agency is given in Melissa Lane, "Autonomy as a Central Human Right and its Implications for the Moral Responsibilities of Corporations," in T. Campbell and S. Miller (eds.) *Human Rights and the Moral Responsibilities of Corporate and Public Sector Organizations* (Dordrecht: Kluwer Academic Publishers), pp.145-63, the concerns of which overlap with those of this chapter.

21. Sorting out the attribution of action and moral responsibility between natural person, role representative, and corporation as artificial person is complicated, but the fundamental connection between these constituents cannot be gainsaid. Indeed, while moral philosophers may worry about whether corporations can have moral responsibilities, or whether only natural persons can, the criminal law is more resistant to "piercing the corporate veil" to hold individuals liable for (their part in) corporate misconduct than it is to the general idea of corporate crime per se.

22. The problem is discussed for individual ethics by Liam B. Murphy, "The Demands of Beneficence," *Philosophy and Public Affairs* 22:4 (1993), who argues for a principle on which all should continue to do their fair share regardless of the compliance of others in certain circumstances.

23. Václav Havel, "The power of the powerless," trans. P. Wilson, in V. Havel, *Living in Truth*, ed. Jan Vladislav (London and Boston: Faber and Faber, 1986), pp. 36–122.

24. Milton Friedman, "The social responsibility of business is to increase its profits," *New York Times* 13 September 1970, pp. 122–6, quoted in Melody Kemp, "Corporate Social Responsibility in Indonesia: Quixotic Dream or Confident Expectation?" UNRISD Technology, Business and Society Programme Paper 6 (December 2001).

25. The question of overriding duties is considered by Green, but neglected by Miller.

26. One is tempted to go further and to point out with Keynes that most stock market activity resembles casino gambling more than it does fiduciary entrusting; the whole fiduciary model is only dubiously applicable to secondary trading in any case.

27. See, for example, Frank H. Easterbrook and Daniel R. Fischel, "Antitrust Suits by Targets of Tender Offers," *Michigan Law Review* 80 (1982), p. 1177 n. 57.

28. Fisse and Braithwaite, *Corporations, Crime and Accountability*, p. 82. Their proposal for avoiding this trap is to include a range of non-monetary penalties, such as continued federal oversight of corporate management or in the extreme case "corporate capital punishment," in the penalty spectrum.

29. I use "responsibly," despite its appearing tautologous, to avoid the loaded term "autonomously," which would plunge us back into the waters of moral agency.

30. The question of whether Nike was contributing to free-speech protected public debate, or engaging in misleading commercial speech, is now being argued before the United States Supreme Court in the case of *Nike v. Kasky*, No. 02-575. See Linda Greenhouse, "Free Speech for Companies on Justices' Agenda," *New York Times*, 20 April 2003.

31. Glyn Morgan emphasized the dangers of discretion to me in discussion of Lane, "Autonomy."

32. A suggestion made by David L. Engel, "An Approach to Corporate Social Responsibility," *Stanford Law Review* 32 (1979–80): 1–98, p. 27 and *passim*.

33. Again, voluntary corporate forbearance from political activity is a proposal considered by Engel, "An Approach to Corporate Social Responsibility," pp. 70–84, though he is skeptical on the grounds that corporations will not know how much political activity is optimal.

CHAPTER 13

Held to Account: Governance in the World Economy[1]

NGAIRE WOODS

Concerns about order and justice in the globalizing world economy have often been addressed to international organizations. Protesters gather in large numbers around meetings of the International Monetary Fund (IMF) and the World Bank in order to highlight perceived injustices wrought by these organizations. More and more, these demonstrations have called for greater accountability.

Do the arguments of these protesters have any merit? The IMF and World Bank were originally designed to stabilize exchange rates and channel investment for new projects in war-torn and developing countries. But their jurisdiction has subsequently expanded to include some of the most basic decisions about the budget and economic structure of a large number of the world's countries. Yet while their responsibilities have increased, their accountability has not. Borrowing countries have only token representation within the decision-making bodies of these organizations, and little real power. The decisions of these organizations are not subject to public review, and in most cases the processes leading to them are not even made public. The procedures of these institutions are not, however, set in stone, and it is time for them to be made accountable in ways that more adequately reflect their increased purview over the world's national economies.

Existing multilateral economic organizations such as the IMF, the World Bank, and, we might add, the World Trade Organization (WTO) face two profound and closely related challenges. The first is a challenge of effectiveness. As global integration takes place among private actors in the world economy, it becomes more and more difficult for these institutions to regulate effectively many aspects of the global economy—such as the structure of transnational enterprises and capital markets—that their mandates require. At the very least, effective institutions need the support of the most powerful states in the system. Yet the support of their most powerful member—the United States—varies with regard both to the multilateral character and mandate of each institution. Even in weaker states where the IMF and World Bank attach conditionality to loans, the experience of these institutions demonstrates that change cannot be imposed on unwilling governments—it simply does not work. Global economic governance requires some degree of genuine consent to be effective.

The second challenge is legitimacy. The rules and institutions governing the global economy are often seen as illegitimate, even coercively imposed by governments of the most economically powerful countries without the consent of substantial segments of the world's population. Paradoxically, the government of the United States demands on behalf of its citizens that the international institutions be more accountable to Washington.[2] Most other countries require—and need to show their citizens—that the institutions are less beholden to the United States. This is because decisions made in these institutions have their most profound effect on people within developing countries. And although these persons are ostensibly represented by their governments on the governing boards of the institutions, this representation is neither direct nor influential. Developing countries are grouped together, with each group of countries being represented by just one executive director. Furthermore, there are increasing calls for particular groups within countries whose livelihoods are affected by the institutions to be included directly in the formulation and implementation of conditionality. For the international institutions the problem is twofold. Calls for participation by civil society take them more deeply into the political arrangements within borrowing countries. Yet it is with respect to these countries that their formal accountability is at its weakest. They are far more accountable to their powerful non-borrowing members. Each of these challenges can be adequately addressed only by improving the accountability of the institutions.

How can governments and peoples better hold the IMF and World Bank to account for their collective, multilateral actions? Answering this question does not require rewriting the charters of the institutions or addressing the wider question of accountability in the global economy outside their realm. For a long time they have been seen as especially effective and capable of action because their governance arrangements are sensitive to the distribution of political power. Political and economic power is made congruent with formal voting power in each institution through a quota system. The justification for giving powerful states more formal influence than others has always been both pragmatic—this will make the institutions effective and normative—justified in terms of a contractual conception of property rights because powerful states contribute more to the loan guarantees that underpin the institutions. Yet the contemporary challenges to the effectiveness and legitimacy of the institutions suggest that global economic governance increasingly requires a more sophisticated understanding of both effectiveness and legitimacy than traditional power politics and contractual property rights.

Improving Accountability

Because accountability is about restraining the exercise of public power, it is inextricably linked to justice and legitimacy in politics. It lies at the core of all systems of governance. When it is argued that democratic governments rule with the consent of the governed, homage is paid to a raft of domestic political institutions that ensure the accountability of the governors to the governed. These include elections, constitutional limits on power, and checks and balances exercised through ombudsmen, courts, and parliaments.

While improving the accountability of an institution is not always sufficient to make it fully just, it can substantially contribute to this goal. Institutions exist to mediate a wide range of views about what is just and unjust, what works and what does not. Politicians, vested interests, and other groups rarely agree on these things. Even within the IMF and World Bank economists often disagree. When policy-makers or economists agree on the goals of economic policy, they often disagree about which policies would best achieve them. And even when they agree on policies, they may still disagree about the order and priority of the policies that are to be implemented. For these reasons, decisions made by institutions—including the IMF and World Bank—have deep implications for politics and justice within and among states.

There are two limitations to accountability that should be specified at the outset. First, improving the accountability of public institutions does not necessarily justify expanding their mandate. A more accountable IMF and World Bank or WTO may seem an obvious vehicle for upholding and enforcing a more expansive agenda of environmental protection, gender equality, and so forth.[3] But no matter how accountable these international institutions are made, they cannot be made as democratic or accountable as national and regional governments. One should be wary of shifting decision making from potentially more accountable governments to the necessarily democratically stunted international organizations.[4] A second caveat is that accountability is not always a good thing. It can be poorly designed and result in such distortions in performance that public officials focus all their capacities on meeting specified indicators to the detriment of their most fundamental goals and mission. Accountability can be abused and prevent or stalemate good decision making, such as when a small, highly organized interest group uses a procedural glitch or loophole to invoke a powerful restriction. Accountability can also be very costly, requiring the diversion of resources into new institutions, officers, and data gathering and distribution; this requires consideration not just of the balance of costs and advantages of additional accountability, but yet more importantly, the question of who bears that cost. In short, what is needed is both the right kind and right amount of accountability for institutions with the right kind of mandate.

Four Kinds of Accountability

At the international level, there are some clear counterparts to domestic limitations on power, including constitutional, political, financial, and internal mechanisms of accountability. The accountability of the World Bank and IMF is limited or distorted in each of these areas. Constitutionally, every international organization is founded on a treaty that defines the powers that have been delegated to it by member states. In a sense these are the constitutional limits within which the organization must act. However, in the international arena there is little, if any, legal redress against an organization that is pushed by one member state to act outside these limits. This is in part because international organizations do not exist in a nest of checks and balances. There is, for example, no judicial oversight of their activities. Indeed, they enjoy immunity from most bodies of law. Individuals or groups affected by the institutions have no standing to bring any action against them, except in cases for which special panels or tribunals have been established.

Political accountability is also limited in international organizations. There is an obvious democratic deficit because people do not directly elect, or throw out, their representatives on the IMF or the World Bank, nor those who represent them in international trade negotiations. Instead, those who live in democracies elect politicians, some of whom form a government, which appoints ministers who represent and choose delegations to represent a country. For this reason, international economic organizations are very far removed from representative government. Even if they so wished, citizens could not use their votes effectively to influence, restrain, or hold to account their government for its actions in an international organization. Parliamentary accountability of multilateral agencies, even in highly politically institutionalized countries in Europe and North America, is weak.

The financial accountability of international organizations is tightly related to their political accountability—and similarly skewed so that developing countries exercise little power. Borrowing members actually pay for most of the running and administration costs of each organization through the charges they pay for loans. Yet these countries have little influence over who is appointed to head each organization, nor have they exercised control over decisions that have led administrative costs to escalate.[5] Conversely, the United States has acquired tremendous unilateral influence each time the bank or fund has sought to expand its resources. With respect to the IMF, the United States has used the process of negotiating increases in the resources of the institution to influence its agenda and structure unilaterally.[6] In the World Bank the United States has similarly exerted influence in negotiations for the funding of the International Development Association (IDA), the concessional lending arm of the bank, which relies on contributions by each member.[7]

Finally, internal accountability is an important element in defining what organizations do and how they do it. The operating rules and decision-making processes of any organization set up lines of responsibility and accountability. In the fund and bank the board of governors, responsible cabinet-level officials from member states who meet once per year, has formal control over each organization. However, most decision-making power is delegated to the executive board of each institution, which sits permanently in Washington, D.C. In turn, the executive board delegates negotiations and the framing of proposals to the staff in each organization. The staff persons are held to account by senior management and by internal operational rules and guidelines. Neither is transparent. The appointment of the head of each organization proceeds by a long-standing political agreement. The operational rules and guidelines of both organizations should be—but are not—fully published and amenable to scrutiny, particularly by those most affected by the decisions.

Principles of Restraint

Improving the accountability of the World Bank and IMF should be guided by two principles: the matching principle and the subsidiarity principle. The matching principle suggests that the accountability of each organization should be congruent with its functions. The more intrusive an organization into the traditional realm of national politics, the more consent from and accountability to the governed it requires. The principle of subsidiarity in global governance implies that authority should rest at the most local and democratic level possible and should not be delegated to higher levels unless absolutely necessary.

The matching principle highlights the extent to which, since their creation, international organizations have dramatically expanded their functions. The IMF and World Bank are no longer concerned with setting targets for exchange rates, achieving macroeconomic stability, and making project loans. The past two decades have witnessed a gradual expansion of each institution into prescribing and requiring measures of structural and institutional reform. For example, whereas in the 1980s borrowing countries were required to conform to, say, six to ten "performance criteria," in the 1990s an average of some twenty-six measures were being required.[8] Similarly, international trade rules have expanded to cover domestic and national rules on foreign direct investment, the entry of foreign personnel, intellectual property rights, trade-related investment measures, food safety measures, technical barriers to trade, subsidies, and anti-dumping and countervailing duties, and now seem set to expand further to include competition policy and government procurement, both of which are being discussed by WTO working groups.[9]

The work of the IMF, World Bank, and WTO now takes these intergovernmental institutions into the heart of domestic politics, advising and monitoring government reforms in areas such as the rule of law, judicial reform, corruption, and corporate governance. Yet their accountability has not expanded to match this. Some changes have been made. The IMF, World Bank, and WTO have opened up to some public scrutiny by publishing more of their work and consulting more with NGOs. In the bank and fund, some degree of independent monitoring is undertaken by the Operations Evaluation Department and the Independent Evaluation Office. The more member-driven WTO has at its core the Trade Policy Review Mechanism, which oversees the compliance of its members. In the World Bank Group internal accountability has been strengthened by the creation of the Inspection Panel, which scrutinizes bank decisions on behalf of adversely affected groups to ascertain whether bank staff members have followed the organization's own rules and guidelines. Several serious gaps remain, however, that are worth investigating more closely.

The second principle, subsidiarity, focuses attention on who is making decisions that expand the jurisdiction of intergovernmental organizations and through what process. In particular, subsidiarity proposes a yardstick against which the legitimacy of international processes might be measured. It proposes that in those areas in which decision making is to be transferred to them, such institutions have to be at least as democratic and accountable as domestic institutions have the potential to be. This is controversial. In much writing about expanding global governance, there is an implicit assumption that international decision making is cleaner and somehow less corrupted by vested interests than national-level decision making. Some argue, for example, that at the national level, "governments risk to become prisoners of the siren-like pressures of organized interest groups," whereas international institutions can imbue them with "the wisdom of Ulysses."[10] This line of reasoning has led many to endorse expansion and strengthening of the mandates of international institutions. Yet there is little evidence that policy-makers come to more rational and selfless conclusions away from the hurly-burly of domestic politics. There is some evidence that international institutions can act as forces of restraint.[11] But in their process of decision making, international negotiators are often equally susceptible to highly organized vested interests. Furthermore, people within developing countries stand even less chance of monitoring and countering such interests in international forums.[12]

Reforming the Institutions

How can the international economic institutions be made more accountable? Let us take up the issues of constitutional, political, financial, and internal accountability. The constitutional accountability of the IMF and World Bank does not confine them to a straightjacket of tasks defined more than fifty years ago and entrenched in their articles of agreement. The spirit of constitutional accountability is that the institutions should act at the behest of their full membership, adapting their role in accordance with their decision-making procedures. For this reason constitutional and political accountability are enmeshed.

The articles of agreement preserve a sense of collective agreement by requiring that special majorities be reached for significant decisions. In reality, however, the special majorities, particularly an 85 percent requirement in some cases, endow the United States with special influence. On its own the United States has just over 17 percent voting power, which is enough to veto any 85 percent majority requirement. The implicit threat of this veto power, coupled with the ability to threaten to withhold additional funding or support for the institutions, permits the United States to manipulate each institution, leaving it inadequately accountable—constitutionally and politically—to its other members. To some degree, this unilateral power reveals a political failure on the part of other members to restrain the United States and counter its informal and formal use of influence within each organization. At the same time, there are some structural features that make this influence all too potent.

In the IMF and World Bank, political accountability lies with the board of governors and the executive board. Ostensibly the boards comprise representatives of member states. Yet these are not direct representatives, nor are they adequately accountable. On the executive board, national finance and central bank officials sit simultaneously as officers of the bank or fund. Their provenance is specified in the articles of agreement, which require countries to deal with the institutions through their domestic institutions such as fiscal agencies, treasuries, and central banks. This form of technical representation was appropriate when the articles were drawn up, but now a clearer system of accountability is required.

Many have proposed more legislative oversight and monitoring of the IMF and World Bank, since they represent an outpost of specific domestic agencies overseen by legislatures.[13] This is a good exhortation, but promises little in practice when one examines how little success legislatures have in overseeing the actions of their own agencies in most countries.[14] Instead, as the IMF and World Bank take on wider tasks, officials in the executive offices of government need to be responsible for the process of setting the objectives of these bodies. There are two reasons for this. First, it clarifies who is ultimately responsible and might be held to account for the direction of the institutions. Second, it avoids a significant problem in the political accountability of the institutions: Finance ministers and central bank governors now have too much incentive to use the institutions to bolster their own positions within domestic political struggles and among vested interests.

At the global level, these and a plethora of other international organizations have increased the scope of their activities in a way that not only impinges on the sovereignty of developing countries, but equally on the work of other international agencies. The result is often crisscrossing and contradictory conditionalities that are costly, counterproductive, and obviating of a more positive and constructive use of international aid and expertise. A modest first step toward accountability would be achieved by some form of reporting within the UN system, such as a Global Report on the Performance and Coherence of International Organizations. At a more ambitious level, this form of accountability could be undertaken by some form of Economic and Social Security Council.[15] At the core of this proposal is the notion of global intergovernmental accountability for the expansion in the activities of international organizations.

The financial accountability of the institutions could be robustly improved, as could the responsibility taken by all members. There is a loose assumption underpinning much thinking about the IMF and the World Bank that industrialized countries pay and therefore the agencies should be accountable to them. This justifies the practice of using threats of exit or the withholding of increases in financial resources as a wedge for exerting political influence. However, the assumption is extremely loose, for in fact the institutions undertake very different kinds of tasks, and different kinds of financial accountability are therefore called for. For example, only one part of the World Bank is engaged in aid policies, meaning lending at below-market rates to its members. This is the IDA, which is funded by periodic donor contributions. There is an arguable case that those who donate the funds for the IDA might rightly demand exclusive accountability for the use of those funds. This kind of philosophical case rests on a robust view of the rights of wealthy nations to their wealth and control over its disposal.[16] Even without engaging in that debate, however, it is a strongly limited case because all other parts of the World Bank and IMF are differently funded.

The main part of the World Bank, the International Bank for Reconstruction and Development (IBRD), is better envisaged as a credit club for its members. It pools the credit rating of all members to raise capital, which it then lends to developing countries at interest rates that cover at least the cost of administering the loans. The IBRD could in principle operate in these functions without the participation of the largest industrialized countries. The experience of regional development banks such as the Andean Development Fund highlights the extent to which this can work in a limited way even exclusively among developing countries.[17] The IMF was also originally conceived precisely to provide club-like mutual assistance, pooling the resources of members to offer funds to any one of them facing a crisis. Small groupings of countries have successfully pooled resources to provide this kind of help, although only to a very limited extent.[18] The underlying lessons for the international financial institutions are that their financial accountability need not be an us-and-them arrangement in which creditors hold borrowers to account. The experience of the Bretton Woods and regional institutions is that members acting collectively tend to take prudential, institution-preserving positions with respect to lending. At the same time, a more active engagement in financial accountability by borrowing members would deepen their sense of ownership and commitment to the strategic decision making in the institutions.

Such decisions take us into the final category of accountability—internal accountability. Operational decisions in the IMF and World Bank are formally made by the executive board. It could be held vastly more to account. At present decisions are made by consensus, and voting is very rare, but the underlying voting power of members is a constant feature of decision making. On contested issues, decisions are made on the basis of an informal tally of votes around the table. The fact that votes are never recorded, and the minutes of the executive board meetings are never published, creates a gap in accountability, since outsiders cannot know who took what position and hold decision-makers responsible. For people in developing countries the gap is yet more egregious. They are not usually represented by an official from their own country who is directly responsible to their own government. Rather they are likely to be represented by an official from another country who has been elected by a constituency of countries and who sits for a fixed term of office.

A more accountable board would have a transparent and published voting record.[19] Indeed, this would be a natural extension of the IMF's current practice of publishing a summary of board discussions on their Web site. Published votes and discussions would permit citizens within member countries to engage with other governments and to know which governments to hold to account for specific decisions—and indeed, for what to hold their own government responsible. Secrecy has long been justified on the presumption that it promotes more frank and open discussion within the board and that it preserves the confidentiality of governments. However, both of these presumptions have become seriously questionable since the successful experience of shifts to greater transparency both within the fund and bank and within national authorities such as the Bank of England's Monetary Policy Committee, which publishes full minutes and decisions shortly after meetings.

More ambitiously, the board could be required to give reasons for its policies. Just as judicial processes in most countries require judges to give the basis for their decisions, the board should justify its actions, demonstrating that alternatives have been considered and why they have been rejected. This would require the staff of each institution to present proposals—analytically justified—to the board. The board would then have to make political judgments as to which of the presented alternatives it would support. Political constraints and politically motivated preferences at the board level currently tend to be hidden within the technical advice of the staff, since proposals are arrived at through an iterative discussion between the staff and the board that results in just one final proposal. If political decisions were made distinct from technical advice, the board and staff could be held accountable for their respective inputs.

The extent to which this is important is highlighted in the debate over professional responsibility. One provocative proposal for improving the accountability of staff persons within international institutions is to hold them to a professional standard and open them up to liability for professional negligence where their advice can be shown to be lacking in sufficient care or due diligence.[20] The problems with such an approach usefully highlight the very shaky form of accountability in present structures. The staff in each institution is directed by and accountable to senior management that is appointed in a nontransparent way. The institutions enjoy legal immunity, which has not been diminished even though state immunity has. Furthermore, it is very difficult to get a consensus on the causes of a financial crisis, for example, much less to establish liability. However, even if this was possible and the fund or bank incurred liability, the resulting accountability would be skewed against developing countries. The costs of penalties would be paid by developing countries through the adverse impact on either the availability of funds or borrowing charges. Furthermore, the latter would likely increase if legal standing to make claims were opened up.[21]

An alternative approach would be to press for clearer operating rules and procedures within the organizations, appointment procedures to senior management jobs, and ways that outsiders can scrutinize and ensure that such rules and procedures are followed. At the top of each institution is a director to whom all staff persons are accountable. The president of the World Bank and the managing director of the IMF not only present the public face of each organization, but also play a crucial role in setting the agendas of board meetings, in directing and managing the staffs, in resolving conflicts within the institutions, and in acting as gatekeepers to outside parties or members wishing to exert undue or specific influence. Indeed, as they sit in Washington, D.C., the relationship of the head of each organization to the United States is particularly important. How these leaders are appointed matters. Yet they, and one tier of senior management, have always been appointed according to a postwar bargain struck by the United States and major European countries. The president of the World Bank is always an American citizen named by the U.S. government, and the managing director of the IMF has always been a European. The accountability of the staff at the fund and bank rests at the end of the line with the head of each organization. Yet the process of that person's appointment embeds no accountability into either organization. An obvious first step in bolstering internal accountability would be to implement a selection procedure for all senior management that is representative of all members and meritocratic so as to underscore both the political legitimacy of the organization and its technical competence.[22]

Below the heads of each organization is the staff, which is guided in its work by internal rules and guidelines. Two serious attempts have been made within the World Bank Group in the past decade to improve public accountability for these rules and guidelines. In 1993, an Inspection Panel was created by the executive board to investigate complaints from groups who believe they have suffered because the bank had failed to follow its own policies and procedures. In 1999, in a different part of the World Bank, a Compliance Advisor/Ombudsman's office (CAO) was created to deal with environmental and social concerns and complaints of people directly impacted by projects financed by the International Finance Corporation or the Multilateral Investment Guarantee Agency.

The existence of the Inspection Panel and CAO has required the bank to clarify and publicize its rules and procedures. Although neither the panel nor the compliance officer can rewrite bank policy if it is exposed as faulty, their investigations can highlight poor rules or guidelines and catalyze appropriate political action to rectify them. Obviously not every country is in an equal position to use such procedures to bring formal complaints. Nor is everyone equally able to use the threat of such actions to keep officials within their mandates and rules. In many cases people in developing countries have relied on northern NGOs to assist in funding and presenting their cases. Critics argue that the process is too easily abused, permitting groups to attack good decisions that suffer minor technical flaws and diverting resources into long, costly, and time-consuming investigations. Nevertheless, the new accountability mechanisms reflect an explicit recognition that the World Bank directly affects the lives of people who are not always adequately represented by their own governments. When a group suffers from a failure of the institution to abide by its own rules, it can demand an investigation. At the very least it can find out the rules that guided the decision.

In the IMF no mechanism yet exists for the external scrutiny of internal rules. Indeed, the fund's operational guidelines and manuals are not accessible to the public. This has important implications. Operational guidelines are there in order to temper the discretion of individual officials and negotiators. Unless they are published it is not clear to outsiders what is an individual discretionary judgment and what is the multilaterally endorsed policy of the institution. For this reason, internal rules within institutions are a vital aspect of public accountability. Practically, for people in developing countries negotiating with fund officials or affected by fund policies, access to such documents is a prerequisite for holding the institutions and their officials to account. More ambitiously, an external form of accountability could be put in place using an ombudsman's office to which affected parties could address complaints. Rather like the bank's Inspection Panel—although with a much more limited range of potential complainants—the ombudsman's office would adjudicate to what extent the staff had adhered to its own guidelines and report back to the executive board.

Transparency, Responsibility, and Democracy

Accountability in international organizations is multifaceted. Each aspect of the accountability of the fund and bank could be improved by better corresponding mechanisms by which officials are held responsible for their tasks and functions. Constitutional accountability could be enhanced by a role for heads of state, overseen by an Economic and Social Security Council, which would hold international organizations to account for expansions in their activities. Political accountability could be bolstered by clear and transparent decision making, including recorded voting and published minutes and perhaps even a requirement to give reasons why a particular choice has been made and to demonstrate that alternatives have been considered. Financial accountability needs to be analyzed on the basis of contributions for specific activities rather than a general and vague presumption that creditors collectively ought to hold debtors collectively to account. In many of their activities the institutions operate more like clubs and could be more effectively held to account through more equal and mutual governance. Finally, the internal accountability of each institution requires transparent and meritocratic appointments to senior management positions and transparent and actionable operating guidelines and internal rules.

Some may wonder whether these reforms go far enough. Surely to shrink the scope of existing institutions or to match their accountability with their current structure is an overly modest and second-best option for reforming global governance. More radical proposals move in the opposite direction, releasing the fund and bank from their strictures not to be political, or replacing them with a system of competing development organizations whose funding would be depoliticized. Such proposals may well be appealing, but they contradict the starting point of this argument, which is that justice in global economic governance is first and foremost about just processes. The reason for this is that different values, means, and ends are pursued within and among the actors of the world economy. Without a legitimate and accountable process, these debates will be resolved as a simple matter of bargaining and power. Even modest procedural changes can therefore significantly enhance the justice of these institutions.

Notes

1. This chapter has benefited from the input of Christian Barry and other discussants present at the Carnegie Council on Ethics and International Affairs seminar, "Held to Account: Governance in the World Economy," New York, October 28, 2002, and from discussions with Robert Keohane.
2. Meltzer Commission, "Report of the International Financial Institutions Advisory Commission" (Washington, D.C., 2000); available at www.house.gov/jec/imf/meltzer.htm
3. David Held, "Law of States, Law of Peoples: Three Models of Sovereignty," *Legal Theory* 8 (March 2002): 1–44.
4. This is more elegantly argued by Robert A. Dahl, "Can International Organizations Be Democratic? A Skeptic's View," in Ian Shapiro and Casiano Hacker-Cordón, eds., *Democracy's Edges* (Cambridge: Cambridge University Press, 1999), p. 33.

5. Devesh Kapur, "Who Gets to Run the World?" *Foreign Policy* (November/December 2000): 44–50; and Miles Kahler, *Leadership Selection in the Major Multilaterals* (Washington, D.C.: Institute for International Economics, 2001).

6. Mary Locke, "Funding the IMF: The Debate in the U.S. Congress," *Finance and Development* 37 (September 2000): 56–9.

7. Catherine Gwin, "U.S. Relations with the World Bank, 1945–1992," in Devesh Kapur, John Prior Lewis, and Richard Charles Webb, eds., *The World Bank: Its First Half Century*, vol. 2 (Washington, D.C.: Brookings Institution Press, 1997), pp. 195–274.

8. Devesh Kapur, "Expansive Agendas and Weak Instruments: Governance Related Conditionalities of the International Financial Institutions," *Journal of Policy Reform* 4, no. 3 (2001): 207–41.

9. World Trade Organization, "Multilateral Agreements on Trade in Goods," 1994; available at ww.wto.org/english/docs_e/legal_e/legal_e.htm#goods

10. See Ernst-Ulrich Petersmann, "The Transformation of the World Trading System through the 1994 Agreement Establishing the World Trade Organization," *European Journal of International Law* 6, no. 2 (1995); available at www.ejil.org/journal/Vol6/No2/art1.html

11. Paul Collier, "Learning from Failure: The International Financial Institutions as Agencies of Restraint in Africa," in Andreas Schedler, Larry Diamond, and Marc Plattner, eds., *The Self-Restraining State: Power and Accountability in New Democracies* (Boulder, Colo.: Lynne Rienner, 1999), pp. 313–32.

12. See my argument against this form of governance in Ngaire Woods, "Global Governance and the Role of Institutions," in David Held and Anthony McGrew, eds., *Governing Globalization: Power, Authority and Global Governance* (Malden, Mass.: Polity Press, 2002), pp. 25–45.

13. See House of Commons Treasury Committee, "International Monetary Fund: A Blueprint for Parliamentary Accountability: Government Response to the Committee's Fourth Report of Session 2000–01," November 26, 2001, House of Commons Paper no. 379 (London: The Stationery Office, 2001); Bretton Woods Project Proposal to the House of Commons Development Committee, "International Development: Appendices to the Minutes of Evidence," Appendix 2, February 10, 2000 (London: The Stationery Office, 2000); and Bank Information Center, "Who is Governing the Governors? Globalization, Governance, and Democracy" (Washington, D.C.: 2000).

14. Indeed, the Commonwealth Secretariat's review of the role of parliaments in holding governments to account makes no mention of overseeing international institutions. See Commonwealth, "Activities"; available at www.thecommonwealth.org/

15. Sam Daws and Frances Stewart, Global Challenges: An Economic and Social Security Council at the United Nations (London: Christian Aid, 2000) proposes such a forum for different, more expansive rather than accountability purposes, as does Erskine Childers, "An Agenda for Peace and an Agenda for Development: The Security Council and the Economic and Social Council in the UN Reform Process" (speech given at "Colloquium on the United Nations at Fifty: Whither the Next Fifty Years?" European Parliament, Brussels, September 8, 1995); available at www.globalpolicy.org/resource/pubs/childer2.htm

16. The counter case has been forcefully argued in Thomas Pogge, "Achieving Democracy," *Ethics & International Affairs* 15, no. 1 (2001): 3–23; in Thomas W. Pogge, *World Poverty and Human Rights: Cosmopolitan Responsibilities and Reforms* (Cambridge: Polity Press, 2002); and in Charles Beitz, *Political Theory and International Relations*, rev. ed. (Princeton, NJ: Princeton University Press, 1999).

17. See Corporación Andina de Fomento, "About CAF," September 11, 2002; available at www.caf.com/view/index.asp?ms=0&pageMs=4306

18. We can contrast the experience of the Latin American Reserve Fund and its difficulties in increasing its members' contributions. See Latin American Reserve Fund, "Who Are We?"; available at www.comunidadandina.org/ingles/who/flar.htm

19. José de Gregorio et al., *An Independent and Accountable IMF* (Geneva: International Centre for Monetary and Banking Studies, 1999); and Great Britain Department for International Development, *Eliminating World Poverty: Making Globalization Work for the Poor: White Paper on International Development* (London: The Stationery Office, 2000).

20. Kunibert Raffer, "Introducing Financial Accountability at the IBRD: An Overdue and Necessary Reform," paper presented at the conference "Reinventing the World Bank," May 14–16, 1999, Northwestern University, Ill.; available at www.worldbank.nwu.edu/papers/raffer.rtf

21. These points are made by Daniel Bradlow. See Working Group on Institutional Reform in Global Financial Governance, "Report of October 2002 Meeting"; available at users.ox.ac.uk/~ntwoods/wg3.htm
22. Devesh Kapur, "Who Gets to Run the World?"; and Kahler, *Leadership Selection in the Major Multilaterals.*

Contributors

Christian Barry is Editor of the journal *Ethics & International Affairs* and directs the program on Justice and the World Economy at the Carnegie Council on Ethics and International Affairs. His publications include "Global Justice: Aims, Arrangements, and Responsibilities" in *Can Institutions Have Duties?* (2003), edited by Toni Erskine; "Redistribution" in the *Stanford Encyclopedia of Philosophy* (2003); "Access to Medicines and the Rhetoric of Responsibility," co-authored with Kate Raworth, in *Ethics & International Affairs* (2002); and "Education and Standards of Living" in the *Blackwell Companion to the Philosophy of Education* (2002). He served as a principal consultant and contributing author to the United Nations Human Development Report for three years.

Michael Green is Assistant Professor of Philosophy and a member of the Human Rights Program at the University of Chicago. His publications include "Global Justice and Health: Is Health Care a Basic Right?" in *Public Health Ethics*, edited by Michael Boylan (2004); "Justice and Law in Hobbes" in *Oxford Studies in Early Modern Philosophy* (2003); "The Idea of a Momentary Self and Hume's Theory of Personal Identity" in the *British Journal for the History of Philosophy* (1999); and "National Identity and Liberal Political Philosophy" in *Ethics & International Affairs* (1996).

David Held is Graham Wallas Professor of Political Science at the London School of Economics. His books on globalization, democracy, and international justice include *Global Transformations: Politics, Economics and Culture* (co-author, 1999) and *Globalization/Anti-Globalization* (co-author, 2002). He also edited, with Anthony McGrew, *The Global Transformations*

Reader (2000) and *Governing Globalization: Power, Authority and Global Governance* (2002). His articles include "Violence, Law and Justice in a Global Age" in *Constellations* (2002); "Law of States, Law of Peoples" in *Legal Theory* (2002); and "Globalisation: The Argument of Our Time" (www.opendemocracy.net, 2002). Twenty years ago, Held co-founded Polity Press, which is now a major presence in social science and humanities publishing.

Susan James is Professor of Philosophy at Birkbeck College London. She is the author of *The Content of Social Explanation* (1985) and *Passion and Action* (1997), and editor of *Beyond Equality and Difference* (1992), *Visible Women* (2002), and *The Political Writings of Margaret Cavendish* (2003). Her chapter in this volume is part of a current project about the place of an understanding of emotion in political philosophy.

Andrew Kuper is a Managing Director at Ashoka—Innovators for the Public, an organization that supports social entrepreneurs around the world. Born and raised in South Africa, he now lives in Washington, D.C. He has been a Fellow of Trinity College, Cambridge University, and a visiting scholar at Harvard and Columbia Universities. As Senior Associate at the Carnegie Council on Ethics and International Affairs, he directed the project on multilateral strategies to promote democracy. He remains closely connected to South Africa, as Co-Director of Kuper Research, a media and sociopolitical consultancy based in Johannesburg. He has published widely on democracy and globalization, the media, international law and institutions, and the role of corporations in development. He is the author of *Democracy Beyond Borders* (Oxford University Press, 2004).

Melissa Lane is University Lecturer in the History Faculty and Fellow of King's College, Cambridge University, where she is also associated as a researcher with the Centre for History and Economics. She has served on the core faculty for the British Petroleum/Cambridge Executive Education Programme and for the BP/New Hall Gender and Leadership Programme. She has been Visiting Professor of Government at Harvard University and visiting fellow at the Research School of Social Sciences, Australian National University. In 2001 she was a paid consultant on ethics to BP, a role that has now ended. Although her books so far reflect her historical research on ancient philosophy and its modern reception—*Method and Politics in Plato's Statesman* (1998); *Plato's Progeny: How Socrates and Plato Still Captivate the Modern Mind* (2001)—she has also published widely on normative political philosophy.

David Miller is Professor of Political Theory at the University of Oxford and an Official Fellow of Nuffield College. His recent books include *On Nationality* (1995), *Principles of Social Justice* (1999), *Citizenship and National Identity* (2000), and *A Very Short Introduction to Political Philosophy* (2003). His current research is focused on the idea of national responsibility and its implications for international justice, and on problems of social justice in multicultural societies.

Onora O'Neill is Principal of Newnham College, Cambridge University. Her books on ethics and political philosophy include *Faces of Hunger: An Essay on Poverty, Development and Justice* (1986); *Constructions of Reason: Exploration of Kant's Practical Philosophy* (1989); *Towards Justice and Virtue* (1996); *Bounds of Justice* (2000); and *Autonomy and Trust in Bioethics* (2002). She delivered the 2002 Reith Lectures, published as *A Question of Trust* (2002). She has been president of the Aristotelian Society (1988–9), a member of the Animal Procedures (Scientific) Committee (1990–4), and a member of the Nuffield Council on Bioethics (1991–8; Chairman 1996–8). She was a member and later acting Chairman of the Human Genetics Advisory Commission of the United Kingdom (1996–9). O'Neill is currently Chairman of the Nuffield Foundation. She was created a Life Peer in January 1999 and sits as a cross-bencher in the House of Lords.

Thomas W. Pogge is Professor of Philosophy at Columbia University and teaches moral and political philosophy at Columbia and Oslo Universities. His recent publications include *World Poverty and Human Rights* (2002); the edited collection *Global Justice* (2001); "What We Can Reasonably Reject" in *NOÛS* (2002); "Can the Capability Approach Be Justified?" in *Philosophical Topics* (2002); "On the Site of Distributive Justice" in *Philosophy and Public Affairs* (2000); and, with Sanjay Reddy, "How Not to Count the Poor" (www.socialanalysis.org). He is editor for social and political philosophy for the *Stanford Encyclopedia of Philosophy* and a member of the Norwegian Academy of Science. Pogge's work was supported by, most recently, the John D. and Catherine T. MacArthur Foundation, the Princeton Institute for Advanced Study, and All Souls College, Oxford.

Amartya Sen is Lamont University Professor at Harvard University and was, until recently, Master of Trinity College, Cambridge University. His publications include *Collective Choice and Social Welfare* (1970); *On Economic Inequality* (1973); *Poverty and Famines* (1981); *On Ethics and Economics* (1987); *Inequality Reexamined* (1992); *Development as Freedom* (1999); and *Rationality as Freedom* (2003). He is a past president of the

American Economic Association, the Indian Economic Association, the International Economic Association, and the Econometric Society. Sen was a founding father of the UNDP's Human Development Report, which is still based on his work on capabilities, and is honorary president of Oxfam. He has received more than forty honorary doctorates. Among his awards are the Frank E. Seidman Distinguished Award in Political Economy, the Senator Giovanni Agnelli International Prize in Ethics, the Alan Shawn Feinstein World Hunger Award, the Jean Mayer Global Citizenship Award, and "Bharat Ratna," the highest honor conferred by the president of India. In 1998, Sen was awarded the Nobel Prize in economics.

S. Prakash Sethi is University Distinguished Professor at the Zicklin School of Business, Baruch College, The City University of New York. He has authored or co-authored 23 books and over 135 articles in scholarly and professional journals. He is internationally known for his work on corporate codes of conduct, reflected in his latest publication, *Setting Global Standards: Guidelines for Creating Codes of Conduct in Multinational Corporations* (2003). He is also the president of a not-for-profit organization, the International Center for Corporate Accountability, an academically affiliated research group and think tank that deals with issues of corporate accountability, voluntary standards for corporate social performance, and transparency of corporate actions.

Peter Singer is De Camp Professor of Bioethics in the University Center for Human Values at Princeton University. His books include *Animal Liberation* (1975), which is commonly credited with triggering the modern animal rights movement; *Practical Ethics* (1979), one of the most widely used textbooks in applied ethics; *How Are We to Live?* (1993); *Rethinking Life and Death* (1995), which received the 1995 National Book Council's Banjo Award for nonfiction; and *One World: Ethics and Globalization* (2002). Two collections of his work have been published: *Writings on an Ethical Life* (2000), which he edited, and *Unsanctifying Human Life* (2002), edited by Helga Kuhse. *Singer and His Critics* (1999), a collection of essays focusing on Singer's work, was edited by Dale Jamieson. Singer was founding president of the International Association of Bioethics and, with Helga Kuhse, founding co-editor of the journal *Bioethics*. Outside academic life, he is president of Animal Rights International and of The Great Ape Project.

Ngaire Woods is a Fellow in Politics and International Relations at University College, Oxford University. She has recently published *The Political Economy of Globalization* (2000); *Inequality, Globalization and World Politics* (1989), co-authored with Andrew Hurrell; and *Explaining International*

Relations Since 1945 (1986). A new book on the IMF and World Bank is forthcoming. She was lead consultant on the UNDP's Human Development Report 2002, and now serves on the HDR Advisory Panel as well as on the Commonwealth Expert Group on Democracy and Poverty. She also chairs a high-level working group on developing countries and the reform of global financial institutions.

Appendix

The editor, contributors, and publisher are grateful to several journals and editors for permission to print copyrighted articles or chapters here.

Christian Barry's "Applying the Contribution Principle" will also appear in *Metaphilosophy* 36 (1/2) and is printed with the permission of Blackwell Publishing, Ltd.

Michael Green's "Institutional Responsibility for Global Problems" appeared in *Philosophical Topics*. Fall 2002; 30 (2): 1–28. Reprinted with permission.

David Held's "Globalization, Corporate Practice and Cosmopolitan Social Standards" appeared in *Contemporary Political Theory*. 2002; 1 (1): 59–78. Reprinted with permission.

Susan James's "Realizing Rights as Enforceable Claims" is a revised and extended version of her "Rights as Enforceable Claims," which appeared in *The Proceedings of the Aristotelian Society*, 2003; CIII. Reprinted with permission.

Andrew Kuper's "Global Poverty Relief: More Than Charity" and "Poverty, Facts, and Political Philosophies" (reprinted here as part of "A Debate with Andrew Kuper") both appeared in *Ethics and International Affairs*. April 2002; 16 (1): 107—20, 125–6. Reprinted with permission.

David Miller's "Distributing Responsibilities" appeared in the *Journal of Political Philosophy*. December 2001; 9 (4): 453–71. Reprinted with permission of Blackwell Publishing, LTD.

Onora O'Neill's "Agents of Justice" appeared in *Metaphilosophy*. 2001; 32 (1/2), and in Thomas Pogge, ed., *Global Justice* (Oxford: Blackwell, 2001). Reprinted with permission of Blackwell Publishing, LTD.

Thomas Pogge's "Human Rights and Human Responsibilities" appeared—with more extensive footnotes—in Ciaran Cronin and Pablo De Greiff, eds., *Transnational Politics and Deliberative Democracy* (Cambridge, MA: MIT Press, 2002). Reprinted with permission.

Amartya Sen's "Open and Closed Impartiality" appeared in the *Journal of Philosophy*. September 2002; 99 (9): 445–69. Reprinted with permission.

S. Prakash Sethi's "Corporate Codes of Conduct and the Success of Globalization" appeared in *Ethics and International Affairs*. April 2002; 16 (1): 89–106. Reprinted with permission.

Peter Singer's "Poverty, Facts, and Political Philosophies" and "One More Try" (reprinted here as part of "A Debate with Andrew Kuper") both appeared in *Ethics and International Affairs*. April 2002; 16 (1): 121–4. Reprinted with permission.

Ngaire Woods, "Held to Account: Governance in the World Economy" appeared in *Ethics and International Affairs*. April 2003; 17 (1): 1–25. Reprinted with permission.

Index